Using Computational Intelligence for the Dark Web and Illicit Behavior Detection

Romil Rawat
Shri Vaishnav Vidyapeeth Vishwavidyalaya, India

Upinder Kaur
Akal University, Talwandi Sabo, India

Shadab Pasha Khan
Oriental Institute of Science and Technology, Bhopal, India

Ranjana Sikarwar
Amity University, Gwalior, India

K. Sakthidasan Sankaran
Hindustan Institute of Technology and Science, India

A volume in the Advances in Digital Crime, Forensics, and Cyber Terrorism (ADCFCT) Book Series

Published in the United States of America by
IGI Global
Information Science Reference (an imprint of IGI Global)
701 E. Chocolate Avenue
Hershey PA, USA 17033
Tel: 717-533-8845
Fax: 717-533-8661
E-mail: cust@igi-global.com
Web site: http://www.igi-global.com

Library of Congress Cataloging-in-Publication Data

Names: Rawat, Romil, 1986- editor. | Sankaran, K. Sakthidasan, 1983-
   editor.
Title: Using computational intelligence for the dark web and illicit
   behavior detection / Romil Rawat, Upinder Kaur, Shadab Khan, Ranjana
   Sikarwar, and K. Sakthidasan Sankaran, editors.
Description: Hershey, PA : Information Science Reference, an imprint of IGI
   Global, [2023] | Includes bibliographical references and index. |
   Summary: "The goal of this monograph is to convey a picture of the Dark
   Web environment, suggest a methodical, computational approach to
   comprehending the difficulties, and define tactics and solutions,
   providing researchers, security professionals, counter-terrorism
   specialists, and strategy developers with useful information"-- Provided
   by publisher.
Identifiers: LCCN 2022020091 (print) | LCCN 2022020092 (ebook) | ISBN
   9781668464441 (h/c) | ISBN 9781668464489 (s/c) | ISBN 9781668464458
   (ebook)
Subjects: LCSH: Anomaly detection (Computer security) | Intrusion detection
   systems (Computer security) | Computer networks--Monitoring. | Computer
   crimes--Prevention. | Dark Web. | Artificial intelligence.
Classification: LCC TK5105.59 .U77 2023 (print) | LCC TK5105.59 (ebook) |
   DDC 005.8--dc23/eng/20220706
LC record available at https://lccn.loc.gov/2022020091
LC ebook record available at https://lccn.loc.gov/2022020092

This book is published in the IGI Global book series Advances in Digital Crime, Forensics, and Cyber Terrorism (ADCF-CT) (ISSN: 2327-0381; eISSN: 2327-0373)

British Cataloguing in Publication Data
A Cataloguing in Publication record for this book is available from the British Library.

All work contributed to this book is new, previously-unpublished material. The views expressed in this book are those of the authors, but not necessarily of the publisher.

For electronic access to this publication, please contact: eresources@igi-global.com.

Advances in Digital Crime, Forensics, and Cyber Terrorism (ADCFCT) Book Series

Bryan Christiansen
Global Research Society, LLC, USA
Agnieszka Piekarz
Independent Researcher, Poland

ISSN:2327-0381
EISSN:2327-0373

MISSION

The digital revolution has allowed for greater global connectivity and has improved the way we share and present information. With this new ease of communication and access also come many new challenges and threats as cyber crime and digital perpetrators are constantly developing new ways to attack systems and gain access to private information.

The **Advances in Digital Crime, Forensics, and Cyber Terrorism (ADCFCT) Book Series** seeks to publish the latest research in diverse fields pertaining to crime, warfare, terrorism and forensics in the digital sphere. By advancing research available in these fields, the **ADCFCT** aims to present researchers, academicians, and students with the most current available knowledge and assist security and law enforcement professionals with a better understanding of the current tools, applications, and methodologies being implemented and discussed in the field.

COVERAGE

- Cryptography
- Cyber Warfare
- Malicious Codes
- Crime Scene Imaging
- Encryption
- Digital surveillance
- Mobile Device Forensics
- Global Threat Intelligence
- Telecommunications Fraud
- Digital Crime

IGI Global is currently accepting manuscripts for publication within this series. To submit a proposal for a volume in this series, please contact our Acquisition Editors at Acquisitions@igi-global.com or visit: http://www.igi-global.com/publish/.

Titles in this Series

For a list of additional titles in this series, please visit: www.igi-global.com/book-series/advances-digital-crime-forensics-cyber/73676

Media and Terrorism in the 21st Century
Elnur Ismayil (Istanbul Medeniyet University, Turkey) and Ebru Karadogan Ismayil (Uskudar University, Trkey)
Information Science Reference • © 2022 • 299pp • H/C (ISBN: 9781799897552) • US $195.00

World Politics and the Challenges for International Security
Nika Chitadze (International Black Sea University, Georgia)
Information Science Reference • © 2022 • 427pp • H/C (ISBN: 9781799895862) • US $195.00

Technologies to Advance Automation in Forensic Science and Criminal Investigation
Chung-Hao Chen (Old Dominion University, USA) Wen-Chao Yang (National Central Police University, Taiwan) and Lijian Chen (Henan University, China)
Information Science Reference • © 2022 • 289pp • H/C (ISBN: 9781799883869) • US $225.00

Intelligence and Law Enforcement in the 21st Century
Eugene de Silva (Virginia Research Institute, USA) and Asanga Abeyagoonesekera (Parliament of Sri Lanka, Sri Lanka)
Information Science Reference • © 2021 • 253pp • H/C (ISBN: 9781799879046) • US $225.00

Social Engineering and Information Warfare Operations Emerging Research and Opportunities
Rhonda L. Johnson (Upper Iowa University, USA)
Information Science Reference • © 2021 • 150pp • H/C (ISBN: 9781799842705) • US $145.00

Evaluating Emerging Threats and New Research Opportunities in Digital Crime and Forensics
Rhonda Johnson (Upper Iowa University, USA)
Information Science Reference • © 2021 • 350pp • H/C (ISBN: 9781799822288) • US $195.00

Confluence of AI, Machine, and Deep Learning in Cyber Forensics
Sanjay Misra (Covenant University, Nigeria) Chamundeswari Arumugam (Sri Sivasubramaniya Nadar College of Engineering, India) Suresh Jaganathan (Sri Sivasubramaniya Nadar College of Engineering, India) and Saraswathi S. (Sri Sivasubramaniya Nadar College of Engineering, India)
Information Science Reference • © 2021 • 248pp • H/C (ISBN: 9781799849001) • US $225.00

Cyber Security Auditing, Assurance, and Awareness Through CSAM and CATRAM
Regner Sabillon (Universitat Oberta de Catalunya, Spain)
Information Science Reference • © 2021 • 260pp • H/C (ISBN: 9781799841623) • US $195.00

701 East Chocolate Avenue, Hershey, PA 17033, USA
Tel: 717-533-8845 x100 • Fax: 717-533-8661
E-Mail: cust@igi-global.com • www.igi-global.com

Table of Contents

Section 3
Anomaly Detection Using Artificial Intelligence and Machine Learning Algorithms

Detailed Table of Contents

Section 1
Traffic Analysis and Network Management

Chapter 1

    P. William, Sanjivani College of Engineering, Savitribai Phule Pune University, India
    Siddhartha Choubey, Shri Shankaracharya Technical Campus, India
    Abha Choubey, Shri Shankaracharya Technical Campus, India
    Apurv Verma, MATS University, India

Security breaches may be difficult to detect because attackers are continually tweaking methods to evade detection and utilize legitimate credentials that have already been deployed in network environments. Many firms have a way to resist the evolving sophistication of attacks in network traffic analysis technology. As cloud computing, DevOps, and the internet of things (IoT) become common, it has become more difficult to maintain network visibility. Automated detection of malicious intent using a weight-agnostic neural network architecture is possible with the authors' unique darknet traffic analysis and network management technology. Intelligent forensics tool for network traffic analysis and real-time identification of encrypted information is powerful. Automated neural network search techniques based on a weight-agnostic neural network (WANNs) approach may be used to discover zero-day threats. Many firms struggle to protect their important assets because of the effort required to identify malicious intent on the darknet manually. The advanced solution proposed here overcomes such obstacles.

Chapter 2

    Prem Mahendra Kothari, Ajeenkya D. Y. Patil University, India
    Ratan Singh Gaharwar, UIT-RGPV Bhopal, India

Due to the drastic and exponential growth of information systems and their use, the technology has taken a quantum leap. To ensure safe data transportation, different protection systems are used, such as intrusion detection systems, intrusion prevention systems, and firewalls. In this chapter, the proposed system has an anomaly-based cyber threats detection system using advanced machine learning algorithms. The anomaly-based detection system was used to analyze repackage signatures of malware which is not predefined. Machine learning with the use of previous datasets and algorithms to make the IDS intelligent. In this chapter, the authors use K-NN, which takes the similarity between new attack footprints and compare it with the older footprints in the dataset, and tell which has a higher resemblance. The major challenges of this IDS are minimization of false alarms and gaining high accuracy. The proposed IDS system is not only tested manually but is tested by automated utilities as well, and minimizing of overfitting and underfitting is also checked.

Chapter 3

Ashwini Dalvi, Veermata Jijabai Technological Instutute, India
Kunjal Shah, Veermata Jijabai Technological Institute, India
Uddhav Jambhalkar, Veermata Jijabai Technological Institute, India
Varun Pawar, Veermata Jijabai Technological Institute, India
Dashank Bhoir, Veermata Jijabai Technological Institute, India
S. G. Bhirud, Veermata Jijabai Technological Institute, India

The dark web contains sensitive data that strategic organizations must identify well in advance to anticipate and handle threats. However, associates will prefer to automate classifying the dark web pages instead of opening them due to their disturbing visual images and dangerous links and attachments. Most research is focused on web page text analysis to infer dark web data. But no visible attempt is observed in the literature that classifies dark web content at the structure level. In the chapter, extended scope of work aims to predict the genre of the webpage without opening the web page. The work converts web pages to their respective DOM (document object model) graphs. DOM graphs essentially represent web page structure. A GNN (graph neural network) is trained with constructed DOM graphs to predict the page's genre. The various graph properties like a number of nodes, edges, etc. for web page DOM graphs are extracted. Unsupervised learning (i.e., k-means clustering) is performed on the dataset to group the web pages into clusters based on similarity in structure.

Section 2
Models for Crime Prediction

Chapter 4

Sonali Gupta, J. C. Bose University of Science and Technology, India

The dark web is termed as the concealed content hidden behind interfaces offering secure chats or mailing applications on the WWW, and exploiting it for illegal practices is termed cybercrimes. As the dark web is enormously big compared to the surface web, cyber-crimes have become one of the biggest challenges to tackle. Predicting them before they actually happen is almost impossible. The work thus deals with predicting the number of cognizable crimes (physical and cybercrimes reported collectively) by National Crime Record Bureau (NCRB), the government-approved agency for maintaining crime records in India. Predicting crimes has become important as they advance to new levels of intelligence and diversification with the increased use of information and communication technology (ICT). This work presents the research based on evidences with ARIMA and LSTM time series models for predicting the cognizable crimes in India. The authors have used root mean squared error and mean absolute error as loss functions for error evaluation, and the results obtained from both the models are presented.

Chapter 5

Om Kumar C. U., Vellore Institute of Technology (VIT) Chennai, India
Dharmala Pranavi, SRM Easwari Engineering College, India
B. R. Aishwarayaa Laxmi, SRM Easwari Engineering College, India
Devasena R., SRM Easwari Engineering College, India

IoT devices are naturally vulnerable to security issues such as botnet attacks that lead to compromised data. Due to the proliferation of network traffic, the existing system demonstrated a mean FPR of 0.007 ± 0.01, but it needs to be updated to be on par with swiftly growing bots. In the proposed system, the authors have deployed various autoencoders for the detection of IoT botnets. This proposed system helps to differentiate malicious attacks from benign ones. To validate the proposed method, they have used NbaIoT dataset infected with the two most widely known IoT-based botnets: Mirai and Gafgyt. The autoencoders are trained using the optimization dataset generated by various smart devices, and when tested, they achieved formidable accuracy for various autoencoders: 96.158% for sparse autoencoder, 86.775% for deep Autoencoder, 96.157% for variational autoencoder, 96.156% for under complete autoencoder, and 79.789% for denoising autoencoder. Compared to many other state-of-the-art botnet detection methods, variational autoencoder has achieved better accuracy with lower false predictions.

Chapter 6

Deepika Chauhan, Swarrnim Startup and Innovation University, India
Chaitanya Singh, Swarrnim Startup and Innovation University, India
Dyaneshwar Kudande, Swarrnim Startup and Innovation University, India
Yu-Chen Hu, Providence University, Taiwan

The dark web is a portion of the deep web that's hidden away from the ordinary user. It contains various tools and techniques that cyber criminals can use to carry out their attacks. The increasing popularity of the internet of things has raised the concerns of various security organizations regarding the security of the systems connected to it. The rapid emergence and success of internet of things devices and their associated services have raised the number of attacks against these devices and services to the alarming level. The need to secure this rapidly changing industry has become a top priority in the cyber defense industry. This chapter aims to provide a comprehensive view of the various threats and attacks targeting the infrastructure of the IoT and to analyze the various cyber defense techniques and solutions that are being used to secure the connected objects.

Section 3
Anomaly Detection Using Artificial Intelligence and Machine Learning Algorithms

Chapter 7

Neha Nitin Gawali, NBN Sinhgad Technical Institute, Pune, India
Shailesh Bendale, NBN Sinhgad Technical Institute, Pune, India

Even with the dark web (DW) being accessible only through special software, global law enforcement agencies are considering it a major problem. The fact that activities happening on DW are completely untraceable has become the main point of attraction for the perpetrators. Also, in certain years, there has been improvement and advancement in the artificial intelligence (AI) as well as machine learning (ML) fields. Therefore, digital security based on AI is of immense benefit for the security industry. Thus, in response to the increasing use of AI and ML technologies, actions were taken against DW crimes, and applications for crime recognition were developed. This chapter is an attempt to discuss and showcase all the different aspects of applications of AI and ML in DW crime recognition. The author sheds light on the enormous benefits of these applications to the security industry as well as the investigators. Considering AI and ML work as double-edged swords in the cyber world, the author also mentions the importance for investigators to understand and practice them carefully.

Chapter 8

    RamaDevi Jujjuri, PVP Siddhartha Institute of Technology, India
    Arun Kumar Tripathi, KIET Group of Institutions, Delhi, India
    Chandrika V. S., KPR Institute of Engineering and Technology, India
    Sankararao Majji, Gokaraju Rangaraju Institute of Engineering and Technology, India
    Boppuru Rudra Prathap, Christ University, India
    Tulasi Radhika Patnala, GITAM University, India

Cybercrime has several antecedents, including the rapid expansion of the internet and the wide variety of users around the world. It is now possible to use this data for a variety of purposes, whether for profit, non-profit, or purely for the benefit of the individual. As a result, tracing and detecting online acts of terrorism requires the development of a sound technique. Detection and prevention of cybercrime has been the subject of numerous studies and investigations throughout the years. An effective criminal detection system based on face recognition has been developed to prevent this from happening. Principle component analysis (PCA) and linear discriminant analysis (LDA) algorithms can be used to identify criminals based on facial recognition data. Quality, illumination, and vision are all factors that affect the efficiency of the system. The goal of this chapter is to improve accuracy in the facial recognition process for criminal identification over currently used conventional methods. Using proposed hybrid model, we can get the accuracy of 99.9.5%

Chapter 9

    Chitra R., Karunya Institute of Technology and Sciences, India
    Anusha Bamini A. M., Karunya Institute of Technology and Sciences, India
    Chenthil Jegan T. M., St. Xavier's Catholic College of Engineering, India
    Padmaveni K., Hindustan Institute of Technology and Science, India

In the biometric authentication, the stored data is used for the verification of used identity. The unique biological traits commonly used for biological authentication are facial characteristics, fingerprints, and retinas. It also offers superior fraud detection and customer satisfaction, compared to all other traditional multi factor authentication. Deep learning algorithms plays a major role in anomaly detection and fraud identification in various real-time applications. RNNs have proven that they work well in analysing and detecting anomalies in time series data. RNNs have the unique ability for each cell to have its own memory of all the previous cells before it. This allows for RNNs to process sequential data in time steps which other machine learning models cannot do. RNNs can also be found sorting through your emails to sort out spam and phishing emails from friendly emails. This chapter reviews the methodologies, purposes, results, and the benefits of RNNs in anomaly detection in biometric authentication.

Section 4
Content Labeling for Hidden Services Using Keyword Extraction

Chapter 10

Ashwini Dalvi, Veermata Jijabai Technological Institute, India
Saurabh Mahesh Raut, Veermata Jijabai Technological Institute, India
Nirmit Joshi, Veermata Jijabai Technological Institute, India
Dhairya Rajendra Bhuta, Veermata Jijabai Technological Institute, India
Saikumar Nalla, Veermata Jijabai Technological Institute, India
S. G. Bhirud, Veermata Jijabai Technological Institute, India

The data investigation of hidden services on the dark web is gaining attention from the research community and law enforcement agencies. However, the anonymity feature of hidden services makes it difficult to index the hidden services for investigation. Therefore, one of the primary focuses of dark web data investigation research is labelling the hidden services so that the labelled services can be classified or indexed further. The methodology deployed in the proposed work is based on keyword extraction using the graph degeneracy method. The proposed work analyzes the text data by extracting keywords from each hidden service document. The accuracy of the proposed method is validated by LDA-based topic modelling approach. The document labelling obtained by the keyword extraction method and LDA model matched with the accuracy of 78. The main intuition behind the keywords extraction method is that central nodes make good keywords. This is because central nodes with high centrality in the GoW of a document correspond to the document's keywords, which are well-understood by humans.

Chapter 11

Shyamala Devi N., Vels Institute of Science, Technology, and Advanced Studies, Chennai,
India
Sharmila K., Vels Institute of Science, Technology, and Advanced Studies, Chennai, India

The neoteric occurrence, the pandemic, and global crisis entails the extensive use of web portals to unfurl information. While this has built the cognizance of the common man, the infinitely unnoticed enumeration of malicious content on the web has escalated copiously. Spurious data and fake information has done more harm than what is actually unraveled to the public; however, scrupulously meticulous measures to agonize their source and delve into mitigating these data has become quite a challenge. This indignation delves into step-wise analysis of identifying the hoax through systematically programmed algorithms using natural language processing.

Chapter 12

Nikhil Chaturvedi, Shri Vaishnav Vidyapeeth Vishwavidyalaya, India
Jigyasu Dubey, Shri Vaishnav Vidyapeeth Vishwavidyalaya, India

Events are critical for comprehending the things that occur in the actual world. The term "events" is frequently used to describe the numerous relationships between people, places, activities, and things. Events-centered modelling entails the representation of several facets of an event in addition to the semantic representation of event facts. Detecting cybersecurity occurrences is important to keep us aware of the rapidly increasing number of such incidents reported via text. The authors focus on cyber security event detection task in this study, specifically on identifying event trigger words and arguments in the cybersecurity area. For this study, they use the CASIE dataset. They propose a system that involves the events identification, event triggers identification, and event arguments extraction. In this section, they divide the cyber security event sentence classification model into two steps: event trigger and argument identification, and cyber security event sentence classification using the training corpus.

Section 5
Assessment of Dark Web Threat Evolution

Chapter 13

P. William, Sanjivani College of Engineering, Savitribai Phule Pune University, India
M. A. Jawale, Sanjivani College of Engineering, Savitribai Phule Pune University, India
A. B. Pawar, Sanjivani College of Engineering, Savitribai Phule Pune University, India
Rahul R. Bibave, Sanjivani College of Engineering, Savitribai Phule Pune University, India
Priyanka Narode, Sanjivani Jr. College, India

Cyber thieves and terrorists use the dark web as one of the most difficult channels to achieve their nefarious goals. There are many similarities between cyber-crimes and real-world crimes taking place on the dark web. However, the dark web's sheer breadth and anonymity are key to tracing the offenders. The first step in finding effective solutions to cybercrime is to assess the different dark web criminal hazards. The investigation of the dark web includes a review of crimes to minimize crime issues. To assist cyber security specialists, the authors used the systematic literature review approach and extracted data from 65 publications from the most relevant internet resources to meet research aims. As a result of an exhaustive investigation, systematic literature review is able to provide a clear picture of how criminal activity on the dark web is expanding and examine the strengths and weaknesses of existing methods for tracking down criminals. This study has showed, to aid law enforcement in the apprehension of criminals, digital evidence must be analyzed as per established standards.

Chapter 14

Vinod Mahor, IES College of Technology, Bhopal, India
Sadhna Bijrothiya, Maulana Azad National Institute of Technology, Bhopal, India
Rakesh Kumar Bhujade, Information Technology, Government Polytechnic, Daman, India
Jasvant Mandloi, Government Polytechnic, Daman, India
Harshita Mandloi, Shri Vaishnav Vidyapeeth Vishwavidyalaya, India
Stuti Asthana, UT Administration of Dadra and Nagar Haveli and Daman and Diu, India

The authors offer an operational method for obtaining cyber intimidation intelligence from diverse social platforms on the internet, notably dark-web and deep-web sites with Tor, in this study. They concentrate their efforts on gathering information from hacker forums and marketplaces that sell harmful hacking-related items and services. They've established an operational mechanism for gathering information from these sites. This system now collects 400 high-quality cyber-intimidation notifications every week on average. These danger alerts provide details on newly generated malware and exploits that have yet to be used in a cyber-attack. This is a valuable service for cyber-surveillance. Various machine learning approaches are used to dramatically improve the system. They can recall 93% of items in marketplaces and 85% of comments on forums about harmful hacking with great precision using machine learning models. They do preliminary analysis on the data gathered, illustrating how it might be used to assist a security professional in improved intimidation analysis.

Chapter 15

Advancement in technology provides numerous solutions to not only legitimate businesses but to illegal trades as well. Selling substances, drugs, and prohibited merchandise and goods on the internet comes under illegal trading. The internet we surf is merely a thin layer of this deeply rooted miraculous mechanism of connecting the world. The dark web is the part of the deep web that utilizes the internet to flourish the illicit intentions of trading illegal items, thereby fostering the ongoing societal devastation. This chapter is exploring anonymous trading on the dark online marketplace using the Silkroad 2.0 dataset. This work aims to analyze the various aspects of dark e-commerce trading and highlight different themes used for trading illicit drugs on Twitter by performing the thematic analysis using Latent Dirichlet Allocation unsupervised machine learning with a 0.44 coherence score. The findings have shown that developed countries are participating in illegal trading, and teenage schoolgoers can be victims of social media drug trading.

Preface

The use of Machine Learning, Artificial Intelligence, and Intelligent Hardware-based design has resulted in cyber warfare between security agencies and cyber criminals (terrorist groups) in order to construct a web shield and protection from tracking. Cyber attack tactics are becoming more advanced, and thwarting an attack is becoming more difficult, regardless of whether a countermeasure is used. Overall, having a forecast of hacker attacks, effective safety measures, and feasible use of cyber intelligence that enables these activities is critical for a successful treatment of the current situation. Malevolent hackers communicate various types of data over specialized networks, such as the dark web, demonstrating that cyberspace has a great deal of intelligence.

This book focuses on gatherings on the black market and proposes a method for dealing with extricate discussions that incorporate significant data or intelligence from massive amounts of gatherings and recognize qualities of each gathering using procedures such as artificial intelligence, regular language handling, and so on. This technique will allow us to obtain a better understanding of the emerging threats in cyberspace and take appropriate countermeasures against malicious activities. Many individuals consider IoT, at least to the extent that they consider the necessity to screen and regulate the hundreds of thousands of different sensors and devices that make up a Machine Learning-based system. The vast majority of people are also aware of ransomware. The results might be undeniably more concentrated and targeted attacks, not built around the basic cycle of getting into a machine with one malware attempt and launching an attack. Rather, it will be based on embedding a large number of Bots within systems to detect exercises, locate weak targets, and overall decide where and when to attack. Cyber lawbreakers, terrorists, and state-sponsored government operatives use the Dark Web to satisfy their illicit thinking processes since it is one of the most challenging and undetectable channels available. Inside the Dark Web, cyber-violence are indistinguishable from current reality wrongdoings. Nonetheless, the Dark Web administrations' sheer size, unique environment, and anonymity are the primary showdowns to track the lawbreakers. Assessing the cruising Dark Web misbehavior hazards is a crucial step in determining the most likely arrangements against cyber-violations.

The Dark Web project is a long-term logical analysis initiative that aims to study and explain global psychological warfare (Jihadist) activities using a computational, data-driven methodology. Web destinations, debates, chat rooms, online diaries, informal communication locations, recordings, virtual worlds, and so on are examples of online gatherings. In order to conduct connect examination, content investigation, web measurements (specialized refinement) examination, notion investigation, origin investigation, and video investigation, we developed several multilingual data mining, text mining, and web mining processes. This venture's approaches and tactics contribute to the advancement of the field of intelligence and security informatics. As a result of these advancements, connected partners will be better able to carry out illegal intimidation and promote international security and concord.

The goal of this monograph is to convey a picture of the Dark Web environment, suggest a methodical, computational approach to comprehending the difficulties, and define tactics and solutions. It will provide researchers, security professionals, counterterrorism specialists, and strategy developers with useful information. The monograph can also be used as background information or reading material in graduate-level courses on data security, data strategy, data validation, data systems, psychological warfare, and public policy.

The book *Using Computational Intelligence for the Dark Web and Illicit Behavior Detection* is divided into five sections that cover a wide range of subjects.

The sections are:

1. Traffic Analysis and Network Management.
2. Models for Crime Prediction.
3. Anomaly Detection Using Artificial Intelligence and Machine Learning Algorithms.
4. Content Labeling for Hidden Services Using Keyword Extraction.
5. Assessment of Dark Web Threat Evolution.

The following paragraphs provide a summary of what to expect from this research reference.

Section 1, "Traffic Analysis and Network Management," serves as a foundation for the approaches defined for suspicious Traffic Analysis and Network Management analysis by addressing techniques used to analyze vulnerable inputs.

Introducing the book is "Darknet Traffic Analysis and Network Management for Malicious Intent Detection by Neural Network Frameworks" by P William, Siddhartha Choubey, Abha Choubey, and Apurv Verma, Malicious contents of dark web identification strategy is presented using Machine Learning approach. Section 1 concludes and leads into the following portion of the book with Tor Hidden Services analysis given in the chapter "Structure Analysis of Tor Hidden Services Using DOM-Inspired Graphs" by Ashwini Dalvi, Kunjal Shah, Uddhav Jambhalkar, Varun Pawar, Dashank Bhoir, and S. G. Bhirud.

Section 2, "Models for Crime Prediction," provides in-depth examination of cyber terrorism Prediction models and design and architecture.

Opening the section is "Time-Series Models for Crime Prediction in India: An Empirical Comparison" by Sonali Gupta. Through Time-series Models for Crime detection, this part sets a robust foundation for future applications of Cyber Terrorism Threats. The section concludes with an excellent work by Deepika Chauhan, Chaitanya Singh, Dyaneshwar Kudande, and Yu-Chen Hu, "Cyber Security for IoT-Enabled Industry 4.0: Systematic Review for Dark Web Environments."

Section 3, "Anomaly Detection Using Artificial Intelligence and Machine Learning Algorithms," presents extensive coverage of the Anomaly Detection techniques for crime analysis using Machine Learning approach.

The first chapter, "Artificial Intelligence and Machine Learning Algorithms in Dark Web Crime Recognition," by Neha Nitin Gawali and Shailesh Bendale, lays a framework for the dark web crime recognition techniques in this section. The section concludes with "Anomaly Detection in Biometric Authentication Dataset Using Recurrent Neural Networks" by Chitra R., Anusha Bamini A. M., Chenthil Jegan T. M., and Padmaveni K.

Section 4, "Content Labeling for Hidden Services Using Keyword Extraction," describes about Keyword extraction of Hidden Services for malicious activities identification.

The first chapter in the section is "Content Labeling of Hidden Services With Keyword Extraction Using the Graph Decomposition Method" written by Ashwini Dalvi, Saurabh Mahesh Raut, Nirmit Joshi, Dhairya Rajendra Bhuta, Saikumar Nalla, and S G Bhirud.

This section covers dark web criminals' online social network presence and activity, as well as research, approaches, frameworks, architectures, theories, and analyses for detecting dangerous content. The section concludes with "Cyber Security Event Sentence Detection From News Articles Based on Trigger and Argument" by Nikhil Chaturvedi and Jigyasu Dubey.

Section 5, "Assessment of Dark Web Threat Evolution," presents coverage of cyber crime threat evolution modeling techniques.

The section begins with "Systematic Approach for Detection and Assessment of Dark Web Threat Evolution" by P. William, M. A. Jawale, A. B. Pawar, Rahul R. Bibave, and Priyanka Narode. Chapters in this section will look into dark web assessment for threat evolution. The section concludes with "Anonymous Trading on the Dark Online Marketplace: An Exploratory Study" by Piyush Vyas, Gitika Vyas, Akhilesh Chauhan, Romil Rawat, Shrikant Telang, and Madhu Gottumukkala.

OBJECTIVES, IMPACT, AND VALUE

The book will highlight Attackers' techniques, crawling of hidden contents, Intrusion detection using advanced algorithms, TOR Network structure, Memex search engine indexing of anonymous contents at Online Social Networks, IoT Platform, and Intelligent systems activities, Artificial Intelligence and Machine Learning framework, and many other topics.

Due to anonymous behaviors for the purpose of information stealing, fake post circulating, international illicit movement promotions, and illegal activities trafficking by keeping distance and hiding from law enforcement agencies, cyber criminals and terrorist activities are more dangerously activating and fluctuating at dark web platform.

The goal of the book is to demonstrate and expose the challenges that academics and practitioners confront owing to a lack of data about the dark web and high-quality content for analysis and future study. The material offered in the book will assist organizations, academics, security agencies, and security practitioners since it has addressed the most significant subjects of interest, which are not included in any book summary. Researchers are now working on dark web crime analysis and publishing research articles at conferences, and the government is also assisting in the fight against crime in the shadows.

Section 1
Traffic Analysis and Network Management

Chapter 1
Darknet Traffic Analysis and Network Management for Malicious Intent Detection by Neural Network Frameworks

P. William

https://orcid.org/0000-0002-0610-0390

Sanjivani College of Engineering, Savitribai Phule Pune University, India

Siddhartha Choubey

Shri Shankaracharya Technical Campus, India

Abha Choubey

Shri Shankaracharya Technical Campus, India

Apurv Verma

MATS University, India

ABSTRACT

Security breaches may be difficult to detect because attackers are continually tweaking methods to evade detection and utilize legitimate credentials that have already been deployed in network environments. Many firms have a way to resist the evolving sophistication of attacks in network traffic analysis technology. As cloud computing, DevOps, and the internet of things (IoT) become common, it has become more difficult to maintain network visibility. Automated detection of malicious intent using a weight-agnostic neural network architecture is possible with the authors' unique darknet traffic analysis and network management technology. Intelligent forensics tool for network traffic analysis and real-time identification of encrypted information is powerful. Automated neural network search techniques based on a weight-agnostic neural network (WANNs) approach may be used to discover zero-day threats. Many firms struggle to protect their important assets because of the effort required to identify malicious intent on the darknet manually. The advanced solution proposed here overcomes such obstacles.

DOI: 10.4018/978-1-6684-6444-1.ch001

INTRODUCTION

Heterogeneous information systems (Yu and Guo,2019) that are interconnected exchange massive amounts of data in a relatively short time. Static and dynamic data are both included in this data. Constant data streams are required by the continuous flow paradigm, which prevents data from being stored either temporarily or permanently. Since of the system's limited memory, it is very difficult to retrieve flow data that has already been processed because it is either discarded or archived. In order to properly build, administer, and monitor the system's vital infrastructure, as well as monitor assaults and perform research on cybercrime, the analysis, monitoring, and categorization of Internet network traffic (Demertzis and Iliadis,2015) need a specialised solution and a useful tool.

Requests, responses, and control data are all examples of data types that may be sent across a network in the form of packets. When evaluating individual network packets, it is very difficult to make conclusions and eliminate safe conclusions since the information sent between network devices is separated into a number of packets that are connected and include all of the data. It is far more difficult to use standard mathematical analysis approaches because of the network traffic's unpredictable and accidental nature, which favours the network traffic modelling approach (LXing et al.,2020).

In order to make better decisions, many companies acquire as much web traffic data as possible and use it to assess and correlate it with the services they represent and to compare it with previous log files. Analyzing network traffic allows for safe inferences about the network, the users, and the total data consumption to be formed, allowing for the modelling of traffic in order to optimise network resources based on monitoring needs, as well as compliance with legal and security standards. There are a number of ways traffic analysis may be utilised in cybersecurity to safeguard services, guarantee the delivery of important data and find random causes of difficulties, modify or strengthen intrusion detection systems and identify cybercriminals (Yang and Liu,2019). Using traffic packet analysis technology has the following drawbacks: (Siswanto et al.,2019)

1. In spite of the fact that the techniques are extremely effective at preventing DoS/DDoS attacks, buffer overflow attacks, and certain types of malwares, they can also be used to launch similar attacks from the adversary side, depending on their mode of operation;
2. They complicate the operation of active network security methods and make them extremely difficult to manage. In addition, they use up more computer resources and severely slow down online transactions, especially encrypted traffic, which necessitates a higher degree of reconstruction of messages and entities;
3. One drawback is the ease with which the recipient or sender of the text being analysed may be recognised, resulting in privacy concerns for both parties.

In the event of a zero-day attack, they are useless. Specialist analytic services are needed to get a thorough picture of the network environment and any risks, as the need for security services grows. With the help of global threat environment cyber threat data, this information allows for a targeted and knowledgeable response to cyber-related issues (Samrin and Vasumathi, 2019).

In essence, a fully automated cybersecurity environment is required for the information ecosystem and its vital applications. It is possible to identify known and new dangers and mitigate the risk to crucial data using a scalable troubleshooting or logging technique in these solutions (Mercaldo et al.,2019).

In order to identify hazardous intent in real time, we have developed a unique darknet traffic analysis and network management system that employs a weight-agnostic neural network architecture. Computational intelligence forensics tool for network traffic analysis, malware decryption and real-time identification of encrypted data is powerful and accurate. Weight agnostic neural networks (WANNs) may be used to perform a wide range of tasks, including the detection of zero-day vulnerabilities. Automating the process of identifying malicious intent on the darknet reduces the skills and effort barrier that prevents many firms from properly safeguarding their most essential assets. In this study, researchers used CIC Darknet2020, a dataset that includes both darknet and conventional traffic from audio-streaming, browsing, chatting and emailing, P2P and file transfers, as well as video-streaming and VOIP. Either Tor or VPN infrastructure is used to distribute this data, or they are not installed at all. It's possible to get more information on the well-known dataset for assessing cyber security risks elsewhere (Lashkari et al.,2020). More and more public benchmark data sets have been generated from various sources, but their structure and eventual adoption as standards have been varied. It is thus unnecessary to continue choosing and curating specific criteria. Since our hypothesis needed to be verified, we employed an established database of comparison to perform reliable comparison experiments.

LITERATURE REVIEWS

Only a small portion of the internet is accessible to the general public through search engines. For those who don't know, the "DeepWeb" is the area of the internet that search engines can't reach. Subclasses of deep webs are known as darknets, which are accessible only via specialised software like the Tor browser (HaddadPajouh et al.,2018). Tor enables users to hide their identity and prevent traffic from being traced back to the source users by routing their traffic via other users' devices. To move data from one layer to the next, Tor has built "relays" on computers across the world that act as data conduits for the network's tunnels. Each of the relays receives the encrypted data. There are three relays along the path of a Tor message before it reaches its final destination. This method uses Tor nodes (consensus) operated by volunteers all over the globe to communicate regularly while maintaining total forward secrecy between the nodes and Tor's hidden services.

In spite of the fact that the Tor network is based on OSI Level 4 (Transport Layer), the onion proxy software offers a Level 5 Socket Secure (SOCKS) interface to its users (Session layer). To further protect the integrity of the network, messages are encrypted before being sent between the retransmission nodes (entry guards, middle relays, and exit relays) (Sun et al.,2018). This prevents anyone along the communication path from being able to decipher the encrypted data and identify either the sender or the recipient. In addition to providing encryption, the Tor network is designed to mimic traditional HTTPS traffic, making the detection of Tor channels difficult even for experienced network engineers or analysts. Whether you want to know if you're communicating with someone who is using the Tor network, you can't just monitor and identify a session based on the TCP port 443, which is also used by HTTPS.

In order to properly detect Tor traffic, statistical analysis and the detection of SSL protocol violations are required. Public-key and symmetric-key cryptography are used to encrypt data using SSL. Before a secure connection (handshake) can be formed, a sequence of messages must be exchanged between the server and the client. Through public-key encryption, the server may verify the identity of the client, and the two parties can then work together to create a symmetric key that can be used to quickly encrypt and decode data sent between them. It is also possible to utilise a handshake to authenticate the

Figure 1. The relationship between the Internet, DeepWeb and DarkWeb

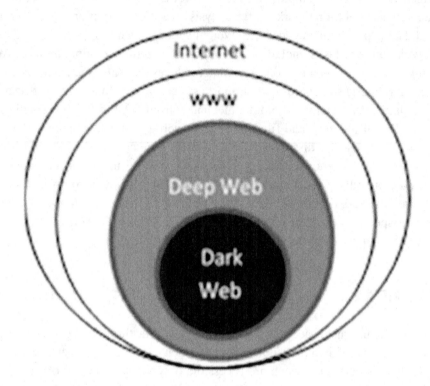

client's identity in the server. SSL certificates created by each Tor client are self-signed, and the random domains generated by each client vary every three minutes, making it possible to identify Tor sessions when paired with HTTPS traffic on a network (Siswanto et al.,2019).

Dark web research is becoming more popular. Network intrusion detection methods accounted for a large section of the cybersecurity literature review (Samrin and Vasumathi, 2019) Machine learning and network traffic analysis have recently received a lot of attention from the IoT (HaddadPajouh et al.,2018), as well as research on network traffic classification (Soysal and Schmidt, 2022)

With the help of Yang et al. (Yang et al.,2019), an analytical system for visualising the links between various forum posts and posters has been developed, enabling researchers to dig deeper into the current dominant dark network communication technique, TOR. Then there's another study (Yang et al.,2019) that presents a framework for hidden threat intelligence using Hadoop. In order to determine the features of important dark network criminal networks, a web crawler uses the anonymous TOR technology to gather data, which serves as a basis for further investigation into dark network activity. The Knowledge Discovery in Databases KDD-Cup 99 dataset was examined by Samrin et al. (Samrin and Vasumathi,2017) who found an effective strategy for classifying and recognising intrusions in these datasets. In (Summerville et al.,2004) Summerville et al. mapped unlabeled trade data into a set of two-dimensional grids and developed a collection of bitmaps that differentiated between regular and abnormal sessions. (Summerville et al.,2004) Many intrusion detection methods as well as data volume reduction techniques were evaluated by Kwon et al. (Kwon et al.,2019). For the most part, these investigations used the KDD-Cup

1999 dataset (Tavallaee et al.,2021)or its successor, NSL-KDD (Demertzis and Iliadis,2014), which has been broadly adopted by the academic community (Sellappan and Srinivasan,2014). Even though the bulk of anomaly-based network intrusion detection systems employ supervised algorithms, Zhang et al. (Zhang and Zulkernine,2006) found that these systems were inefficient and presented an unsupervised outlier identification strategy to overcome these inefficiencies. For example, Singh et al. (Singh and Venkatesan, 2018) coupled random forest classification with k-means clustering methods while Song et al. (Song et al.,2017) presented an ensemble k-nearest neighbour graph-based anomaly detector with a deep autoencoder as part of their hybrid approach to intrusion detection systems. According to Soysal et al. in (Soysal and Schmidt,2010), Bayesian networks and decision trees were determined to be suitable for high-speed traffic flow categorization in their review. Using a thorough analysis of traffic classification methodologies for machine learning, Pacheco et al. in (Pacheco et al,2018) identified some trends, while Dhote et al. in (Dhote et al.,2015) assessed the strengths and weaknesses of three prominent methods for categorising different types of Internet traffic. An intrusion detection system (HAST-IDS) based on spatial–temporal features is also proposed (hierarchical spatial–temporal feature-based), which learns low-level spatial network features from network traffic by using deep convolutional neural networks (CNNs), before learning high-level temporal network features by using long short-term memory networks.

The proposed method offers a low false alarm rate (FAR) and a good accuracy and detection rate, according to the authors. In (HaddadPajouh et al.,2018), HaddadPajouh et al. provide a fast and large-scale monitoring system for darknet traffic monitoring. Pre-processing and a classifier make up the system.

There are 17 distinct darknet traffic characteristics encoded in the feature vector created by the pre-processing portion. Known distributed denial-of-service (DDoS) attack traffic features are used to train classifier data for faster online learning. DDoS backscatter packets were successfully identified using the recommended technique, according to the study's authors, who provided measurement data. It's also quite quick to learn how to deal with new threats. As a matter of fact, new study has found a flaw in the popular assumption that training machine learning models relies on independent and equally distributed data samples. Research on data poisoning, model improvement, and machine learning model explanation has been prompted by this. (Zhang et al.,2020)Since a machine learning model's decision-making process relies on trust and transparency, it is becoming more important to be able to explain why a given prediction was made. For every prediction, Shapley values add a certain weight to each characteristic (Zhang and Gao,2011). Model-independent interpretability of two explanations based on Shapley values was assessed by Messalas et al. (Messalas et al.,2019), for example, who introduced the top similarity approach. The Shapley value, which is a game-theoretic solution concept that quantifies how each network component contributes to the overall performance of the network, is also discussed in this chapter. Pruning more parts of the network at once may speed up the execution process and enhance results. The network is fine-tuned using an evolutionary hill-climbing approach after each simplification.

METHODOLOGY AND DATASET

Recently, it has been shown that advanced machine learning algorithms, such as neural networks, may benefit industries and manufacturing processes across the board. Their success depends on the thorough analysis of data that reflect the functioning of a system. For example, by seeing patterns in the data that has been collected, it is possible to extract valuable information that may be used to anticipate the future and so increase the value of a certain industry. There are many linear layers in a multilayer neural network, which is considered the simplest learning architecture. There are a total of three levels, each of which takes a previous level input and runs it through an activation function before generating the level's output through a combination of weights and a bias vector. This procedure is continued until the final level's classification result is obtained. To calculate the sorting error, an appropriate loss function is used. Stochastic gradient descent is used to adjust the weights at each level successively in order to minimise the loss. Even still, putting it into practise in the actual world remains a complex and specialised task (Leon,2014). For this reason, a variety of variables are coordinated by data scientists utilising publicly available training datasets. This is a time-consuming, labor-intensive, and costly procedure.

MetaLearning

Automating and solving the problem of machine learning algorithms being employed in specialised ways, MetaLearning is a breakthrough comprehensive technique. Machine learning algorithms and hyperparameters may be discovered via automated machine learning, which is the goal of this project (Kerschke et al.,2019). It's possible to think about machine learning in particular as a search problem, aiming to solve for an unknown underlying mapping function. To a varying extent, the search space, algorithmic parameters (weights), hyper-parametric features, and their inherent unpredictability all influence how far one can map out a workable function. Techniques such as MetaLearning allow for quick new task learning utilising different sorts of information, such as the issue, the method employed (e.g. performance metrics), or patterns drawn from data from a prior problem to find the linkages between the datasets. To put it another way, they use cognitive information from unknown cases selected from the distribution and examples from the real world to enhance the result of the learning process. As a result, it's possible to use many learning algorithms to solve a certain problem effectively.

A meta-learning system should handle three issues (Xu et al.,2019).:

1. The system must have a learning subsystem;
2. Experience must be gleaned from metadata connected with the dataset being processed or from previously completed learning assignments in related or unrelated fields.
3. The selection of the learning bias must be dynamic.

Meta-learning models that can be trusted should be trained on a variety of learning tasks and fine-tuned for better performance on generalising tasks, including ones that may include previously unknown scenarios. supervised learning tasks are related to a dataset D, which includes attribute vectors and class labels. Here are the model's best parameters:

Each tag belongs to a certain group of L tags.

Assuming a limited collection of rapid learning assistance, the goal is to reduce prediction error in data samples with unknown tags. According to one interpretation of fast learning, it is possible to accomplish rapid learning by creating an artificial dataset with a restricted subset of tags (to prevent disclosing all tags in the model) and making tweaks to the optimization process.

There are a total of two data points for each sample pair (SL/BL). As a consequence, the model gets honed to be applicable to new datasets that aren't familiar to it. Meta-learning symbols have been included into the supervised learning model to provide the following function. LSTM, for example, is not regarded a meta-learning technique since it does not have an external memory. On the other hand, neural architecture search is the best meta-learning architecture for neural networks (NAS) (Hu et al.,2020).

Figure 2. Search strategies of three neural architectures

Neural Architecture Search

Machine learning's most widely used area, artificial neural networks, may now be built automatically. By using NAS, it is possible to build networks that are on par with or even better than those that are made by hand alone! The categorization of NAS techniques is based on the search space, the search strategy, and the performance evaluation mechanism used. (Hu et al.,2020).:

1. Identifying several different types of neural networks that can be constructed and optimised in order to determine the optimal type of neural network for solving the given problem, for example, a forward neural network (FFNN), a recurrent neural network (RNN), and so on, is the first step in the search area.
2. The search strategy specifies how the search space will be explored, i.e., the structure of the architectural design within an internal search field of hyperparameters (levels, weights, learning rate, and so on);
3. The performance appraisal strategy quantifies the performance of a potential neural network without constructing or training it; 4. The performance evaluation strategy quantifies the performance of a potential neural network without constructing or training it.

It is possible to investigate the many levels of standard design using a variety of NAS methodologies that examine both micro and macro components. Three NAS techniques and hierarchical search approaches are shown in Figure 2. If you're looking for an answer in a hierarchical search that has several levels, the first level consists of the most fundamental functions, the second level is a directed acyclic graph that connects the primitive functions, and so on.

A subfield of automated machine learning, NAS adheres to the best practises for reducing programme load, providing stable and simple environments, minimising the number of actions required for use, and providing a clear methodology for discovering knowledge in unfamiliar environments (Bublea and Caleanu,2020). It is the goal of this study to find the optimal neural network that is the least expensive in the dataset D, given a search space for neural architectures F and input data D divided into Dtrain and Dval.

As part of the NAS process, a neural network architecture is created that can learn from the input dataset and precisely coordinate optimal hyperparameters to produce an accurate model that can generalise well to data outside of the training and testing sets. Techniques such as SGD, Adam, and regularisation are commonplace in hyperparameter tuning and optimization (Hu et al.,2020). Basically, they allow for the formulation of the most effective learning techniques, with high performance outcomes, with less effort and knowledge required.

This approach may be used with tactics that are more natural, such as those that emphasise the importance of instinct over teaching, such as the NAS method. Many species in biology, such as predators, are born with the ability to perform complex motor and sensory tasks, and this is frequently more than enough for the species' long-term survival. As opposed to training real neurons, it is more common to employ learning algorithms to find the weight parameters of an architecture that is judged suitable for modelling the job at hand. It is possible to design a neural network based on natural social behaviours that is capable of achieving a certain job even when weight parameters are randomised, enabling them to operate effectively without training while simultaneously being taught to perform even better.

Proposed Method

A weight-agnostic neural network (WANN) was employed in this study (Zhong et al.,2020). With this strategy, the neural network may perform a certain task without regard to the weights of the connections between the network's building blocks, which means that no training is required (WLee et al.,1996). In the hunt for architectural neural networks with specific biases capable of categorising a given problem even when random weights are applied, the notion of deploying WANNs is crucial. An examination of such a design may uncover variables that perform well in their interaction context even without prior training, allowing for the development of an effective cyber-security system that can detect zero-day attacks with confidence.

Based on this research's analysis of WANN architectural frameworks, it is clear that inductive bias is fully exploited to provide biased outcomes as a consequence of assumptions/choices made for either a case space representation or an engine description. Theoretically, there is no limit to the unbounded space of conceivable possibilities. This space is limited, which introduces the first level of bias, by stating the kind of knowledge, i.e., the representation. There's a good chance that the search area is still too large to conduct an extensive search, however. When searching for a new solution, the search algorithm does not go through every possible option; instead, it uses heuristic or probabilistic methods to get an answer. Random selection is superior than a learning system when these other options are available.

This bias is compounded by the selection procedure and underlying assumption that this data will have a uniform distribution under all circumstances, which are both flawed in their own right. As a result, it may be concluded that a model constructed from a modest set of training data would be equally as good at describing unique, unknown cases. All learning algorithms have inherent biases in their representations, methods and data. This is a fundamental, essential trait that must be taken into consideration while exploring ideal neural network architectures. Another crucial step in choosing the best architecture for a specific problem is analysing the interpretability of the approaches used.

The model's global interpretability may be seen as a whole. In order to understand the model's decisions and determine its most important traits, one must first understand how it makes those decisions. The explanations at the universal level include a wide global description of the model that is neither detailed nor true due to the difficulties of gaining a perfect understanding in reality. Also known as "local interpretability," this refers to the ability to deduce the model's logic for certain choices by looking at just a small portion of the information. Predictions based on little amounts of data are more likely to be linear or monotonic than complex, depending on a small number of parameters. When it comes to understanding cooperative/coalitional game theory, Shapley values (Zhang et al.,2020) are a great way to get at it. There is an actual function that allocates values to groups of players in order to calculate the payoff/gain for cooperative gaming participants. WANN architectural structures provide a significant barrier for those who want to comprehend Shapley values. Using WANN architectures, it is possible to describe the dataset's profit function as a cooperative game in which each player represents a feature of a particular WANN architectural structure. As a result, the model's selection is explained by the Shapley values, which show the relative relevance of each feature.

This equation (Phillips and Marden,2018) yields the Shapley value of a characteristic I in a neural network model f, in which F is the set of attributes, S is a subset of F, and M is the total of F. Each characteristic's contribution to the prediction is calculated and subtracted using this connection, which measures its significance. This connection. Weighted average of all possible subsets S in F, M! is the result. SHP (Molnar,2020) explains model selections by using Shapley values as an explanation. SHAP is unique in that it works as a linear model and, more accurately, as a feature addition approach.

The SHAP technique, on the surface, seems to use a local linear approach to explain behaviour. While the model as a whole may be sophisticated, determining whether or not a given variable is present or not is relatively straightforward. Thus, the Pearson's R correlation table may be used to establish the degree of linear correlation between the set's independent and dependent variables, with dispersion s2X and s2Y, respectively, and the covariance sXY= Cov(X,Y) = E(X,Y) E(X)E(Y), which is calculated by calculating the Pearson's R correlation table:

The predictive power score (PPS) methodology (Wetschoreck et al.,2020) was utilised in this work to establish predictive associations between available data since the aforementioned method could not uncover nonlinear correlations such as sinus waves and quadratic curves and investigate the links between important variables. To describe non-linear relationships and categorical data, PPS differs from the correlation matrix in that asymmetric connections between variables A and B may be modelled using PPS. In practise, scoring is a measure of the model's ability to anticipate a variable objective using off-sample variable prediction, which implies that this technique may considerably enhance the efficiency of discovering hidden patterns in the data and picking appropriate forecast variables.

Obtaining a local explanation for models that are initially capable of performing without training and then strengthened via teaching is another key component of the PPS approach. Since huge data dimensions and model hyper-parameter values may have a significant impact on how well SHAP performs, feature selection must be done before using the approach. Since of the difficulty in solving the challenge, the model's predictions are much more difficult to produce because they demand a great deal of explanation for each of the model's characteristics and the distances between them. A feature selection strategy based on this understanding was utilised to choose the most important characteristics while reducing their overall number to preserve as much useful information as possible. If low-resolution characteristics are selected, the subsequent learning system will function badly, but if relevant information is selected, the system will be simple and efficient. This step is important. Overall, the goal is to choose traits that result in big variations across groups and minimal distinctions between classes.

The PPS method was used to identify features, and the MAE metric was utilised to determine the PPS for numerical variables. It is computed as follows: where fi is the estimated value and yi is the real value. The MAE is a measure of estimation or prediction error. The absolute inaccuracy of their connection is defined as the average of their absolute values of the quotient. These F-score metrics (harmonic means) were used for categorical variables, and the higher the F-score was, the higher these two metrics were. The value is calculated using the following relationship:

NAS creation using the WANN approach and Shapley value explanations, after the PPS method was utilised to precede the feature selection process, was applied to establish a cybersecurity environment with completely automated solutions capable of detecting material from the darknet.

Table 1. Traffic Details of Darknet Network

ID	Traffic Category	Applications Used
0	Audio-Stream	Vimeo and YouTube
1	Audio-Stream	Crypto streaming platform
2	Browsing	Firefox and Chrome
3	Chat	ICQ, AIM, Skype, Facebook, and Hangouts
4	Email	SMTPS, POP3S and IMAPS
5	P2P	uTorrent and Transmission (BitTorrent)
6	File Transfer	Skype, SFTP, FTPS using FileZilla and an external service
7	File Transfer	Crypto transferring platform
8	Video-Stream	Vimeo and YouTube
9	Video-Stream	Crypto streaming platform
10	VOIP	Facebook, Skype, and Hangouts voice calls

Dataset

To access the darknet, one must have specialised software, configurations, or licencing, as well as communication protocols and ports that are not commonly used. The network's passive behaviour in processing incoming packets makes it unreachable to regular web browsers, and any connection to the darknet is treated with suspicion.

In order to categorise real-time applications, classification of darknet data is essential, and analysis of this traffic allows both pre- and post-attack monitoring of malware. Choosing, designing, or comparing machine learning algorithms in new techniques may be a difficult task depending on the target problem and research aims. Some of these public datasets are real-world and simulated, although their structure and acceptability as standards vary widely from one to the next.

It is thus unnecessary to continue choosing and curating specific criteria. In order to run an accurate comparison experiment, we will require a well-known benchmark dataset. When analysing CICDarknet2020, researchers were able to see all of the many types of traffic that can be found on the darknet as well as the usual traffic associated with other types of services such as audio/browsing/chat/email/P2P/transfer/video/VOIP/files/session/authentication. Table 1 shows the final categories and the applications that implement them. Information about datasets, their selection, and evaluation may be found in (Lashkari et al.,2020).

EXPERIMENTS AND RESULTS

For multi-class classification, all of the indices below should be calculated in a one-vs.all method. True positive (FP) and true negative (FN) indexes in the confusion matrix reveal the level of incorrect categorisation. The FP is the number of times we get a false positive, and the FN is the opposite. As an alternative, the true positive (TP) statistic measures the number of records where we get the right answer. The actual negative contrast is what we mean when we talk about the contrast (TN). Total accuracy (TA) may be calculated using the following equations: True positive rate (TPR), True negative rate (TNR), Total accuracy (TA)

Table 2. Classification Performance Metrics

Classifier	Accuracy	AUC	Recall	Precision	F1	Kappa	MCC	TT (s)	RAM-H
Extreme Gradient Boosting (XGB)	0.9012	0.9953	0.7500	0.9014	0.8990	0.8751	0.8756	441.61	0.054
CatBoost	0.8927	0.9942	0.7227	0.8936	0.8894	0.8642	0.8648	606.07	0.0662
Decision Tree	0.8858	0.9477	0.7406	0.8845	0.8849	0.8561	0.8562	1.90	0.00016
Random Forest	0.8846	0.9848	0.7245	0.8829	0.8835	0.8545	0.8545	19.83	0.00145
Gradient Boosting	0.8801	0.9916	0.7106	0.8797	0.8764	0.8482	0.8488	645.38	0.0681
Extra Trees	0.8775	0.9677	0.7201	0.8756	0.8762	0.8455	0.8455	11.61	0.00115
k-Neighbors	0.8504	0.9663	0.6748	0.8462	0.8466	0.8105	0.8108	7.45	0.00091
Light Gradient Boosting Machine	0.7826	0.8986	0.5387	0.7911	0.7808	0.7247	0.7259	17.41	0.00137
Ridge Classifier	0.6664	0.0000	0.3276	0.6672	0.6221	0.5659	0.5727	0.40	0.00006
Linear Discriminant Analysis	0.6497	0.9136	0.4400	0.6439	0.6231	0.5535	0.5575	2.01	0.00025
Quadratic Discriminant Analysis	0.3858	0.8710	0.4026	0.6325	0.4394	0.2936	0.3144	0.71	0.000087
Logistic Regression	0.3174	0.6756	0.1226	0.3089	0.2753	0.1237	0.1433	126.46	0.0135
Naïve Bayes	0.2974	0.6328	0.1281	0.2303	0.2278	0.0960	0.1120	0.13	0.00019
SVM—Linear Kernel	0.1937	0.0000	0.1037	0.2419	0.1248	0.0379	0.0485	130.74	0.0138
Ada Boost	0.1626	0.7142	0.1521	0.0501	0.0713	0.0788	0.1193	14.27	0.00129

AUC: Area under the Curve; MCC: Matthews Correlation Coefficient; TT: Training Time.

Table 2 was generated using the information in Section 3.4 to identify and categorise network traffic in Tor, non-Tor, VPN, and non-VPN services to compare the recommended approach. In Figure 4, each algorithm's categorization approach is laid out in depth. We used CPU time or speed (the total CPU time utilised by the process since it started, precise to hundredths of a second) and memory usage as RAM hours as further estimations of computational resource utilisation (RAM-H). We used a shell script based on the "top" command to keep tabs on Linux processes and resource use.

ROC curves, a confusion matrix, and a class prediction error diagram for the XGBoost method, which had the highest success rate, are shown in Figures 5–7. (Accuracy 90 percent).

Figure 3 depicts the receiver operating characteristic (ROC) curves for each axis in a color-coded fashion. The connection between the true-positive rate (sensitivity) and the false-positive rate (1—specificity) when the threshold is altered is shown by the receiver operating characteristic (ROC) curve. Points in the upper-left corner of the test would be optimal and the test would have 100 percent sensitivity and specificity.

Figure 4 shows the darknet dataset's confusion matrix. Accuracy may be observed in the green squares and the light green regions, which show a high percentage of correct answers and low percentage of incorrect answers. Figure 5 depicts the accuracy of our classifier in predicting the proper classes, as represented by the class prediction error curve. The number of training samples for each class in the fitted classification model is shown in this image as a stacked bar chart. Each bar shows the proportion of predictions for that class (including FN and FP). With the use of class prediction error, we were able to see the classes our classifier had trouble with, as well as the incorrect answers it provides for each one. In this way, the strengths and weaknesses of alternative models, as well as difficulties specific to our dataset, may be better understood.

DISCUSSION AND CONCLUSIONS

A innovative, reliable, low-demand, and highly efficient network traffic analysis system based on sophisticated computational intelligence technologies is presented in this paper. Cyber-attacks are typically the

Figure 3. Receiver operating characteristic curves of the XGBoost classifier.

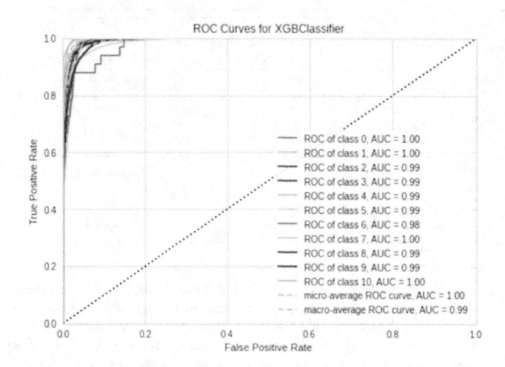

Figure 4. Confusion matrix of the XGBoost classifier.

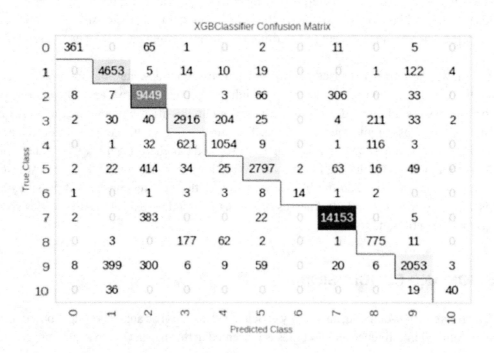

Figure 5. Class prediction error of the XGBoost classifier

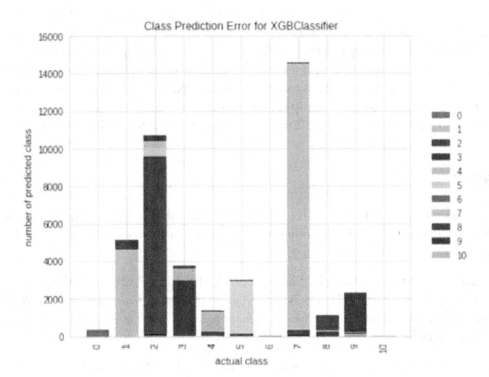

cause of network traffic anomalies, and the proposed framework utilises the advantages of metalearning in order to identify these anomalies and their causes.

A comprehensive dataset that includes both legitimate and malicious network traffic was used to test the effectiveness of the recommended digital security solution. This study's goal was to examine how neural network architecture can codify solutions and imitate a certain activity without prior learning. No human interaction is required to capture an unknown mapping function between input data and output data using the suggested holistic approach, which automates and solves the challenge of using neural network discovering methods to address specific problems without needing system training.

A weight-agnostic neural network architecture for darknet traffic monitoring, big data analysis and network management, with the purpose of automating the process of identifying hazardous intent in real time, is presented in this paper. For the first time, a new architecture for developing adaptive pattern recognition systems is proposed in the literature, and it is now being implemented and published for the first time. To emphasise, the proposed approach simplifies the operation of NAS strategies since it employs multiple features of special techniques to produce meaningful intermediate representations from complex neural network design. Increased training stability and excellent classification accuracy are achieved by the initial use of the independent variables' predictive potential.

When designing neural networks that can be understood, the response should be directly included into the network architecture rather than being trained as a weight. The proposed architecture is more resistant to changes in node inputs than current learning algorithms, establishing the basis for a formidable defence against adversarial attacks or even completely destroyed networks.

There should be a focus on automating pre-training technique parameter optimization in order to achieve even more efficient, accurate, and speedy classification processes. In addition, a more complex architecture based on Siamese neural networks in a parallel and distributed computing environment (Demertzis et al.,2020) or through blockchain (Rantos et al.,2019) might be used to study the system's progress. In addition, the operation of a network using methods of self-improvement and parameter definition could be investigated in the direction of future expansion, so that the process of selecting architectural hyper-parameters can be fully automated in order to identify dark web services (Marin et al.,2018), dark web exploits (Cherqi et al.,2018), and malicious traffic from this network (He et al.,2019).

REFERENCES

Ahmad, M., Abdullah, M., & Han, D. (2019). A novel encoding scheme for complex neural architecture search. *Proceedings of the 2019 34th International Technical Conference on Circuits/Systems, Computers and Communications (ITC-CSCC),* 1–4.

Almukaynizi, M., Grimm, A., Nunes, E., Shakarian, J., & Shakarian, P. (2017). Predicting cyber threats through hacker social networks in Darkweb and Deepweb forums. In *Proceedings of the 2017 International Conference of the Computational Social Science Society of the Americas (CSS 2017)*. Association for Computing Machinery.

Almukaynizi, M., Paliath, V., Shah, M., Shah, M., Shakarian, P., & Cryptocurrency, F. (2018). Attack indicators using temporal logic and Darkweb data. *Proceedings of the 2018 IEEE International Conference on Intelligence and Security Informatics (ISI)*, 91–93.

Austin, J., Kennedy, J., & Lees, K. (1995). A neural architecture for fast rule matching. *Proceedings of the Second New Zealand International Two-Stream Conference on Artificial Neural Networks and Expert Systems*, 255–260.

Bublea, A., & Caleanu, C. D. (n.d.). *Deep Learning based Eye Gaze Tracking for Automotive Applications: An Auto-Keras Approach*. Academic Press.

Buehner, M., & Young, P. (2006). A tighter bound for the echo state property. *IEEE Transactions on Neural Networks*, *17*(3), 820–824. doi:10.1109/TNN.2006.872357 PMID:16722187

Cherqi, O., Mezzour, G., Ghogho, M., & el Koutbi, M. (2018). Analysis of hacking related trade in the Darkweb. *Proceedings of the 2018 IEEE International Conference on Intelligence and Security Informatics (ISI)*, 79–84.

Coulombe, J. C., York, M. C. A., & Sylvestre, J. (2017). Computing with networks of nonlinear mechanical oscillators. *PLoS One*, *12*(6), e0178663. doi:10.1371/journal.pone.0178663 PMID:28575018

Dale, M., Miller, J. F., Stepney, S., & Trefzer, M. A. (2016). Evolving carbon nanotube reservoir computers. *Lecture Notes in Computer Science*, 49–61. doi:10.1007/978-3-319-41312-9_5

Demertzis, K., & Iliadis, L. (2014). A hybrid network anomaly and intrusion detection approach based on evolving spiking neural network classification. *Communications in Computer and Information Science*, 11–23. doi:10.1007/978-3-319-11710-2_2

Demertzis, K., & Iliadis, L. (2014). Evolving computational intelligence system for Malware detection. In *Lecture Notes in Business Information Processing* (pp. 322–334). Springer. doi:10.1007/978-3-319-07869-4_30

Demertzis, K., & Iliadis, L. (2015). Evolving smart URL filter in a zone-based policy firewall for detecting algorithmically generated malicious domains. *Lecture Notes in Computer Science*, 223–233. doi:10.1007/978-3-319-17091-6_17

Demertzis, K., & Iliadis, L. (2020). GeoAI: A model-agnostic meta-ensemble zero-shot learning method for hyperspectral image analysis and classification. *Algorithms*, *13*(3), 61. doi:10.3390/a13030061

Demertzis, K., Iliadis, L., & Anezakis, V.-D. (2018). *A dynamic ensemble learning framework for data stream analysis and real-time threat detection*. In Lecture Notes in Computer Science. Springer. doi:10.1007/978-3-030-01418-6_66

Demertzis, K., Iliadis, L., & Bougoudis, I. (2020). Gryphon: A semi-supervised anomaly detection system based on one-class evolving spiking neural network. *Neural Computing & Applications*, *32*(9), 4303–4314. doi:10.100700521-019-04363-x

Demertzis, K., Iliadis, L., Tziritas, N., & Kikiras, P. (2020). Anomaly detection via blockchained deep learning smart contracts in industry 4.0. *Neural Computing & Applications*, *32*(23), 17361–17378. doi:10.100700521-020-05189-8

Demertzis, K., Iliadis, L. S., & Anezakis, V.-D. (2018). Extreme deep learning in biosecurity: The case of machine hearing for marine species identification. *Journal of Information and Telecommunication*, *2*(4), 492–510. doi:10.1080/24751839.2018.1501542

Department of Health. (2020). https://www.unb.ca/cic/datasets/dohbrw-2020.html

Dhanabal, L., & Shantharajah, D. S. P. (2015). A study on NSL-KDD dataset for intrusion detection system based on classification algorithms. *International Journal of Advanced Research in Computer and Communication Engineering*, *4*, 7.

Dhote, Y., Agrawal, S., & Deen, A. J. (2015). A survey on feature selection techniques for Internet traffic classification. *Proceedings of the 2015 International Conference on Computational Intelligence and Communication Networks (CICN)*, 1375–1380.

Ding, J., Guo, X., & Chen, Z. (2020). Big data analyses of ZeroNet sites for exploring the new generation DarkWeb. In *Proceedings of the 3rd International Conference on Software Engineering and Information Management (ICSIM2020)* (pp. 46–52). Association for Computing Machinery.

Dyrmishi, S., Elshawi, R., & Sakr, S. (2019). A decision support framework for AutoML systems: A meta-learning approach. *Proceedings of the 2019 International Conference on Data Mining Workshops (ICDMW)*, 97–106.

HaddadPajouh, H., Dehghantanha, A., Khayami, R., & Choo, K.-K. R. (2018). A deep Recurrent Neural Network based approach for Internet of Things malware threat hunting. *Future Generation Computer Systems*, *85*, 88–96. doi:10.1016/j.future.2018.03.007

He, S., He, Y., & Li, M. (2021). Classification of illegal activities on the dark web. In *Proceedings of the 2019 2nd International Conference on Information Science and Systems (ICISS 2019). Electronics*. Association for Computing Machinery.

Hu, W., Li, M., Yuan, C., Zhang, C., & Wang, J. (2020). Diversity in neural architecture search. n *Proceedings of the 2020 International Joint Conference on Neural Networks (IJCNN)*, 1–8.

Huang, G., Zhu, Q., & Siew, C. (2006). Extreme learning machine: Theory and applications. *Neurocomputing, 70*(1–3), 489–501. doi:10.1016/j.neucom.2005.12.126

Hyndman, R. J., & Athanasopoulos, G. (2018). *Forecasting: Principles and practice* (2nd ed.). OTexts.

Jin, H., Song, Q., & Hu, X. (2019). *Auto-keras: An efficient neural architecture search system*. https://arxiv.org/abs/1806.10282

Kerschke, P., Hoos, H. H., Neumann, F., & Trautmann, H. (2019). Automated algorithm selection: Survey and perspectives. *Evolutionary Computation, 27*(1), 3–45. doi:10.1162/evco_a_00242 PMID:30475672

Kwon, D., Kim, H., Kim, J., Suh, S. C., Kim, I., & Kim, K. J. (2019). A survey of deep learning-based network anomaly detection. *Cluster Computing, 22*(S1), 949–961. doi:10.100710586-017-1117-8

Lashkari, A. H., Kaur, G., & Rahali, A. (2020). DIDarknet: A contemporary approach to detect and characterize the Darknet traffic using deep image learning. In *Proceedings of the 10th International Conference on Communication and Network Security (ICCNS 2020)* (pp. 1–13). Association for Computing Machinery.

Lee, Bartlett, & Williamson. (1996). Efficient agnostic learning of neural networks with bounded fan-in. *IEEE Transactions on Information Theory, 42*(6), 2118–2132. doi:10.1109/18.556601

Lekamalage, C. K. L., Song, K., Huang, G., Cui, D., & Liang, K. (2017). Multi layer multi objective extreme learning machine. *Proceedings of the 2017 IEEE International Conference on Image Processing (ICIP)*, 1297–1301.

Leon, F. (2014). Optimizing neural network topology using Shapley value. *Proceedings of the 18th International Conference on System Theory, Control and Computing (ICSTCC)*, 862–867.

Lundberg, S., & Lee, S.-I. (2017). *A unified approach to interpreting model predictions*, arXiv:170507874, Ar.Xiv.

Makmal, A., Melnikov, A. A., Dunjko, V., & Briegel, H. J. (2016). Meta-learning within projective simulation. *IEEE Access: Practical Innovations, Open Solutions, 4*, 2110–2122. doi:10.1109/ACCESS.2016.2556579

Manjunath, G., & Jaeger, H. (2013). Echo state property linked to an input: Exploring a fundamental characteristic of recurrent neural networks. *Neural Computation, 25*(3), 671–696. doi:10.1162/NECO_a_00411 PMID:23272918

Marin, E., Almukaynizi, M., Nunes, E., Shakarian, J., & Shakarian, P. (2018). Predicting hacker adoption on Darkweb forums using sequential rule mining. *Proceedings of the 2018 IEEE International Conference on Parallel and Distributed Processing with Applications, Ubiquitous Computing and Communications, Big Data and Cloud Computing, Social Computing and Networking, Sustainable Computing and Communications (ISPA/IUCC/BDCloud/SocialCom/SustainCom)*, 1183–1190.

Marin, E., Almukaynizi, M., Nunes, E., & Shakarian, P. (2018). Community finding of Malware and exploit vendors on Darkweb marketplaces. *Proceedings of the 2018 1st International Conference on Data Intelligence and Security (ICDIS)*, 81–84.

Mercaldo, F., Martinelli, F., & Santone, A. (2019). Real-time SCADA attack detection by means of formal methods. *Proceedings of the 2019 IEEE 28th International Conference on Enabling Technologies: Infrastructure for Collaborative Enterprises (WETICE)*.

Messalas, A., Kanellopoulos, Y., & Makris, C. (2019). Model-agnostic interpretability with Shapley values. *Proceedings of the 2019 10th International Conference on Information, Intelligence, Systems and Applications (IISA)*, 1–7.

Molnar, C. (2020). *Interpretable machine learning*. Lulu Press.

Montieri, A., Ciuonzo, D., Bovenzi, G., Persico, V., & Pescapé, A. (2020). A dive into the DarkWeb: Hierarchical traffic classification of anonymity tools. *IEEE Transactions on Network Science and Engineering*, *7*(3), 1043–1054. doi:10.1109/TNSE.2019.2901994

Pacheco, F., Exposito, E., Gineste, M., Baudoin, C., & Aguilar, J. (2018). Towards the deployment of machine learning solutions in network traffic classification: A systematic survey. *IEEE Communications Surveys and Tutorials*, *21*(2), 1988–2014. doi:10.1109/COMST.2018.2883147

Phillips, M., & Marden, J. R. (2018). Design tradeoffs in concave cost-sharing games. *IEEE Transactions on Automatic Control, 63*(7), 2242–2247.

Pustokhina, I. V., Pustokhin, D. A., Gupta, D., Khanna, A., Shankar, K., & Nguyen, G. N. (2020). An effective training scheme for deep neural network in edge computing enabled Internet of medical things (IoMT) systems. *IEEE Access: Practical Innovations, Open Solutions, 8*, 107112–107123. doi:10.1109/ACCESS.2020.3000322

Rantos, K., Drosatos, G., Demertzis, K., Ilioudis, C., & Papanikolaou, A. (2021). *Blockchain-based consents management for personal data processing in the IoT ecosystem*. https://www.scitepress.org/PublicationsDetail

Rantos, K., Drosatos, G., Demertzis, K., Ilioudis, C., Papanikolaou, A., & Kritsas, A. (2019). *ADvoCATE: A consent management platform for personal data processing in the IoT using Blockchain technology*. In Lecture Notes in Computer Science. Springer. doi:10.1007/978-3-030-12942-2_23

S, D., & S, R. (2014). Performance Comparison for Intrusion Detection System using Neural Network with KDD dataset. ICTACT Journal on Soft Computing, 4(3), 743–752. doi:10.21917/ijsc.2014.0106

Samrin, R., & Vasumathi, D. (2017). Review on anomaly based network intrusion detection system. *Proceedings of the 2017 International Conference on Electrical, Electronics, Communication, Computer, and Optimization Techniques (ICEECCOT).*

Shaikh, F., Bou-Harb, E., Crichigno, J., & Ghani, N. (2018). A machine learning model for classifying unsolicited IoT devices by observing network telescopes. *Proceedings of the 14th International Wireless Communications and Mobile Computing Conference (IWCMC)*, 938–943.

Singh, P., & Venkatesan, M. (2018). Hybrid approach for intrusion detection system. *Proceedings of the 2018 International Conference on Current Trends Towards Converging Technologies (ICCTCT)*, 1–5.

Siswanto, A., Syukur, A., Kadir, E. A., & Suratin, E. A. (2019). Network traffic monitoring and analysis using packet sniffer. *Proceedings of the 2019 International Conference on Advanced Communication Technologies and Networking (CommNet).*

Song, H., Jiang, Z., Men, A., & Yang, B. (2017, November 15). A hybrid semi-supervised anomaly detection model for high-dimensional data. *Computational Intelligence and Neuroscience, 8501683*. Advance online publication. doi:10.1155/2017/8501683 PMID:29270197

Soysal, M., & Schmidt, E. G. (2010). Machine learning algorithms for accurate flow-based network traffic classification: Evaluation and comparison. *Performance Evaluation, 67*(6), 451–467. doi:10.1016/j.peva.2010.01.001

Summerville, D. H., Nwanze, N., & Skormin, V. A. (2004). Anomalous packet identification for network intrusion detection. *Proceedings of the Fifth Annual IEEE SMC Information Assurance Workshop*, 60–67.

Sun, X., Gui, G., Li, Y., Liu, R. P., & An, Y. (2018). ResInNet: A novel deep neural network with feature Re-use for Internet of things. *IEEE Internet of Things Journal, 6*(1), 679–691. doi:10.1109/JIOT.2018.2853663

Tavabi, N., Goyal, P., Almukaynizi, M., Shakarian, P., & Lerman, K. (2018). *DarkEmbed: Exploit prediction with neural language models.* https://ojs.aaai.org/index.php/AAAI/article/view/11428

Tavallaee, M., Bagheri, E., Lu, W., & Ghorbani, A. A. (2009). A detailed analysis of the KDD CUP 99 data set. *Electronics, 10*(781), 1–6.

Tu, E., Zhang, G., Rachmawati, L., Rajabally, E., Mao, S., & Huang, G. (2017). A theoretical study of the relationship between an ELM network and its subnetworks. *Proceedings of the 2017 International Joint Conference on Neural Networks (IJCNN)*, 1794–1801.

Wetschoreck, F., Krabel, T., & Krishnamurthy, S. (2020). *Ppscore:* Zenodo *release* (1.1.2 version). *Zenodo.*

Xing, L., Demertzis, K., & Yang, J. (2020). Identifying data streams anomalies by evolving spiking restricted Boltzmann machines. *Neural Computing & Applications, 32*(11), 6699–6713. doi:10.100700521-019-04288-5

Xu, Z., Cao, L., & Chen, X. (2019). Learning to learn: Hierarchical meta-critic networks. *IEEE Access: Practical Innovations, Open Solutions, 7*, 57069–57077. doi:10.1109/ACCESS.2019.2914469

Yang, B., & Liu, D. (2019). Research on Network Traffic Identification based on Machine Learning and Deep Packet Inspection. *Proceedings of the 2019 IEEE 3rd Information Technology, Networking, Electronic and Automation Control Conference (ITNEC)*, 1887–1891.

Yang, Y., Yang, L., Yang, M., Yu, H., Zhu, G., Chen, Z., & Chen, L. (2019). Article. In *Proceedings of the 2019 IEEE 8th Joint International Information Technology and Artificial Intelligence Conference (ITAIC)* (pp. 1216–1220). IEEE.

Yang, Y., Yu, H., Yang, L., Yang, M., Chen, L., Zhu, G., & Wen, L. (2019). Hadoop-based dark web threat intelligence analysis framework. *Proceedings of the IEEE Publications 3rd Advanced Information Management, Communicates, Electronic and Automation Control Conference (IMCEC)*.

Yu, X., & Guo, H. (2019). A survey on IIoT Security. *Proceedings of the 2019 IEEE VTS Asia Pacific-Wireless Communications Symposium (APWCS)*, 1–5.

Zhang, J., & Zulkernine, M. (2006). Anomaly based network intrusion detection with unsupervised outlier detection. *Proceedings of the 2006 IEEE International Conference on Communications*, 5, 2388–2393.

Zhang, K., Wang, Q., Liu, X., & Giles, C. L. (2020). Shapley homology: Topological analysis of sample influence for neural networks. *Neural Computation*, 32(7), 1355–1378. doi:10.1162/neco_a_01289 PMID:32433903

Zhang, L., & Gao, Z. (2011). The Shapley value of convex compound stochastic cooperative game. *Proceedings of the 2011 2nd International Conference on Artificial Intelligence, Management Science and Electronic Commerce (AIMSEC)*.

Zhong, S., Liu, D., Lin, L., Zhao, M., Fu, X., & Guo, F. (2020). A novel anomaly detection method for gas turbines using weight agnostic neural network search. *Proceedings of the 2020 Asia-Pacific International Symposium on Advanced Reliability and Maintenance Modeling (APARM)*, 1–6.

Chapter 2
Information System for Cyber Threat Detection Using K–NN Classification Model

Prem Mahendra Kothari
Ajeenkya D. Y. Patil University, India

Ratan Singh Gaharwar
UIT-RGPV Bhopal, India

ABSTRACT

Due to the drastic and exponential growth of information systems and their use, the technology has taken a quantum leap. To ensure safe data transportation, different protection systems are used, such as intrusion detection systems, intrusion prevention systems, and firewalls. In this chapter, the proposed system has an anomaly-based cyber threats detection system using advanced machine learning algorithms. The anomaly-based detection system was used to analyze repackage signatures of malware which is not predefined. Machine learning with the use of previous datasets and algorithms to make the IDS intelligent. In this chapter, the authors use K-NN, which takes the similarity between new attack footprints and compare it with the older footprints in the dataset, and tell which has a higher resemblance. The major challenges of this IDS are minimization of false alarms and gaining high accuracy. The proposed IDS system is not only tested manually but is tested by automated utilities as well, and minimizing of overfitting and underfitting is also checked.

INTRODUCTION

As the world is moving to a more digital environment, information security has become the most essential yet challenging task for researchers. Due to the unexpected turn of the event due totheCovid-19 pandemic(Ciottietal.,2020), there has been a huge increase in the number of digital platforms related to different businesses solutions, education, medical science, transport, federal organizations, e-commerce, and many more applications have been introduced to an online mode which made exponential growth in

DOI: 10.4018/978-1-6684-6444-1.ch002

the digital records. Although there have been many introductions of many good changes never forget a coin as two faces, due to this exponential growth in the digital market many cybersecurity-related threats such as scams, money scandals, data thefts, data breaches, and many such cyberattacks. The recent security breaches and cyber threats have become challenging, and critical for modern threat detection systems. These threats successfully exploited vulnerabilities in the server and systems. Many security solutions are used here to get secure or prevent such attacks, which are not competent enough. Machine Learning (ML)(Zhanget al,2020) is the application of Artificial Intelligence (AI)(Russell and Norvig,2002), Machine Learning (ML)(Zhang et al,2020) is made with the sole purpose of creating a smart digital environment that can focus on automated advancements of the system. The main objective of Machine Learning (ML)(Zhang et al,2020) is to aim to be sub-par with the human mind, and also remove the factor of stagnancy of the process of operation (Business/work). It also removes the factor of human error.

There is a big part of the Internet that is hidden from popular search engines like Google, Bing, Yahoo, etc that part is called as Dark Web. It is predicted that 96% of WWW is a dark web(Nazah et al., 2020). The dark web is used for most criminal activities like drug dealing, weapons selling, and more. After a data breach of any organization that data will be available on the dark web for example Dominos faced a data breach in 2021 where customers mobile number, address, email id, payment, order history everything was freely available on the dark web. Such attacks and data breachesarea big point of concern. All big organizations have IDS in their network to avoid such big data breaches.

In modern Information Security practice,the dark web is the most critical section for intrusion detection. Nowadays threats are advancing their nature and signatures very drastically. Conversational intrusion detection prevention systems are based in signature-based while modern cyberspace or dark web needs very advanced or AI-based Intrusion detection prevention systems. These systems must be capable to analyze networks, packet trafficking in the dark web, and anomaly-based analysis. A major challenge is to capture and decode darkweb traffic. In this research paper traffic is classified into two categories a) Benign traffic, b) malicious traffic.Benign traffic is natural traffic that is free from intrusions and Malicious traffic is abnormal traffic. This classification is performed based on AI algorithms.In this research paper, an exclusive method is used which is based on AI concepts.

An Intrusion Detection System (IDS) is a tool or software which is used to monitor a system and gives an alarm when it finds any unusual or suspicious activity. In this paper, an IDS is proposed which is based on machine learning(Zhang et al,2020). IDS is used to scan each data packet and if any suspicious activity is detected it will be reported and prevented. Deploying an IDS with high accuracy is challenging due to many factors used for attack detection. IDS can be classified as Anomaly-based, Signature-based, Behavior-based, host-based, and network-based.

In this paper, an Intrusion Detection System is proposed, the proposed IDS System is tested using Standard NSL KDD Dataset. The standard dataset has multiple networks originated attacks like DDoS, DoS, Port Scanner, etc. the selection of the dataset is a Crusius task because the accuracy and correctness of the proposed system are dependent on the used dataset. NSL KDD is an updated version of KDD 99 and it is highly accurate. IDS isan Intrusion Detection System that monitors the system and detects suspicious or malicious activity.

There are 2 types of IDS based on their location/configuration:

1. Network-Based: It deploys on the network for monitoring the traffic so it can detect and prevent any unusual things happening in the network.

Figure 1. Block diagram of the process

2. Host-Based: it deploys on the server/host itself so it can monitor each port of the server to prevent any further attacks.

In recent times, the frequency of cyberattacks has been increased and it is getting challenging because of the increase in attacks like Anomaly Based Attacks. In response to minimize it, we need to step up our game by using Machine Learning(Zhang et al,2020) and Artificial Intelligence (Russell and Norvig,2002)in our IDS, so it will get to learn from the previous attacks and also will prepare itself for new attacks with new footprints. There is a different type of ML algorithms that we can use in this case like K-means, Linear Regression, Decision Tree and list goes on. In this paper, we will mainly target on KNN algorithm.

KNN comes in the lazy learning category, where it takes time to compute data but gives us high accuracy. I have many attributes in my dataset which gives me sufficient knowledge of the domain. In this scenario where I want high accuracy and have nice knowledge about the data, KNN is the best algorithm. This makes KNN perfect algorithms that can predict accurately to find malicious traffic in the network.

KNN Algorithm (Kozma et al,2008)can be used for both classification and regression. This is the simplest algorithm where classification is done based on the majority. Let's have a look at the simple word KNN which means K- Nearest Neighbors. To predict a new point, KNN will check the majority of K points that are near to that particular point and will place that point in that particular group, where K is the number of points. In a simple life example, predicting a person's behavior by his friend circle where he is most of the time.

Figure 1 shows the block diagram of the processes which has been followed for the output of the result. It gives a basic idea about how the ML-based IDS has been created. The first stage is of data preprocessing in which dataset will be taken and all prerequisites will be done like merging datasets, making it in polynomial data type, etc. next step will be splitting off the dataset into two to train and test the model next step is to train the model with K-NN algorithm and then test the same model with the testing dataset. The last step will be to evaluate the performance of the model with various parameters.

LITERATURE REVIEW

In this literature, multiple respective literatures are reviewed. These Literatures are shown in table 1 and the reference section. The review Literature belongs to Intrusion Detection System using multiple or different machine learning and AI models. (Chandre et al.,2018) have proposed a novel method or tool named AVISPA for Intrusion Detection using the Machine Learning approach. AVISPA is an IDS tool that is developed but not tested with a standard dataset as well as not used multiple attacks. (RIBEIRO et al.,2020) proposed a HIDROIDS system which is android based Intrusion Detection System and can be used for host-based identification. HIDROID has upto 90% accuracy and limitations such as not covering network-based attacks well as not testing standard attacking liability. (Ahmad et al.,2018) proposed a detailed comparison among Machine Learning models for Intrusion Detection Systems such as SVM, Random Forest, and ELM. In this paper, the NSL KDD dataset was used in a 60:40 ratio for testing and training purposes. (Constantinides et al.,2019) discussed the incremental learning approach for intrusion detection using the classification machine learning approach. In this system accuracy is upto 97% but the system is not tested using the standard library and considers limited attacks. This system needs to be in a standard environment. (Yerima et al.,2013)proposed an Analysis of Bayesian classification-based approaches for Android malware detection and the accuracy of the system is upto 95%. This system can be tested using the anomaly-based method.

In table 1 there are 15 different IDS its technics used, paper, and author from which it referred, accuracy, and limitation

PROPOSED METHODOLOGY

In this paper, RapidMiner software(Hofmann and Klinkenberg,2016) is used to build and test our IDS. RapidMiner is data science software that gives you a very user-friendly GUI to build any model. It has an operator section that gives you all functionality at your fingertip by just dragging and dropping. The first task was to download the dataset, for this paper we used the IDS-2017 dataset which was downloaded from NSL-KDD after downloading all the CSV files that were merged in one CSV file. After merging replaced Benign traffic with 0 and malicious traffic with 1 in the 'Label' column, so RapidMiner can classify and predict it easily. RapidMiner doesn't understand the comma in numeric attributes so it should be converted to Polynomial. The next task was to set the label role to our 'Label' column where we have set '0' and '1' value for benign malicious traffic and it acts as a target attribute for learning and predicting data. Now to train and test the model it is needed to split data. K-NN algorithm has been applied to the model to train with training data. On the trained model testing data has been sent to see what it is predicting. The predicted value parameters like accuracy, Classification Error, Weighted Mean Recall, Weighted Mean Precision, and Root Mean Squared Error have been checked and noted.

Figure 2 shows the process in RapidMiner in that Retrieve testing is our dataset which is going to numeric to a polynomial operator to make all values to polynomial so it won't give any error when we give input to the k-NN operator. K-NN operator needs a column with a label, for that set role operator is used. In our dataset 'Label' column is assigned as a label role. To split the dataset into 2 i.e., training and testing, a split data operator is used. Training data is sent to the k-NN operator and it is applied to the model to teach it what is benign and which one is suspicious or malicious. Testing data that was previously split is given as an input to apply the model operator to test it. For checking the accuracy and other parameters performance operator is used and then the result is displayed.

As multiple authors discussed IDS with different Machine Learning and Artificial Intelligence algorithms, in this research paper also we will discuss IDS, with K-NN Algorithm. To simulate the idea, the proposed model is shown below:

Figure 3 shows the flow of the process. The steps to deploy this model is discussed below:

Table 1. Different intrusion detection system

Sr. No.	Technic and Method used	Paper Name	Results	Limitation	Author Name
1.	IDS using AVISPA	Machine Learning Based Novel Approach for Intrusion Detection and Prevention System: A Tool Based Verification	Upto 95%	The system does not use a standard dataset and all attacks are not tested	(Chandre et al.,2018)
2.	Host-based IDS (HIDROID)	HIDROID: Prototyping a Behavioral Host-Based Intrusion Detection and Prevention System for Android (HIDROID)	Upto 90%	The system is tested on the local network and needs to test with the standard dataset.	(RIBEIRO et al.,2020)
3.	Drozer	HIDROID	N.A.	Uses a command-line interface that is not user friendly	(RIBEIRO et al.,2020)
4.	Kmeans	HIDROID	90.9%	Accuracy is comparatively less.	(RIBEIRO et al.,2020)
5.	Crowdriod	HIDROID	N.A.	Needs root access and analyzes one application at a time	(RIBEIRO et al.,2020)
6.	Gaussian	HIDROID	91.4%	Need to test with standard datasets.	(RIBEIRO et al.,2020)
7.	Andromly	HIDROID	N.A.	Requires labeled data and only has been tested against malicious data collected from a few artificial malware	(RIBEIRO et al.,2020)
8.	SVM(SUPPORT VECTOR MACHINE)	Performance comparison of support vector machine, random forest, and extreme learning machine for intrusion detection	95.5-99.5%	it includes the requirements of a Gaussian function for each instance of the training set, thereby increasing training time and performance degradation on very large	(Ahmad et al.,2018)
9.	Random Forest	Performance comparison of support vector machine, random forest, and extreme learning machine for intrusion detection	92.49%	Complexity requires more computational resources, time-consuming than other algorithms.	(Ahmad et al.,2018)
10.	Aurasium	HIDROID	N.A.	Uses repackaging modifies the original application, can be treated as malware by other IDSs	(RIBEIRO et al.,2020)
11.	Extreme Learning Machine	Performance comparison of support vector machine, random forest, and extreme learning machine for intrusion detection	97.79%	Standard dataset testing is not performed. Multiple attacks not included.	(Ahmad et al.,2018)
12.	SOINN	A Novel Online Incremental Learning Intrusion Prevention System	94.05%	The system is tested on the local network and needs to test with the standard dataset.	(Constantinides et al.,2019)
13.	n-SOINN-WTA-SVM	A Novel Online Incremental Learning Intrusion Prevention System	78.23-89.67%	Mathematical model not describe	(Constantinides et al.,2019)
14.	Bayesian	Analysis of Bayesian classification-based approaches for Android malware detection	0.9, 0.92, 0.93	Mathematical model not describe	(Yerima et al.,2013)
15.	Kirin	HIDROID	N.A.	Analyzes the application in install time and is not designed for monitoring the application behavior in runtime	(RIBEIRO et al.,2020)

a) Dataset: Dataset is a collection of instances and is used to train machine learning models. For IDS testing, a dataset is a very crucial part as the performance and accuracy of IDS depend on it.

b) Convert to Polynominal- This will convert the selected attribute into a polynomial type.

Figure 2. K-NN model

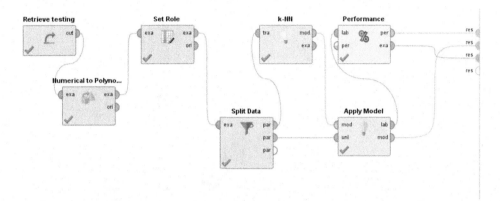

c)   Set Role- This function gives the role to one or many selected attributes. It defines how other operators handle that attribute. For example, for prediction, it needs to set label attribute for the model so with the help of other attributes it will predict the value where the role is set to label.

d)   Split data- Created model should be trained and tested with one dataset so it's needed to split data into training and testing data to have an idea of how the model will perform in real-time traffic.

e)   K-NN Algorithm- This is an algorithm that has been used in this paper to train the model with training data.

f)   Apply Model- For testing the model, testing data has been sent to the trained model for predicting the value.

g)   Result- Predicted Value will be checked with the original value in the dataset and a result is displayed with parameters like accuracy, root mean squared error, etc.

RESULT

In this research paper I have analyzed the standard Intrusion Detection Data for the detection of the intrusion based on certain attacks as mentioned below:

1.   DDoS:DDoS refers to distributed denial of service which targets a webserver and sends multiple requests to the webserver intending to exceed its capacity so that its website won't operate properly.

2.   Port Scanner: Port scanner is used by hackers to find the open ports in the system which not only helps hackers for further attack processes but also reveals whether the port or system has a firewall or other security measures.

3.   Bot:A bot isan automated software that keeps the webserver busy with a certain pattern of requests. Many bots request together to keep the whole capacity of the webserver busy and this leads to a halt in getting responsesto benign traffic.

4.   Brute Force: Brute Force guesses login info encrypted keys and also finds hidden pages in web applications.

5.   XSS: XSS is Cross-Site Scripting, it is a type of injection attack which injects malicious script into a trusted website to get some unauthorized access or to harm it

Figure 3. Flow of K-NN based intrusion detection system

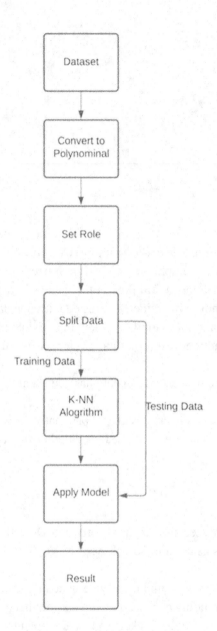

6. SQL Injection:SQL injection is the most common one among all these attacks, basically,in it,attackers take SQL code and try to access data from the database or manipulate it.
7. FTPPatator: FTP Patator is a modular Brute Forcerthat tries to crack FTP passwords by guessing them.
8. SSHPatator: SSH Patator try common Username and Password on thousands of server till they get a match.
9. DoS Hulk: DoS Hulk tool attack on webserver by generating unique and obfuscated traffic volume.

Table 2. Splitting of data for both models

Splitting of Data	70:30 Model	60:40 Model
Training Data	6,94,294	5,95,109
Testing Data	2,97,554	3,96,739
Total	9,91,848	9,91,848

10.   DoS GoldenEye:GoldenEye is an HTTP DoS attack that exploits HTTP Keep-Alive and No-cache.

This attack is determined using the K-NN method KNN i.e., K-Nearest Neighbor which sees the number of neighbors (k) nearby and classifies or predicts the value on that basis of neighbor. I have utilized this algorithm with various k values like k= 4,5,6,7,8,9,10,15 to understand the overfitting and underfitting of the data. The data sample has 9,91,848 entries. Two models were created based on splitting that is 70:30 where 70% is for training and 30% is for testing, in a similar purpose we did 60:40 also, where 60% is training and 40% is testing to understand the overfitting of the result. We found that both models have identical accuracy with 70:30 slightly ahead. The table below shows you how much data is for training and testing for both models.

In 70:30 model training data is 6,84,294 and that of 60:40 is 5,95,109. For testing data, 2,97,554 is 1of 70:30 model and 3,96,739 of 60:40 model as you can see in table 2

IDS was run on both models with different k values and found a very minimum variation of parameters which we mentioned in the performance attribute. All the results which we found for both models are mentioned below:

Table3 shows the results of the 70:30 model with the parameters like accuracy, Classification Error, Weighted Mean Recall, Weighted Mean Precision, and Root Mean Squared Error.

Figure 4 shows how stable the accuracy is for the 70:30 model which says that it fits perfectly without overfitting or underfitting of data. Figure 5 is a zoomed version of figure 3 to make it easy to understand. Graph took the peak with the k value as 10 and accuracy is 99.25% which is very good for Intrusion Detection System (IDS). And it is lowest with the k value 15 with an accuracy of 98.58%.

Confusion Matrix

Above Table 4 shows the confusion matrix of the 70:30 model which shows there were 2194 false-positive and 601 false-negative predictions.

Table 5 shows the results of the 60:40 model with the parameters like accuracy, Classification Error, Weighted Mean Recall, Weighted Mean Precision, and Root Mean Squared Error.

Figure 6 shows in the 60:40 model have the k value increases accuracy decreases slightly. In the 60:40 model, we have the highest accuracy at k=4 and lowest at k=15 i.e.98.94% and 98.12% respectively.

Table 6, shows a comparison of KNN IDS with some other techniques which were mentioned in the literature review. It can be observed KNN shows better accuracy than other methods which shows there is no overfitting and underfitting of data. Other IDS with ML algorithms like K-Means, Gaussian, and Random Forest was having an accuracy of 90.9%, 91.4%, and 92.48% respectively whereas KNN was having 99.25% of accuracy when the k value was 10 in the 70:30 model.

Table 3. Result table of 70:30 K-NN IDS model

K-value	Accuracy (70:30)	Classification Error	Weighted Mean Recall	Weighted Mean Precision	Root Mean Squared Error
4	99.06%	0.94%	99.13%	98.61%	0.087
5	98.92%	1.09%	98.92%	98.11%	0.085
6	99%	1.00%	99.10%	98.17%	0.090
7	98.67%	1.33%	98.76%	97.62%	0.092
8	98.92%	1.08%	98.92%	98.11%	0.093
9	98.83%	1.17%	98.87%	97.94%	0.095
10	99.25%	0.75%	99.26%	98.68%	0.093
11	99.00%	1.00%	98.98%	98.28%	0.000
12	99.00%	1.00%	98.98%	98.28%	0.000
13	98.83%	1.17%	98.50%	98.27%	0.097
14	98.83%	1.17%	98.50%	98.27%	0.099
15	98.58%	1.42%	98.22%	97.87%	0.101

Figure 4. Accuracy graph of 70:30 model

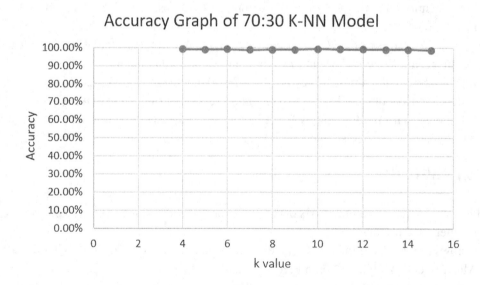

This system was proposed after the analysis of multiple classification algorithms and their respective accuracy from different literature review works. This system implements the KNN model which provides more than 99% accuracy. This system achieved high accuracy and better performance as compared to other classification models shown below the table.

Figure 5. Accuracy graph of 70:30 model (Zoomed)

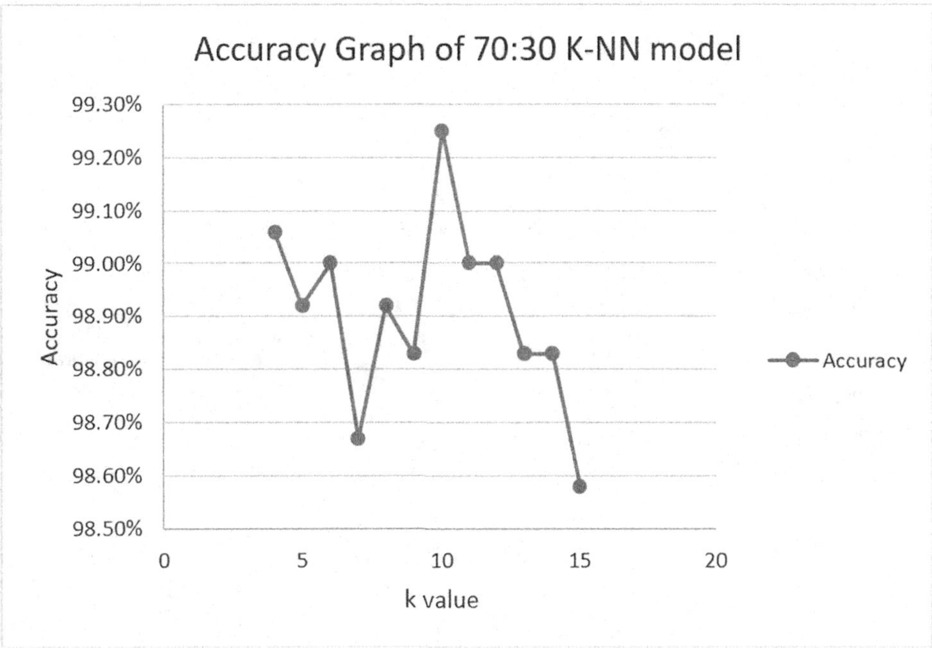

Table 4. Confusion matrix for k=4 in the 70:30 model

True:	0 (Benign)	1
0:	208672	601
1:	2194	86087

Table 5. Result table of 60:40 K-NN IDS model

K value	Accuracy (60:40)	Classification Error	Weighted Mean Recall	Weighted Mean Precision	Root Mean Squared Error
4	98.94%	1.06%	99.12%	98.00%	0.096
5	98.56%	1.44%	98.78%	97.34%	0.099
6	98.62%	1.38%	98.92%	97.39%	0.103
7	98.25%	1.75%	98.58%	96.75%	0.104
8	98.56%	1.44%	98.78%	97.34%	0.105
9	98.56%	1.44%	98.69%	97.42%	0.104
10	98.69%	1.31%	98.96%	97.51%	0.105
11	98.50%	1.50%	98.74%	97.22%	0.107
12	98.50%	1.50%	98.74%	97.22%	0.108
13	98.44%	1.56%	98.43%	97.32%	0.109
14	98.56%	1.44%	98.51%	97.57%	0.109
15	98.12%	1.88%	97.86%	97.01%	0.109

Figure 6. Accuracy graph of 60:40 (Zoomed)

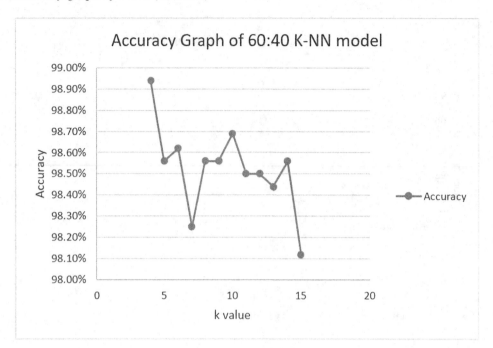

Table 6. Comparison with other IDS

Methods	Features	Efficiency / Detection rate	References
K-means	Training and tuning did in one step	90.9%	(RIBEIRO et al.,2020)
Gaussian	Dataset was split 5:1 for training and testing	91.4%	(RIBEIRO et al.,2020)
Random Forest	Few chances of overfitting	92.49%	(Ahmadet al.,2018)
K-NN (k Nearest Neighbour)	NSL KDD 2017 Dataset RapidMiner	99.25% (k=10)	------------

CONCLUSIONS

In the past, many researchers and enthusiasts worked on IDS using different types of ML and AL-based algorithms. Many papers discuss many methods of ML-based IDS that are discussed in the literature review. In this paper, we deploy K-NN-based Intrusion Detection which certainly got high accuracy i.e., the 70:30 model has 98.91% accuracy whereas the 60:30 model has 98.52% accuracy. Both the model had a stabile accuracy which indicates that there is no underfitting or overfitting of data. It proves that K-NN is also suitable for big data. As a limitation concern of this research paper, this intrusion detection system technique performs well with multiple datasets and multiple attacks and also to use on real-time data.

REFERENCES

Agarap, A. F. M. (2018, February). A neural network architecture combining gated recurrent unit (GRU) and support vector machine (SVM) for intrusion detection in network traffic data. In *Proceedings of the 2018 10th International Conference on Machine Learning and Computing* (pp. 26-30). 10.1145/3195106.3195117

Ahmad, I., Basheri, M., Iqbal, M. J., & Rahim, A. (2018). Performance comparison of support vector machine, random forest, and extreme learning machine for intrusion detection. *IEEE Access: Practical Innovations, Open Solutions*, 6, 33789–33795. doi:10.1109/ACCESS.2018.2841987

Bhatia, V., Choudhary, S., & Ramkumar, K. R. (2020, June). A Comparative Study on Various Intrusion Detection Techniques Using Machine Learning and Neural Network. In *2020 8th International Conference on Reliability, Infocom Technologies and Optimization (Trends and Future Directions)(ICRITO)* (pp. 232-236). IEEE. 10.1109/ICRITO48877.2020.9198008

Burguera, I., Zurutuza, U., & Nadjm-Tehrani, S. (2011, October). Crowdroid: behavior-based malware detection system for android. In *Proceedings of the 1st ACM workshop on Security and privacy in smartphones and mobile devices* (pp. 15-26). 10.1145/2046614.2046619

Chandre, P. R., Mahalle, P. N., & Shinde, G. R. (2018, November). Machine learning based novel approach for intrusion detection and prevention system: A tool based verification. In *2018 IEEE Global Conference on Wireless Computing and Networking (GCWCN)* (pp. 135-140). IEEE. 10.1109/GCWCN.2018.8668618

Ciotti, M., Ciccozzi, M., Terrinoni, A., Jiang, W. C., Wang, C. B., & Bernardini, S. (2020). The COVID-19 pandemic. *Critical Reviews in Clinical Laboratory Sciences*, 57(6), 365–388. doi:10.1080/10408363.2020.1783198 PMID:32645276

Constantinides, C., Shiaeles, S., Ghita, B., & Kolokotronis, N. (2019, June). A novel online incremental learning intrusion prevention system. In *2019 10th IFIP International Conference on New Technologies, Mobility and Security (NTMS)* (pp. 1-6). IEEE. 10.1109/NTMS.2019.8763842

Fang, W., Tan, X., & Wilbur, D. (2020). Application of intrusion detection technology in network safety based on machine learning. *Safety Science*, 124, 104604. doi:10.1016/j.ssci.2020.104604

Faruki, P., Bharmal, A., Laxmi, V., Ganmoor, V., Gaur, M. S., Conti, M., & Rajarajan, M. (2014). Android security: A survey of issues, malware penetration, and defenses. *IEEE Communications Surveys and Tutorials*, 17(2), 998–1022. doi:10.1109/COMST.2014.2386139

Gaharwar, R. S., & Gupta, R. (2020, February). Android data leakage and anomaly based Intrusion detection System. In *2nd International Conference on Data, Engineering and Applications (IDEA)* (pp. 1-5). IEEE. 10.1109/IDEA49133.2020.9170738

Gaharwar, R. S., & Gupta, R. (2020). Review of cyber security threats and proposed trustworthy memory acquisition mechanism. *Journal of Discrete Mathematical Sciences and Cryptography*, 23(1), 137–144. doi:10.1080/09720529.2020.1721877

Gaharwar, R. S., & Gupta, R. (2020). Vulnerability assessment of android instant messaging application and network intrusion detection prevention systems. *Journal of Statistics and Management Systems*, *23*(2), 399–406. doi:10.1080/09720510.2020.1744314

Kozma, L. (2008). k Nearest Neighbors algorithm (kNN). Helsinki University of Technology.

Musavi, S. A., & Hashemi, M. R. (2019). HPCgnature: A hardware-based application-level intrusion detection system. *IET Information Security*, *13*(1), 19–26. doi:10.1049/iet-ifs.2017.0629

Nazah, S., Huda, S., Abawajy, J., & Hassan, M. M. (2020). Evolution of Dark Web threat analysis and detection: A systematic approach. *IEEE Access: Practical Innovations, Open Solutions*, *8*, 171796–171819. doi:10.1109/ACCESS.2020.3024198

Ribeiro, J., Saghezchi, F. B., Mantas, G., Rodriguez, J., & Abd-Alhameed, R. A. (2020). Hidroid: Prototyping a behavioral host-based intrusion detection and prevention system for android. *IEEE Access: Practical Innovations, Open Solutions*, *8*, 23154–23168. doi:10.1109/ACCESS.2020.2969626

Ribeiro, J., Saghezchi, F. B., Mantas, G., Rodriguez, J., Shepherd, S. J., & Abd-Alhameed, R. A. (2020). An autonomous host-based intrusion detection system for android mobile devices. *Mobile Networks and Applications*, *25*(1), 164–172. doi:10.100711036-019-01220-y

Russell, S., & Norvig, P. (2002). *Artificial intelligence: A modern approach*. Academic Press.

Yerima, S. Y., Sezer, S., & McWilliams, G. (2013). Analysis of Bayesian classification-based approaches for Android malware detection. *IET Information Security*, *8*(1), 25–36. doi:10.1049/iet-ifs.2013.0095

Yerima, S. Y., Sezer, S., & Muttik, I. (2015). High accuracy android malware detection using ensemble learning. *IET Information Security*, *9*(6), 313–320. doi:10.1049/iet-ifs.2014.0099

Zhang, X. D. (2020). Machine learning. In *A Matrix Algebra Approach to Artificial Intelligence* (pp. 223–440). Springer. doi:10.1007/978-981-15-2770-8_6

Chapter 3
Structure Analysis of Tor Hidden Services Using DOM–Inspired Graphs

Ashwini Dalvi
Veermata Jijabai Technological Instutute, India

Varun Pawar
Veermata Jijabai Technological Institute, India

Kunjal Shah
Veermata Jijabai Technological Institute, India

Dashank Bhoir
Veermata Jijabai Technological Institute, India

Uddhav Jambhalkar
Veermata Jijabai Technological Institute, India

S. G. Bhirud
Veermata Jijabai Technological Institute, India

ABSTRACT

The dark web contains sensitive data that strategic organizations must identify well in advance to anticipate and handle threats. However, associates will prefer to automate classifying the dark web pages instead of opening them due to their disturbing visual images and dangerous links and attachments. Most research is focused on web page text analysis to infer dark web data. But no visible attempt is observed in the literature that classifies dark web content at the structure level. In the chapter, extended scope of work aims to predict the genre of the webpage without opening the web page. The work converts web pages to their respective DOM (document object model) graphs. DOM graphs essentially represent web page structure. A GNN (graph neural network) is trained with constructed DOM graphs to predict the page's genre. The various graph properties like a number of nodes, edges, etc. for web page DOM graphs are extracted. Unsupervised learning (i.e., k-means clustering) is performed on the dataset to group the web pages into clusters based on similarity in structure.

INTRODUCTION

Most of the deep web is engaged in harmless information exchange; there is part of the deep web "Dark Web" involved in illegal activities. The dark web and darknet terms are used interchangeably, but in a

DOI: 10.4018/978-1-6684-6444-1.ch003

nutshell, the darknet is a network beneath the dark web, which constitutes illegal information and service exchange.

The luring aspect of the dark web is anonymity. The anonymization technologies keep the user's identity hidden while performing notorious activities. The services hosted to enhance the hidden activities are considered as Hidden Services. The researchers and law enforcement agencies are actively investigating this portion of the hidden web to comprehend the extent of the dark web. The range of dark web content is vast, from availability leaked data, drugs, weapons, hacking exploits for sale to offering assassination services.

The dark web requires a rigid authentication process to access it. The registration process and complex encryption mechanism justify the term dark to access this part of the web. The different users participate in dark web Forums and Marketplace to exchange unlawful communication. The communication involves but is not limited to demand and supply for malwares, ransomwares, zero- day exploits, personal data, pornographic material, drugs, assassination service, etc. The extremist and terrorists also use the dark web to spread their propaganda.

The anonymity feature of the dark web makes it a safe place to harbour terrorists and other criminals. Researcher Chen H offered the pioneering study on the dark web, covering technical and web connectivity intricacies on the dark web (Chen,2011). Also, content analysis is discussed by blending data mining approaches. In 2016, a study (Moore and Rid,2016) attempted to map out behavioural tendencies on the dark web, including drugs, hacking, pornography, and many such illicit activities. The study might not be accurate to a great extent since only about 5000 dark web pages were taken into account, but it managed to give a good overview of the general tendencies shown on the dark web.

The attempts like (Beshiri and Susuri,2019) are more accommodating to address research questions like how to know the size and reach of dark web users? What are activities carried on the dark web? How to estimate users' statistics like country, Number of requests? How to measure performance evaluation of Tor services? The answers were attempted by data sampled by two dark web search engines - Ahima and Onion City search. Not complete, but directing answers were attained through the conducted study.

The researchers have acknowledged the dark web as a potential data source to investigate various crimes. Thus, individual research attempts have been made to comprehend how the academic research community has studied the dark web for various crimes. For example, in (Rawat et al.,2021) the researchers presented a systematic literature review on drug trafficking on the dark web. However, the researchers point out that a more detailed and focused study is required to research and document the prevalence of drugs and other crimes on the dark web. Similarly, in work (Broadhurst et al.,2018), authors discussed deep and dark web markets along with malware trends, search queries used to search, the statistical distribution-based analysis to comprehend the spread of drugs and exchange of malware and hacker software's on the marketplace and the reach of hacker forums, cryptocurrency on the dark web.

However, the study in (Alghamdi and Selamat,2022) offered a concentrated research review on techniques discussed in the literature to identify terrorism-related content on the dark web. Forty dark web data sets were analysed. The study concluded that feature selection and extraction approaches are helpful for content analysis and text identification. Further, the content analysis could be strengthened by topic modelling. Thus, the research community is proactive in gathering information from the dark web. The common way to collect information from the dark web is by designing a dark web crawler. The dark web crawlers are designed to be an artificial intelligence agent. For example, in work (Dalvi et al.,2021), the crawler fed data to a natural language processing (NLP) trained module for categorizing dark web crawled data in related categories.

In work (Iliou et al.,2017), authors proposed 11 different hyperlink selection methods to find the most relevant sites on a given topic. These methods are based on the dynamic linear combination of hyperlink and web page (parent and destination page) classification. In work (Kawaguchi and Ozawa,2019), authors developed a crawler to collect links from the dark web. The study's purpose was to employ an ML-based approach to identify malicious sites from collected crawled dark web links. The work succeeded in predicting harmful links with an accuracy of 0.82 in the F1 score.

Researchers (Zhang and Chow,2020) discussed the threat intelligence analysis framework that helps law enforcement agencies analyse crimes and criminals' relevant information related to the dark side of the World Wide Web or dark web. The framework implemented to carry out this analysis is the Dark Web Threat Intelligence Analysis (DWTIA) Platform. The DWTIA framework implemented as the traditional network investigation method based on IP address finds it challenging to trace the cybercriminal's identity. DWTIA provides access to a large volume of information, combining the surface web and dark web. It does so by providing or using the OnionScan Dark Web crawler that collects more than 8,000 sites on the dark web. DWTIA platform adopts the standard STIX 2.0 for data acquisition and sharing. The platform collects and processes critical data such as TOR Web Site Dynamic List, TOR relay list, critical information, correlation analysis and Threat Intelligence Centre Feedback. The platform consists of a Data Acquisition module, Indexing Module, Data Analysis Module and Data Visualization Module that assist in collecting and processing the data. The mining and correlation analysis assists in identifying the relationship between vendors and buyers for keywords like drugs, fraud, etc.

In this era of the internet and data, Cyber-threat Intelligence (CTI) tools help identify, monitor and gather data from the underlying dark web where potential threats vectors could collaborate, communicate and plan future attacks. The analysis and prior knowledge of threats, vulnerabilities and indicators of an impending attack and security tools enhance the projection of dark web crimes. Thus, comprehension of dark web data is critical.

The dark web contains sensitive data that strategic organizations must identify well in advance to anticipate and handle threats. However, associates will prefer to automate classifying the dark web pages instead of opening them due to their disturbing visual appearance and dangerous links and attachments. Furthermore, in a working dark web crawling setup, the crawler can gather data at high velocity. Thus, dark web crawled data has characteristics of volume, velocity and variety. Most research focused on web page text analysis to infer dark web data.

Most dark web analysis work performs text analysis by extracting text features with related algorithms. But no visible attempt is observed in the literature that classifies dark web content at the structure level. Thus, novelty of the proposed work is as follows:

- Analysing dark web typically TOR hidden services at the structure level
- Clustering the similar DOM graphs using the unsupervised algorithm
- Conforming the label of clustered graphs with the supervised learning algorithm
- Proposal to effective content search mechanism for crawled dark web data having big data characteristics

In the proposed work, the analysis of dark web data is intended to establish beyond text classification. The extended scope of work aims to predict the genre of the webpage without opening the web page. The proposed work converts web pages to their respective DOM (Document Object Model) graphs. DOM graphs essentially represent web page structure. A GNN (Graph Neural Network) is trained with constructed DOM graphs to predict the page's genre. The various graph properties like a number of nodes, edges, etc., for web page DOM graphs are extracted. Unsupervised learning, viz. K-Means clustering is performed on the dataset to group the web pages into clusters based on similarity in structure.

BACKGROUND

Machine Learning Based Approach Implementation on the Dark Web

The early works on dark web data include a feature of rich text representation, identification and measurement of the sentiment polarities using machine learning techniques and affect the intensities of forum communication in the dark web because hacker forums are used for communication of attacks (Chen,2008). The authors have selected Al-Firdaws and Montada, two web forums of the dark web, for analysis. Crawling programs were used to extract the information from the two web forums of the dark web. A score was assigned to each line: (violence, anger, hate, racism, sentiment) and the training set was prepared, and different models were designed with a weight to each model. Later, the focus is divulged to sentiment analysis, which uses NLP and machine learning (ML) to interpret and classify emotions in subjective dark web data.

The work (Ghosh et al.,2017) then proposed three approaches for discovering and categorizing onion sites. The first approach is Automated keyword discovery (ATOL Keyword) using NLP in the limited dataset. Second, classification with limited training data (ATOL Classifier) based on ATOL Keywords. The third task is categorizing an onion Clustering with external supervision (ATOL Cluster) in case of less data and using keyword weights inferred by the previous algorithm ATOL re-weighted training data and made classifiers like Naive Bayes, SVM, etc.

In work (Ding et al.,2020), researchers proposed a distributed crawling infrastructure termed Zero-Crawler, which spontaneously crawls and updates ZeroNet websites in real-time. Named Automated Multi-Categorization Labelling (AMCL), it learns descriptive and discriminative keywords for various categories, gets a probability distribution of the keywords for multiple categories, and uses these terms to map ZeroNet website content to many labels. In addition, AMCL can learn categories on previous websites that do not have any labels.

Sometimes due to large dimensions, data cannot be efficiently analysed. Accuracy can get reduced due to the same. In (Faizan and Khan,2020), authors proposed a two-step dimensionality reduction: Mutual information were computed, features and scores were ranked, and k best features were selected. Natural language processing has found a place in dark web data analysis. In (He et al.,2019), researchers prepared a dataset from legal documents and rules and regulations, and manual labelling was done for five categories (counterfeiting credit cards, pornography, drugs, weapons, hackers). A test set was prepared from the dark web using the Python-based crawler. A Bag of words vector was created for each document from the dataset, and TFIDF (Term frequency-inverse document frequency) to was applied detect how important a word is, and classifiers were trained.

The Covid-19 pandemic has also accelerated dark web activities and hence research done on the web. For example, researchers (Bracci et al.,2008) have analysed 472,372 listings extracted from 23 Dark Web Marketplaces between January 1, 2020, and July 7, 2020. The findings of research work suggested that there were 518 listings on the dark web marketplace directly associated with Covid-19 products and other essential services.

Thus, the research trends on dark web information highlight the effort of researchers to draw as much information as possible from the dark web with divers of text feature identification and classification. Furthermore, the proposed work aims to extend the scope of dark web services identification with web structure analysis.

Role of Document Object Model in Web Structure Analysis

The WWW consortium built up a DOM model (Document Object Model), which functions as an object-based framework. It produces an XML and HTML document as a memory tree layout. The programming software utilizes these XML documents through the memory tree. The DOM additionally assists the clients with crossing and altering the XML documents powerfully. Each page of HTML is a DOM tree, with the labels being inner nodes and the leaf nodes containing instructive writings, images and hyperlinks.

The present work attempted to predict a deep and dark web page category without opening it directly, i.e., using its DOM graph, which essentially represents its structure. Nevertheless, these mechanisms can benefit stakeholders who do not wish to open any dark web page due to security concerns. Moreover, the literature survey hints an indication to attempt question: Is the HTML tag structure of the dark web pages helpful in getting more details about the topic of the web page?

Each page of HTML is a DOM tree, with the labels being inner nodes and the leaf nodes containing instructive writings, images and hyperlinks. The HTML page of reports is split into two different types: topic-based web pages and image-based web pages. Topic-based pages have a vast quantity of words with only a few images for the secondary function. In the image-based web pages, images are the important presentation, and the words describe the narration of the images.

The researchers (Yu and Jin,2017) proposed a method supported by the tree structure of the DOM to split one page into many blocks structure and get the insight of content blocks with numerical content rather than ML practice and guided tagging. They implemented a method with DOM structure, Page segmentation and statistical information. Statistical information is used to know the content importance of every block. Also, statistical data is used to demonstrate the algorithm's execution using F1 Score, Recall, and Precision. This algorithm provides excellent implementation in the mentioned concepts.

An algorithm was proposed to convert the HTML-DOM tree of any HTML document (Sarma and Mahanta,2019). It took input as all web pages, which were nothing but HTML web pages, parsed each document from start to end; this algorithm was implemented using a recursive approach. It used a recursive call that performed the pre-order traversal. This pre-order traversal traversed all nodes in the HTML DOM-Tree of every webpage file in depth-first fashion and subsequently extracts the names of the HTML nodes, and eventually prints the node name separated by comma (,). Whenever the algorithm encounters a leaf node, backtracking is done to the parent node of that leaf node and subsequently marks the backtracking by a ($). There are four distance methods named Qgram distance, Cosine distance, Jaccard distance, Jaro distance, out of which two measures were used for clustering performance evaluation Purity and Entropy. The algorithm ran on two datasets and got the best results. In both datasets, 25 web pages were used.

Researchers proposed approaches of news automated duplication on internet sites are located on the syntactical and linguistic review of the HTML web page source text (Galushka et al.,2017). To analyse main tags or traits of HTML web pages and to disclose web pages those allow to understand duplication of the news which is already added on the web page of news with particular apps and free from human interaction. The step called parsing practices the DOM structure of HTML web pages to look for content where the concern is and split the information from the pattern defined by HTML tags, attributes, etc. DOM is a global and general web page structure narrative, and that page has a tree structure that includes HTML tags as a node of the tree, and the twigs are the links among nodes. In other work, the authors of (Ma et al.,2012) proposed a crawling mechanism based on Document Object Model (DOM). The crawler at first fed with a URL. Then, the URL is sent straight to the finder. The finder extracts all accessible links from the initial page, push them into the TO-DO list and the current URL into the Visited list. The finder then, in a loop, visits the URLs in the TO-DO list one by one, pushing links on the current page into the TO-DO list, sending the current URL to the downloader, and throwing it into the Visited list. The existing URL in both the TO-DO list and the Visited list won't be inserted again into the TO-DO list. Finally, the downloader downloads the pages with the received URLs into the HTML storage, then sends a done flag back to the finder to ensure it is successfully downloading. Further, the HTML pages are converted to XML pages with a DOM parser. Finally, the XML pages are analysed and interpreted with text analysis. The focus of the study is to employ a DOM parser to separate deep web query interfaces like login form and AJAX-based pages. The author cited that creating the DOM tree facilitated better visual analysis.

In the present work, the HTML DOM structure significance is evaluated to predict dark web page genre classification. The following section offers a brief overview of the literature survey to classify the web page genre.

Web Page Genre Classification

In web mining, classifying web pages without opening them is researched. The web page genre matches similar web page's types to respond to input queries and avoid topic contamination while harvesting links for search engine output.

The research directions are regarding features used, classification algorithms and genres referred for web page genre classification. Typically, the web page genre is classified based on the subject/topic of the web page. For example, web pages can be considered political, sports, and business. Further, web page features such as the home page and forum page could be classified. The other category of web page classification is sentiment recognition of the web page. The web page genre classification is attempted to improvise search engine performance. The proposed work aims to label the category of web pages in predefined categories without opening the page.

One common feature of classifying web page genres is URL pattern and its part recognition. But a handful of researchers explored the role of DOM (Document Object Model) termed Tag Tree in grouping similar kinds of web pages. The Document Object Model (DOM) sets out the structure of documents and how a document is approached and manoeuvred.

In work (Chakrabarti,2001), the author discussed DOM structure in improved topic distillation by mapping DOM to the relevant query from mixed hub structure. In another work (Chakrabarti et al.,2001), authors considered DOM at element level as one of the factors along with HTML text and hyperlink structure among web pages to avoid topic drift and contamination problems concerning input queries.

The chapter covers dark web page genre classification with web page structure analysis in further discussion.

Figure 1. Proposed methodology for analysing web pages at the structural level

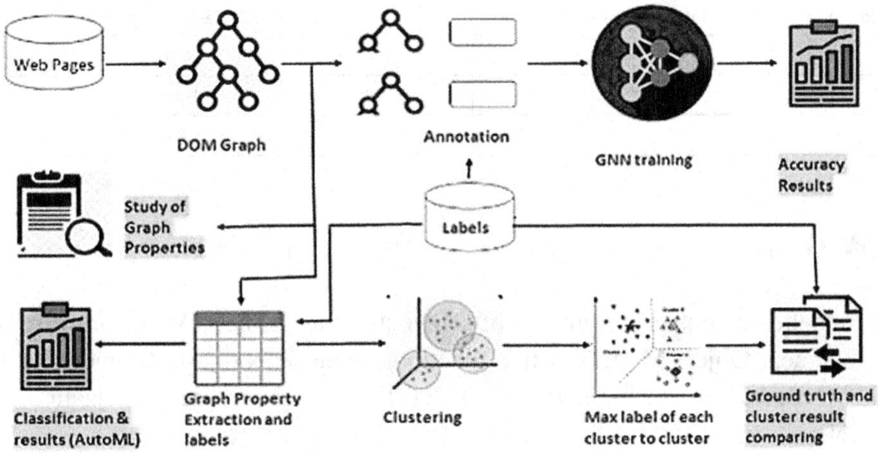

METHODOLOGY

Figure 1 shows a functional block diagram for analysing web pages at the structural level.

The functions covered in the figure are as follows:

1. Clustering DOM graphs with GNN
    a. Constructing DOM graphs for each web page
    b. Annotating labels to the graph of web page
    c. Training graph neural network for similar DOM clustering
2. Extracting graph properties
    a. Applying clustering algorithms to form clusters of the graphs with related properties
    b. Assigning labels to cluster
3. Classifying web pages in classes using AutoML
4. Confirming relevancy of labels with clusters

Data Preparation

The indigenous python-based crawler is developed to crawl the tor dark web. The crawler collected the 44 thousand onion hidden service web pages for one week. Table 1 shows the number of hidden service pages.

Most of the hidden services were HTML and PHP pages, and the rest were CGI and other formats.

The proposed work aims to predict the domain of onion links without opening the page. The challenge lies in determining how to label unlabelled data. Thus, the task of labelling the collected data is undertaken initially. Though to establish the relevance of labels to web pages, the discussion includes clustering DOM graphs first.

Table 1. Data collection

Hidden Service Web Page format	Number of Hidden Service Web Pages
HTML	34367
PHP	10026
Other	91

Creating DOM Graphs

Proposed work modelled web pages as graphs of DOM structures. The WWW consortium built up a DOM model (Document Object Model), which functions as an object-based framework. It produces an XML and HTML document as a memory tree layout. Figure 2 shows the visualization of the DOM structure in a graph.

In the structure of DOM using a web page, the dependent route to the information of the initial content can be scripted and free from any HTML attributes. e.g., HTML Body of the web page initial content of a page, where initial content is the first paragraph and first tag from all tag data sets. Overall, it can be written as: Root of the tree . . .. Parent of the child . . .. Tag/attributes. The potential of such demand for the information for the automated duplication can be avoided by modifying the DOM structure of the web page by increasing some arbitrary number of extra tags before the content is displayed.

Therefore, in the DOM tree structure, an additional tag/attribute will be extra to the equivalent width of the tree as the guarded structure. Therefore, they appointed a method as "additional width of DOM structure". The second method is an additional depth of the DOM structure tree, including the additional levels increasing to the HTML web page structure of the blocks.

To define the tree twig, two issues are directed. The one issue is one it should be on a similar level of the tree structure as the vertices, which includes a guarded content twig can be extra level over the vertex about guarded information, given that it adds one of the parent vertexes. The mixture of the narrative methods of the web page DOM growth is supported on utilization of random standards of recognition of HTML elements as tags. One more modification is adding its levels and breadth, denying the offender a chance to invent and compose methods of the web pages parsing for the division in the important element of current content that in turn forms it unfeasible it's automated duplication. The HTML page of reports is split into two different types: topic-based web pages and image-based web pages. Topic-based pages have many words with only a few images for the secondary function. In the image-based web pages, images are the important presentation, and the words describe the narration of the images.

Supervised Learning Approach to Label the Data

The supervised learning model is created with surface web data. However, there is no formal data set to label the website in different categories. Thus, the model is trained with manually labelled data to label the crawled data. More than 100 websites were visited for each category to create the manual dataset. A dataset consists of different websites, including URL, the name of the website, parsed website text. The collected data is labelled under sixteen categories viz. 'Adult', 'Business/Corporate', 'Computers and Technology', 'E-Commerce', 'Education', 'Food', 'Forums', 'Games', 'Health and Fitness', 'Law

Figure 2. Document object model (DOM) graph

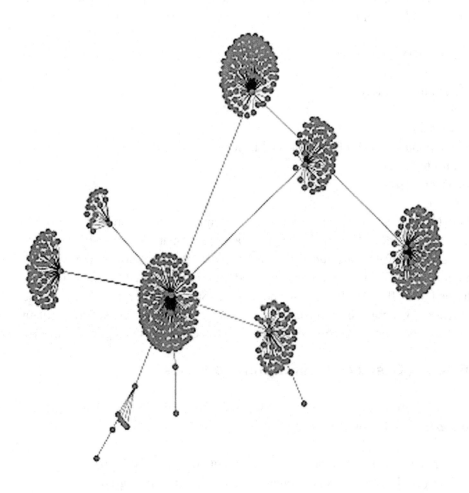

and Government', 'News', 'Photography', 'Social Networking and Messaging', 'Sports', 'Streaming Services', 'Travel'.

For the present discussion, the authors choose all pages belonging to categories - Streaming Services, Forums, Social Networking and Messaging, E-Commerce.

Graph Neural Network for Web Page Prediction

A graph neural network introduced in (Zhang et al.,2018) is implemented on created DOM graphs. The researchers have considered simple graphs in discussed work, i.e., a graph with no self-loops and a symmetrical adjacency matrix to represent the edge between the vertices of the given graph. Furthermore, the author has considered every vertex as a feature vector of c-dimensions and used the information matrix of every node to represent a vertex.

The classification used in the proposed work is Graph Neural Network (GNN). Each HTML page was created into a DOM graph which is then converted into a specific format and served as the input to the GNN. The GNN then classifies the web pages based on the training data provided to the GNN. The processing of the graph neural network can be summarized into the following stages:

1. Web Page to DOM graph creation
2. DOM to GNN input format
3. Graph Convolutional Layer
4. Sort Pooling
5. 1D Convolutional Layer
6. Several maxpooling and 1D Convolutional Layers
7. Fully connected layer
8. Softmax layer

Referred GNN model accepted input in a specific format. Thus, the proposed work faced two challenges, i.e., the conversion of DOM structure the data into a format acceptable by the GNN and training the model with a vast number of a graph. But both the challenges were addressed by authors. For feeding the DOM graph into the GNN, the authors converted it into the required text data format.

GNN is trained with 10,000 web pages that belonged to Streaming Services, Forums, Social Networking and Messaging, E-Commerce for 100 epochs with an 80:20 ratio of train and test split on an NVIDIA GPU on DGX-1 supercomputer. Accuracy of around 86 per cent on the testing set achieved on the dataset.

Graph Clustering Based on DOM Graph Properties

Depending on the structure, the graph comes with various properties used to characterize the graph. The proposed work extracted the following properties of graphs:

1. Number of nodes (n): The Number of nodes presents within a given graph
2. No. of edges (m): Number of edges connecting vertices in a given graph
3. Radius r(G): The lowest eccentricity out of all the vertices is deemed for the radius of Graph G (Graph theory basic properties, 2022)
4. Diameter d(G): The maximum eccentricity out i of all the vertices is deemed for the diameter of Graph G. The greatest from all distances within a vertex to all diverse vertices is considered the diameter of Graph G
5. Density D: The ratio of the Number of edges |E| concerning the utmost feasible edges. For undirected uncomplicated graphs, the graph density is depicted in figure 3.

Figure 3. Density for uncomplicated undirected graph

$$D = \frac{|E|}{\binom{|V|}{2}} = \frac{2|E|}{|V|(|V| - 1)}$$

where D is the density of Graph, V is no. of vertices, and E is no. of edges, while for directed simple

Figure 4. Density for simple directed graph

$$D = \frac{|E|}{|V|(|V| - 1)}$$

graphs, the graph density is defined as depicted in figure 4.

where |E| - No. of edges; |V| - No. of vertices in the graph.

Note that the maximum number of edges is as depicted in figure 5

Figure 5. Maximum number of edges (wiki/Dense graph, 2022)

$$D = \frac{|V|(|V| - 1)}{2}$$

6.   Average Eccentricity e(v):

Let G be a connected graph of order n. Then, the eccentricity e(v) of a vertex v is the separation from v to a vertex uttermost from v. The maximum distance among a vertex to all diverse vertices is deemed the eccentricity of the vertex (Das et al.,2017). The average eccentricity of G - mean of all eccentricities in G is depicted in figure 6.

Figure 6. Average eccentricity

$$\text{avec}(\text{G}) = \frac{1}{n} \sum_{i=1}^{n} \varepsilon_i$$

where G is a given graph, n is the number of vertices; ε is epsilon, and 'i' is iterator among the list of vertices.

7. Average Shortest Path Length l(G)

The average shortest path length is a concept in the network topology defined as the average Number of steps along the shortest paths for all possible pairs of network nodes. It measures the efficiency of information or mass transport on a network (Wikipedia Average path length,2022). The equation is depicted in figure 7.

Figure 7. Average shortest path length

$$l(G) = \frac{1}{n(n-1)} \sum_{i \neq j} d(v_i, v_j)$$

where n is the number of vertices in graph G; di represents the degree of vertex i in graph G

8. Number of cliques ω(G):

The clique number of a graph is the number of vertices in a maximum clique of a Graph where the clique of the graph is defined as the complete subgraph of the given graph. The equation is depicted in figure 8.
Equivalently, it is equal to the size of the largest clique or maximal clique of the graph (mathworld. wolfram.com/CliqueNumber, 2022).

Figure 8. Number of cliques

$$\omega(G) \geq \sum_{i=1}^{n} \frac{1}{n - d_i}$$

where n is the number of vertices in graph G; di represents the degree of vertex i in a graph

9. Average Number of maximal cliques:

It is defined as the average of the Total Number of cliques such that they cannot be extended by including one more adjacent vertex, i.e., the clique considered should not be a subset of a larger clique (mathworld.wolfram.com/ MaximalClique, 2022).

10. Number of periphery nodes:

It is the Number of sets of nodes with eccentricity equal to the diameter (networkx.algorithms.distance measures, 2022).

11. Maximum degree:

The maximum degree of the graph is the degree of the vertex with the most significant number of edges incident to it (the-maximum-and-minimum-degrees-of-a-graph,2022).

12. Degree assortativity coefficient r:

Pearson's correlation coefficient of the degree between pairs of linked nodes in a graph is called the Assortativity coefficient (Assertivity,2022). The formula is shown in figure 9.

Figure 9. Assortativity coefficient

$$r = \frac{\sum_{jk} jk(e_{jk} - q_j q_k)}{\sigma_q^2}$$

where qk is the distribution of the remaining degree

13. Estrada index EE or EE(G):

The Estrada index of Graph (G) is defined as some bottommost and uppermost bounds of all vertices, edges and randic index are obtained (Kasim et al.,2013).
The equation is depicted in figure 10.

Figure 10. Estrada index EE

$$EE = EE(G) = \sum_{i=1}^{n} e^{\delta i}$$

where 1 = Lower bound n = upper bound delta(i) = Eigen values

14. Biconnected graphs

A graph which is connected and not separable then that graph called as Biconnected Graph (wiki/Biconnected_graph,2022).

15.   Global efficiency of the graph

The graph's global efficiency is the average efficiencies over all pairs of vertices (Ek et al.,2015). The equation is depicted in figure 11.

Figure 11. Global efficiency of the graph

$$E_{glob}(G) = \frac{1}{n(n-1)} \sum \cdot_{i \neq j} \in (v_i, v_j)$$

where v(i),v(j) = vertices i,j = vertex number; n = number of vertices

16.   Wiener index W(G):

It is a summation of distances among all graph vertices (Eliasi et al.,2012). The equation is depicted in figure 12.

Figure 12. Wiener index

$$W(G) = \sum \cdot_{u,v \subseteq V(G)} d(u, v)$$

The DOM graphs were further analyzed based on graph properties with reference to (Samtani et al.,2020) and NetworkX documentation (networkx.org,2021).

Along with Node and Network, Graph is also a category. Table 3 shows related remarks, if any, on graph metric.

Referring to node, network and graph properties data set is prepared. For example, figure 13 depicts the graph properties data set. On this curated dataset, an unsupervised learning algorithm is performed.

Clustering is a well-known unsupervised technique that groups data points into a predetermined quantity of dissociating clusters. The authors have chosen the K-means clustering algorithm as the unsupervised technique in the proposed work. In the algorithm, 'K' relates to the whole quantity of groups stated earlier in the initialization process of the clustering algorithm. Several algorithmic parameters are ready to define which point is allotted to one particular cluster. The proposed work aimed to implement clustering on Web pages supported by Document Object Model structure of Web Documents, since the HTML web pages - DOM tree structure of every Web document has been described as an HTML Tags, structure of the webpage and later on implementing K-means clustering algorithm on the DOM

Table 2. Shows node and network properties

Category	Metric		Definition	Remarks
Node	Number of nodes		# of nodes in the network	A number of tags in a page; a page with too many tags can be a dynamic one, while one with fewer tags can be simply a static page with little content (Samtani et al.,2020)
	Number of edges		# of edges in network	A number of tags in a page; a page with too many tags can be a dynamic one, while one with fewer tags can be simply a static page with little content (Samtani et al.,2020)
	Betweenness		# of shortest paths passing through a node divided by all shortest paths	A node with high betweenness centrality indicates that it has many children, i.e. a tag with a lot of children tags, for example, a very big table, etc. (networkx.algorithms. distancemeasures, 2022, graph theory basic properties, 2022)
	Overall Degree		Sum of a node's in and out-degree	The overall importance of each threat term within the vocabulary
	Eigenvector		Summed connections to others weighted by the centrality	A node with high betweenness centrality indicates that it has many children, i.e., a tag with a lot of children tags, for example, a very big table, etc. (Tudisco, F., & Higham, D. J., 2021)
	Closeness		Avg. # of hops required to reach every other node on the network	The more central a node is, i.e., higher the closeness value, the more central that tag is on the page
Network	Graph Density		Sum of edges divided by the number of possible edges	Relationship and inter-dependence of tags on a page: more the density, more the tags and hence it can be a social networking site
	Eccentricity		Maximum geodesic distance from a node to all other nodes	Similar to closeness; it measures how quickly a threat term can reach another
	Diameter		Maximum eccentricity	It indicates the breadth and diversity of various tags. It can also indicate the maximum distance between two tags at the top and bottom of the page
	Radius		Minimum Eccentricity	It indicates the breadth and diversity of various tags. It can also indicate the maximum distance between two tags at the top and bottom of the page
	Avg. path length		Average distance between two nodes	It identifies the average dependencies between tags. If the tag distance is very low, it is probably a small page and could be a forum. If the tag distance is considerable, then it is an extensive page with multiple components and probably can be a darknet marketplace or a social networking website
	Clustering Coefficient		Identifies how nodes tend to cluster together	Pinpoints how tags cluster together indicates the amount of closely connected components, e.g., table on a page

structure of web pages. Using various graph properties, authors decided to prepare a dataset and then performed unsupervised learning.

Agglomerative Clustering, Birch, Spectral Clustering and Gaussian Mixture, the specified cluster n=4, i.e., four clusters to be generated.

DBSCAN algorithm automatically generated four clusters. For MeanShift, it generated 18 clusters. For OPTICS, it generated around 273 clusters.

Table 3. Graph properties

Category	Metric	Remark
Graph	Bipartite	The web page can be distinctly divided into two parts or two sections.
	Size of the largest clique	-----------
	Number of cliques	-----------
	Largest maximal size	-----------
	Avg No of maximal cliques	-----------
	Transitivity	-----------
	Connectivity	-----------
	Number of connected components	-----------
	Directed Acyclic	-----------
	Number of periphery nodes	There are many tags and contents on the borders of web pages example, at the top, there is a menu, and at the bottom, there is contact information, etc.
	Is eulerian	-----------
	If the graph is semi- Eulerian	-----------
	If the graph has an Eulerian path	-----------
	Wiener Index	-----------

Figure 13. Data set created by calculating values of DOM graphs

Page	No of nodes	No of edges	Radius	Diameter	Avg Eccentricitiy	Density	Avg shortest path length	No of cliques	Avg No of maximal cliques	No of periphery nodes	Maximum degree	Degree assortativity coefficient
crawled/ar-ar.facebookcorewwwi.onion/P8FDOC0E0...	479	478	4	8	6.716075	0.004175	3.751784	478	1.995825	92	121	-0.757233
crawled/ar-ar.facebookcorewwwi.onion/P9CDF8CE3...	386	385	5	10	7.396373	0.005181	4.262930	385	1.994819	23	162	-0.523293
crawled/ar-ar.facebookcorewwwi.onion/P9q20C9XC...	461	460	4	8	6.726681	0.004336	3.783495	460	1.995662	90	109	-0.777539
crawled/ar-ar.facebookcorewwwi.onion/PB0zBDK8D...	393	392	4	8	6.638677	0.005089	3.791868	392	1.994911	69	104	-0.729413
crawled/ar-ar.facebookcorewwwi.onion/PB5250F40...	275	274	4	8	6.727273	0.007273	4.063132	274	1.992727	45	72	-0.763838
crawled/zqktlwiuavvvqqt4ybvgvi7tyo4hjl5xgfuvpd...	178	177	5	9	7.050562	0.011236	4.210944	177	1.988764	19	61	-0.531743
crawled/zqktlwiuavvvqqt4ybvgvi7tyo4hjl5xgfuvpd...	127	126	4	7	5.811024	0.015748	3.495563	126	1.984252	37	56	-0.586220
crawled/zqktlwiuavvvqqt4ybvgvi7tyo4hjl5xgfuvpd...	199	198	4	8	6.195980	0.010050	3.942033	198	1.989950	21	63	-0.542826
crawled/zqktlwiuavvvqqt4ybvgvi7tyo4hjl5xgfuvpd...	1272	1271	6	11	8.365566	0.001572	3.801714	1271	1.996428	32	590	-0.644174
crawled/zvvtba2a37mcydnntjkzy26lrv3y5effyotr4g...	195	194	5	9	7.969231	0.010256	5.493101	194	1.989744	63	37	-0.726532

The labelled clusters were compared with the labelled class. Table 4 shows similarities in the Jaccard index between cluster and class labels.

The result confirms that around 59% of clusters were labelled correctly. Thus, considering the massive data set undertaken for clustering, attained accuracy could be acceptable.

Table 4. Clustering results (indicates that the number of clusters was selected automatically)*

Clustering Algorithm	Jaccard Index
K-Means	0.593
Agglomerative Clustering	0.595
Birch	0.599
DBSCAN*	0.5
MeanShift*	0.51
OPTICS	0.78
Spectral Clustering	0.64
Gaussian Mixture	0.61

Classifying Web Pages in Classes using AutoML

AutoML systems are helpful machine learning assistants developed to go through data for new features, choose correct supervised learning models and hyper tune the specific parameters. One of the Auto ML tools is the Tree-based Pipeline Optimization Tool (TPOT).

1. TPOT's present operators comprise:
2. Sets of feature pre-processors
3. Feature transformers
4. Feature selection techniques
5. Supervised classifiers and regressors.

TPOT automates the stressful and lengthy process of designing an optimized machine learning pipeline by representing pipelines as binary expression trees with machine learning operators as basics. TPOT automatically selects the best pipeline available for the particular dataset by genetic algorithms (mutation and cross-over).

1. The procedure for utilizing the TPOT library is:
2. The extracted various properties like Number of nodes, Number of edges, etc., from the DOM structure graphs and prepared a dataset in a CSV file.
3. The prepared dataset needs to be split into X and Y train and test sets and fit into the TPOTClassifier.
4. The TPOT library automatically searches for the best pipeline using genetic algorithms (mutation and cross-over).
5. Once TPOT finishes searching, it offers the Python code for the best pipeline it has found so far.
6. Finally, the exported pipeline can be fitted with the dataset to infer the categories of web pages in the testing set.
7. As mentioned earlier, TPOT automatically selects the best pipeline available for the particular dataset by genetic algorithms (mutation and cross-over) and hence achieved around 97.6% accuracy with the current dataset. It is one of the efficient AutoML approaches to Machine Learning.

Analysing Graph Properties

The proposed work presented a theoretical study of the various graph properties and their implication for deciding upon the web page structure. For example, considering the property 'Number of nodes' implies a number of tags in a page; a page with too many tags can be a dynamic one, while one with fewer tags can be simply a static page with little content. For example, the result showed the average Number of nodes for Social Networking and Streaming Services pages are higher than those of E-Commerce and Forum based pages.

The present work studied six properties and their implications for web page structure. Table 5 lists properties considered along with their implications.

Table 5. Graph properties and properties and their implications for web page structure

Property	Definition	Implications	
Number of nodes	# of nodes in the network	Number of tags in a page; a page with too many tags can be a dynamic one, while one with fewer tags can be simply a static page with little content (Samtani et al.,2020)	
Number of edges	# of edges in the network	Number of tags in a page; a page with too many tags can be a dynamic one, while one with fewer tags can be simply a static page with little content (Samtani et al.,2020)	
Betweenness	# of shortest paths passing through a node divided by all shortest paths	A node with high betweenness centrality indicates that it has many children, i.e. a tag with a lot of children tags, for example, a very big table, etc. (Betweenness Centrality - an overview, 2022)	
Eigenvector	Added associations with others weighted by the centrality	A node with high eigenvector centrality indicates that it has many children, i.e. a tag with a lot of children tags, for example, a very big table, etc. (Tudisco and Higham,2021)	
Closeness	Avg. # of hops required to reach every other node on the network	The more central a node is, i.e. higher the closeness value, the more central that tag is on the page (closeness-centrality, 2022)	
Eccentricity	Maximum geodesic distance from a node to all other nodes	Like closeness, gauges how rapidly a dangerous term can come to another (Hage and Harary,1995)	

Table 6 contains the values for the graph properties extracted from the DOM graphs for the web pages. Few observations were made regarding the DOM:

1. The average Number of nodes is more for graphs belonging to dynamic pages like 'Social Networking and Messaging' and 'Streaming Services' than for graphs belonging to static pages like 'E- Commerce' and 'Forums.'
2. The average Number of edges is more for graphs belonging to dynamic pages than for graphs belonging to static pages.
3. The average diameter is more for graphs belonging to dynamic pages than for graphs belonging to static pages.
4. The average Number of periphery nodes is more for 'E-Commerce' type pages and less for others.
5. The Wiener index is more for graphs belonging to dynamic pages than for static pages

Table 6. Values obtained for discussed graph properties of DOM graph dataset

Property or Category	Social Networking and Messaging	Streaming Services	E-Commerce	Forums
No of nodes	421.9310153	366.7154878	348.2179487	278.745614
No of edges	420.9310153	365.7154878	347.2179487	277.745614
Radius	4.743810848	4.465089834	4.538461538	4.035087719
Diameter	9.035883171	8.835569707	8.641025641	7.850877193
Avg Ecentricitiy	6.998182315	6.94195582	6.983255845	6.208269526
Density	0.006034384	0.005931816	0.010365514	0.007719547
Avg shortest path length	3.979102892	3.861603892	3.834842961	3.614774773
No of cliques	420.9310153	365.7154878	347.2179487	277.745614
Avg No of maximal cliques	1.993965616	1.994068184	1.989634486	1.992280453
No of periphery nodes	47.05312935	41.92085513	61.62820513	13.5877193
Maximum degree	148.6625869	125.1187173	145.3846154	103.2631579
Degree assortativity coefficient	-0.624349507	-0.647356354	-0.663699958	-0.73867083
Estrada index	12736033562	-16500232174	6.29008E+11	324448.0596
No of biconnected item	420.9310153	365.7154878	347.2179487	277.745614
Avg global efficiency of the graph	0.301058442	0.305064226	0.321803268	0.324296325
Wiener index	415619.2292	283783.2556	351439.3718	156037.6579

The Observations from the Proposed Work Offered the Following Lemmas

Lemma 1: The Number of nodes for dynamic pages like social networking and streaming is more than that of static pages like forums.

Lemma 2: Weiner index of dynamic pages like social networking and streaming is more than that of static pages like forums.

Lemma 3: Diameter is more for dynamic graphs like those belonging to Social Networking and Streaming Pages than static graphs belonging to Forum.

The proofs for lemmas are presented as follows.

Lemma: The Number of nodes for dynamic pages like social networking and streaming is more than that of static pages like forums.

Proof:

While converting a web page into its DOM graph, each web page tag is represented as a node in the graph. This shows that a large number of nodes in the DOM graph indicates a large number of tags on the web page.

Moreover, many tags indicate an enormous amount of content on the page. Dynamic pages can have more extensive content like links and elements on the web page than static pages, with a straight title and some comments.

Also, observe that the average Number of nodes is vast for dynamic pages like Social Networking

(421) and Streaming Services (366) rather than that of static pages like E-Commerce (348) and Forums (278), shown in table 6.

Thus, the Number of nodes for dynamic pages like social networking and streaming is more than that of static pages like forums.

Lemma: Weiner index of dynamic pages like social networking and streaming is more than that of static pages like forums.

Proof:

From table 6, it is observed that an average number of edges for social networking pages (426) is more than the average Number of edges for forums (277). Since the Weiner index includes dG(u, v) is the distance between two vertices and u, v∈V (G) is the minimum Number of edges on a path in G between u and v.

Thus, it is observed that the Wiener Index is greater for dynamic pages than that of static pages.

Lemma: Diameter is more for dynamic graphs like those belonging to Social Networking and Streaming Pages than static graphs belonging to Forums

Proof:

A graph's diameter D is the largest Number of vertices that must be traversed to travel from one vertex to another. The average Number of nodes is very large for dynamic pages like Social Networking (421) and Streaming Services (366) rather than that of static pages like E-Commerce (348) and Forums (278), shown in table 6. Thus, a large number of nodes may indicate a lot of content on the page.

The DOM graph is nothing but a tree, having a large number of nodes, and they are not compact since a DOM tree is usually a long one with parent-child relation for each tag and its subsequent tags.

The trees with a large number of nodes possibly have a larger diameter than trees with a lesser number of nodes. Hence, with a large diameter, the web page may have a lot of content like a dynamic one rather than a page with meagre content like a static one.

Thus, diameter is more for dynamic graphs like those belonging to Social Networking and Streaming Pages than static graphs belonging to Forums.

CONCLUSION

The dark web contains sensitive data that strategic organizations must identify well in advance to anticipate and handle threats. However, due to disturbing visual content and dangerous links and attachments, it is not preferable to open dark web data without possible filtering. Therefore, the present work offered a hypothesis for exploring the categories of web pages without opening them, i.e. analyzing web pages based on their structure. First, the web pages were converted to their DOM (Document Object Model) graphs, representing their structure. Then, a graph neural network (GNN) is trained with these graphs.

Further, various graph properties like the Number of nodes, edges, etc., for these web page DOM graphs were measured. On the DOM graph property dataset, supervised and unsupervised learning is performed. Finally, the chapter presented a theoretical study of the various graph properties and their implication for deciding upon the web page structure, supplemented with present observations.

The proposed approach can predict the category of any hidden onion service web page using proposed models with around 80% accuracy. However, the data's loss in accuracy is because of some inconsistencies since the data in the dark web does not mandatorily follow any markup language standards.

Modelling web pages as DOM graphs can successfully represent their structure. Hence it is possible to successfully predict types of web pages using their structure properties, i.e. without directly opening the pages.

There is a marked difference in the characteristics of graphs belonging to static pages and of those belonging to dynamic pages. This difference can help in better analysis of the web pages.

REFERENCES

Alghamdi, H., & Selamat, A. (2022). *Techniques to detect terrorists/extremists on the dark web: a review.* Data Technologies and Applications. doi:10.1108/DTA-07-2021-0177

Beshiri, A. S., & Susuri, A. (2019). Dark web and its impact in online anonymity and privacy: A critical analysis and review. *Journal of Computer and Communications*, 7(03), 30–43. doi:10.4236/jcc.2019.73004

Bracci, A., Nadini, M., Aliapoulios, M., McCoy, D., Gray, I., Teytelboym, A., ... Baronchelli, A. (2008). *The COVID-19 online shadow economy.* Academic Press.

BroadhurstR.LordD.MaximD.Woodford-SmithH.JohnstonC.ChungH.W.SabolB.(2018).*Malware trends on 'darknet' crypto-markets: Research review.* doi:10.2139/ssrn.3226758

Chakrabarti, S. (2001, April). Integrating the document object model with hyperlinks for enhanced topic distillation and information extraction. In *Proceedings of the 10th International Conference on World Wide Web* (pp. 211-220). 10.1145/371920.372054

Chakrabarti, S., Joshi, M., & Tawde, V. (2001, September). Enhanced topic distillation using text, markup tags, and hyperlinks. In *Proceedings of the 24th Annual International ACM SIGIR Conference on Research and Development in Information Retrieval* (pp. 208-216). 10.1145/383952.383990

Chen, H. (2008, June). Sentiment and affect analysis of dark web forums: Measuring radicalization on the internet. In *2008 IEEE International Conference on Intelligence and Security Informatics* (pp. 104-109). IEEE.

Chen, H. (2011). *Dark web: Exploring and data mining the dark side of the web* (Vol. 30). Springer Science & Business Media.

Dalvi, A., Paranjpe, S., Amale, R., Kurumkar, S., Kazi, F., & Bhirud, S. G. (2021, May). SpyDark: Surface and Dark Web Crawler. In *2021 2nd International Conference on Secure Cyber Computing and Communications (ICSCCC)* (pp. 45-49). IEEE.

Das, K. C., Maden, A. D., Cangül, I. N., & Çevik, A. S. (2017). On average eccentricity of graphs. *Proceedings of the National Academy of Sciences. India. Section A, Physical Sciences*, 87(1), 23–30. doi:10.100740010-016-0315-8

Ding, J., Guo, X., & Chen, Z. (2020, January). Big data analyses of zeronet sites for exploring the new generation darkweb. In *Proceedings of the 3rd International Conference on Software Engineering and Information Management* (pp. 46-52). 10.1145/3378936.3378981

Ek, B., Ver Schneider, C., & Narayan, D. A. (2015). Global efficiency of graphs. AKCE. *International Journal of Graphs and Combinatorics, 12*(1), 1–13. doi:10.1016/j.akcej.2015.06.001

Eliasi, M., Raeisi, G., & Taeri, B. (2012). Wiener index of some graph operations. *Discrete Applied Mathematics, 160*(9), 1333–1344. doi:10.1016/j.dam.2012.01.014

Faizan, M., & Khan, R. A. (2020). A Two-Step Dimensionality Reduction Scheme for Dark Web Text Classification. In *Ambient Communications and Computer Systems* (pp. 303–312). Springer. doi:10.1007/978-981-15-1518-7_25

Galushka, V., Marshakov, D., & Fathi, V. (2017). Dynamic document object model formation technique for corporate website protection against automatic coping of information. In *MATEC Web of Conferences* (Vol. 132, p. 05001). EDP Sciences. 10.1051/matecconf/201713205001

Ghosh, S., Das, A., Porras, P., Yegneswaran, V., & Gehani, A. (2017, August). Automated categorization of onion sites for analysing the darkweb ecosystem. In *Proceedings of the 23rd ACM SIGKDD International Conference on Knowledge Discovery and Data Mining* (pp. 1793-1802). ACM.

Hage, P., & Harary, F. (1995). Eccentricity and centrality in networks. *Social Networks, 17*(1), 57–63. doi:10.1016/0378-8733(94)00248-9

He, S., He, Y., & Li, M. (2019, March). Classification of illegal activities on the dark web. In *Proceedings of the 2019 2nd International Conference on Information Science and Systems* (pp. 73-78). 10.1145/3322645.3322691

Iliou, C., Kalpakis, G., Tsikrika, T., Vrochidis, S., & Kompatsiaris, I. (2017). Hybrid focused crawling on the Surface and the Dark Web. *EURASIP Journal on Information Security, 2017*(1), 1–13.

Kasim, M., Zhang, F., & Wang, Q. (2013). Estrada Index of Graphs. Academic Press.

Kawaguchi, Y., & Ozawa, S. (2019, December). Exploring and identifying malicious sites in dark web using machine learning. In *International Conference on Neural Information Processing* (pp. 319-327). Springer.

Ma, W., Chen, X., & Shang, W. (2012, June). Advanced deep web crawler based on Dom. In *2012 Fifth International Joint Conference on Computational Sciences and Optimization* (pp. 605-609). IEEE.

Moore, D., & Rid, T. (2016). Cryptopolitik and the Darknet. *Survival, 58*(1), 7–38.

Rawat, R., Kumar, A., Chouhan, M., Telang, S., Pachlasiya, K., Garg, B., & Mahor, V. (2021). *Systematic literature Review (SLR) on social media and the Digital Transformation of Drug Trafficking on Darkweb.* Available at SSRN 3903797.

Samtani, S., Zhu, H., & Chen, H. (2020). Proactively identifying emerging hacker threats from the dark web: A diachronic graph embedding framework (d-gef). *ACM Transactions on Privacy and Security, 23*(4), 1–33.

Sarma, M. K., & Mahanta, A. K. (2019, April). Clustering of Web Documents with Structure of Webpages based on the HTML Document Object Model. In *2019 IEEE International Conference on Intelligent Techniques in Control, Optimization and Signal Processing (INCOS)* (pp. 1-6). IEEE.

Tudisco, F., & Higham, D. J. (2021). *Node and Edge Eigenvector Centrality for Hypergraphs.* arXiv preprint arXiv:2101.06215.

Wikipedia Average path length. (n.d.). https://bit.ly/3b8hwxn

Yu, X., & Jin, Z. (2017, October). Web content information extraction based on DOM tree and statistical information. In *2017 IEEE 17th International Conference on Communication Technology (ICCT)* (pp. 1308-1311). IEEE.

Zhang, M., Cui, Z., Neumann, M., & Chen, Y. (2018, April). An end-to-end deep learning architecture for graph classification. *Thirty-Second AAAI Conference on Artificial Intelligence.*

Zhang, X., & Chow, K. P. (2020). A framework for dark Web threat intelligence analysis. In Cyber Warfare and Terrorism: Concepts, Methodologies, Tools, and Applications (pp. 266-276). IGI Global.

Section 2
Models for Crime Prediction

Chapter 4
Time–Series Models for Crime Prediction in India:
An Empirical Comparison

Sonali Gupta

https://orcid.org/0000-0001-5885-0612

J. C. Bose University of Science and Technology, India

ABSTRACT

The dark web is termed as the concealed content hidden behind interfaces offering secure chats or mailing applications on the WWW, and exploiting it for illegal practices is termed cybercrimes. As the dark web is enormously big compared to the surface web, cyber-crimes have become one of the biggest challenges to tackle. Predicting them before they actually happen is almost impossible. The work thus deals with predicting the number of cognizable crimes (physical and cybercrimes reported collectively) by National Crime Record Bureau (NCRB), the government-approved agency for maintaining crime records in India. Predicting crimes has become important as they advance to new levels of intelligence and diversification with the increased use of information and communication technology (ICT). This work presents the research based on evidences with ARIMA and LSTM time series models for predicting the cognizable crimes in India. The authors have used root mean squared error and mean absolute error as loss functions for error evaluation, and the results obtained from both the models are presented.

INTRODUCTION

Crime is an act done by a person which is against the laws of the country. The offenders of law commit crime in any form at any location irrespective of the time of the day. Crime Rate in India has reached alarming figures and the figures does not dimmish even after adopting stringent measures and continuous efforts put in by the Government. It is one of the most challenging social problems in the country as it hampers the socio-economic development of the nation and its citizens.

While most of the world including India was struggling with the Corona spectre in the year 2020, many sensational crimes also dominated the headlines. They managed to grab attention along with tea

DOI: 10.4018/978-1-6684-6444-1.ch004

time discussions and social media. The news of arrest of the Kanpur gangster Vikas Dubey who ambushed eight policemen with heavy gunfire from rooftops in his village was the biggest crime story that shocked the people of India. The audacity of the crime prompted a look into how he rose through the ranks of UP mafia. The police records shows that the history-shooter Vikas Dubey entered the crime world with snatching and robberies but later on involved himself in murder cases.

Another news that raised alarm in the society was the murder of a 21-year-old woman, identified as Nikita Tomar was shot dead outside her college in Haryana's Faridabad district by a man who first tried to abduct her. When she resisted, one of the accused pulled out a revolver and fired at her. The number of urban murders reported are really disturbing and thus the challenge lies in busting crimes and ensure conviction for murderers.

In 2016, it was the Nirbhaya gangrape case (Nirbhaya, 2016), in 2018 it was the Kathua case (Kathua gangrape-murder case, 2019), in 2019 the rape and murder of a Hyderabad vet and in 2020 it was the Hathras gangrape and murder case. These rape and murder cases shake the country to its core, provoke public anger and force us to reason for the uptick in murders in India.

Likewise, Dark Web Crime cannot be overlooked as India ranks second amongst the countries most affected by cyber attacks during 2016-2018 and fourth out of the top 10 targeted countries in the world (Nazah et al., 2020). Some of the biggest cyberattacks worth mentioning include the 2018-Cosmos Bank Cyber Attack in Pune, 2018-UIDAI Aadhaar data breach and 2019 Hacker attack on Indian HealthCare Websites (Cyber Threat Report, 2019). Factually, Deep Web is another layer of the WWW which cannot be easily accessed online (Bergman, M. 2001,Gupta & Bhatia, 2017) and can be characterized by the Unknown—unknown depth, breadth, users and content. The Dark Web is a furthest corner of this Deep Web having content that has been intentionally concealed and the crime on the Dark Web deals with exploiting this content for illegal practice (Finklea, K. 2017).

Every year large volume of crime and prison related data is generated by the National Crime Records Bureau (NCRB) in association with Government of India (GoI) but analysing this data for future decision making remains a major challenge for them. Steep rise has been witnessed in the crime rate in India during the past decade. As per the reports by NCRB, the largest increase of approximately 63% was seen in cognizable crimes (Personal & Archive, 2009). Thus, controlling crime rate has become the topmost priority of the law enforcement agencies and government police department in recent years (Hendricks et al., 2000). But for effective decision making and policy generation, gaining insights into the factors responsible for the crime, is crucial.

Machine learning models have achieved wide success in classifying and categorizing different crime types. But with the steady increase in the number, type and volume of crime data, deep learning methods overtook the traditional ML models. Deep learning models like Multi-Layer Perceptron (MLP), Long-Short Term Memory (LSTM) networks have been successfully employed for modelling the sequential nature of the crime data.(*No Title*, n.d.) Time-series forecasting models deal with analysis of a data series gathered over time (Douglas, L. J., Montgomery, C., and Kulahci, 2015). ARMA and ARIMA models have attained wide success for forecasting crime incidents (Yadav & Kumari Sheoran, 2018; Yuki et al., 2019) and locations based on latitudinal and longitudinal information available in crime data released by many countries (Stalidis et al., 2021). However, no such information is available for Indian Crime data.

In this paper, time-series models ARIMA and LSTM have been used to forecast the future number of cognizable crimes in India. Different types of crime from thefts and robberies to cyberattacks are included within these cognizable crimes as reported in India. The models are based on the assumption that the previous pattern of figures of cognizable crimes can be considered for extracting the future behaviour as well.

The rest of the paper is organized as follows: firstly, a review of literature for crime prediction has been presented in section 2, then the methodology of time series models, with an introduction to ARIMA and LSTM are presented in section 3. In section 4, the proposed approach to crime forecasting has been presented and then in section 5, experiments are carried out to forecast the number of cognizable crimes in. Finally, the conclusion is given in section 6.

LITERATURE

Cognizable crimes are those in which the police has direct responsibility to take immediate action on receipt of a complaint, visit the crime scene, investigate the facts, apprehend the offender and arraign him in a court of jurisdiction. Criminal acts are often divided into Violent Crimes, property crimes, financial crimes, cybercrime etc. Violent crimes are those that result in physical or mental harm to another person. They include crimes like murders or attempt to murders, suicides, kidnapping & abduction, assault, rape, child abuse, domestic abuse etc. Property crimes typically involve interference with the property of another and include theft, burglary, robbery, shoplifting etc. White Collar Crimes comprise of Criminal breach of trust, cheating and counterfeiting, involving deception or fraud, money laundering, tax evasion etc.

Cybercrime is a high-tech form of crime that consists of intrusion into business and personal computers with the goal of financial gain (bank fraud, credit card fraud) but some have goals other than financial gain also like copyright infringement; buying and selling illegal items, say drugs; transmitting and receiving illegal content like child pornography etc. The use of systems that offer better communication and mobility had further widened the scope of criminal activities. The quality of life has certainly improved with the advances in technology. But this has also opened doors to new ways of committing crimes be it physical attacks or cyber-attacks, causing severe personal and financial losses. Cyber-attacks include everything from electronic wracking to denial-of-service attacks and covers crimes like credit card frauds, distribution of pirated software, email-spoofing, child pornography, cyber -terrorism, online drugs sale/purchase, spam mails /messages etc.(Narnolia, n.d.).

Cyber-crimes involve gaining access to the content that has been intentionally concealed which might be due to legitimate reasons or reasons to conceal malicious or otherwise criminal activities. This concealed portion of the Web which is exploited for illegal practices is called the Dark Web. Detecting illegal activities is difficult on the Dark Web as individuals communicate through secure chat, personal messages and mailing applications that anonymizes user's content and activity. As a result, it becomes difficult to identify the attack and its perpetrator(Bilen & Özer, 2021) leaving these crimes hidden behind the Deep Web. The problem is further enhanced in a developing country like India where majority of cyber-crimes go unreported owing to the victim's reluctance for defamation relating their unawareness of digital means(Kumari, n.d.) and unawareness of actually being a victim of these attacks.

(Chun et al., 2019) investigate criminal behaviour based on its history using deep learning techniques. To accurately predict the crime reoccurrence based on criminal history, Graph-based progression analyses was performed. Using pairwise progression, crime trajectory was deigned over time. They have developed a deep neural network to build the prediction model for multilabel classification (level 1,2,3 and no crime) using soft-max classifier and gradient descent approach.

(Sangani et al., 2019)build a systematic approach for crime prediction and analysis to help law agencies for maintaining safety. They have designed a technique based on simple k-means clustering algorithm that gives information on predicting and stopping crime. For visualization, Graph plotting is used on crime type and location. This work provides a platform for law agencies to find information about crime, like how many crimes of a type occurs in any city and identify the areas that are more sensitive to each crime type.

(ToppiReddy et al., 2018) used various visualizing techniques and machine learning algorithms for predicting crime distribution over an area. He purposes a web mapping & visualization-based crime prediction tool using multiple libraries to analyse the pattern of crime.

(Rumi et al., 2018) uses historical features, Geographic features, Demographic features, and dynamic feature to find the correlation among these features and with different crime type events. Using Historical feature, Crime density is calculated for every region based on near-repeat theory. Crime Event Density is then used to find the crime events in past x days at region r. Crime Event Trend is used to find crime patterns in a particular region. Polynomial Regression is used to build the model.

(Kadar,Cristina, IriaJ., Pletikosa, 2016) uses Foursquare data for crime prediction. In this paper, the author selected spatial and dynamic feature based on feature extraction techniques for the investigation and Prediction of crimes in New York City for 5 years. The features were derived on the basis Foursquare check-ins.

(Ramirez-alcocer et al., 2019) et al. used the LSTM deep learning approach to classify incidents of crime through predictive analysis. The predictive model relies on an LSTM neural network that's trained with a short range of attributes of data set, enabling the prediction of the category label in the validation phase. Deep learning techniques have proven their capability of discriminative strength in comparison with other learning methods.

TIME-SERIES MODELLING

If huge amount of data is available, then it is often recommended to analyse the data along the time axis. Any structured data format that consists of a time component and some value associated with each listed instance of time is called a 'Time-Series' (Almuammar & Fasli, 2019; Iqbal et al., 2020). As time acts as a primary axis for recording the data, we can have two types of series: a discrete time series Where the data is recorded for periodic or non-periodic discrete points in time; a continuous time series where the data is recorded continuously along a time axis. The examples of discrete time series might include the crime statistics/ financial records where values of different attributes are recorded at regular intervals of time. However, the real-time data gathered from IOT devices /sensors form an example of continuous time -series data

Also, for any such series, if the mean, variance and covariance remain relatively constant over time, then it is classified as a stationary time-series, the one that does not display any trend (Tariq et al., 2021). Typically in real world, a stationary time-series rarely exists and most of the time-series models assume the series to be stationary. So, pre-processing is needed to convert the non-stationary data into stationary time-series data.

Autocorrelation (ACF) and Partial Auto Correlation (PACF) helps to examine the strength of relation between the values at different lags of the time-series. To observe, the strength between the current observation and some past observations of the time series, autocorrelation needs to be computed and if we need to examine the correlation between two time lags that are separated by some specified number of periods so as to ignore relation with the immediate previous time lag, PACF is often computed. As a next step in order to forecast values during future time stamps of the time-series, description of the two popular time-series forecasting models, ARIMA and LSTM have been presented next.

ARIMA

It is a popular time-series forecasting model which originated from a combination of Auto-Regressive (AR) model and Moving Average (MA) model. Auto-regressive model predicts the future value of a variable based on the linear combination of past values of some selected variables whereas the Moving Average models predicts the future values based on errors in past predictions.

The ARIMA model is described by a three parametric tuple (p,d,q) where p,q respectively represent the order of AR and MA models and d represent the degree of differencing used to convert the series into a stationary time-series data [9][11]. The autocorrelation (ACF) and partial autocorrelation functions (PACF) are computed to get a summary of the statistics of the series at a specific time lag. This helps to obtain the order of AR and MA.

An autoregressive AR(p) model of order p can be written as:

$$y_t = c + \varnothing_1 y_{t-1} + \varnothing_2 y_{t-2} + \ldots\ldots \varnothing_p y_{t-p} + \varepsilon_t \tag{1}$$

And a moving average MA(q) model with q number of lagged forecast errors can be written as:

$$y_t = c + \varepsilon_t - \theta_1 \varepsilon_{t-1} - \theta_2 \varepsilon_{t-2} - \ldots\ldots - \theta_q \varepsilon_{t-q} \tag{2}$$

Where in equation (1) and (2), c is a constant, εt is a white noise, $\phi = (\varnothing_1, \varnothing_2, \varnothing_3, \ldots \varnothing_p)$ is vector of coefficients of AR(p) model, $\theta = (\theta_1, \theta_2, \theta_3, \ldots, \theta_q)$ is a vector of coefficients of MA(q) model with p and q being non-negative integers.

Thus, the combined ARIMA(p,d,q) model using degree of differencing, d can be written as in Equation (3):

$$y_t - 2y_{t-1} - \ldots - y_{t-d} = c + \varnothing_1 y_{t-1} + \varnothing_2 y_{t-2} + \ldots\ldots \varnothing_p y_{t-p} + \varepsilon_t - \theta_1 \varepsilon_{t-1} - \theta_2 \varepsilon_{t-2} - \ldots\ldots - \theta_q \varepsilon_{t-q} \tag{3}$$

At the order p, ACF tails off but PACF cuts off whereas at the order q, ACF cuts off and PACF tails off. So ARIMA models provides results with an upper and lower limit on forecasted values.

LSTM

It belongs to the family of Recurrent Neural Networks used typically for modelling Sequential data [9]. They differ from other feed forward neural networks as it has feedback connections which help in

Figure 1. Structure of a LSTM network model

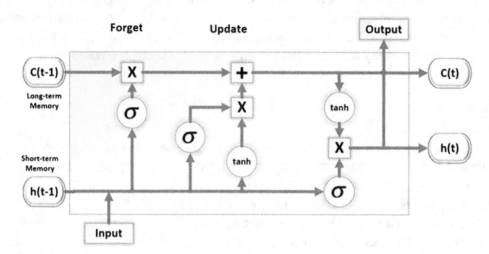

explaining its working on a single data point in the dataset as well as the entire dataset (Almuammar & Fasli, 2019; Tariq et al., 2021). As can be seen from the structure of the LSTM network in Figure 1, it consists of a hidden state and a memory cell with three gates that named as forget, input or write gate and output or read gate. The cell helps in memorizing values during each time-interval and the gates help in flow of input and output. The forget gate controls the traversal of information that seems unnecessary for training the network. Input Gate makes sure that new information is passed to the cell and the output gate ensures that some output reaches the next hidden state. They are good at handling the problem of vanishing gradient that arises during training process using back-propagation as in MLPs.

The number of neurons and the hidden layers in the work are selected heuristically for performance comparison as per the standard configuration in the deep learning library Pytorch or tensor flow available in Python.

OVERVIEW OF THE PROPOSED APPROACH

This section discusses the step by step approach followed to build a successful model for crime prediction using the different time-series models as illustrated in figure 2.

In the first phase of Data Acquisition, Crime data from different web sources like zipnet delhi police, ncrb, data.gov.in, newsfeed, rss feeds is collected for the years 1952-2020. The data acquired from these disparate and unstructured sources is cleaned against missing, Null and erroneous values and converted into a structured form (.csv) suitable for processing. The cleaned data is then fused and integrated to gather meaningful insights of the data. The independent and dependent variables are identified. Also, the different scales of the values of these variables might increase the complexity of the model being generated and thus the model can learn large values for weights. But such a neural network model iterates many times before converging or may even fail to converge. Such an unstable model yields poor performance leading to large generalization error. Thus, the data is normalized to have the values of all the variables in the range 0 to 1(mean=0, variance =1). Normalization also facilitates comparison amongst different prediction models.

Figure 2. Proposed approach to forecast the number of cognizable crimes in India

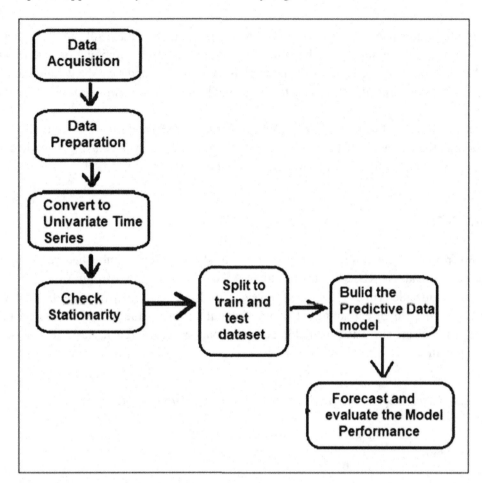

Scikit-learn preprocessing object, MinMaxScaler has been used in this work for the said purpose and the transformation is given by

$$X_{std}^i = \frac{X^i - X_{min}}{X_{max} - X_{min}} \qquad (4)$$

Where X_{min}, X_{max} are the minimum and maximum range values of the ith attribute/column.

For univariate analysis, the data values need to be sequential having utmost one data point. So for each year in the duration 1952-2020, the number of cognizable crimes is taken while ignoring the crimes under Social and Local Laws(SLL) as the data was not reported for certain years .

To check the stationarity, the data distribution is plotted for the years 1952-2020 and Augmented Dickey Fuller's test is performed. The mean and variance need to be noticed to conclude if the series is stationary or not. If the series is not stationary, them it is converted into a stationary series before applying the Time-series network model. Differencing is applied to the time-series until it becomes stationary. The following equation is used iteratively to achieve stationarity.

Z(t)=Z(t)-Z(t-1)   (5)

Before training the ARIMA or LSTM models for prediction, the data is split into training and test sets where two-third of the dataset has been used for training and the remaining one-third is used for testing and evaluation purpose. Training the network model involves updating the weights and identifying the hyperparameter 'learning rate' so as to reduce the loss each time. An initial rate of learning was set to 0.001.

The error was measured using Root Mean Square Error (RMSE) and Mean Absolute Error (MAE). RMSE measures the deviation of the predicted values from the true values using Euclidean distance whereas MAE is defined as the average over all prediction errors.

EXPERIMENTS

Crime record from different volumes of Crime in India (statistics report published yearly by National Crime Records Bureau, NCRB, Ministry of Home Affairs, Government of India) is integrated to get the number of cognizable crimes recorded each year from 1952-2020. Any missing data values for the duration was also made up by extracting data from other publicly available authorized sources like zipnet delhi police, data.gov.in. The data is stored in comma separated values (crimes.csv) format suitable for analysis using python

Figure 3a. Sample snapshot of .csv file from python showing Crime record statistics

Date	cogniable crime Under IPC	SLL	Total Number ofcogniable crime	Murder	Kidnapping	Thefts
1952-01-01	612010	NaN	NaN	10343	5157	251816.0
1953-01-01	601964	NaN	NaN	9802	5261	256567.0
1954-01-01	556912	NaN	NaN	9765	5514	223866.0
1955-01-01	535236	NaN	NaN	9700	5529	212028.0
1956-01-01	585217	NaN	NaN	10025	5905	236214.0

Figure3 (a) shows the first five rows of crime.csv that was considered for predicting the number of cognizable crimes under IPC . A plot of the number of cognizable crime vs year has been shown in the graph in Figure 3(b). The graph shows a linear rise in the numebr of crimes every year which can be attributed to the rise in Indian population since 1952. As a next step, the trend, seasonal components of the data series were analyzed to gain insights into data from 1952-2020 as shown in Figure 4.

Initially, the data is decomposed into four different components: Observed, Trend, Seasonal, Residual (anything else in the time-series) to improve understanding of the crime data with time-series nature and improve the accuracy of forecasting. This has been done using the seasonal_decompose function within the Python 'statsmodels' As can be observed from the four graphs shown in Figure 4(a), the trend patterns of the crime dataset has a fixed linear-parametric form and an overall increasing trend with no much effect of seasons.

Figure 3b. A Graph generated using matplotlib python library to show the number of cognizable crimes for each year from 1952 to 2020.

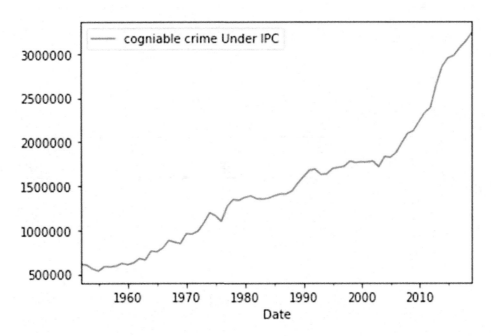

Figure 4a. Graphs reflecting Trend analysis of the Indian crime data

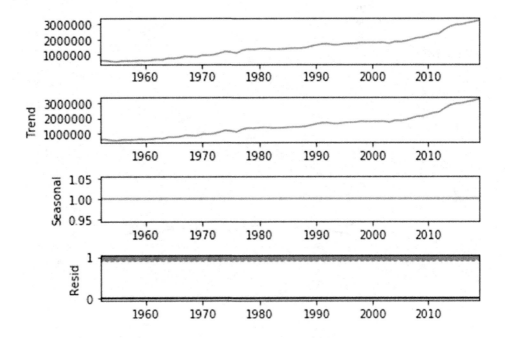

Figure 4b. Graph showing autocorelation with time lags.

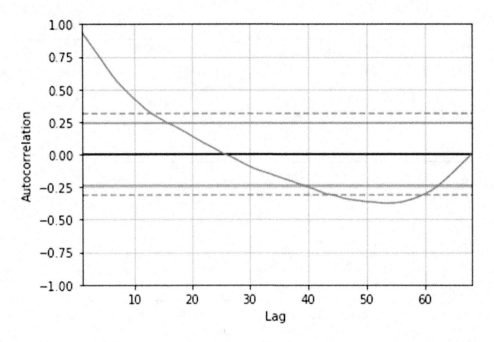

Figure 5a. Rolling mean Statistics of the crime.csv file.

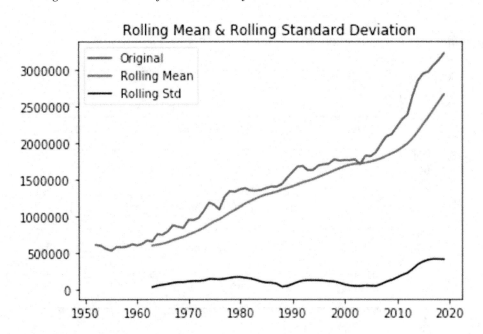

Figure 5b. python code used to generate the statistics in (a).

```
rolling_mean = df2.rolling(window = 12).mean()
rolling_std = df2.rolling(window = 12).std()
plt.plot(df2, color = 'blue', label = 'Original')
plt.plot(rolling_mean, color = 'red', label = 'Rolling Mean')
plt.plot(rolling_std, color = 'black', label = 'Rolling Std')
plt.legend(loc = 'best')
plt.title('Rolling Mean & Rolling Standard Deviation')
plt.show()
```

Table 1. Augmented Dickey Fuller's test statistics

ADF Statistic: 3.23231401293 79335		p-value: 1.0	
Confidence level	99%	95%	90%
Critical Values	-3.530398990560757	-2.9050874099328317	-2.5900010121107266

The two common method for checking the stationarity are through Visualization and the Augmented Dickey Fuller test (DF test). To check for stationarity, the statistical properties of the dataset like mean, variance and autocorrelation are extracted and checked for changes with time as shown in Figure 4(b).

Also, the rolling mean and variance are plotted to see if there is a substantial change in standard deviation over time as in Figure 5(a). Python code for the fetching the same has been shown in Figure 5(b). If the values don't seem to change over time, then the dataset can be considered stationary.

Rolling mean is clearly not stationary. Though the standard deviation seems to be constant but the scale of y-axis is so large that it is difficult to conclude that the data is stationary by viewing the above graph. So, the Dickey fuller test is now applied to determine if the data is stationary with different levels of confidence. The Dickey-Fuller test compares the critical values and performs a hypothetical testing. The critical values are as obtained in Table 1.

Crime data for any country is often not stationary and so is the case with Indian Crime dataset. As a next step, we need to make the data stationary through mathematical transformations so that time series forecasting models can be fit. By applying just first order differencing, stationarity was achieved.

ARIMA and LSTM models were used to predict the number of cognizable crimes. The achieved results of ARIMA (5,1,0) model have been summarized in Figure 6(a) whereas the predicted values and expected values of the data are shown in Figure 6(b). A RMSE of 76156.527 was reported for test data using the specified ARIMA model.

LSTM model with specifications listed in Table 2 has been used to model the trend and distribution pattern for cognizable crimes in the country. On the temporal dimensions, the data was available from 1952 to 2019. Adaptive Moment Estimation (Adam) optimization is used in the LSTM configuration to calculate the adaptive learning rate of the weights rather than using a single learning rate for all the weights as in gradient descent.

Table 3 shows the values of the evaluation metric used for checking the accuracy of the LSTM model. The graph in Figure 8 presents the predicted and the actual values of the number of cognizable crimes

Figure 6a. Model summary of ARIMA(5,1,0)

```
print(model_fit.summary())

                       ARIMA Model Results
========================================================================
Dep. Variable:    D.cogniable crime Under IPC   No. Observations:           67
Model:                       ARIMA(5, 1, 0)     Log Likelihood         -827.405
Method:                               css-mle   S.D. of innovations    55675.078
Date:                     Mon, 17 May 2021      AIC                     1668.809
Time:                             22:38:37      BIC                     1684.242
Sample:                         01-01-1953      HQIC                    1674.916
                              - 01-01-2019
========================================================================
                                    coef     std err       z      P>|z|     [0.025    0.975]
------------------------------------------------------------------------
const                            3.901e+04   1.39e+04    2.805    0.005    1.18e+04   6.63e+04
ar.L1.D.cogniable crime Under IPC   0.2365    0.122    1.934    0.053    -0.003    0.476
ar.L2.D.cogniable crime Under IPC  -0.0523    0.125   -0.419    0.676    -0.297    0.192
ar.L3.D.cogniable crime Under IPC   0.2873    0.120    2.396    0.017     0.052    0.522
ar.L4.D.cogniable crime Under IPC   0.0920    0.125    0.734    0.463    -0.154    0.338
ar.L5.D.cogniable crime Under IPC  -0.0353    0.123   -0.287    0.774    -0.276    0.205
                                   Roots
========================================================================
              Real       Imaginary       Modulus      Frequency
------------------------------------------------------------------------
AR.1        1.3095       -0.0000j        1.3095        -0.0000
AR.2       -0.3474       -1.3919j        1.4346        -0.2889
AR.3       -0.3474       +1.3919j        1.4346         0.2889
AR.4       -2.3961       -0.0000j        2.3961        -0.5000
AR.5        4.3907       -0.0000j        4.3907        -0.0000
------------------------------------------------------------------------
```

(a)

Figure 6b. Predicted versus expected values using ARIMA(5,1,0)

```
            obs = test[t]
            history.append(obs)
            print('predicted=%f, expected=%f' % (yhat, obs))

    predicted=1715351.106167, expected=1709576.000000
    predicted=1724098.228192, expected=1719820.000000
    predicted=1758141.802176, expected=1779111.000000
    predicted=1808877.867384, expected=1764629.000000
    predicted=1771135.190822, expected=1771084.000000
    predicted=1817791.582422, expected=1769308.000000
    predicted=1787861.632046, expected=1780330.000000
    predicted=1810767.722972, expected=1716120.000000
    predicted=1731911.688490, expected=1832015.000000
    predicted=1883107.899758, expected=1822602.000000
    predicted=1815255.236183, expected=1878293.000000
    predicted=1913344.302920, expected=1989673.000000
    predicted=2007587.270128, expected=2093379.000000
    predicted=2087331.761002, expected=2121345.000000
    predicted=2151979.675501, expected=2224831.000000
    predicted=2265168.993695, expected=2325575.000000
    predicted=2340695.872937, expected=2387188.000000
    predicted=2418722.249624, expected=2647722.000000
    predicted=2739065.049373, expected=2851563.000000
    predicted=2936983.327295, expected=2949400.000000
    predicted=3090348.326336, expected=2975711.000000
    predicted=3076260.334614, expected=3062579.000000
    predicted=3125295.033525, expected=3132954.000000
    predicted=3165484.829717, expected=3225701.000000
```

(b)

Figure 7a. plot of predicted values vs. actual values (blue indicates the predicted values whereas actual values are indicated in orange) for ARIMA (5,1,0) over different time durations. The graph in (a) was generated for the purpose of validation and

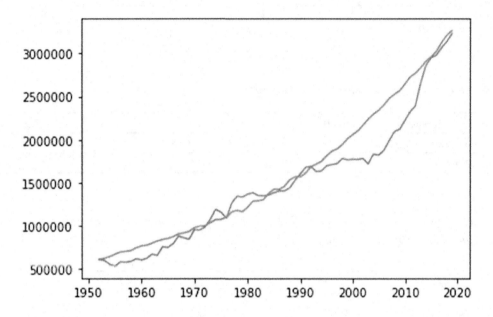

Figure 7b. was generated for predicting crimes over the upcoming years.

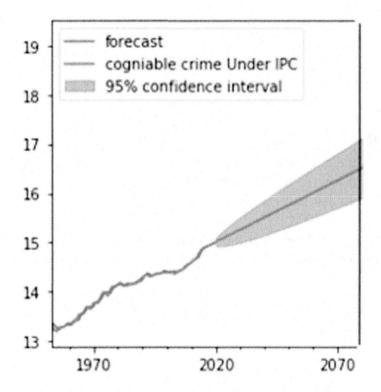

Table 2. Configuration of LSTM model used for predicting the number of cognizable crimes across India

Neural Network	Neurons in Hidden layer	Learning Rate	Activation	Optimizer	No. of Epochs
Long-Short Term Memory model (LSTM)	100	.001	ReLu	Adam	150

Table 3. Evaluation metric of resulting LSTM model.

Evaluation Metric (LSTM)	Values
Root Mean Square Error	6.858700
Mean Absolute Error	10.013511

Figure 8. Actual vs predicted values for LSTM model. Red indicates predicted values, blue indicates expected values of the cognizable crimes for the year 2000 to 2020

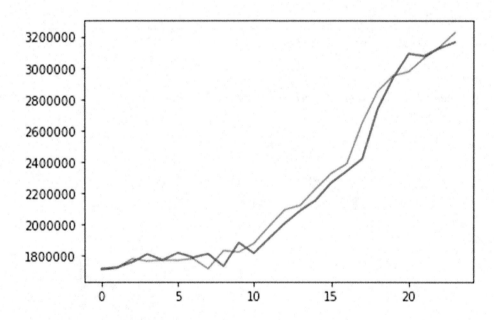

using LSTM model. Here, red represents the predicted values and the blue line represents the actual values Using the said configuration of the LSTM model, a RMSE of 6.858700 was observed.

CONCLUSION

In this work, the popular time-series models were demonstrated to predict the number of cognizable crimes in India. And LSTM model gave satisfactory results during the experiments conducted in this study. It exhibits low error rates showing capability of better generalization. In future, microscopic features from social media and local community will be taken into consideration during data-pre processing for improving prediction. And comprehensive evaluation with other popular models of predictive modeling will be done.

REFERENCES

Almuammar, M., & Fasli, M. (2019). Deep Learning for Non-stationary Multivariate Time Series Forecasting. *2019 IEEE International Conference on Big Data (Big Data)*, 2097–2106. 10.1109/Big-Data47090.2019.9006192

Bilen, A., & Özer, A. B. (2021). Cyber-attack method and perpetrator prediction using machine learning algorithms. *PeerJ. Computer Science*, 7, e475. doi:10.7717/peerj-cs.475 PMID:33954249

Chun, S. A., Avinash Paturu, V., Yuan, S., Pathak, R., Atluri, V., & Adam, R., N. (2019). Crime Prediction Model using Deep Neural Networks. *Proceedings of the 20th Annual International Conference on Digital Government Research*, 512–514. 10.1145/3325112.3328221

DouglasL. J.MontgomeryC.KulahciM. (2015). https://www.wiley.com/en-us/Introduction+to+Time+Series+Analysis+and+Forecasting%2C+2nd+Edition-p-9781118745113

Gupta, S., & Bhatia, K. K. (2017). Optimal query generation for hidden web extraction through response analysis. *The Dark Web: Breakthroughs in Research and Practice*, *2001*, 65–83. doi:10.4018/978-1-5225-3163-0.ch005

Hendricks, C., Hendricks, J. E., & Kauffman, S. (2000). *Literacy, Criminal Activity, and Recidivism.* https://www.americanreadingforum.org/yearbook/yearbooks/01_yearbook/pdf/12_hendricks.pdf

Iqbal, N., Technology, C., & Lanka, S. (2020). *COVID-19 Outbreak Forecast Model using FbProphet.* Academic Press.

Kadar, C., Iria, J., & Pletikosa, I. (2016). KDD - Urban Computing WS '16. doi:10.1145/1235

KumariS. (n.d.). https://timesofindia.indiatimes.com/readersblog/legal-writing/cyber-crimes-in-india-and-its-legal-remedies-35244/

NarnoliaN. (n.d.). https://www.legalserviceindia.com/legal/article-4998-cyber-crime-in-india-an-overview.html

Nazah, S., Huda, S., Abawajy, J., & Hassan, M. M. (2020). Evolution of Dark Web Threat Analysis and Detection: A Systematic Approach. *IEEE Access: Practical Innovations, Open Solutions*, 8, 171796–171819. doi:10.1109/ACCESS.2020.3024198

No Title. (n.d.). http://www.deeplearningbook.org

Personal, M., & Archive, R. (2009). *Munich Personal RePEc Archive Determinants of crime rates : Crime Deterrence and Growth in.* Academic Press.

Ramirez-alcocer, U. M., Tello-leal, E., & Mata-torres, J. A. (2019). *Predicting Incidents of Crime through LSTM Neural Networks in Smart City Domain.* Academic Press.

Rumi, S. K., Deng, K., & Salim, F. D. (2018). Crime event prediction with dynamic features. *EPJ Data Science*, *7*(1), 43. doi:10.1140/epjds13688-018-0171-7

Sangani, A., Sampat, C., & Pinjarkar, V. (2019). Crime Prediction and Analysis. SSRN *Electronic Journal.* doi:10.2139/ssrn.3367712

Shipping, F. W. (2017). The dark web: Breakthroughs in research and practice. *The Dark Web: Breakthroughs in Research and Practice*. doi:10.4018/978-1-5225-3163-0

Stalidis, P., Semertzidis, T., & Daras, P. (2021). Examining Deep Learning Architectures for Crime Classification and Prediction. *Forecasting*, *3*(4), 741–762. doi:10.3390/forecast3040046

Tariq, H., Hanif, M. K., Sarwar, M. U., Bari, S., Sarfraz, M. S., & Oskouei, R. J. (2021). Employing Deep Learning and Time Series Analysis to Tackle the Accuracy and Robustness of the Forecasting Problem. *Security and Communication Networks*, *2021*, 1–10. doi:10.1155/2021/5587511

ToppiReddy, H. K. R., Saini, B., & Mahajan, G. (2018). Crime Prediction & Monitoring Framework Based on Spatial Analysis. *Procedia Computer Science*, *132*, 696–705. doi:10.1016/j.procs.2018.05.075

Yadav, R., & Kumari Sheoran, S. (2018). Crime Prediction Using Auto Regression Techniques for Time Series Data. *2018 3rd International Conference and Workshops on Recent Advances and Innovations in Engineering (ICRAIE)*, 1–5. 10.1109/ICRAIE.2018.8710407

Yuki, J. Q., Sakib, M. M. Q., Zamal, Z., Habibullah, K. M., & Das, A. K. (2019). Predicting Crime Using Time and Location Data. *Proceedings of the 2019 7th International Conference on Computer and Communications Management*, 124–128. 16/1210.1145/3348445.3348483

Chapter 5
Variational Autoencoder for IoT Botnet Detection

Om Kumar C. U.

https://orcid.org/0000-0003-2866-0281

Vellore Institute of Technology (VIT) Chennai, India

Dharmala Pranavi

SRM Easwari Engineering College, India

B. R. Aishwarayaa Laxmi

SRM Easwari Engineering College, India

Devasena R.

SRM Easwari Engineering College, India

ABSTRACT

IoT devices are naturally vulnerable to security issues such as botnet attacks that lead to compromised data. Due to the proliferation of network traffic, the existing system demonstrated a mean FPR of 0.007 ± 0.01, but it needs to be updated to be on par with swiftly growing bots. In the proposed system, the authors have deployed various autoencoders for the detection of IoT botnets. This proposed system helps to differentiate malicious attacks from benign ones. To validate the proposed method, they have used NbaIoT dataset infected with the two most widely known IoT-based botnets: Mirai and Gafgyt. The autoencoders are trained using the optimization dataset generated by various smart devices, and when tested, they achieved formidable accuracy for various autoencoders: 96.158% for sparse autoencoder, 86.775% for deep Autoencoder, 96.157% for variational autoencoder, 96.156% for under complete autoencoder, and 79.789% for denoising autoencoder. Compared to many other state-of-the-art botnet detection methods, variational autoencoder has achieved better accuracy with lower false predictions.

INTRODUCTION

The advancements in technology has led to an increase in cyber-crime. Dark web(Paffenroth et.al,

DOI: 10.4018/978-1-6684-6444-1.ch005

2019), is one of the common places where cyber-crime transpires as it provides complete anonymity of network traffic. Dark web provides a place for users to perform any kind of activity ranging from legal ones like journalism to illegal criminal schemes like drugs, stolen identities and weapons trading. It acts as a breeding ground for cyber threats with many tools and techniques available for compromising companies and individuals using DDoS or other attacks. Tor anonymity network aided in increasing the Mevade Botnet users to up to 5 million per day (Mirea et.al, 2019). Apart from this, Tor network also acts as a source of ransomware applications.

Classic methods like traffic analysis and web-crawling were initially used to identify malicious traffic and websites. Recent crime pattern detection using Machine learning involves signature-based analysis. In (Paffenroth et.al, 2019), for pattern detection or pattern recognition of DDoS attacks they have mentioned two methods. Method 1 is a variation of the classic SVM known as robust Support Vector Machine(SVM) which is used to classify anomalies i.e, Method 2 is about detecting anomalies using the Random Forest approach where an abnormality detector was established to boost a subsequent threat classifier. Other deep learning methods like Robust PCA and RDAs can be utilized for DDoS anomaly detection.

The Internet of Things (IoT) devices are predicted to reach upto 75 milliard by 2030 (Louis Columbus, 2016). The network administrators are faced with novel security issues due to the augmented increase in use of IoT devices. Majority of the IoT appliances are naturally exposed to security threats like botnet attacks. A botnet framework generally consists of malignant software replicated onto miscellaneous devices connected to a network. Each hijacked device is extensively administered from the command and control server to perform macroscale automated attacks. These IoT devices commonly face security issues because of security flaws such as installation of vulnerable IoT devices directly tethered to the web, weak passwords, manufacturer and user's lack of perceptibility about IoT functionality and security and especially due to unavailability of secure firmware updates for the existing IoT devices.

From the year 2016 to 2017, a six-hundred percent surge in the IoT attacks was observed (Symantec, 2018). In the year 2016, prominently known botnet "Mirai" converted chiliads of IoT appliances into zombie devices. The Reaper botnet was predominantly exploiting hidden susceptibilities to enslave devices in 2017 (Andy Greenberg, 2017). Between January to May 2018, HideNSeek has infected upto 90,000 unique devices (CatalinCimpanu, 2018). As per a report from Nozomi Networks, there was a proliferate rise in attacks and threats engineered by IoT botnets in the first half of 2020 owing to the current ongoing world-wide pandemic (Nozomi, 2020). Due to this ongoing pandemic, the workers are forced to stay at home, and the substantial number of hacktivists who now have ingress to vulnerable IoT devices have revolutionized increasingly more sophisticated tools for deploying botnet attacks (Om Kumar C.U, 2019) (Rawat, 2021). Expeditious identification of these IoT botnet attacks promotes network security as it alerts and disconnects the malicious botnets from the network, thereby terminating the botnets from disseminating further and prohibiting the further spread of attacks(Ahmed et.al, 2020) (Bhardwaj et.al, 2020) (Jagadeesan et.al, 2021) (Ko et.al, 2020) (Kunang et.al, 2021) (Moodi et.al, 2021) (Sadaf et.al, 2020).

This rapid growth of the IoT devices is directly proportional to botnet attacks that occur to these smart devices(Tsogbaatar et.al, 2021) (Yang et.al, 2020). Timely detection of botnets is necessary to enhance network security. Therefore, the objective of this paper is to increase the network security and to develop an efficient method to detect botnet attacks.

To overcome this problem, we propose Autoencoder's to detect the malicious activities in the network traffic. Autoencoder's are mainly applied for attribute extraction and dimensionality mitigation. We have employed the N-BaIoT dataset (Y.Meidan et.al, 2019), which contains data that has been collected from different smart devices infected by two popular bots such as Mirai and Gafgyt. The Autoencoder's are trained using N-BaIoT dataset and test data samples are given to the Autoencoder to predict the malicious ones from the benign onesas shown in Figure 1. So, to mitigate the threats caused by the botnets, our Autoencoder detects botnet attacks and differentiates anomalous(malicious) ones from the legitimate(benign) ones.

The contributions of this paper is as follows:

- By applying five different Autoencoder's, we've compared the overall performance of these systems on the N-BaIoT dataset, and found out that Sparse Autoencoder and VariationalAutoencoder demonstrate relatively higher accuracies of 96.158% and 96.157%.
- Our proposed system, VariationalAutoencoder exhibits a mean FPR of 0.00241. This FPR is much lower in comparison with the results of (Y.Meidan et.al, 2019), whose deep Autoencoder showed a mean FPR of 0.007±0.01. Even though our Sparse has better accuracy, Variational outperformed Sparse Autoencoder (0.00248) in terms of FPR.

Figure 1. Overall system design

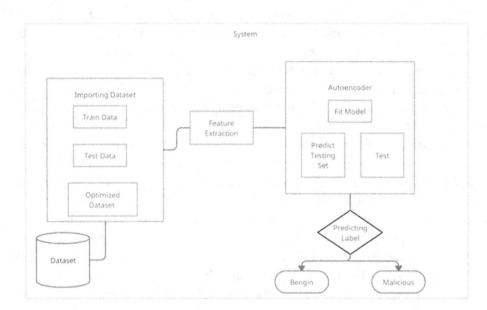

RELATED WORK

Autoencoder's for IoT Botnet detection have already been proposed in some works. While probabilistic methods were originally developed to identify bots, machine learning algorithms were used in later stages to detect bots.

In (Y.Meidan et.al, 2019) a network-based technique is formulated for detection of anomalies. It extricates snapshots of the network behavior and utilizes deep AE to identify malignant traffic emerging from infected IoT appliances. To analyse the system, they have tainted 9 widely used IoT appliances with the two popular botnets, Mirai and Gafgyt, and collected the dataset from these infected smart IoT devices (N-BaIoT Dataset). The above method raised only a few false alarms. It exhibited a stable and reduced mean False Positive Rate of 0.007 ± 0.01, in comparison to the SVM (0.026 ± 0.029). This model needed 174-212 ms to identify the botnet attacks which is lower compared to state-of-the art methods.

Sparse Autoencoder with SVM is used in (Al-Qatf et.al, 2018) the experimental results exhibit that their proposed system bespeaks improved training and evaluation time and ameliorate accuracy. Their model has exhibited improved efficiency in the 2-category and the 5-category classification. It requires improvised techniques for feature depiction and mitigation in dimensionality. Furthermore, the time taken by the proposed system for training and evaluation can be minimized by implementing the model in parallel computers or Graphics Processing Unit acceleration.

(Asadi et al., 2020)proposed a concoction of PSO algorithm and BD-PSO-V, that includes an SVM, DNN algorithm, and DT C4.5. It showed a progress of 0.42% and 0.17% in average accuracy for the Bot-IoT and ISOT dataset respectively. This model suffered from a drop in accuracy rate upon estimating the efficacy of 6 prominent adversarial attacks on the above mentioned datasets.

In (Cil et.al, 2021) they have proposed a DNN model that identifies Distributed Denial of Service attacks on packet fragments recorded from network traffic. The experiments were carried out using the CICDDoS2019 dataset consisting of DDoS attacks generated in 2019. A classification model that extracts features effectively is considered for improved accuracy. They have achieved an accuracy rate of 94.57% for the DDoS attacks which is comparatively lesser than the state of art methods.

In (Dahal et.al, 2019) they have proposed a system for domain detection that makes use of deep learning such as Dynamically Generation Algorithm. They have invented a new concept called Mean Activation Encoder Units (MAEU) which makes their model adaptable to fresh classes of Dynamically Generation Algorithm without training it anew. A 16-bit encryption of the input features is generated by applying Autoencoder's and classification is done using a combination of SVM and NN.The Amazon collated dataset, Alexa-1M was used for the benign domain and py script contributed by Endgame was used for the malignant domains. The accuracy of their model is 88% which is not revolutionary for detection of DGA in the field of DL.

In (Erhanet.al, 2020) they have proposed a stratagem for DDoS detection framework using the MP algorithm for determining resource exhaustive Distributed Denial-of-Service attacks. The CAIDA dataset was used for evaluation and the model comparison is done with the BOUN dataset. A distinctive feature representation vector that is generated from a meld of multiple 1-D traffic characteristics had been introduced by them. With the BOUN dataset, their proposed method performs efficiently illustrating an FPR lesser than 0.7%.

In (J. Kim et.al,2020) they have proposed the RVAE that is used for identifying botnets through subsequential features of network traffic. In this paper, they have used the CTU-13 dataset. They have selected a testing dataset that contains botnets varying from the training set. The disadvantage of this method is that random forest shows better performance compared to recurrent variational AE. The particular reason for the circumstance is that the data used to train and test the VAE share identical attributes, whereas for the same datasets the RF is constructive in discovering preponderant features. To improve the performance, routines to handle instances where botnets have minuscule inaccuracies in reconstruction need to be developed.

In (M. R. Shahid et.al, 2019), they have proposed a group of sparse AEs that are used to detect illegitimate transmission of information in IoT networks. Here an experimental smart home is set up that consists of 4 IoT appliances: a TP-Link smart bulb, a D-Link motion sensor, TP-Link smart plug, and a Nest security camera. A network is constructed to detect malicious communications and drop them without interrupting the service of the device. Bidirectional TCP flows are drawn out to characterize the network. Its behaviour is described using the first N network packet proportions transmitted and received, together with data corresponding to the inter-arrival times amidst packets. Based on the N value, the accuracy in detecting the botnets ranges from 86.9% to 91.2%, and FPR ranging from 0.1% to 0.5%.

In (N. Shone et.al, 2018), AE with non-symmetrical hidden layers (NDAE) is stacked and combined with Random Forest to form a classification system. This model was used for detecting network intrusion systems using the NSL-KDD and KDD Cup '99 dataset. The drawback is that the stacked Non-symmetric deep auto-encoder model needs an enormous quantity of data to train. Since the proportion of training data at hand is inadequate, the obtained outcome is inconsistent.

In (Q. P. Nguyen et.al, 2019), they have utilized a system called GEE to detect network anomaly by analysingNetFlow records. GEE is made up of 2 parts: a VAE for anomaly detection and gradient-based fingerprints for describing abnormalities. The UGR16 dataset consisting of NetFlow traces recorded from a Tier 3 ISP was used. The GEE model is efficacious in identifying various attacks of the UGR16 dataset. This approach, however, utilizes benign data obtained by eliminating abnormalities from the original data to train the VAE, which is strenuous to do in real-time.

In (Rahman et.al, 2021), the proposed system involves the use of unsupervised Autoencoder for deep feature abstraction and utilizes a heterogeneous combination of strategies such as NB, SVM, and DT for selecting important features. This system accomplishes upto 99.95% accuracy in detecting anomalies on the Aegean Wi-Fi Intrusion Dataset but it lacks data relevant to the latest IoT malwares like Mirai and Bashlite.

In (Rodríguez-Ruiz et.al, 2020), one-class classification is deployed to accelerate identification of bots on Twitter. This system is capable of new bot account identification. This model exhibited performance issues as classifiers constructed for identification of a particular type of bot had a better performance than one-class classifiers.

In (S. Zavrak et.al, 2020) an AE and VAE employed together with One-Class SVM(OCSVM) is used for detecting an anomaly in the network intrusion system. The NSL-KDD dataset and KDD Cup '99 dataset are used here. VAE Detection rates are much better than AE and OCSVM but to further increase the detection rates these techniques need to be reinforced by supervised learning mechanisms owing to their excessive false alarms rates.

In (W. Wang et.al 2020) they have proposed a system that consists of a Stacked CAE for extraction of prominent attributes and Support Vector Machine (SVM) for detection of malicious attacks in the cloud environment. This model is evaluated using the KDD Cup 99 dataset and NSL-KDD dataset. It procures propitious performance for categorization of six different metrics but the SVM cannot successfully detect some novel attacks prevailing in the dataset used for testing. It can be further enhanced by improving the classifier.

BOTNET DETECTION THROUGH VAE

To detect IoT Botnets, we propose Autoencoder's (AE). An AE is a neural architecture in which a bottleneck is imposed in the network that in turn forces a compressed representation of the original input. A bottleneck restricts the amount of data that will flow through the network, coercing an assimilated compression of the input.

An Autoencoder consists of 3 layers which are: the input layer, hidden layer and output layer. The input and hidden layers form the encoder part. The data fed into the encoder is constricted into a latent-space representation. The decoder consists of a hidden layer or a coded layer and an output layer. The objective of the decoder is to rebuild the input. The original input is given to the encoder and the output obtained from the encoder is the input of the decoder which in turn reconstructs the compressed representation of the original input.

In this paper, we have used a variety of Autoencoder's such as DenoisingAutoencoder, Sparse Autoencoder, Deep Autoencoder, UndercompleteAutoencoder, VariationalAutoencoder.

VariationalAutoencoder

Among the proposed five Autoencoders, we consider VariationalAutoencoder to be best fit for IoT Botnet Detection because they can produce coding or feature representation that is more robust to noise. A variationalautoencoder is a deep generative technique, which incorporates deep learning and variational inference.

One drawback with the vanilla Autoencoder's is that they encode each input sample separately. This means that the samples belonging to the same class might learn very different latent features. Due to this issue, our network might suffer in reconstructing related unseen data samples.

To overcome these issues, we use VAE as it ensures that the points in close neighborhood in the latent space, are representing very similar data samples. Thus it is a substantial method for assimilating representations of high dimensional data which is effective as the datasets for each IoT device consists of 115 features subsequently making our model's prediction more challenging while detecting botnets.

Figure 2 displays a variationalAutoencoder with 64 intermediate nodes and 2 hidden nodes. Initially, the encoder splits the input into two latent space parameters: a vector of Zμ and another vector of Zlogσ. In addition, homogenous points z are sampled on a random basis, originating at the latent space that is presumed to generate the data, using the sum of Zμ and the product of epsilon ε with an exponent of Zlogσ where ε is a random normal tensor. Ultimately, the decoder maps these points once again to the original input.

Algorithm

Step 1: Read datasets pertaining to the IoT device and concatenate them into a single dataset. Split this into X_train, X_opt and X_test.

Step 2: Using functional API, create the VAE model by initializing 115 nodes for the input and output layers.

Step 3: Set the intermediate nodes as 64 and hidden nodes as 2.

Step 4: Set the activation of hidden layers to 'relu' and the activation of the output layer as 'sigmoid'.

Step 5: Train the model using X_train dataset by applying 'Adam' optimizer. For every record in X_train dataset:

Step 5a: The input features are passed into the dense layer.

Step 5b: These features are converted into two vectors - Zμ and Zlogσ.

Step 5c: Using random normal tensor epsilon, Zμ and Zlogσ, random homogeneous points are sampled using sampling function

Figure 2. Architecture of VariationalAutoencoder

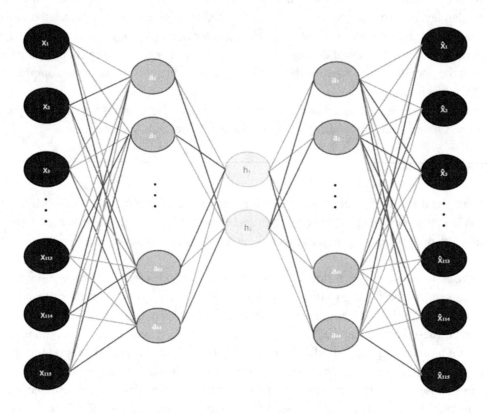

Step 5d:The decoder uses Bernoulli probability distribution to map these points once again to the original input.

Step 6: Predict the output of trained model using X_opt dataset.

Step 7: Calculate MSE and compute its mean and standard deviation using:

$$MSE = \frac{1}{n} \sum_{i=1}^{n} \left(Xi - \widehat{Xi} \right)^2$$

978-1-6684-6444-1.ch005.g01

Step 8: Initialize best_acc=0 and best_n=0. For every value of n from 1 to 30 do:

Step 8a: Set Tr= μMSE + n*σMSE

Step 8b: Calculate the accuracy(acc) of the mode using the set Tr.

Step 8c: If acc>best_acc, set best_acc = accand best_n = n.

Step 9: Set the threshold using the best_n value obtained.

Step 10: For every record in the X_test dataset

Step 10a: Determine the output X and calculate the MSE for that output.

Step 10b: If MSE > threshold, label it as a botnet (1).

Step 10c: Else label it as benign traffic (0).

From these hypotheses, we presume that VariationalAutoencoder surpasses all the other Autoencoder's in terms of achieving good results. When compared to many other state-of-art botnet detection methods, sparse Autoencoder's are known to produce better accuracy with lower false predictions. After scrutinizing the existing systems, a model was proposed to such a degree that it resolves an amount of issues in the existing system and produces better results.

IMPLEMENTATION

Datasets pertaining to six IoT devices: Danmini Doorbell, Baby Monitor B120N10, PT 737E Security Camera, Ecobee Thermostat, PT 838 Security Camera and XCS7 1002 WHT Security Camera, are extracted from the N-BaIoT dataset. Each IoT device consists of traffic data collected by infecting the devices with two common botnet families: Gafgyt and Mirai. The traffic data is divided into ten attacks, 5 each of Gafgyt namely COMBO, Junk, Scan, TCP, UDP and Mirai such as Ack, Scan, Syn, UDP, UDPplain including one file of benign. The dataset is split into train(X_train), optimize(X_opt) and split(X_test) with each containing instances of both malicious and benign classes. The train dataset is used to train the model, optimize dataset is applied to predict and set the MSE threshold for anomaly detection and test dataset is utilized to evaluate the Autoencoder model's learning process.

For detecting the botnet attacks, we have used Autoencoders, an efficient type of neural network. The basic idea behind Autoencoder's is that, when a set of features are fed into the neural net, it understands the relationship between these features and tries to reconstruct the input. In this project, we exploit the fact that failure of reconstruction of input implies that anomalies exist i.e. the IoT device is infected with a botnet and behaving abnormally.

We have used five different autoencoders namely, UndercompleteAutoencoder, Sparse Autoencoder, VariationalAuoencoder, Deep Autoencoder and DenoisingAutoencoder separately for each device to evaluate their performance for the detection of botnets. Using tensorflow, we have created models for the specified autoencoders by defining the two main components: encoder and decoder. The last layer uses 'sigmoid' activation since we need the outputs to be in between 0 and 1. All the other layers use the 'relu' activation function that returns 0 for negative values and the same value for positive values.

Before feeding the input to the encoder, the X_train dataset is standardized in order to obtain desirable results from the model. The model is configured with mean squared error loss and adam optimizer. The MSE is used to measure the deviation in the learning process. Adam optimizer is applied to adjust the input weights by comparing the loss function and prediction. It is much more efficient compared to other optimizers as it utilizes the benefits of both AdaGrad and RMSProp. The model is trained using the fit() function. In this phase, the model uses the input data and learns the relationship between various features and comprehends the important features required for effective regeneration of input. Since Autoencoder's reconstruct the input as the output, both input and target provided to the fit function will be the X-train dataset. Each model is set to train for 100 epochs.

The Early Stopping function is used to monitor the "val_loss" and stop the epochs when there is no improvement in val_loss for five contiguous epochs. Once the training is completed, the function restores model weights from the epoch with the optimum value of the monitored quantity. This is beneficial in preventing overfitting or underfitting of the model and also saving computational resources. The time() function is used to calculate the time taken by the model for learning by considering the start and end time of training.

Table 1. Accuracy comparison

Dataset/Model	Deep Autoencoder	Sparse Autoencoder	VariationalAutoencoder	DenoisingAutoencoder	UndercompleteAutoencoder
Baby Monitor	0.892603	0.997749	0.997749	0.787277	0.997766
Provision PT737E security camera	0.861932	0.998504	0.998504	0.999855	0.998504
Provision PT838 Security Camera	0.869998	0.998736	0.998691	0.999924	0.998736
Thermostat	0.880577	0.998513	0.998170	0.500686	0.998284
Danmini Doorbell	0.897342	0.897251	0.897251	0.500000	0.897251
SimpleHome XCS7 1002 WHT Security Camera	0.804076	0.878711	0.879033	0.999614	0.878807

Threshold Optimization

For the autoencoder to classify the result as benign (0) and malicious (1), we need to set a threshold for the output. The threshold is calculated as:

$$\text{Tr} = \mu_{MSE} + n *_{MSE} \tag{1}$$

The model trained in the previous module is used to predict the results of the X_opt dataset. The MSE is obtained from the difference between the X_opt dataset and the reconstructed output of the model for the X_opt dataset. We then calculate the average and SD of the MSE obtained.

We evaluate the result as following:

- If the MSE (inaccuracy in reconstruction) is larger in comparison to the said threshold, then it means that there is an abnormality in the device's behavior. Thus we can categorize the output as malicious (1).
- If the reconstruction error is less than the said threshold, then the device is acting normally, hence the output can be categorized as benign (0).

The threshold needs to be well tuned in order to produce accurate results. As shown in equation (1), we multiply another balancing factor n with the σMSE. The n value is ranged between 1 to 30. We iterate through each n value and use the same X_opt dataset to predict the label (0 or 1). For each n value, the accuracy score, precision, recall and confusion matrix is also determined. At the end of the iteration, the n value that produces the best accuracy score is considered. This best n value is used to set the optimized threshold value used for label prediction.

Finally, the model's learning is put to test. The X_test dataset is divided into two parts, feature set X_set that contains data from the 115 feature columns and Y_test which contains the label to be predicted. The model is tested by providing only the feature set. MSE for the test dataset is calculated and compared with the optimized threshold, if it is greater than threshold then the label is 1, otherwise 0.The labels predicted (y_pred) by the model are compared with the actual labels, Y_test. This data is used to determine:

- Accuracy: measure of fraction of correct predictions.
- Recall: measure of True Positives being identified correctly by the model.
- Precision: measure of positive values identified by the model that are originally part of the positive class
- Confusion matrix: measure the performance of a model using TP, TN, FP, FN values in case of a binary classification (0 or 1) problem.

These four factors are considered for all the five models used and compared to determine the best performing model out of the five. This is done separately for each IoT device and the final scores are put together to calculate the average accuracy for each smart device and the top model is selected.

To measure the performance of the models, we have considered the accuracy score of all the models for each dataset. The average accuracy is determined for each model and from Figure 3, we can establish that VariationalAutoencoder has an overall accuracy of 96.157% closely followed by Sparse Autoencoder and UndercompleteAutoencoder with 96.158% and 96.156% average accuracy respectively. Deep Autoencoder has demonstrated a mean accuracy of 86.775% with DenoisingAutoencoder exhibiting a poor performance with an overall accuracy of 79.789%.

False Positive Rate is the probability of raising a false alarm i.e. a negative value will be predicted as positive. In the context of our project, it means that a benign value will be classified as malicious, which is something that we'd prefer to avoid in order to develop an efficient method for detecting botnets. Thus, a lower FPR implies that our model would be better in enhancing IoT device's security.

Since we have established the fact that VariationalAutoencoder and Sparse Autoencoder exhibit nearly the same performance in terms of accuracy Figure 3, we further explore by taking into account the FPR of Sparse Autoencoder and VariationalAutoencoder for each dataset. The average FPR for Sparse Autoencoder and VariationalAutoencoder are evaluated to be 0.00248 and 0.00241 respectively. Thus, we can infer that VariationalAutoencoder demonstrates a lower and better FPR collated to Sparse Autoencoder. From Figure 4, we can ascertain that VariationalAutoencoder displays the lowest FPR approximating to 0.00036 for Damini Doorbell dataset while the Baby Monitor dataset has the highest FPR of 0.00421.

This variation may also be attributed to the difference in number of samples used for testing. Taking into consideration the FPR of VariationalAutoencoder for all the six datasets used, the average FPR corresponds to 0.00241 which is significantly lower and more consistent than 0.007 ± 0.01 produced by the Deep Autoencoder model proposed by Y. Meidan et al[17].

CONCLUSION

In this paper, we have posited an analysis of various Autoencoder's for detecting IoT botnet attacks. Different Autoencoder's are trained and tested to differentiate between malicious and legitimate traffic. As we discussed above, Autoencoder's are applied for dimensionality reduction and feature extraction. If the Autoencoder's are not able to reconstruct the features during the testing, it implies that there exists some abnormality in the network traffic and the output is classified to be "malicious". After performing training and testing on various Autoencoder's, the VariationalAutoencoder provides the best average accuracy of 96.157% in predicting the results for the data obtained from the N-BaIoT dataset. The above-mentioned system demonstrates a 99.86% outstanding accuracy for the Provision PT838 security camera dataset

Figure 3. Average accuracy comparison

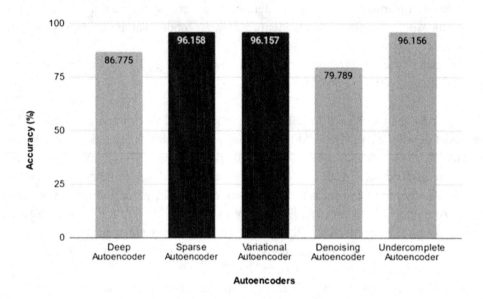

with a precision of 0.9979 and recall value of 0.9995. The False Positive Rates (FPR) in the proposed model are much lower (0.00241) compared to Deep Autoencoder's used in the existing model.

For future work, our model should be tested on real-time traffic to measure the performance since we have applied these models on the existing processed dataset above. One should also consider the case of extending our proposed model to an all-purpose network encompassing a wide range of devices such as

Figure 4. FPR comparison for VariationalAutoencoder

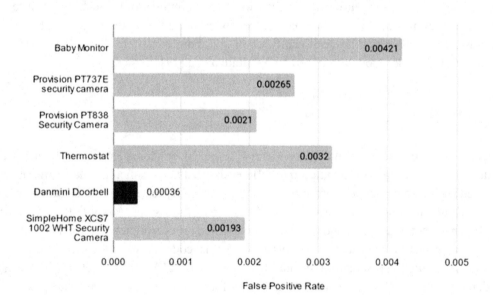

PCs, laptops and mobile phones. Ensemble learning methods can be exerted to improve the resilience of the proposed system.

ACKNOWLEDGMENT

This research received no specific grant from any funding agency in the public, commercial, or not-for-profit sectors.

REFERENCES

Abbasi, M., Shahraki, A., & Taherkordi, A. (2021). Deep learning for network traffic monitoring and analysis (ntma): A survey. *Computer Communications*, *170*, 19–41. doi:10.1016/j.comcom.2021.01.021

Aburomman, A. A., & Reaz, M. B. I. (2016). A novel SVM-kNN-PSO ensemble method for intrusion detection system. *Applied Soft Computing*, *38*, 360–372. doi:10.1016/j.asoc.2015.10.011

Aceto, G., Ciuonzo, D., Montieri, A., & Pescapé, A. (2019). Mobile encrypted traffic classification using deep learning: Experimental evaluation, lessons learned, and challenges. *IEEE eTransactions on Network and Service Management*, *16*(2), 445–458. doi:10.1109/TNSM.2019.2899085

Aceto, G., Ciuonzo, D., Montieri, A., & Pescapé, A. (2021). DISTILLER: Encrypted traffic classification via multimodal multitask deep learning. *Journal of Network and Computer Applications*, *183-184*, 102985. doi:10.1016/j.jnca.2021.102985

Ahmed, A. A., Jabbar, W. A., Sadiq, A. S., & Patel, H. (2020). Deep learning-based classification model for botnet attack detection. *Journal of Ambient Intelligence and Humanized Computing*, *2020*, 1–10. doi:10.100712652-020-01848-9

Al-Qatf, M., Lasheng, Y., Al-Habib, M., & Al-Sabahi, K. (2018). Deep learning approach combining sparse autoencoder with SVM for network intrusion detection. *IEEE Access: Practical Innovations, Open Solutions*, *6*, 52843–52856. doi:10.1109/ACCESS.2018.2869577

Andy Greenberg. (2017). *The Reaper IoT Botnet Has Already Infected a Million Networks*. https://www.wired.com/story/ reaper-iot-botnetinfected-million-networks/

Asadi, M., Jamali, M. A. J., Parsa, S., & Majidnezhad, V. (2020). Detecting botnet by using particle swarm optimization algorithm based on voting system. *Future Generation Computer Systems*, *107*, 95–111. doi:10.1016/j.future.2020.01.055

Bamakan, S. M. H., Wang, H., & Shi, Y. (2017). Ramp loss K-Support Vector Classification-Regression; a robust and sparse multi-class approach to the intrusion detection problem. *Knowledge-Based Systems*, *126*, 113–126. doi:10.1016/j.knosys.2017.03.012

Bhagoji, A. N., Cullina, D., & Mittal, P. (2017). *Dimensionality reduction as a defense against evasion attacks on machine learning classifiers*. arXiv preprint arXiv:1704.02654

Bhardwaj, A., Mangat, V., & Vig, R. (2020). Hyperband Tuned deep neural network with well posed stacked sparse AutoEncoder for detection of DDoS attacks in cloud. *IEEE Access: Practical Innovations, Open Solutions*, *8*, 181916–181929. doi:10.1109/ACCESS.2020.3028690

Chen, C., Liu, B., Wan, S., Qiao, P., & Pei, Q. (2021). An edge traffic flow detection scheme based on deep learning in an intelligent transportation system. *IEEE Transactions on Intelligent Transportation Systems*, *22*(3), 1840–1852. doi:10.1109/TITS.2020.3025687

Cil, A. E., Yildiz, K., & Buldu, A. (2021). Detection of DDoS attacks with feed forward based deep neural network model. *Expert Systems with Applications*, *169*, 114520–114530. doi:10.1016/j.eswa.2020.114520

Cimpanu. (2018). *Hide and Seek Becomes First IoT Botnet Capable of Surviving Device Reboots*. https://www.bleepingcomputer.com/news/security/hide-and-seekbecomes-first-iot-botnet-capable-of-surviving-device-reboots/

Comar, P. M., Liu, L., Saha, S., Tan, P. N., & Nucci, A. (2013, April). *Combining supervised and unsupervised learning for zero-day malware detection. In 2013 Proceedings IEEE INFOCOM*. IEEE.

Dahal, B., & Kim, Y. (2019). AutoEncoded domains with mean activation for DGA botnet detection. *International Conference on Global Security, Safety and Sustainability IEEE*, 208-212. 10.1109/ICGS3.2019.8688037

Erhan, D., & Anarim, E. (2020). Hybrid DDoS detection framework using matching pursuit algorithm. *IEEE Access: Practical Innovations, Open Solutions*, *8*, 118912–118923. doi:10.1109/ACCESS.2020.3005781

Jagadeesan, S., & Amutha, B. (2021). An efficient botnet detection with the enhanced support vector neural network. *Measurement*, *176*, 109140–109151. doi:10.1016/j.measurement.2021.109140

Kim, J., Sim, A., Kim, J., & Wu, K. (2020). Botnet Detection Using Recurrent VariationalAutoencoder. *GLOBECOM IEEE Global Communications Conference IEEE*, 1-6.

Ko, I., Chambers, D., & Barrett, E. (2020). Adaptable feature-selecting and threshold-moving complete autoencoder for DDoS flood attack mitigation. *Journal of Information Security and Applications*, *55*, 102647–102657. doi:10.1016/j.jisa.2020.102647

Kunang, Y. N., Nurmaini, S., Stiawan, D., & Suprapto, B. Y. (2021). Attack classification of an intrusion detection system using deep learning and hyperparameter optimization. *Journal of Information Security and Applications*, *58*, 102804–102814. doi:10.1016/j.jisa.2021.102804

Louis Columbus. (2016). *Roundup Of Internet Of Things Forecasts And Market Estimates*. https://www.forbes.com/sites /louiscolumbus/2016/11/27/roundup-ofinternet-of-things-forecasts-and-market-estimates-2016/

Meidan, Y., Bohadana, M., Mathov, Y., Mirsky, Y., Breitenbacher, D., Shabtai, A., & Elovici, Y. (2018). N-BaIoT: Network-based Detection of IoT Botnet Attacks Using Deep Autoencoders. *IEEE Pervasive Computing*, *17*(3), 12–22. doi:10.1109/MPRV.2018.03367731

Mirea, M., Wang, V., & Jung, J. (2019). The not so dark side of the darknet: A qualitative study. *Security Journal*, *32*(2), 102–118. doi:10.105741284-018-0150-5

Moodi, M., Ghazvini, M., & Moodi, H. (2021). A hybrid intelligent approach to detect Android Botnet using Smart Self-Adaptive Learning-based PSO-SVM. *Knowledge-Based Systems*, *222*, 106988–106996. doi:10.1016/j.knosys.2021.106988

Nguyen, Q. P., Lim, K. W., Divakaran, D. M., Low, K. H., & Chan, M. C. (2019). GEE: A Gradient-based Explainable Variational Autoencoder for Network Anomaly Detection. *IEEE Conference on Communications and Network Security*, 91-99. 10.1109/CNS.2019.8802833

Nozomi Networks. (2020). *Webinar: OT/IoT Security Report 2020*. https://www.nozominetworks.com/past-events/webinar-ot-iot-security-report-2020/

Om Kumar, C. U., & Ponsy, R. K. (2019). Detecting and confronting flash attacks from IoT botnets. *The Journal of Supercomputing*, *75*(12), 8312–8338. doi:10.100711227-019-03005-2

Paffenroth, R. C., & Zhou, C. (2019). Modern Machine Learning for Cyber-Defense and Distributed Denial-of-Service Attacks. *IEEE Engineering Management Review*, *47*(4), 80–85. doi:10.1109/EMR.2019.2950183

Rahman, M. A., Asyhari, A. T., Wen, O. W., Ajra, H., Ahmed, Y., & Anwar, F. (2021). Effective combining of feature selection techniques for machine learning-enabled IoT intrusion detection. *Multimedia Tools and Applications*, *2021*(20), 1–19. doi:10.100711042-021-10567-y

Rawat, R., Mahor, V., Chirgaiya, S., Shaw, R. N., & Ghosh, A. (2021). Analysis of Darknet Traffic for Criminal Activities Detection Using TF-IDF and Light Gradient Boosted Machine Learning Algorithm. In *Innovations in Electrical and Electronic Engineering* (pp. 671–681). Springer. doi:10.1007/978-981-16-0749-3_53

Rodríguez-Ruiz, J., Mata-Sánchez, J. I., Monroy, R., Loyola-González, O., & López-Cuevas, A. (2020). A one-class classification approach for bot detection on Twitter. *Computers & Security*, *91*, 101715–101727. doi:10.1016/j.cose.2020.101715

Sadaf, K., & Sultana, J. (2020). Intrusion detection based on autoencoder and isolation Forest in fog computing. *IEEE Access: Practical Innovations, Open Solutions*, *8*, 167059–167068. doi:10.1109/ACCESS.2020.3022855

Shahid, M. R., Blanc, G., Zhang, Z., & Debar, H. (2019). Anomalous Communications Detection in IoT Networks Using Sparse Autoencoders. *International Symposium on Network Computing and Applications IEEE*, 1-5. 10.1109/NCA.2019.8935007

Shone, N., Ngoc, T. N., Phai, V. D., & Shi, Q. (2018). A Deep Learning Approach to Network Intrusion Detection. *IEEE Transactions on Emerging Topics in Computational Intelligence*, *2*(1), 41–50. doi:10.1109/TETCI.2017.2772792

Symantec. (2018). *Internet Security Threat Report*. https://www.symantec.com /content/dam/symantec/docs/reports/istr23-2018-en.pdf

Tsogbaatar, E., Bhuyan, M. H., Taenaka, Y., Fall, D., Gonchigsumlaa, K., Elmroth, E., & Kadobayashi, Y. (2021). DeL-IoT: A deep ensemble learning approach to uncover anomalies in IoT. *Internet of Things*, *14*, 100391–100403. doi:10.1016/j.iot.2021.100391

Wang, W., Du, X., Shan, D., Qin, R., & Wang, N. (2020). *Cloud Intrusion Detection Method Based on Stacked Contractive Auto-Encoder and Support Vector Machine. IEEE Transactions on Cloud Computing.* doi:10.1109/TCC.2020.3001017

Yang, Y., Zheng, K., Wu, B., Yang, Y., & Wang, X. (2020). Network intrusion detection based on supervised adversarial variational auto-encoder with regularization. *IEEE Access: Practical Innovations, Open Solutions, 8*, 42169–42184. doi:10.1109/ACCESS.2020.2977007

Zavrak, S., & İskefiyeli, M. (2020). Anomaly-Based Intrusion Detection From Network Flow Features Using VariationalAutoencoder. *IEEE Access: Practical Innovations, Open Solutions, 8*, 108346–108358. doi:10.1109/ACCESS.2020.3001350

Chapter 6
Cyber Security for IoT–Enabled Industry 4.0:
Systematic Review for Dark Web Environments

Deepika Chauhan

Swarrnim Startup and Innovation University, India

Chaitanya Singh

iD https://orcid.org/0000-0002-1384-8495

Swarrnim Startup and Innovation University, India

Dyaneshwar Kudande

iD https://orcid.org/0000-0003-3410-5102

Swarrnim Startup and Innovation University, India

Yu-Chen Hu

Providence University, Taiwan

ABSTRACT

The dark web is a portion of the deep web that's hidden away from the ordinary user. It contains various tools and techniques that cyber criminals can use to carry out their attacks. The increasing popularity of the internet of things has raised the concerns of various security organizations regarding the security of the systems connected to it. The rapid emergence and success of internet of things devices and their associated services have raised the number of attacks against these devices and services to the alarming level. The need to secure this rapidly changing industry has become a top priority in the cyber defense industry. This chapter aims to provide a comprehensive view of the various threats and attacks targeting the infrastructure of the IoT and to analyze the various cyber defense techniques and solutions that are being used to secure the connected objects.

DOI: 10.4018/978-1-6684-6444-1.ch006

INTRODUCTION

The rapid emergence and evolution of the Internet of Things has raised the concerns of system administrators about the security of their industrial systems. This paper explores the various considerations involved in integrating smart devices into existing industrial platforms. In 2011, the term Industry 4.0 was coined to describe the digital revolution that's happening in today's world. It's a new wave of technological innovation that's constantly happening. In Industry 4.0, digital records are collected by devices that are attached to industrial machines. The data they collect provides insight into how thoughts and feelings are expressed. Second, the analytical capabilities of the devices are combined with background operations to create a visual representation of the data (K. FERENCZ et al., 2021).

The Dark Web is a network that enables users to hide their identity and gain control over their network traffic. It is often used by criminals to distribute goods and services. Dark Web operators typically use special software to hide their identities and conduct business. Dark Web platforms are also used by criminals to carry out their criminal activities, such as buying and selling cryptocurrencies. Some of them act as intermediaries to make it easier for others to carry out their activities (S. Samtani et al., 2020). Dark Web marketplaces are often rife with tools and products that are designed to organize attacks. Some of these include tools that allow hackers to perform distributed denial of service (DDoS) and phishing attacks. Dark Web marketplaces are populated by hackers and buyers with varying levels of expertise (R. Liggett et al., 2020). Some of these individuals are experienced in creating and selling sophisticated hacking tools. In this environment, some companies provide security services to help protect their users from potential attacks. While it's possible for hackers to create and sell their own tools, they often rely on the collective skills of their accomplices to carry out their activities. These networks and marketplaces are often referred to as peer ship networks or colleagueship's networks (E. R. Leukfeldt and T. J. Holt, 2020). Instead of having their own servers, they act as intermediaries between the buyers and the hackers. The main characteristics of Dark Web markets are that they allow hackers to sell their products and services through encrypted communication methods. Due to the existence of such marketplaces, it is believed that the focus of hackers is financial gain.

The need to acquire information instantly has led to the emergence of new computing paradigm such as Big Data and Blockchain. This is enabled by the emergence of the Internet of Things (IoT) (Karmakar KK et al., 2019, Alenezi M et al., 2019, Bao Z et al., 2018). Aside from humans, some of the interconnected entities include sensors and machines. The Internet of Things (IoT) refers to the transformation of various objects from analog to smart devices through the use of various technologies. Some of these include energy management, home monitoring, and transportation. The former allows customers to connect their devices to the Internet and monitor their usage (Sharma PK et al., 2017, Tyagi N et al., 2016). Smart grid and smart metering are some of the applications of the Internet of Things. These include monitoring the consumption of electricity and determining how much of it is used (Zhang N et al., 2019, Khandpur et al., 2017). Water meters are also being utilized to improve the quality of drinking water. Data broadcast in an IoT system can expose various details such as location, battery life, and memory usage. It can also lead to the exploitation of various systems (Li et al., 2016). Industry 4.0 refers to the evolution of manufacturing through the use of intelligent systems, which are composed of Cyber-Physical Systems and the Internet of Things. Cyber-attacks are very dangerous when used in Industry 4.0 networks. Since these systems are vulnerable to attacks, manufacturers should implement effective cyber-security measures to prevent these risks (Cheng et al., 2013, Zanero et al., 2008).

Table 1. Review of various types of dark web attacks in IoT

Dark web Attack	Year of Attack	Country	Ref
Attack on Mail System of Belgium ministry of defense	2021	Belgium	Schwartz, H. (2022)
Ransomware attack on Australian Utility using dark web	2021	Australia	Schwartz, H. (2022)
Unauthorized Webmail Access Sale Detected for An Insurance Firm from Colombia on The Dark Web	2022	USA	SOCRadar (2022)
Database of Canada-Saskatoon City Airport Published on The Dark Web	2022	Canada	SOCRadar (2022)
Unauthorized Shell Access for An E-Commerce Company from Spain Put on Sale	2022	Spain	SOCRadar (2022)
An Investment Company from Switzerland Crippled by Cuba Ransomware	2022	Switzerland	SOCRadar (2022)
Credential stuffing Attack	2021	New York	Bannister, A. (2022)
Route Device trafficking through VPN	2021	USA	Leyden, J. (2021)
Information Leakage of 20,000 Indian	2021	India	Rajaharia, R. (2022)
7595 Website Hack Attack	2020	World	Winder, D. (2022)

According to a Security researcher (R. Rajaharaa,2022), thousands of individuals in India had their personal data, including their names, mobile number, and address, leaked. The information was posted on the Raid Forums website by cyber criminals.

(SocRacer,2020) released a report "The week in Dark Web" targeting the latest dark web incident. On January 13, a dark web vendor tried to sell unauthorized access to a financial firm's webmail account. The vendor, who was identified as a customer, offered to give the attacker access to over 300 thousand messages and 315 GB of email. The following day, SOCRadar detected a post claiming to have a stolen database of Skyxe Airport, which included sensitive contracts and financial documents. The vendor that owned the database said that it was obtained on December 3, 2021. On January 14, another vendor offered to sell access to a Spanish e-commerce company for $200. The vendor did not provide the details of the transaction, but noted that 70% of the funds used were credit cards. On January 13, a post claiming to be from a ransomware group called Lapsus$ Group was detected in a channel monitored by SOCRadar. The group, which was created in 2021, could leak all of the victims' data if they refuse to negotiate. Table presents the various types of attacks accomplished by the Dark Web.

Due to the increase in the attacks using dark web table 2 present review of Machine Learning based methods used for detection and identification of cyber threats in dark web environment.

Due to the exponential increase in the number of people accessing cyberspace, the demand for cyber security has also increased. Cybercriminal activities have become more prevalent. The increasing number of Web applications has raised the concern of cyber security (Werner et al., 2017). Cyber security has become a global issue that has become more significant over the years. Although many organizations have implemented various security measures to protect themselves from cyber-attacks, they are not sufficient enough to prevent these types of attacks (Masi, et al., 2011, Okutan, et al., 2017). Table 3 shows the famous cyber-attacks in history targeting critical cyber infrastructure.

Table 2. Review of Machine Learning based methods used for detection and identification of cyber threats in dark web environment

Reference	Year	Detecting of Cyber Attacks	Predicting Cyber Attacks	Detection of Community	Identification of Hacker behavior	Detection & Identification of Malicious Attachment
Huang et al.	2021	●		●		●
Koloveas et al.	2021		●		●	
Ampel et al.	2020	●		●		●
Ebrahimi et al.	2020		●	●		
Koloveas et al.	2019	●		●	●	
Marin et al.	2019		●	●		●
Queiroz et al.	2019	●	●		●	●
Zenebe et al.	2019		●	●	●	
Pastrana et al.	2018	●	●		●	●
Narayanan et al.	2018	●		●		●
Marin et al.	2018	●	●	●	●	

REVIEW METHODOLOGY

This study aims to provide a comprehensive and detailed analysis of the various types of cyber security issues and the solutions available to address them. It will also identify the most common and severe cyber security issues and the effective ways of mitigating them. Our mapping study address the research questions formulated.

Objectives and Research Questions

The goal of this study is to investigate the various techniques and solutions that can be used to secure Internet of Things systems from large-scale attacks. Firstly, we discuss about the What are common security threats and vulnerability of IoT enabled industry 4.0. Secondly research focused on What are common IoT enabled application of industry 4.0 vulnerable to cyber-attacks. Lastly, we identified various mitigation techniques for IoT enabled application of industry 4.0.

RQ1: What are common security threats and vulnerability of IoT enabled industry 4.0 in relation to dark web.

The main RQ is to determine the frequency of the key security vulnerabilities that are most likely to occur in the chosen studies. This step will help researchers to formulate their main research areas.

RQ2: What are common IoT enabled application of industry 4.0 vulnerable to cyber-attacks in relation to dark web.

The question that follows is which applications were the targets of cybercrimes during the study. This list will provide insight into the users of these applications so that they can protect themselves from attacks.

RQ3: Discuss various mitigation techniques for IoT enabled application of industry 4.0 to overcome issues.

Table 3. The famous cyberattacks in the history targeted critical cyber infrastructure

Cyber Attack	Year	Country	Target	Method	Description	Ref.
TRITON	2017	Saudi	ICS	Spear Phishing	This attack was discovered in a Saudi petrochemical plant, which allowed hackers to take over the facility's safety instrument systems. It was the first time that a malicious code was designed to cause a fatal explosion.	(Sandberg, H. 2021)
CPC Corp	2020	Taiwan	Payment System using Flash Drive	Ransomware Attacks	Last year, Taiwan's CPC Corp, which is also known as Liquid Natural Gas, was hit by a ransomware attack. The incident caused its payment system to crash, which affected gas station customers.	(MELANI. 2021)
Israel water Pump Attack	2020	Israel	ICS Command and control	Reconnaissance, packet sniffing, ping sweeping, port scanning, phishing, social engineering and internet information queries	The Israeli water system was targeted by a number of cyber-attacks in mid-2020. The attackers exploited weaknesses in the systems' command and control systems to launch attacks that attempted to disrupt the supply of chlorine and other harmful chemicals.	(Associates, A. 2021).
Nippon Telegraph and Telephone	2020	Japan	Data Breach	Phishing Attack/ Ransomware Attacks	NTT Communications, a telecommunications company that provides data centers in over 20 countries, recently suffered a data breach that was reportedly carried out by multiple attackers. The company believes that machine learning and AI were used in the attack.	(NTT Com, 2021)
Moderna	2020	US	Vaccine development department	Reconnaissance, packet sniffing, ping sweeping, port scanning, phishing, social engineering and internet information queries	The hackers were able to infiltrate Moderna through its network and target specific users with enhanced security permissions. They were also able to steal data through various exploitation techniques.	(Taylor, M 2021)
Unnamed US natural Gas Operator	2020	US	IT Network	Phishing Attack/ Ransomware Attacks	A gas facility in the US was attacked by ransomware that encrypted its communications and control systems. The criminal first used a Spear Phishing link to gain access to the facility's network. Once inside, the attackers were able to install and activate the ransomware.	(CISA. 2021)
Ukrain's Power Grid (Black Energy 3)	2016	Ukrain	IT Network	Multi-Vector Attacks (KillDisk,Spear Phising,Credential Theft,VPN,DoS attack, Remote access exploit)	In 2016, a massive cyber-attack affected a power facility in Ukraine. The attack, which was carried out by the Sandworm group, left half of the population without power. It was considered one of the most dangerous attacks in recent memory.	(Searle, J. 2021)
San Francisco's MUNI light rail system	2016	San Francisco's	ICS	Mamba Ransomware	In 2016, hackers infiltrated San Francisco's Municipal rail system (MUNI) and launched a ransomware attack called Mamba. The attack, which crippled the transit agency's operations for several days, left customers with no choice but to type "Out of Order" or "Free Rides" in order to access their tickets.	(Abrams, L. 2021)
Iranian Cyber Attack on New York Dam	2013	New York	Supervisory Control And Data Acquisition (SCADA) Systems	Vulnerabilities in cellular network	The Iranian hackers, who were backed by the country's Ministry of Science and Technology, exploited the weaknesses in the system by accessing its cellular modem connection. They were also able to remotely control the system's controllers. The attack was conducted to test the various security controls in the pipeline.	(Thompson, M. 2013)
Unnamed American Water Authority	2021	Florida	Cellular Networks	Packet Sniffing, Ping Sweeping, Port Scanning	The attackers used the cellular routers of the water authority to jack up the cellular data bills of the customers. The clue was revealed later that year after the DHS discovered a flaw in the routers' firmware.	(BBC News. 2021)
Colonial Oil Pipeline	2021	US	ICS	Ransomware Attacks	On May 7, 2021, the Colonial Oil pipeline was hit by a ransomware attack. The attack crippled its operations and left thousands of gas stations without fuel. The hacker group Dark Side was able to steal over 100GB of data from Colonial's servers, and they only surrendered control after the company paid $5 million in cryptocurrency. The rising cost of gasoline is also believed to be the cause of the attack.	(The Guardian. 2021)

The goal of this question is to provide a list of cyber security mitigation techniques that are commonly used to prevent attacks. This list will help researchers gain a better understanding of the various techniques available to address these threats.

Table 4. Search criteria

Key	Criteria's
Search String	Cyber security (cyber OR Privacy OR {cyber security} OR {cyber physical} OR {Network security} OR {Internet security} OR {computer security} OR {IT Security} OR {software Security}). Attack (vulnerability OR {cyber threat} OR {cyber-Crime} OR {cyber-attack} OR challenge OR risks OR violence). (IoT OR "internet of things") AND Security AND (DDOS or "distributed denial of service" or botnet or attack) Cyber OR Privacy OR {cyber security} OR {cyber physical} OR {Network security} OR {Internet security} OR {computer security} OR {IT Security} OR {software Security}) AND (vulnerability OR {cyber threat} OR {cyber-Crime} OR {cyber-attack} OR challenge OR risks OR violence).
Limiters	Full Text +Print/ Scholarly (Peer Reviewed) Journals, Published date: 2016-2021 Language= English
Expanders	Apply relevant synonyms and words.
Search Modes	Search all the relevant search terms.

Search Criteria

A search for the phrase "Internet of Things" or "security" is then narrowed down to the most relevant search terms. The terms "DDoS" and "Bots" are then added to the list to enable users to query for more detailed information about the attacks that are against the systems. Table 4 shows the search criteria for the selection of articles.

The databases were selected for their prominent positions in the cyber security research community Science Direct, Springer, ACM, PubMed, IEEE

Publication Selection Criteria

This section also details the process used to select the appropriate publications. It highlights the various criteria that were used to select the most appropriate ones. The inclusion criteria were only used for the publications that were published after 2016. Inclusive criteria for studies include Empirical studies on vulnerabilities in IoT infrastructure-based applications and Studies proposing solutions to the IoT vulnerabilities.

Exclusive criteria for the studies include: Duplicate studies, Studies not proposing solution to the existing vulnerabilities, Studies where solutions are not evaluated empirically, Studies in form of abstract and PPT's, Book Chapters, Paper written in other than English Language, Introductory research articles in workshop, special issues and books.

SECURITY THREATS AND VULNERABILITY OF IOT ENABLED INDUSTRY 4.0 IN RELATION TO DARK WEB.

The concept of the Internet of Things requires the establishment of a framework to control and manage the various processes that are being carried out by various components of the system. The framework can be easily visualized as a set of rules that are responsible for handling the exchange of data between various hosts. The users can easily access various IoT services through various means, such as availing them through a web browser or a mobile device. The framework can be developed depending on the

Figure 1. Types of security threats

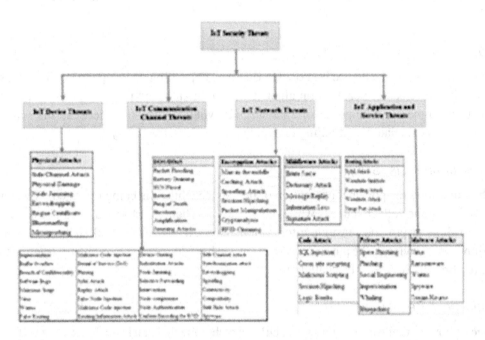

requirements of the target organization. Security is the biggest issue that the Internet of Things (IoT) has to address. It is typically focused on protecting the devices and the data they contain from unauthorized access. According to the forecasts, by 2020, the total number of connected devices will reach 50 billion (Middleton, P. 2021). Although security is the biggest challenge for an Internet-connected network, it is also an area where the vendor can offer the most effective solutions. Figure 1 show below various types of security IoT threats in the cyber space.

IoT Device Security

There is a huge effort being put in improving the hardware security of the critical system. Various initiatives are being taken to implement hardware-based encryption, secure boot, and other security measures. Attacks like Side Channel Attack (SCA) are becoming more prevalent, which can be easily exploited by anyone. Deep neural network models are also vulnerable to SCA attacks. Although there are various countermeasures that can be implemented to prevent these attacks, they are more dangerous for devices that rely on low-power CPUs. Due to the nature of these attacks, they have become more prevalent.

Side Channel Attack (SCA)

Aside from direct attacks on the processor, side-channel attacks can also expose sensitive data. These attacks happen when the processor consumes excessive power or has an electromagnetic emanation. Side channel attacks are focused on the leakages in the system (Yan, Y. 2019). These include the timing and power supply of the device, as well as the various electromagnetic signals. An attacker can use SCA to extract sensitive information from a device. There are various types of side channel attacks occur in the IoT devices.

Power attack

The power consumption of a device is known to fluctuate depending on its operation. This characteristic can be exploited to break the encryption algorithms commonly used in computer systems. A 50-ohm resistor is used to measure the power of a device. The voltage difference between the supply and the resistance value is calculated by dividing the value by the clock frequency.

Simple power analysis (SPA)

This technique shows the power consumption of the device while it is being operated. Power analysis is done by analyzing the collected traces while the operation is being performed. It can be used to identify hidden algorithms or provide sensitive information. This attack uses manual analysis to extract secret information from a device. If the power consumption can be reduced or varied, then extracting the desired information through SCA may be challenging.

Differential power analysis (DPA)

Difference of Power Analysis, also known as DP, is a technique that can be utilized for statistical analysis and data processing. It uses the same concept as SPA but it consumes less power. The power consumption of a particular hardware component is associated with the target bit's configuration. The target bit is calculated by dividing the trace's zero-bin value by the target bit's 1. The mean of the traces in the zero-and one-bin is computed, and the difference between the two is computed. The power consumption of the system is then linked to the guess. This attack is usually carried out by an attacker without having the system's internal knowledge.

Correlation power analysis (CPA)

The Correlation Power Analysis method was developed in SCA studies to be more effective than the Data Analysis Program (DAP). This method is performed by taking into account the number of power traces and the distance between the device and the power source.

Electromagnetic (EM) attack

This is an attack against a device involves taking advantage of its electromagnetic emissions. This procedure works by measuring the frequency of the emitted electromagnetic field. The goal of SCA is to collect and analyze the signals that are being sent by an attacker. This method allows the attacker to extract the secret information that is being stored in the system (J. Danial, et al. 2020).

Timing attack

The execution timing of a device operation is dependent on the data inputs that are computed. An attacker can exploit this difference to either extract or guess the sensitive data.

Cache attack

An attacker uses the leaked information to determine the timing of the cache access. The attacker knows that the data is being accessed, and they can use this information to extract it. Spectre and Meltdown are two of the most severe types of security attacks that affected Intel's hardware. *Differential fault attack*

These attacks usually involve generating a faulty system fault. They can also exploit the complexity of the device's design and its possible causes of failure. Various factors such as voltage, clock glitching, etc., can cause a faulty component to appear. A fault attack is performed to identify the operation that caused the issue.

IoT Communication Channel threats

Sybil Attack

Most networks are characterized by the assumption that each node represents an identity. When an insecure node is hijacked, it can enforce many identities on the network. This phenomenon, known as Sybil attack, can occur when a network is suddenly attacked. Another method is to use verified and valid certification. This method requires a huge number of resources and bandwidth to thoroughly test and validate the correctness of the certificate. The test is carried out to determine if the collected data is from an individual or group of nodes (Alsaedi, N., 2017). Table 5 shows types of Sybil attacks and their purpose.

Categories of sybil attack

SA-1 Sybil Attack: In SA-1, invaders make relations within the Sybil community. However, they fail to connect with other honest nodes. This means that they have no substantial connection with the community.

SA-2 Sybil Attack: Unlike SA-1, SA-2 can easily create social relations between users and other nodes. This capability makes it capable of launching attacks against users' social structures. SA-2 can generate numerous positive and negative reviews for services or for any evaluation system. This behavior can be replicated frequently.

SA-3 Sybil Attack: SA-3 mainly aims to reduce the duration of mobile phone calls. Due to the dynamics of cellular networks, it is not possible for users to have long-term connections and central authority anytime.

Detection of Sybil Attack

Various methodologies are used for the detection of Sybil attack. Figure 2 present the techniques used for the detection.

Social graph based detection

The goal of SGSD is to enable a known honest node to label a non-named individual as "Sybil" or "honest" without requiring the community to detect the presence of a known suspicious node (M. Baza et al., 2020).

Table 5. Types of sybil attacks in IoT

Sybil Attack Category	Region	Purpose	Behavior	Mobility	Domain
SA-1	Same region and limited number of edges	Control full system using malicious code or information	Perform as normal user and repeat specific behavior frequently.	No	Sensing
SA-2	Open Platforms/ Fake ratings & Reviews/ Recommender System.	Attack user privacy and malware dissemination.	Purposely repetition of specific behavior with high frequency.	No	Social
SA-3	Absence of central Identity for verification and authentication	Hinder privacy via manipulation in local environment.	Repetition of specific behavior frequently.	Yes	Mobile

Social network based sybil detection (SNSD)

Social community detection is proposed to enable the detection of Sybil. The concept of social network partitioning (SNSD) is presented as a graph partitioning problem. In this, we partition the social graph into two parts, one being the honest and the bastard. The more nodes that are tightly connected with the known ones, the higher their rank would be in the algorithm. However, if they are slightly disconnected from the known ones, it is more likely to be detected. This is because the algorithm only works if the nodes are connected to each other.

Social community based sybil detection (SCSD)

Social community detection is proposed to enable the detection of Sybil. This method is based on the concept of partition partitioning, where the nodes are ranked according to their social connections. On the other hand, if the nodes are tightly connected with known trusted ones, their ranking would improve significantly. However, if the nodes are slightly disconnected from the known ones, their ranking would still be affected by the algorithm.

Behavior classifier-based detection

The main activities of users of the Ren Ren Ren operating system are summarized below. These include sharing content with others, creating new social connections, and monitoring and blocking attacks. The

Figure 2. Techniques of detection of sybil attacks

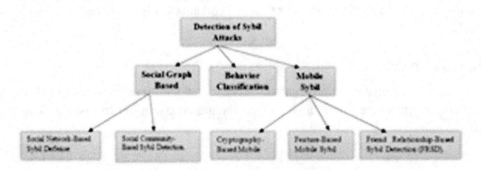

main activities of normal users are mostly focused on clicking photos. This paper presents a method that enables the users to be identified through graph clustering. This method works by modeling the click transitions using a Markov chain. Instead of just detecting Sybil, a distributed system is proposed. It can detect various types of attacks, such as SA-2 based on the user's behavior and classification. (Baza, M. et al., 2020).

Mobile sybil detection

In this section, we introduce the various defense schemes that are used to prevent Sybil attacks in mobile networks.

Friend relationship based sybil detection (FRSD)

Due to the complexity of the mobile network defense, it is quite different from the online networks. In order to defend against Sybil attacks, mobile users should have their communities matched with those in the community. Through friendship, it is possible to detect Sybil attacks. Hailes and Quercia propose an MSD scheme that would identify the users from the mobile user communities and label them as Sybil attackers. This method would work if the two lists contain the same user, and if the latter is not in the trusted communities. If a user is not in a trusted community, they would be considered as a Sybil user. This scheme assumes that the users are in different communities and rely on the community matches to detect them. However, this method requires users to maintain their trusted community data in advance (Casey, W et al., 2018).

Cryptography based mobile sybil detection

For more advanced attacks, such as Sybil, cryptography is another useful tool. In this section, we will discuss some crypto-MSD schemes that can defend against the attacks known as SA-3. The local vehicle users cannot effectively detect Sybil attackers until the attacker is revoked by the TA. Therefore, every user should implement group signature to prevent invalid signatures. Then, they can be linked to other users and be detected as Sybil attackers (Hamdan et al, 2021). Instead of requiring the vehicles to disclose their identity, the system can passively overhear them and prevent Sybil attacks. Using a smart phone, users can shop for deals and services nearby without relying on traditional sources such as brick-and-mortar stores and online reviews. However, these services are not secure from Sybil attacks since local service providers (LSPs) cannot independently verify the truthfulness of the reviews submitted by their users. TSE enables mobile users to sync their mobile reviews with the tokens generated by LSPs. After receiving a token, a user ui can only tie his or her reviews to one token. The same token can then be circulated among users. If ui uses multiple pseudonyms, both the user and the LSP can easily verify the submitted reviews (Medjek, F et al., 2017). Also, the revealed pseudonyms can be linked to the user's real identity. Aside from the basic cryptography solutions, a user can also prevent himself or herself from being attacked by creating a large number of reviews with the same username.

Feature based mobile sybil attack

Some specific features of mobile networks, such as channel characteristics, mobility features, and physical-layer authentication, can be studied to classify users who are most likely to attack Sybil. If a network node always receives the same packet with a similar RSS, it is probably a Sybil attack. Another method that uses mobile network features to defend against Sybil attacks is called MSD (James, J. Q. et al., 2020). Since the vehicle's neighbors measure the signal strength of the particular signal, the accuracy of the location estimation can be significantly improved. A lightweight algorithm for detecting Sybil attacks is proposed. The system relies on the mobility of the nodes and the channel conditions to identify the attackers. The techniques used to detect mobile network attacks vary depending on the environment and the complexity of the attack. Mobile ad hoc networks are typically used to detect mobile network attacks.

Denial of Service Attack (DoS)/ Distributed Denial of Service Attack (DDoS)

DoS attacks are usually carried out on the Internet of Things (IoT). They can be performed in various ways, such as saturating a network or blocking a device. A common strategy used by attackers is jamming, which targets a network with too many devices. A DoS attack could cause a packet to crash due to a small change in its checksum. Also, an adversary could trick the transport layer into thinking that a certain device is sending a request. The application layer is also vulnerable to a path-based attack, which occurs when a packet containing spurious data is sent to a destination. An attacker could then use this technique to drain the network's bandwidth. The site's response time when a large number of users visit it could be affected by the influx of traffic.

TYPES OF DDOS ATTACK

UDP flood

This attack uses multiple UDP packets to flood a target server. Due to the lack of a handshaking mechanism, HTTP connections are typically limited when it comes to addressing requests. An exploitation that uses multiple UDP packets can drain a host's resources.

ICMP flood

An ICMP flood attack sends packets containing fake Echo requests to a resource target. The victim's servers then try to respond using their own Echo replies, which consumes both outgoing and incoming bandwidth. This attack causes the system to crash.

SYN flood

The attack exploits the three-way handshake, which is a technique used to establish a connection between a host and a client. When a hacker succeeds in creating a flood of SYN requests, the receiving server gets severely affected by the overload.

Ping of death

A ping of death attack occurs when an attacker sends multiple malformed or malicious IP packets to a computer. The attacker can execute arbitrary code to cause the packet size to overflow. In a typical Ping of Death attack, the recipient gets an IP packet that is larger than the frame size of 65,535 bytes.

Slow loris

Slow Loris is a highly targeted attack that allows one web server to take down a nearby server without affecting the other services on the target network. It does so by creating multiple connections to the server and only sending a partial request.

NTTP amplification

An amplification attack is a type of network traffic attack that exploits publicly-accessible NTP servers. It can generate a high-volume, highly-complex attack by overloading a server with arbitrary traffic.

HTTP flood

An HTTP flood is a type of distributed denial of service attack that uses seemingly-legitimate HTTP requests to attack a website or application. It uses less bandwidth than other attacks.

Zero day attack

Zero-day refers to all the unpatched vulnerabilities that are exploited without a patch being released. An attacker uses uncatalogued vulnerability in a web server or network to take advantage of it. It is a daunting task to prevent these types of attacks.

Detection of DDos attack

Detection of DDos can be perform by integrating of machine learning and big data. Figure 4 and Figure 5 depicts the categorization of machine learning and big data-based methodologies used for the attack detection.

Machine learning based detection

Machine learning is an advanced artificial intelligence technique that can detect and respond to different types of attacks. It can also provide a defensive policy that can prevent exploitation. In 2018, the authors presented their findings on different attack models involving the use of machine learning techniques for the security of the Internet of Things (L. Xiao et al., 2018). They mentioned their possible solutions based on various attack models. In a review article published in 2020, the authors of the paper discussed the characteristics of Internet of Things (IoT) devices and their limitations when it comes to securing them (Zeadally, S. et al., 2020). RL techniques can help prevent jamming attacks on the Internet of Things. In this study, a method was proposed to prevent aggressive jamming attacks carried out by using a centralized system scheme. In this paper, a peer-to-peer security scheme has been proposed that prevents clients from accessing an Internet of Things (IoT) system without first being registered to a cloud server. Also, a novel strategy has been presented to prevent exploitation of the collected data. Various supervised machine learning algorithms are being used to detect network security attacks such as DoS and DDoS. In one study, an NN algorithm was used to detect DoS activities in an Internet of Things (IoT) network. Miettinen et al. (2017) presented an approach for classifying the devices belong-

Figure 3. Types of DDoS attacks

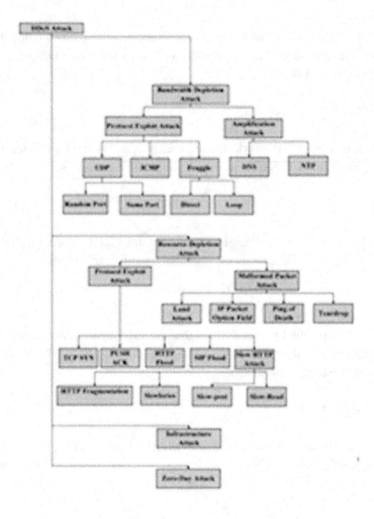

ing to the Internet of Things (IoT) network by using an algorithm that secures them from unauthorized access. A similar method was used by Meidanet et al. (2017), which classifies the non-IoT devices according to their connection to the network. Figure shows various machine learning techniques used for the detection of DDoS.

Big data

Big Data DDoS is a type of defense that uses big data technology to detect and mitigate distributed denial of service attacks. It combines cloud-scale techniques with deep packet analysis to collect and analyze large amounts of network traffic. A distributed denial of service attack is a type of attack that targets networks and applications. Its goal is to limit or deny access to legitimate users. The complexity of the attack makes it impossible to identify and block all of its targets. Automated or manual detection techniques are used by DDoS defense to prevent attacks from consuming too much bandwidth. They can also be used to filter or block traffic that has been identified as suspicious.

Phising Attack

Phishing is a type of attack that uses fraudulent email to steal a user's credentials. It is becoming more sophisticated and popular due to the increasing number of companies that have experienced phishing attacks. Phishing is a type of cyber-attack that uses various communication mediums such as email, websites, instant messages, and mobile applications. As a result, these attacks are becoming more sophisticated and designed to look like real emails. Figure discuss types of phishing attacks.

Types of phishing attacks

There are various types of phishing attacks affecting the system now days. Fig shows categories of phishing attacks.

Spear attack

Spear phishing is a type of email attack that uses embedded links and attachments to trick victims into clicking on a link or clicking on an attachment. These attacks use specially designed emails that contain sensitive information.

Tabnabbing

Tabnabbing is a type of phishing attack that was introduced by Aza Raskin of Firefox in 2010. It works by tricking the victim into opening a malicious website in another browser window. The attack is carried out using a social engineering tool created by the lab.

Whaling

Whaling is a type of attack that uses the victim's high-level access to information to carry out a more aggressive attack. Usually, in this type of attack, the phisher sends a link or download an attachment in order to trick the victim into clicking on it.

Drive by download

This technique works by visiting a malicious website or clicking on an email to expose a malicious shell code. The code then goes to a web page that exploits a web browser vulnerability. The resulting infection sends the infected system's contents to the botnet.

Social engineering

Social engineering is a type of phishing attack that uses the victim's confidence to steal their personal information. It focuses on diverting the victim's attention away from making informed decisions and causing them to make irrational ones.

Detection of phishing attack

Phishing tools are often used by hackers to gain access to sensitive information about users. Unfortunately, many security tools that rely on an existing blacklist often suffer from low detection accuracy and false alarms. Figure 7 present detail view of the methodology used for the detection of phishing attack.

Figure 4. Machine learning techniques used for the detection of DDoS

User training approach

Through user training, end-users can improve their understanding of phishing techniques and prevent them from committing cybercrimes. This is contrary to the concept of preventative training, which suggests that users should only be trained to prevent them.

Figure 5. Bigdata based DDoS attack detection

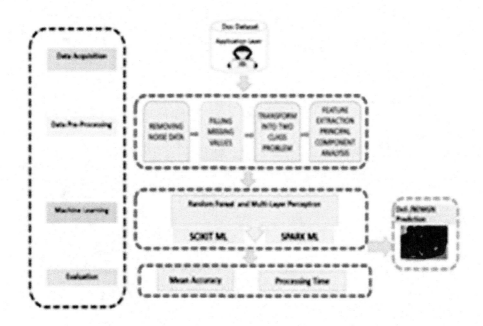

Figure 6. Types of Phishing attacks

Figure 7. Phishing attack detection techniques

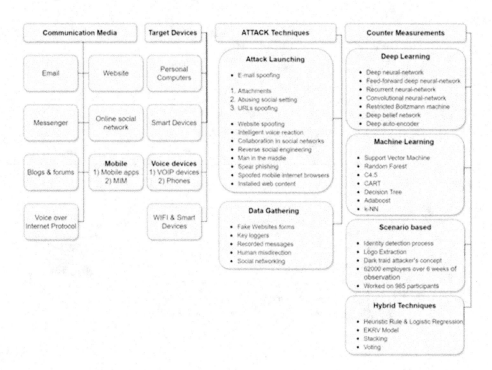

Software classification approach

These approaches are focused on mitigating phishing and legitimate messages sent on behalf of the user. They are mainly used to bridge the gap between the user and the system.

Virus/Worm/Trojan Horse Attack: An adversary can damage a system by creating a virus by sending emails containing links to infected files. The virus can replicate itself without any human intervention.

Malicious Node Injection: Malicious Node Injection occurs when an attacker physically injects a malicious node into more than one node. It then modifies the data that the other nodes receive. In this attack, the attacker uses multiple nodes to execute.

Node Jamming Attack: An attacker can use the WSNs to jam the radio frequencies of the sensor nodes and prevent them from communicating with each other. This attack is similar to the attack known as Radio Frequency Interference.

IoT Network Threats

Botnet: Cyber-criminals can easily compromise the security of IoT devices by taking over their computing power and launching attacks on them. They can also use these devices to carry out various types of attacks such as spam and phishing.

Ransomware: This is a type of malware that tries to lock down a device or a file system until a ransom is paid. Most of the time, this type of attack works by tricking users into believing that they are not allowed to access critical data.

AI Based Attacks: Over a decade ago, bad actors started using AI in cyberattacks. Now, it is becoming more prevalent, and the tools needed to build AI-capable systems are often available on the dark web.

IoT Layer Attacks

The biggest challenge in implementing an Internet of Things (IoT) system is to ensure the protection of user privacy. Understanding the various layers of an IoT architecture should start with an understanding of its various layers and their respective security aspects. Table 6 and Table 7 present the survey of various threats and vulnerabilities based on the layer architecture of IoT and types of attacks that infect the layered architecture.

Sensing Layer: The sensing layer is the part of the IoT that processes the data collected from different domains. There are various types of attacks that can affect the integrity and availability of a network.

Transport Layer: The transport layer is composed of various entities that are not designed for connection purposes. The goal of the Internet of Things is to establish an environment where these entities can interact with each other. An attacker can modify the information stored in the interaction process, which can affect the integrity of the system. The security of networks is divided into three layers: core network security, wireless security, and local area network security.

Application Layer: Security is the most prominent issue in the application layer. There are various types of services that are used for securing IoT devices.

Heterogeneous nature of the Internet of Things (IoT) networks makes them vulnerable to various threats. The table7 shows the various types of vulnerabilities that are common to both the internal and external systems of Internet of Things (IoT) devices.

IoT and Integrated Technology Issues

Blockchain Technology: The current blockchain architecture is not suitable for large-scale Internet networks due to its limited number of nodes and bandwidth. Its development is in its infancy and involves the development of consensus algorithms that can prevent excessive processing power. Due to various factors, it is not feasible for businesses to adopt blockchain technology at the global level. Establishing regulations is also necessary to make it easier for people to implement blockchain in their businesses.

Fog Computing: Feedback loops between distributed and centralized networks can be rationalized through end-to-end systems. Designing end-to-end systems can prevent the exploitation of untrustworthy nodes. Developing fog nodes with intelligent capabilities can allow them to handle the load requests and provide better connectivity.

Edge Computing: Devices at the edge of the network are typically resource-constrained and are prone to various attacks. An attack on these devices can lead to the entire Internet of Things ecosystem crashing. Since the implementation of security mechanisms on edge computing devices is an overhead that consumes a significant amount of time and energy, there has been no standard naming mechanism for this field.

Deep Learning: One of the main challenges in developing deep learning systems for the Internet of Things is training them for high-level representations of the physical world. This issue can be solved by developing networks that can handle large volume of data and make decisions efficiently.

Table 6. Survey of architectural layer-based industry 4.0 security threats and vulnerability

Layer	2021	2020	2019	2018	2017
Sensing Layer	Mrabet et. al, Gonzalez-Amarillo et. al, Saha, H. N et. al and Patnaik, R. et. al.	Mrabet et al., Phalaagae et al., Liu et al. and Sandeep al.	Khattak et al., Zhang N et al., Khattak HA et al. and Zhang J et al.	Burhanuddin et al., Burhan et al., Hamamreh et al., Lin J et al. and Jameel et al.	Tomić et al., Krishna et al., Puthal et al., Soni et al. and Frustaci et al.
Transport Layer	Claeys T. et. al, Gunnarsson et. al and Ahmad et. al	Li P et. al, AF Khan et. al and Mrabet et. al.	Khattak et al., Dizdarevic J et. al, Mars D et. al.	Banerjee et. al, Unwala et. al, Kamble et. al and Y Yilmaz et. al.	A Haroon et al., K Sha et al., S Deshmukh et al. and Y Yang et al.
Application Layer	M. Jamali et al., H Mrabet et al. and A. Raghuvanshi et al.	G Nebbione et al., A. Bhattacharjya et al. and A Tewari et al.	Khattak et al., Hofer-Schmitz et al., M. A da Cruz et al. and M Ahmad et al.	A Kamble et al., Burhan et al., Y Qian et al. and S.Rizvi et al.	Nastase L et al., Swamy SN et al., S Swamy et al., L Nastase et al. and S Vashi et al.

IoT Enabled Application of Industry 4.0 Vulnerable to Cyber-Attacks.

The various applications of the Internet are endless, as it can provide various useful information about its operation. Some of these include monitoring different activities and even controlling them from a distance.

Healthcare

Although the Internet of Things is still in its early stages, it has already developed many useful applications in healthcare. Some of these include monitoring UV radiation levels and temperature. The emergence of the Internet of Things enabled remote monitoring of healthcare has raised the bar for delivering effective and safe care. It has also improved the efficiency of healthcare by reducing costs and improving patient satisfaction. There are a variety of applications in healthcare. Table 8 shows the IoT enabled healthcare tools used for the real-time applications.

IoT for Patients: Wearable devices are becoming more prevalent in today's world. They allow patients to monitor and control their vital signs and get personalized attention.

IoT for Physicians: With the help of wearable devices and home monitoring equipment, healthcare professionals can monitor patients' health and provide them with the most effective treatment and follow-up care.

IoT for Hospitals: Aside from monitoring patients, hospitals also benefit from using the Internet of Things. Aside from monitoring their patients, hospitals also benefit from using the devices for other applications such as asset management and security. Real-time data collection enabled by the Internet of Things is used to monitor and secure the locations of medical equipment such as oxygen pumps and wheelchair-mounted defibrillators.

IoT for Health Insurance Organizations: Health insurers can use the data collected through IoT-connected devices to improve their operations and identify fraudulent claims. This data will help them identify potential customers and minimize risk. Insurers can offer incentives to their customers who use and share the data generated by the Internet of Things (IoT) devices. These devices can help improve the quality of their health care services and lower claims.

Table 7. Types of security attacks and vulnerabilities in the Layered architecture of 4.0 industry

Layer	Sensing Layer	Transport Layer	Application Layer	Physical Layer	Network Layer
Malicious Code Injection		✖	✖		
Denial of Service (DoS)	✖	✖	✖	✖	✖
Phising		✖		✖	✖
Sybil Attack	✖				✖
Replay Attack	✖		✖	✖	✖
False Node Injection	✖				✖
Malicious Code Injection	✖	✖	✖		
Device Cloning	✖			✖	✖
Substitution Attacks	✖	✖			
Node Jamming	✖	✖	✖	✖	✖
Selective Forwarding	✖	✖			
Intervention	✖		✖	✖	✖
Node compromise	✖				
Node Authentication	✖		✖	✖	✖
Uniform Encoding for RFID	✖	✖			✖
Side Channel Attack	✖		✖	✖	
Synchronization attack	✖			✖	✖
Eavesdropping	✖	✖	✖		✖
Spoofing	✖	✖	✖	✖	✖
Connectivity		✖	✖		✖
Compatibility		✖		✖	✖
Sink Hole Attack		✖			
Routing Information Attack		✖			✖
False Routing		✖	✖	✖	✖
Impersonation		✖	✖		✖
Buffer Overflow		✖	✖		✖
Breach of Confidenciality	✖	✖	✖		✖
Software Bugs	✖		✖		
Malicious Script	✖	✖	✖		✖
Virus	✖		✖	✖	✖
Worms	✖		✖	✖	✖
Spyware	✖	✖	✖	✖	✖

Challenges and Issues

Due to the nature of the Internet of Things (IoT), healthcare providers have many challenges when it comes to protecting their patients' data. Most of the devices that are used for monitoring and processing data have no security protocols or requirements. This makes them vulnerable to exploitation. Table present in detail review of research about the challenges and issues faced by IOT enabled healthcare applications.

Table 8. List of IOT enabled healthcare tools

Name of tool	Description	Ref.
QuardioCore	The Philips Health Tracker is a wearable device that provides continuous data about a person's health condition. It works by telling the user's doctor about their condition, allowing them to take immediate action. Aside from monitoring a person's health, it also sends data to a healthcare center.	(QardioCore., 2021)
Zanthion	A medical alert system is worn by a patient as a piece of clothing or jewelry. It uses a series of sensors to measure the wearer's health and welfare.	(zanthion, 2021)
Screencloud	There are plenty of healthcare organizations that are already using digital signage to improve the patient experience. For instance, hospitals can benefit from using video art to create stress-relieving videos for their patients.	(ScreenCloud, 2021)
Up by Jawbones	Instead of just keeping track of steps and calories, the Fit Tracker can also be used to monitor other aspects of a person's health, such as their sleep patterns and overall physical activity levels. It's also being used by patient groups to support those with health issues.	(Prnewswire,2021)
Sensor Metrix	These machines are used in hospitals and laboratories to maintain the proper temperature for the storage of medical samples and supplies.	(The Matrix, 2021)
UroSense	UroSense is a smart device that monitors the body temperature and urine output of patients during a catheterization. It can detect when a patient has a fever and alert the doctor.	(The Matrix, 2021)
Smart Thermometer	Kinsa's smart thermometer is a device that can detect the presence of illness and collect data on its users. It can also map human illness and provide helpful analysis.	Koehler, E., & Van, P. (2021)

Protocol diversity

Aside from the various devices that are connected to the same network, the lack of a uniform communication protocol also makes it hard to gather data from the various devices. This issue also affects the overall operations of the connected healthcare industry.

Security and privacy

One of the main issues with the Internet of Things is security. Due to the variety of protocols and the lack of clear regulations regarding the ownership of data, it is prone to exploitation.

Data overloading

Due to the varying communication protocols and standards used for data aggregation, it is hard to get a full view of the vast amount of data that is collected by the Internet of Things. This issue has become a real concern for doctors as it affects their quality of decision-making.

COUNTER MEASURES AND MITIGATION TECHNIQUES FOR IOT ENABLED APPLICATION OF INDUSTRY 4.0.

Defense Mechanism against SCA Attacks

Although it is very difficult to prevent side channel attacks (SCA), implementing several countermeasures can make them harder to achieve. On the hardware side, physical unclonable functions and shielding

Table 9. Challenges faced by IoT/IoMT enabled healthcare industry

Category	Reference	Description
IoT device security Challenge	(O'Neill, M. et al., 2016).	This article present IoT device security challenges and proposed solutions for various types of challenges mentioned which includes hijacking, automation in device, insufficient testing & updations etc.
Network Segmentation	(Huang, C. et al., 2021)	The draft provides a fault-resistant network segmentation algorithm that can handle the recovery of various systems components of the Internet of Things. It avoids the use of centroids and the dependence on kernel matrices.
Legacy system	(Cam-Winget, N. et al., 2016)	The rapid emergence and evolution of Big Data and the Internet of Things have presented Modern Industrial Systems with new challenges and opportunities.
Media Jacking	(Dhanda, S. S et al., 2020)	The study on the use of lightweight cryptography in Internet of Things (IoT) has been presented.
User imprisonment	(Alghazo, J. et al., 2020)	Blockchain technology has been widely used in healthcare systems to keep track of the activities of the patients. Through biometric methods, it is possible to identify the individuals or groups of people who have been visiting the facilities and are related to the patients.
Traffic Interception	(Hussain, F. et al., 2021)	This study proposed framework, that generated a healthcare dataset which consists of both normal and cyber-attack traffic. After analyzing the data, they applied machine learning techniques to detect and prevent the cyber-attacks.
Authentication & Authorization	(Moustafa Mamdouh et al., 2021)	The goal of this study is to provide a comprehensive review of the various aspects of the IoHT or Internet of Medical Things.
Confidentiality	(Sadek I et al., 2019)	This study discusses some of the main features of the existing sleep trackers and the most common security and privacy concerns associated with them.
Integrity	(Sadek I et al., 2019)	The article aims to provide an overview of the various security and privacy considerations that are related to the data flow in MIoT.

from electromagnetic radiation are some of the most commonly used techniques to prevent these attacks. The power consumption of the device should be independent of the operating instructions. Some techniques are to use differential signals or to hide power spikes. Side-channel attacks are mainly focused on the relationship between leaked information and secret data. They can be prevented by either reducing the release of such information or making the leaked data uncorrelated to the secret data. Under the first category, displays have gained special shielding to reduce their electromagnetic emissions. They can also be protected from power-line conditioning and filtering. A noise jam is a countermeasure that prevents an adversary from accessing or launching a timed attack on a network. It works by reducing the amount of noise in the channel. In the case of timing attacks, the best countermeasure is to design software that is isochronous, which means it runs in an exact constant amount of time. This eliminates the need for secret values. One partial countermeasure against power attacks is to design software that is designed to be secure in its execution path. This means that all conditional branches are based on public information, and not on secret values. Another way to avoid non-isochronous code is to avoid accessing frequently used information in a cache. Doing so could reveal information about the frequency of memory use. Some of the solutions include hardware-based and software-based countermeasures. The former is more effective and can be deployed quickly, while the latter require manual work and may be prone to failure. The program counter and the constant-time 1 policies are commonly used to protect against side-channel attacks. These policies require that the control-flow of a program does not depend on secret secrets. Aside from being easy to implement, software-based countermeasures can also be supported by robust enforcement methods. Generally, they are defined in terms of an information flow policy that records leak information.

Sybil Defensive Measure Techniques

The time and location of vehicles and systems can be easily defended against Sybil attacks. Securing hardware is used to verify the authenticity of the user. Table 10 presents the comparison of Sybil attack detection methodologies.

Cooperative Sybil Defense: Due to the lack of knowledge or the capability of the users, the defense mechanism against Sybil attacks can be ineffective in some scenarios. One possible solution is to involve the mobile users in the defense efforts. They can easily detect the suspicious behavior of the users by sending their details to the servers. The servers could also confirm the detection of Sybil from mobile users. The cooperation between mobile users can also help prevent the exploitation of Sybil. The servers could detect the presence of Sybil attacks by monitoring the mobile users' activities. The users' cooperation could also help gather more knowledge about the attackers.

Privacy and Sybil Defense: Since many security tools collect various details of a user's activities, such as browsing history, contact history, and clickstream, it is important to prevent the privacy leakage during the defense. With proper cryptographic encryption, it can hide the real details of the cipher text, but it can also enable additional operations on the ciphertext. However, such an approach can require a huge increase in computational overheads.

Sybil Defense in MSNs: Some off-the-shelf solutions could not effectively detect Sybil attacks due to the lack of historical and global social graph data to learn about the attackers. Also, the lack of security measures for MSNs could make it hard to detect the attackers. One possible solution is to build a tight social structure within mobile users. This would help prevent the exploitation of their trust relationships. Mobile users would also be differentiated from the normal users due to their behavior.

Phishing Defensive Measure Techniques

Due to the nature of the phishing problem, it is important that we visualize the life cycle of the attacks, which is based on the types of phishing techniques and their lifecycle. We use the perspective of anti-phishing techniques to describe the life-cycle of the campaigns. The ability to detect phishing campaigns can be enhanced by learning from past campaigns. This method can be performed by a human observer or a machine learning algorithm.

Offensive Defense

This strategy is usually used to attack phishing campaigns that are designed to steal sensitive information. It works by flooding websites with fake credentials in order to make it harder for attackers to find the real ones. There are two main types of solutions that can be used for detecting and preventing phishing attacks: content-based solutions and non-content-based solutions.

Non-Content-Based Methods: non-content-based methods are those that classify email and web pages based on the information that's not part of the message or the webpage. These approaches can be used to prevent phishing attacks.

Table 10: Sybil detection technique comparison

Scheme	Attack Type	Feature	Assumption	Technique
SNSD	SA-1	Centralized	Assumption-I	Random Walk, Social Graph Partition
SCSD		Centralized and De-centralized	Assumption-II	Community Detection
BCSD	SA-2	Centralized and De-centralized	Behavior difference	Behavior Classification
FR MSD	SA-3	De-centralized	Trusted community features	Profile Matching & community Detection
Feature-MSD		De-centralized	Wireless channel	Feature Classification/Channel Estimation
Crypto MSD		De-centralized	Security of Cryptography	Cryptography

Content Based Methods: The content of a page or an email is often classified according to its contents (Zhang et al., 2007). Most of the time, these methods rely on the information contained within the page or the email. Other methods include visual similarity and machine learning (ML).

Spam Filtering Techniques: Spam filtering techniques such as statistical classifiers and spam filtering are also used to identify phishing emails. The various technical solutions for anti-phishing attacks are available at various levels of delivery chain. These include mail servers, Internet Service Providers, and web browser tools. Techniques such as scanning the web to detect fake websites. Another type of phishing attack is called content-based phishing, which is carried out by analyzing the various elements of a website. Techniques to prevent phishing attacks from reaching the user's system. An anti-spam tool can block suspicious emails. Also, it can prevent users from clicking on links in emails. Techniques such as grammar correction and spelling check are commonly used to detect fake emails. A new algorithm that uses the Random Forest algorithm was developed to identify phishing emails. The algorithm can also classify them depending on their various features.

Corrective Defense

Correction techniques are focused on taking down a phishing campaign. In most cases, this involves suspending a website or removing phishing files. Securing a domain name from phishing attacks is also a correction method. Social networking services such as Facebook and Twitter can be used to target victims and trick them into revealing their passwords. The shutdown of these services can be initiated by various organizations that provide services related to security, such as email accounts and web hosting. Some of these include banks and financial firms. The following procedures are used to prevent the exploitation of bots and other harmful software: Totrace back and shutdown of compromised email accounts. They can also be initiated by organizations that offer services that are used by phishing attackers. To take down a compromised website, its content should be redirected to a secure server, and its Internet Service Provider should block it. This process is carried out to prevent users from getting victimized by phishing. Phishing providers can also voluntarily take these sites down by notifying them through takedown notices.

Preventive Defense

Different phishing prevention techniques are defined differently depending on the context. As a result, the terms phishing attack prevention and phishing detection techniques can be confusing. Due to the complexity of the investigations, it can take a long time to complete. Therefore, it is usually beneficial to avoid resorting to more drastic measures such as spamming techniques.

- Learn how to identify phishing attacks and how to avoid clicking on links that are fake. Also, be aware that the domain name of the website that's being used for the phishing attack is not the same as the company's domain.
- Many spam filters can be used to prevent emails from being sent from suspicious sources. Two factor authentication should also be implemented to prevent unauthorized users from accessing accounts.
- Authentication and authorization techniques are used to prevent exploitation of a protected resource. These procedures verify the identity of the user before they can access it.
- Security tools that are embedded in the browser to warn the users about suspicious websites. Some of these tools can also block known phishing sites. A study conducted in 2006 revealed that various anti-phishing tools performed well against known phishing sites. However, they were not able to prevent people from falling victim to fraudulent activities.

CONCLUSION

Due to the increasing popularity of cyber security, research in this field is required to address the many security issues that arise when an insider attack is performed. This paper aims to provide a comprehensive review of the current state of cyber security research and to provide new directions for the study of this field. Cyber security vulnerability lists are organized by the frequency of their occurrence. They are usually triggered by denial-of-service attacks and malware. The percentage of organizations that were attacked has shown the need for a comprehensive information security framework. There is also a need to create a transparent and secure mechanism to prevent attacks on sensitive information.

The study on security challenges in IoT and industry 4.0 was carried out to analyze the various aspects of securing the connected supply chains. One of the most critical factors that will affect the success of the industrial revolution is the security of the data collected by the devices. Despite the advantages of the Internet of Things, it still faces many security challenges. To overcome these obstacles, the use of computational intelligence techniques such as Evolutionary Computation will play an important role in the development of smart manufacturing and cyber intelligent applications. Furthermore, due to the complexity of the IIoT's operations and the need to manage the varying dimensions of data, implementing effective and efficient data management techniques is a must. Although the encryption and key management techniques are already widely used in the IIoT environment, their implementation is still subject to various constraints and can be very time-consuming.

REFERENCES

Abrams, L. (2021). *HDD Cryptor Ransomware Overwrites Your MBR Using Open Source Tools*. Retrieved 20 October 2021, from https://www.bleepingcomputer.com/news/security/hddcryptor-ransomware-overwrites-your-mbr-using-open-source-tools/

Ahmad, M., Riaz, Q., Zeeshan, M., Tahir, H., Haider, S. A., & Khan, M. S. (2021). Intrusion detection in internet of things using supervised machine learning based on application and transport layer features using UNSW-NB15 data-set. *EURASIP Journal on Wireless Communications and Networking, 2021*(1), 1–23. doi:10.118613638-021-01893-8

Ahmad, M., Younis, T., Habib, M. A., Ashraf, R., & Ahmed, S. H. (2019). A review of current security issues in Internet of Things. *Recent trends and advances in wireless and IoT-enabled networks*, 11-23.

Alenezi, M., Almustafa, K., & Meerja, K. A. (2019). Cloud based SDN and NFV architectures for IoT infrastructure. *Egypt Inform J., 20*(1), 1–10. doi:10.1016/j.eij.2018.03.004

Alghazo, J., Rathee, G., Gupta, S., Quasim, M. T., Murugan, S., Latif, G., & Dhasarathan, V. (2020). A Secure Multimedia Processing through Blockchain in Smart Healthcare Systems. *ACM Trans. Multimedia Comput. Commun. Appl.*. doi:10.1145/3396852

Alsaedi, N., Hashim, F., Sali, A., & Rokhani, F. Z. (2017). Detecting sybil attacks in clustered wireless sensor networks based on energy trust system (ETS). *Computer Communications, 110*, 75–82. doi:10.1016/j.comcom.2017.05.006

Ampel, B., Samtani, S., Zhu, H., Ullman, S., & Chen, H. (2020). Labeling hacker exploits for proactive cyber threat intelligence: a deep transfer learning approach. *Proceedings of the 2020 IEEE International Conference on Intelligence and Security Informatics (ISI)*, 1–6. 10.1109/ISI49825.2020.9280548

Associates, A. (2021). *Piping botnet: Researchers warns of possible cyberattacks against urban water services*. Retrieved 19 October 2021, from https://securityaffairs.co/wordpress/75389/hacking/piping-botnet-water-services.html

Banerjee, U., Juvekar, C., Wright, A., & Chandrakasan, A. P. (2018, February). An energy-efficient reconfigurable DTLS cryptographic engine for End-to-End security in iot applications. In *2018 IEEE International Solid-State Circuits Conference-(ISSCC)* (pp. 42-44). IEEE. 10.1109/ISSCC.2018.8310174

Bannister, A. (2022). *New York Attorney General flags 1.1 million online accounts compromised by credential stuffing attacks* [Blog]. Retrieved 24 January 2022, from https://portswigger.net/daily-swig/new-york-attorney-general-flags-1-1-million-online-accounts-compromised-by-credential-stuffing-attacks

Bao, Z., Shi, W., He, D., & Chood, K. K. R. (2018). *Iotchain: A three-tier blockchain-based iot security architecture*. arXiv preprint arXiv:1806.02008.2018

Barthe, G., Grégoire, B., & Laporte, V. (2018). Secure Compilation of Side-Channel Countermeasures: The Case of Cryptographic "Constant-Time". *2018 IEEE 31st Computer Security Foundations Symposium (CSF)*, 328-343. doi: 10.1109/CSF.2018.00031

Baza, M. (n.d.). Detecting Sybil Attacks using Proofs of Work and Location in VANETs. *IEEE Transactions on Dependable and Secure Computing*. Advance online publication. doi:10.1109/TDSC.2020.2993769

Baza, M., Nabil, M., Mahmoud, M. M. E. A., Bewermeier, N., Fidan, K., Alasmary, W., & Abdallah, M. (2020). Detecting sybil attacks using proofs of work and location in vanets. *IEEE Transactions on Dependable and Secure Computing*.

BBC News. (2021). *Hacker tries to poison water supply of Florida city*. Retrieved from https://www.bbc.com/news/world-us-canada-55989843

Bhattacharjya, A., Zhong, X., Wang, J., & Li, X. (2020). CoAP—application layer connection-less lightweight protocol for the Internet of Things (IoT) and CoAP-IPSEC Security with DTLS Supporting CoAP. In *Digital Twin Technologies and Smart Cities* (pp. 151–175). Springer. doi:10.1007/978-3-030-18732-3_9

Burhan, M., Rehman, R. A., Khan, B., & Kim, B. S. (2018). IoT elements, layered architectures and security issues: A comprehensive survey. *Sensors (Basel)*, *18*(9), 2796. doi:10.339018092796 PMID:30149582

Burhanuddin, M. A., Mohammed, A. A. J., Ismail, R., Hameed, M. E., Kareem, A. N., & Basiron, H. (2018). A review on security challenges and features in wireless sensor networks: IoT perspective. *Journal of Telecommunication, Electronic and Computer Engineering (JTEC)*, *10*(1-7), 17-21.

Cam-Winget, N., Sadeghi, A. R., & Jin, Y. (2016, June). Can IoT be secured: Emerging challenges in connecting the unconnected. In *2016 53nd ACM/EDAC/IEEE Design Automation Conference (DAC)* (pp. 1-6). IEEE.

Casey, W., Kellner, A., Memarmoshrefi, P., Morales, J. A., & Mishra, B. (2018). Deception, identity, and security: The game theory of sybil attacks. *Communications of the ACM*, *62*(1), 85–93. doi:10.1145/3190836

Cheng, M., Crow, M., & Erbacher, R. F. (2013). Vulnerability analysis of a smart grid with monitoring and control system. In *Proceedings of the Eighth Annual Cyber Security and Information Intelligence Research Workshop*. ACM. 10.1145/2459976.2460042

Claeys, T., Vučinić, M., Watteyne, T., Rousseau, F., & Tourancheau, B. (2021). Performance of the Transport Layer Security Handshake Over 6TiSCH. *Sensors (Basel)*, *21*(6), 2192. doi:10.339021062192 PMID:33801018

Cutting-edge Tech Solutions for Seniors and Caregivers. (2021). Retrieved 27 November 2021, from https://zanthion.com/about-us/

Da Cruz, M. A., Rodrigues, J. J., Lorenz, P., Solic, P., Al-Muhtadi, J., & Albuquerque, V. H. C. (2019). A proposal for bridging application layer protocols to HTTP on IoT solutions. *Future Generation Computer Systems*, *97*, 145–152.

Danial, J., Das, D., Ghosh, S., Raychowdhury, A., & Sen, S. (2020). SCNIFFER: Low-Cost, Automated, Efficient Electromagnetic Side-Channel Sniffing. *IEEE Access: Practical Innovations, Open Solutions*, *8*, 173414–173427. doi:10.1109/ACCESS.2020.3025022

Deshmukh, S., & Sonavane, S. S. (2017, March). Security protocols for Internet of Things: A survey. In *2017 International conference on Nextgen electronic technologies: Silicon to software (ICNETS2)* (pp. 71-74). IEEE.

Dhanda, S. S., Singh, B., & Jindal, P. (2020). Lightweight cryptography: A solution to secure IoT. *Wireless Personal Communications, 112*(3), 1947–1980.

Dizdarevic, J., Carpio, F., Jukan, A., & Masip-Bruin, X. (2019). A survey of communication protocols for internet of things and related challenges of fog and cloud computing integration. *ACM Computing Surveys, 51*(6), 1–29,116.

Ebrahimi, M., Nunamaker, J. F., & Chen, H. (2020). Semi-supervised cyber threat identification in dark net markets: A transductive and deep learning approach. *Journal of Management Information Systems, 37*(3), 694–722.

Ferencz, Domokos, & Kovács. (2021). Review of Industry 4.0 Security Challenges. *2021 IEEE 15th International Symposium on Applied Computational Intelligence and Informatics (SACI)*, 245-248. doi: 10.1109/SACI51354.2021.9465613

Frustaci, M., Pace, P., Aloi, G., & Fortino, G. (2017). Evaluating critical security issues of the IoT world: Present and future challenges. *IEEE Internet of Things Journal, 5*(4), 2483-2495.

Gonzalez-Amarillo, C., Cardenas-Garcia, C., Mendoza-Moreno, M., Ramirez-Gonzalez, G., & Corrales, J. C. (2021). Blockchain-IoT Sensor (BIoTS): A Solution to IoT-Ecosystems Security Issues. *Sensors (Basel), 21*(13), 4388.

Gunnarsson, M., Brorsson, J., Palombini, F., Seitz, L., & Tiloca, M. (2021). Evaluating the performance of the OSCORE security protocol in constrained IoT environments. *Internet of Things, 13*, 100333.

Hamamreh, J. M., Furqan, H. M., & Arslan, H. (2018). Classifications and applications of physical layer security techniques for confidentiality: A comprehensive survey. *IEEE Communications Surveys and Tutorials, 21*(2), 1773–1828.

Hamdan, S., Hudaib, A., & Awajan, A. (2021). Detecting Sybil attacks in vehicular ad hoc networks. *International Journal of Parallel, Emergent and Distributed Systems, 36*(2), 69–79.

Hamed, A., & Khalek, A. A. (2019). Acoustic Attacks in the Era of IoT - A Survey. *2019 Amity International Conference on Artificial Intelligence (AICAI)*, 855-858. 10.1109/AICAI.2019.8701340

Haroon, A., Akram, S., Shah, M. A., & Wahid, A. (2017, September). E-Lithe: A lightweight secure DTLS for IoT. In *2017 IEEE 86th Vehicular Technology Conference (VTC-Fall)* (pp. 1-5). IEEE.

Hofer-Schmitz, K., & Stojanović, B. (2019, November). Towards formal methods of IoT application layer protocols. In *2019 12th CMI conference on cybersecurity and privacy (CMI)* (pp. 1-6). IEEE.

Huang, C., Guo, Y., Guo, W., & Li, Y. (2021). HackerRank: Identifying key hackers in underground forums. *International Journal of Distributed Sensor Networks, 17*(5). doi:10.1177/15501477211015145

Huang, C., Zong, Y., Chen, J., Liu, W., Lloret, J., & Mukherjee, M. (2021). A deep segmentation network of stent structs based on IoT for interventional cardiovascular diagnosis. *IEEE Wireless Communications*, *28*(3), 36–43.

Hussain, F., Abbas, S. G., Shah, G. A., Pires, I. M., Fayyaz, U. U., Shahzad, F., Garcia, N. M., & Zdravevski, E. (2021). A Framework for Malicious Traffic Detection in IoT Healthcare Environment. *Sensors (Basel)*, *21*, 3025. https://doi.org/10.3390/s21093025

IEC 61784-1:2014: Industrial communication networks – Profiles – Part 1: Fieldbus profiles. 2014https://webstore.iec.ch/publication/5878

ISA99. Developing the Vital ISA/IEC 62443 Series of Standards on Industrial Automation and Control Systems (IACS) Security. 2001http://isa99.isa.org/

ISA99. Developing the ISA/IEC 62443 Series of Standards on Industrial Automation and Control Systems (IACS). 2017http://isa99.isa.org/ISA9920Wiki/ Home.aspx/

ISO/IEC 27019 Information technology – security techniques – information security controls for the energy utility industry. 2017https://www.iso.org/standard/68091.html

ISO/IEC 27033-1:2015 Preview Information Technology-Security techniques –Network security – Part 1: Overview and concepts. 2015https://www.iso.org/standard/63461.html

ISO/IEC 29180: 2012 Information technology – Telecommunications and information exchange between systems – Security framework forubiquitous sensor networks. 2012https://www.iso.org/standard/45259.html

ISO/IEC TR 27019:2013: Information technology – security techniques – information security management guidelines based on ISO/IEC 27002 for process control systems specific to the energy utility industry. 2013https://www.iso.org/standard/43759.html

Jamali, M. A. J., Bahrami, B., Heidari, A., Allahverdizadeh, P., & Norouzi, F. (2020). IoT security. In *Towards the Internet of Things* (pp. 33–83). Springer.

Jameel, F., Wyne, S., Kaddoum, G., & Duong, T. Q. (2019). A comprehensive survey on cooperative relaying and jamming strategies for physical layer security. *IEEE Communications Surveys and Tutorials*, *21*(3), 2734–2771.

James, J. Q. (2020). Sybil attack identification for crowdsourced navigation: A self-supervised deep learning approach. *IEEE Transactions on Intelligent Transportation Systems*.

Jawbone Announces New UP App for Smartphones, Smartwatches and Wearables. (2021). Retrieved 20 December 2021, from https://www.prnewswire.com/news-releases/jawbone-announces-new-up-app-for-smartphones-smartwatches-and-wearables-274541851.html

Kamble, A., & Bhutad, S. (2018, January). Survey on Internet of Things (IoT) security issues & solutions. In *2018 2nd International Conference on Inventive Systems and Control (ICISC)* (pp. 307-312). IEEE.

Karmakar, K.K., Varadharajan, V., Nepal, S., & Tupakula, U. (2019). SDN enabled secure IoT architecture. In *2019 IFIP/IEEE symposium on integrated network and service management (IM)* (pp. 581-585). IEEE.

Khan, A. F., & Anandharaj, G. (2020). A Multi-layer Security approach for DDoS detection in Internet of Things. *International Journal of Intelligent Unmanned Systems*.

Khandpur, R. P. (2017). Crowdsourcing cybersecurity: Cyber-attack detection using social media. In *Proceedings of the 2017 ACM on Conference on Information and Knowledge Management*. ACM.

Khattak, H. A., Shah, M. A., Khan, S., Ali, I., & Imran, M. (2019). Perception layer security in internet of things. *Future Generation Computer Systems*, *100*, 144–164.

Khattak, H. A., Shah, M. A., Khan, S., Ali, I., & Imran, M. (2019). Perception layer security in Internet of Things. *Future Generation Computer Systems*, *100*, 144–164.

Koehler, E., & Van, P. (2021). *Shop Award-Winning Smart Thermometers | Kinsa Health*. Retrieved 27 November 2021, from https://kinsahealth.com/shop

Koloveas, P., Chantzios, T., Alevizopoulou, S., Tryfonopoulos, S., & Tryfonopoulos, C. (2021). INTIME: A machine learning-based framework for gathering and leveraging web data to cyber-threat intelligence. *Electronics (Basel)*, *10*(7), 818.

Koloveas, P., Chantzios, T., Tryfonopoulos, C., & Skiadopoulos, S. (2019). A crawler architecture for harvesting the clear, social, and dark web for IoT-related cyber-threat intelligence. *Proceedings of the 2019 IEEE World Congress on Services*, 3–8.

Krishna, B. S., & Gnanasekaran, T. (2017, February). A systematic study of security issues in Internet-of-Things (IoT). In *2017 International Conference on I-SMAC (IoT in Social, Mobile, Analytics and Cloud)(I-SMAC)* (pp. 107-111). IEEE.

Leukfeldt & Holt. (2020). Examining the social organization practices of cybercriminals in -e Netherlands online and offline. *International Journal of Offender 'erapy and Comparative Criminology*, *64*(5), 522–538.

Leyden, J. (2021). *Tor Project unveils plans to route device traffic through Tor anonymity network with new VPN-like service* [Blog]. Retrieved 24 January 2022, from https://portswigger.net/daily-swig/tor-project-unveils-plans-to-route-device-traffic-through-tor-anonymity-network-with-new-vpn-like-service

Li, P., Su, J., & Wang, X. (2020). iTLS: Lightweight Transport-Layer Security Protocol for IoT With Minimal Latency and Perfect Forward Secrecy. *IEEE Internet of Things Journal*, *7*(8), 6828–6841.

Li, Z., Zou, D., Xu, S., Jin, H., Qi, H., & Hu, J. (2016). VulPecker: an automated vulnerability detection system based on code similarity analysis. In *Proceedings of the 32nd Annual Conference on Computer Security Applications* (pp. 201–213). ACM.

Liggett, Lee, Roddy, & Wallin. (2020). -e dark web as a platform for crime: an exploration of illicit drug, firearm, CSAM, and cybercrime markets. In *Palgrave Handbook of International Cybercrime and Cyberdeviance*. Palgrave Macmillan.

Lin, J., Yu, W., Zhang, N., Yang, X., Zhang, H., & Zhao, W. (2017). A survey on internet of things: Architecture, enabling technologies, security and privacy, and applications. *IEEE Internet Things J.*, *4*(5), 1125–1142.

Liu, J., Hu, Q., Suny, R., Du, X., & Guizani, M. (2020, June). A physical layer security scheme with compressed sensing in OFDM-based IoT systems. In *ICC 2020-2020 IEEE International Conference on Communications (ICC)* (pp. 1-6). IEEE.

Mamdouh, M., Awad, A. I., Khalaf, A. A. M., & Hamed, H. F. A. (2021). Authentication and Identity Management of IoHT Devices: Achievements, Challenges, and Future Directions. *Computers & Security, 111.* doi:10.1016/j.cose.2021.102491

Marin, E., Almukaynizi, M., & Shakarian, P. (2019). Reasoning about future cyber-attacks through socio-technical hacking information. *Proceedings of the 2019 IEEE 31st International Conference on Tools with Artificial Intelligence (ICTAI)*, 157–164.

Mars, D., Gammar, S. M., Lahmadi, A., & Saidane, L. A. (2019). Using information centric networking in internet of things: A survey. *Wireless Personal Communications*, *105*(1), 87–103.

Masi, D., Fischer, M. J., Shortle, J. F., & Chen, C.-H. (2011). Simulating network cyber-attacks using splitting techniques. ACM. In *Proceedings of the Winter Simulation Conference* (pp. 3217–3228). Winter Simulation Conference.

Medjek, F., Tandjaoui, D., Romdhani, I., & Djedjig, N. (2017, June). A trust-based intrusion detection system for mobile RPL based networks. In *2017 IEEE International Conference on Internet of Things (iThings) and IEEE Green Computing and Communications (GreenCom) and IEEE Cyber, Physical and Social Computing (CPSCom) and IEEE Smart Data (SmartData)* (pp. 735-742). IEEE.

Middleton, P., Graham, C., Blackmore, D., Sharpington, K., Singh, H., Velosa, A., & Lheureux, B. (2021). *Forecast: IT Services for IoT, Worldwide, 2019-2025*. Retrieved 28 October 2021, from https://www.gartner.com/en/documents/4004741/forecast-it-services-for-iot-worldwide-2019-2025

Millenson, M. (2021). *'The Matrix' Meets Medicine: Surveillance Swoops Into Health Care*. Retrieved 20 December 2021, from https://khn.org/news/matrix-meets-medicine/

Molnar, D., Piotrowski, M., Schultz, D., & Wagner, D. A. (2005). The program counter security model: Automatic detection and removal of control-flow side channel attacks. *Information Security and Cryptology - ICISC 2005 8th International Conference*, 156-168.

Mrabet, H., Belguith, S., Alhomoud, A., & Jemai, A. (2020). A survey of IoT security based on a layered architecture of sensing and data analysis. *Sensors (Basel)*, *20*(13), 3625.

Nastase, L. (2017, May). Security in the internet of things: A survey on application layer protocols. In *2017 21st international conference on control systems and computer science (CSCS)* (pp. 659-666). IEEE.

Nastase, L. (2017). Security in the internet of things: a survey on application layer protocols. In *2017 21st International Conference on Control Systems and Computer Science (CSCS)* (pp. 659-666). IEEE.

Nebbione, G., & Calzarossa, M. C. (2020). Security of IoT application layer protocols: Challenges and findings. *Future Internet*, *12*(3), 55.

NTT Com confirms possible information leak due to unauthorized access. (2021). Retrieved 19 October 2021, from https://www.ntt.com/en/about-us/press-releases/news/article/2020/0702.html

O'Neill, M. (2016). Insecurity by design: Today's IoT device security problem. *Engineering*, 2(1), 48–49.

Okutan, A., Yang, S. J., & McConky, K. (2017). Predicting cyber-attacks with bayesian networks using unconventional signals. In *Proceedings of the 12th Annual Conference on Cyber and Information Security Research* (p. 13). ACM.

Patnaik, R., Padhy, N., & Raju, K. S. (2021). A systematic survey on IoT security issues, vulnerability and open challenges. In *Intelligent System Design* (pp. 723–730). Springer.

Phalaagae, P., Zungeru, A. M., Sigweni, B., Chuma, J. M., & Semong, T. (2020). Iot sensor networks security mechanisms/techniques. In *Green Internet of Things Sensor Networks* (pp. 97–117). Springer.

Puthal, D., Ranjan, R., Nepal, S., & Chen, J. (2017). IoT and big data: An architecture with data flow and security issues. In *Cloud infrastructures, services, and IoT systems for smart cities* (pp. 243–252). Springer.

Qian, Y., Jiang, Y., Chen, J., Zhang, Y., Song, J., Zhou, M., & Pustišek, M. (2018). Towards decentralized IoT security enhancement: A blockchain approach. *Computers & Electrical Engineering*, 72, 266–273.

Queiroz, A. L., Mckeever, S., & Keegan, B. (2019). Detecting hacker threats: performance of word and sentence embedding models in identifying hacker communications. *Proceedings of the 27th AIAI Irish Conference on Artificial Intelligence and Cognitive Science AICS 2019*, 116–127.

Raghuvanshi, A., & Singh, U. K. (2020). Internet of Things for smart cities-security issues and challenges. *Materials Today: Proceedings*.

Rajaharia, R. (2022). Covid-19 Related Data Of 20,000 Indians Leaked Online. *Outlook India*. Retrieved 24 January 2022, from https://www.outlookindia.com/

Ransomware Impacting Pipeline Operations | CISA. (2021). Retrieved 20 October 2021, from https://us-cert.cisa.gov/ncas/alerts/aa20-049a

Reporting and Analysis Centre for Information Assurance MELANI. (2021). *Situation in Switzerland and internationally*. National Cybersecurity Centre NCSC & Federal Intelligence Service FIS. Retrieved from https://www.newsd.admin.ch/newsd/message/attachments/63536.pdf

Rizvi, S., Kurtz, A., Pfeffer, J., & Rizvi, M. (2018, August). Securing the internet of things (IoT): A security taxonomy for IoT. *2018 17th IEEE International Conference On Trust, Security And Privacy In Computing*.

Rosenberg, J. (2017). Embedded security. *Rugged Embedded Systems*, e1-e74. doi:10.1016/b978-0-12-802459-1.00011-7

Sadek, I., Rehman, S. U., Codjo, J., & Abdulrazak, B. (2019). Privacy and Security of IoT Based Healthcare Systems: Concerns, Solutions, and Recommendations. In J. Pagán, M. Mokhtari, H. Aloulou, B. Abdulrazak, & M. Cabrera (Eds.), Lecture Notes in Computer Science: Vol. 11862. How AI Impacts Urban Living and Public Health. ICOST 2019. Springer. https://doi.org/10.1007/978-3-030-32785-9_1.

Saha, H. N., Roy, R., Chakraborty, M., & Sarkar, C. (2021). IoT-Enabled Agricultural System Application, Challenges and Security Issues. *Agricultural Informatics: Automation Using the IoT and Machine Learning*, 223-247.

Samtani, S., Abate, M., Benjamin, V., & Li, W. (2020). Cybersecurity as an industry: a cyber threat intelligence perspective. In Palgrave Handbook of International Cybercrime and Cyberdeviance. Palgrave Macmillan.

Sandberg, H. (2021). *A Risk Management Approach to Cyber-Physical Security in Networked Control Systems*. Retrieved 19 October 2021, from https://cnls.lanl.gov/External/GSSlides2021/Sandberg.pdf

Sandeep, C. H., Naresh Kumar, S., & Pramod Kumar, P. (2020). Significant Role of Security in IOT Development and IOT Architecture. *Journal of Mechanics of Continua and Mathematical Sciences*, *15*(6), 174–184.

Schwartz, H. (2022). *Significant Cyber Incidents*. Center for Strategic and International Studies. Retrieved 24 January 2022, from https://www.csis.org/programs/strategic-technologies-program/significant-cyber-incidents

ScreenCloud – Digital Signage Software for Any Screen or TV. (2021). Retrieved 27 November 2021, from https://screencloud.com/

Searle, J. (2021). *Industrial Control Systems (ICS)*. SANS Institute. Retrieved 20 October 2021, from https://www.sans.org/industrial-control-systems-security/

Sha, K., Errabelly, R., Wei, W., Yang, T. A., & Wang, Z. (2017, May). Edgesec: Design of an edge layer security service to enhance iot security. In *2017 IEEE 1st International Conference on Fog and Edge Computing (ICFEC)* (pp. 81-88). IEEE.

Sharma, P. K., Singh, S., Jeong, Y. S., & Park, J. H. (2017). Distblocknet: A distributed blockchains-based secure sdn architecture for IoT networks. *IEEE Communications Magazine*, *55*(9), 78–85.

Smart Wearable, E. C. G. (2021). *EKG Monitor - QardioCore*. Retrieved 26 November 2021, from https://www.qardio.com/qardiocore-wearable-ecg-ekg-monitor-iphone/

Soni, A., Upadhyay, R., & Jain, A. (2017). Internet of Things and wireless physical layer security: A survey. In *Computer communication, networking and internet security* (pp. 115–123). Springer.

Swamy, S. N., Jadhav, D., & Kulkarni, N. (2017, February). Security threats in the application layer in IOT applications. In *2017 International conference on i-SMAC (iot in social, mobile, analytics and cloud)(i-SMAC)* (pp. 477-480). IEEE.

Swamy, S. N., Jadhav, D., & Kulkarni, N. (2017). Security threats in the application layer in IOT applications. In *2017 International Conference on ISMAC (IoT in Social, Mobile, Analytics and Cloud (I-SMAC)* (pp. 477-480). IEEE.

Taylor, M., & Bing, C. (2021). *Exclusive: China-backed hackers 'targeted COVID-19 vaccine firm Moderna'*. Retrieved 20 October 2021, from https://www.reuters.com/article/us-health-coronavirus-moderna-cyber-excl/exclusive-china-backed-hackers-targeted-covid-19-vaccine-firm-moderna-idUSKCN24V38M

Tewari, A., & Gupta, B. B. (2020). Security, privacy and trust of different layers in Internet-of-Things (IoTs) framework. *Future Generation Computer Systems, 108*, 909–920.

The Guardian. (2021). *How the Colonial Pipeline hack is part of a growing ransomware trend in the US.* Retrieved from https://www.theguardian.com/technology/2021/may/13/colonial-pipeline-ransomware-attack-cyber-crime

The Week in Dark Web. (2022). *Access Sales and Data Leaks.* SOCRadar® Cyber Intelligence Inc. Retrieved 24 January 2022, from https://socradar.io/the-week-in-dark-web-17-january-2022-access-sales-and-data-leaks/

Thompson, M. (2013). Iranian Cyber Attack on New York Dam Shows Future of War. *TIME*, 1-2. Retrieved from https://time.com/4270728/iran-cyber-attack-dam-fbi/

Tomić, I., & McCann, J. A. (2017). A survey of potential security issues in existing wireless sensor network protocols. *IEEE Internet of Things Journal, 4*(6), 1910–1923.

Tyagi, N. (2016). A reference architecture for IoT. *Int J Comput Eng Appl., 10*(1).

Unwala, I., Taqvi, Z., & Lu, J. (2018, April). Thread: An iot protocol. In *2018 IEEE Green Technologies Conference (GreenTech)* (pp. 161-167). IEEE.

Vashi, S., Ram, J., Modi, J., Verma, S., & Prakash, C. (2017, February). Internet of Things (IoT): A vision, architectural elements, and security issues. In *2017 international conference on I-SMAC (IoT in Social, Mobile, Analytics and Cloud)(I-SMAC)* (pp. 492-496). IEEE.

Werner, G., Yang, S., & McConky, K. (2017). Time series forecasting of cyber-attack intensity. In *Proceedings of the 12th Annual Conference on cyber and information security research* (p. 18). ACM.

Winder, D. (2022). Hack Attack Takes Down Dark Web Host: 7,595 Websites Confirmed Deleted. *Forbes*. Retrieved 24 January 2022, from https://www.forbes.com/sites/daveywinder/2020/03/30/hack-attack-takes-down-dark-web-7595-websites-confirmed-deleted/?sh=4b96a9241435

Xiao, L., Wan, X., & Han, Z. (2018, March). PHY-Layer Authentication With Multiple Landmarks With Reduced Overhead. *IEEE Transactions on Wireless Communications, 17*(3), 1676–1687. doi:10.1109/TWC.2017.2784431

Yan, Y. (2019). *Side Channel Attacks on IoT Applications (Ph.D)*. The University of Bristol.

Yang, Y., Wu, L., Yin, G., Li, L., & Zhao, H. (2017). A survey on security and privacy issues in Internet-of-Things. *IEEE Internet of Things Journal, 4*(5), 1250–1258.

Yilmaz, Y., Gunn, S. R., & Halak, B. (2018, July). Lightweight PUF-based authentication protocol for IoT devices. In *2018 IEEE 3rd international verification and security workshop (IVSW)* (pp. 38-43). IEEE.

Zanero, S. (2008). Ulisse, a network intrusion detection system. In *Proceedings of the 4th annual workshop on Cyber security and information intelligence research: developing strategies to meet the cyber security and information intelligence challenges ahead* (p. 20). ACM.

Zeadally, S., Adi, E., Baig, Z., & Khan, I. A. (2020). Harnessing artificial intelligence capabilities to improve cybersecurity. *IEEE Access: Practical Innovations, Open Solutions, 8*, 23817–23837.

Zenebe, A., Shumba, M., Carillo, A., & Cuenca, S. (2019). Cyber threat discovery from dark web. *Proceedings of the 28th International Conference on Software Engineering and Data Engineering.*

Zhang, J., Rajendran, S., Sun, Z., Woods, R., & Hanzo, L. (2019). Physical layer security for the internet of things: Authentication and key generation. *IEEE Wireless Communications, 26*(5), 92–98.

Zhang, N., Chen, D., Ye, F., Zheng, T. X., & Wei, Z. (2019). Physical layer security for internet of things. *Wireless Communications and Mobile Computing, 2019,* 1–2.

Zhang, N., Chen, D., Ye, F., Zheng, T. X., & Wei, Z. (2019). Physical layer security for internet of things. *Wireless Communications and Mobile Computing, 2019,* 1–2.

Section 3

Anomaly Detection Using Artificial Intelligence and Machine Learning Algorithms

Chapter 7
Artifical Intelligence and Machine Learning Algorithms in Dark Web Crime Recognition

Neha Nitin Gawali
https://orcid.org/0000-0003-0545-5189
NBN Sinhgad Technical Institute, Pune, India

Shailesh Bendale
NBN Sinhgad Technical Institute, Pune, India

ABSTRACT

Even with the dark web (DW) being accessible only through special software, global law enforcement agencies are considering it a major problem. The fact that activities happening on DW are completely untraceable has become the main point of attraction for the perpetrators. Also, in certain years, there has been improvement and advancement in the artificial intelligence (AI) as well as machine learning (ML) fields. Therefore, digital security based on AI is of immense benefit for the security industry. Thus, in response to the increasing use of AI and ML technologies, actions were taken against DW crimes, and applications for crime recognition were developed. This chapter is an attempt to discuss and show-case all the different aspects of applications of AI and ML in DW crime recognition. The author sheds light on the enormous benefits of these applications to the security industry as well as the investigators. Considering AI and ML work as double-edged swords in the cyber world, the author also mentions the importance for investigators to understand and practice them carefully.

INTRODUCTION

AI was turned into a hotly debated issue of logical discussion in 1950, owing to the way sci-fi books represent it. Fast-forwarding to the 21st century, AI and ML applications are becoming a powerful tool against DW crimes. This technology holds great promise for crime detection in the future. ML applications (Das,2019) have proved their significance in crime detection from time to time. Therefore, these

DOI: 10.4018/978-1-6684-6444-1.ch007

applications are becoming an indispensable part for all investigators online. To get the most out of this application one needs to understand these applications and make sure that these applications are in proper hands. With the increase in technology use, there is an increase in cybercrimes most specifically in DW crimes. Therefore, AI and ML applications are luxuries for the security industry and investigators. Applications such as Artificial Neural Networks (ANN), clustering, regression, Waikato Environment for Knowledge Analysis (WEKA), Support vector, black widow, etc. are some of the many applications that are used for dark web crime recognition. These applications are of huge help to investigators and have really leveled up the crime investigation game.

WHAT IS THE DARK WEB AND IS IT ILLEGAL?

DW is a larger part of the internet but completely different from the normal internet. DW is accessed only through certain encrypted browsers which allows it to remain in the shadow of the internet enclosed by encryptions. The activates and websites are completely inaccessible and there is no option of finding them through search engines. Perpetrators use this special feature of DW for conducting various illegal activates this became a major issue in the security industry and global law enforcement agencies. DW uses encryption to allow the users to remain anonymous, which gives DW its advantages and disadvantages. Since it is attractive to people included in illegal activities but is also important and useful for higher authorities, authoritarian states wishing to contact the outside world, media officials, and many similar masses. This is the exact reason that DW is not illegal but some of the activities conducted there are.(Findlaw,2021) Websites on DW are accessible through a special browser commonly through TOR ("The onion routing" project) browser. Some more browsers include I2P (it is not universal), Subgraph OS, Firefox, ISP (Invisible Internet Project). [4] To conclude, DW is not illegal to access or to use but the kind of activities one intends to carry on DW can be categorized into illegal or legally. The fact that DW is inaccessible is both a pulse point and a negative point which completely depends on the user's intentions. Therefore, one can conclude that the activities on DW are illegal but accessing or using DW is completely legal.

DIFFERENCE BETWEEN DARK WEB AND DEEP WEB

The deep web and dark web, both being completely anonymous and intractable by search engines, are often mistaken to be the same. When in reality both the deep web and the DW are patently different. Most of the time Dark web is also confused as "Dark internet" whereas the Dark internet consists of raw data which is used for scientific research and is not similar to the Dark web. Below are some major differences between "Dark Web" and "Deep Web".(O'hare,2020)

DARK WEB CRIMES

Various crimes take place on DW because of its ability to keep the user completely anonymous. Even though not all the users on DW are criminals but because DW web provides the undue advantage to

Table 1. Difference between deep web and dark web

Deep web	Dark web
The deep web is not the part of the dark web .	The dark web is the part of the deep web.
The deep web includes news sites existing behind paywalls, content of personal email or social media accounts, and similar pages.	Dark web includes websites with hidden IP addresses, small and big network that are completely anonymous operated by individuals or public organizations.
Regular search engines are not allowed(blocked) to index the content on deep web.	Content on the dark web can be accessed through specific encrypted browsers or networks.
One can access the deep web through valid password and username.	It is only accessible through special software or encrypted browsers.
It is 1000-2000X larger than the surface web.	It is 500X times larger than the surface web.

perpetrators the number of crimes is huge. Some of them include: hiring a murderer, illegal or child pornography, Blackmailing, selling of illegal drugs and arms, sex trafficking, terrorism, and many more.

Finance Fraud

Most dark web crimes include phishing through cloned sites and using scam websites which are often promoted via spoofed URLs. These frauds can be analysed by detecting consumers' method of transaction and recent patterns. ML and AI applications can analyze at a higher speed and can provide more accurate results if compared to humans. A huge amount of information can also be processed in less time without any human errors for detecting finance frauds and even a small change in consumers' behavior can be noted. This can help to stop this fraud even before taking place.

Illegal or Child Pornography

The content most popular on the dark web is illegal/child pornography. Even though it is difficult to access on the dark web too, 80% of traffic is there for this specific reason. Being anonymous advantage these site owners but various operations were carried against these criminals. Many sites with an abundance of followers were taken down after investigation. Investigators worldwide are looking up to these AI and ML applications as these applications have provided solutions against these crimes.

Blackmailing

Blackmailing is one of the majority of crimes that take place on the dark web on large scale. As bitcoin has become new-age money and has higher values, blackmailing has users of the dark web become easier. Perpetrators ask for an amount of bitcoin or cryptocurrency in exchange for information, passwords, or any personal information that one can get through the dark web by hacking or through illegal means.

Human Trafficking

A dark web website named Black Death gives rise to human trafficking. The majority of Survivors of human trafficking were for trafficking labor and sex states a 2017 survey report. Black death is a site known to conduct this crime by often changing the untraceable URLs.

Contract Killer

The dark web consists of several websites where one can hire a professional killer or murderer. Taking the advantage of the dark web being anonymous these professionals are not traceable but using AI and ML applications investigators can trace the chat as well as transactions done as payments to the killers, which results in tracing these perpetrators and thus stopping the crime.

Terrorism

Terrorists found the internet in the early 1990s, however, the dark web became the biggest benefit for these organizations. Chatting platform on the dark web is used to inspire and plan terrorist activities. Some content also includes "how-to" tutorials all about becoming a terrorist. With the introduction to Bitcoin, the terrorist also used DW for funds as well as receiving financial support while being completely anonymous.

Social Media

The dark web also contains social media apps very similar to WWW(world wide web) on the surface internet. This Dark web social network works like normal social media apps and sites. Even social media apps like Facebook are now trying to make their dark web versions so that they can address problems with regular platforms. But these network platforms do not need any personal information and can keep the user completely anonymous.

Dark Web Markets

Selling drugs and weapons on the dark web is easy for perpetrators. These markets not only sell various illegal information like information of payment cards, important blueprints, medical history to blackmail the person, and many more but they also include trading dangerous and illegal commodities which include stolen items, harmful weapons, drugs, endangered species of animals and various dangerous goods that one can not even expect.

CHALLENGES IN DW CRIME RECOGNITION

The biggest issue while recognizing and investigating the crimes on DW is that the large amount of data on the DW is instructed and formless. So, to investigate and recognize the crimes, investigators need to first collect and arrange the data. But that's not possible as DW users are completely anonymous and the sites used for committing crimes are untraceable. Not on users and URLs of the website but also the activity that can be considered as crime is completely hidden. Collecting huge data and tracing similar patterns related to a crime can be done with the help of AI and ML applications. The second biggest challenge can be to identify the target individual or the group conducting the crime. As DW is of complete underground nature, there's no data set available for investigators to investigate which means for every other crime, investigators need to investigate from the beginning with raw information. This problem again can be solved with AI and ML applications as this application stores data and can analyze more faster as compared to humans. As perpetrators keep changing the URLs, it makes tracing them harder for investors, and again storing data and observing behavior patterns of users by AI and ML can be the solution to this challenge.

Investigators Challenges

When investigating a case, investigators need pieces of evidence and proof in various forms. It becomes more difficult to investigate DW as these pieces of evidence are completely unavailable and the data collected cannot be considered as proof. Investigators need a complete understanding of the dark web, unstructured and structured data, and also access to the right browsers before investigation. The investigator needs to have the right understanding of IP address, cryptocurrency wallets, location, hashtags, websites, URLs, including others in order to use the data as support or evidence related to the case. Information found online should be further forwarded to a cycle of intelligence and on to various processes. Irrelevant information should be discarded and then proceed to solve the case. With all this complex process, there is no chance of error as one error can result in an unsolved case and the perpetrator walking away freely. (O'hare,2020) This is exactly when AI and ML applications come into the frame by eliminating human errors and making the process quick and less complex.

ARTIFICIAL INTELLIGENCE AND MACHINE LEARNING

Artificial Intelligence

Artificial intelligence (AI) (Builtin,n.d) focuses on building smart applications and machines that can perform various tasks that generally need human intelligence. There exist four different types of AI which include Reactive Machines, Limited Memory, Theory Of Mind, Self-Awareness.

1. *Reactive Machines*

It follows the basic principles of AI and, as the name states, it can only perceive the information and react to information in front. Being a reactive machine, it cannot store the information nor can depend on experiences in past for making decisions.

Examples:

    a.   Deep blue, a famous reactive chess-playing machine that was designed in the 1990s by IBM.
    b.   AlphaGo. A reactive machine that plays games and was designed by Google.
        2.   Limited Memory

It can store earlier data and make predictions while collecting information. It provides more possibilities and is highly complex compared to reactivate machines. Limited Memory needs training by individuals or a team to learn to analyze and utilize new and raw data. It can also be trained by creating an environment in which the machine can get trained automatically.

Examples:

a. Reinforcement learning.

b. Long short-term memory (LSTM).

c. Evolutionary Generative .

d. Adversarial Networks (E-GAN).

3. Theory of Mind

Humans are not yet able to reach this greater level of AI. It is just as its name says, Theoretical. As humans and animals have emotions and thought which affect one's behavior, the theory of mind is a step to achieve the same for machines.

4. *Self-Awareness*

After achieving the Theory of Mind, the last step will be machines being self-aware. These machines will have consciousness of human-level.

AI is widely used in daily life in the form of Siri, Alexa, Self-driving cars, email spam filters, Netflix recommendations, Google search, and many more. AI falls under two different and wide categories which are Narrow AI and Artificial General Intelligence (AGI).

Machine Learning

Machine learning (ML) is a part of AI which in general allows machines to learn and think like humans. ML applications improve by learning from past experiences. It uses various data, identifies vivid patterns, and also needs a bit of human involvement. From automating tasks like manually entering data, to more complicated situations like detecting fraud, ML has a large range of applications. The major ability of ML is, it can detect that which the human eye can miss. Complicated patterns that can be missed while analyzing by humans, can be detected with the help of machine learning. Perpetrators use a similar method over and over again once they found out that it is the safe way out from the investigators. ML applications can trace these repeating patterns or completely new patterns and can use this same data for crime recognition as well as crime prevention. (Algorithmia,2017)

Advantages

- It can help investigators detect crimes and understand users of the Dark web or any consumers of any website.
- By collecting and analyzing the data it can provide accurate results without any human errors.

Disadvantages

- It is expensive.
- These projects are typically done by data scientists, which generally take high salaries.
- Sometimes it can provide biased decisions.

Figure 1. Understanding AI, ML and deep learning

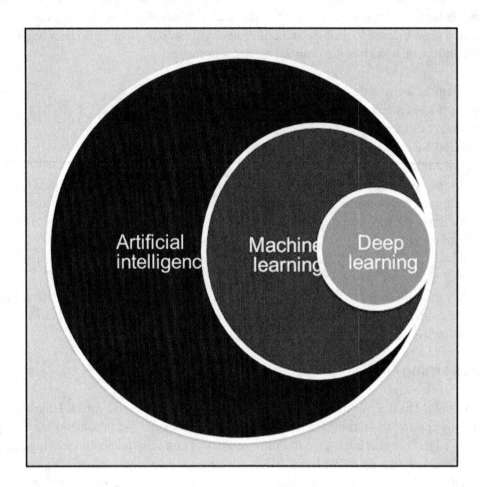

APPLICATIONS OF AI AND ML

Various AI and ML applications are used in the recognition of crimes. This revolutionary step changed the way investigators tackle crimes. AI is used to predict illegal activities by using applications like' Artificial Neural Networks'. AI can be used to recognize specific crimes such as child pornography, fraud, money laundering, or sex trafficking, by training and scanning through volumes of information. Using these applications gave the investigators an edge high above the perpetrators. These applications not only complete the investigation with high accuracy but also require less time. As a result, demand for these applications in the investigation field is increasing. (innefuLabs) Even though there are some drawbacks, these applications are improving and various researches are taking place to make the most out of these algorithms. Below are some applications of AI and ML in detail.

Artificial Neural Networks (ANN)

Investigators can predict the future moves with artificial neural networks, of even unidentified perpetrators who were able to tackle the investigators using a traditional system. ANN is trained by individuals by giving various examples and probabilities. Seemingly unrelated databases are linked to data points by these artificial neural networks. These data points exist in millions which makes it harder for humans to classify but work of a minute or less for AI. ANN has broadly distributed into two types namely feedback ANN and Feed-forward ANN. These AI tools are used to predict various crimes on DW such as money laundering, predicting the next moves of the criminals, and other similar frauds.

Different characters of ANN include:

- Model choice. Depending on the application and representation of data this decision can be taken.
- Algorithm learning. It is easy to select and train the algorithm if one has proper data. But, selection based on different experiments can also be done if data is not available.
- Sturdiness. With the right algorithm learning, model, and function of cost, a sturdy ANN can be achieved.

Advantages:

- It can multitask. In other words to process more than one value simultaneously.
- It can even work without complete knowledge or information provided.
- It can distribute memory.

Disadvantages:

- It does not have any proper structure.
- As why and how did it conclude the answers remain anonymous, this network can be doubtful sometimes.
- It is dependent on hardware such as processors.

Advancement in technologies has benefited the world in many different ways but the way AI and ML are upgrading in their field is magnificent. ML learning applications can be trained to recognize and identify anomalies and specific, repeating patterns which can be useful to track the crime more quickly as compared to traditional methods. ML applications such as supervised, semi-supervised, and unsupervised learning methods. (Sarker,2021)

Supervised Learning

Examples and predictions given to ANN are known as "inputs" and sometimes "results". This training is monitored by checking the difference between the predicted output and the original output. This difference is termed as "error". The network keeps updating and improving using this error value and also following other learning rules. This continuous improvement helps ANN to make the decision very close to the determined output. This is known as Supervised learning. Choice of model, learning algorithm, and robustness are some of the characteristics of ANN. ANNs over a period of time have

Figure 2. Schematic diagram of neural networks

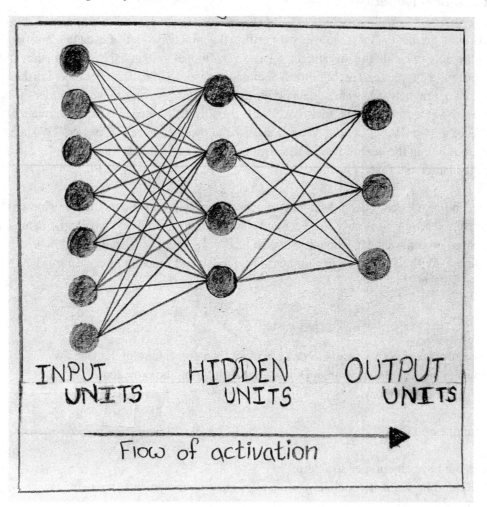

evolved into various types starting from simplest, dynamic, and more complicated, where some of the types completely operate in hardware and vise versa. Patterns that are difficult for humans to identify are identified using various AI tools which generally include Artificial Neural Networks. Examples include recognizing images and identifying objects or living things.

Advantages:

- Model is able to predict the output with the help of previous data and experience.
- Exact classes of objects are known in supervised learning.
- It helps solve various problems of the real world.

Disadvantages:

- Complex tasks are not suitable for this algorithm.
- If training data and test data are slightly different, the accuracy of output can vary.

- Great knowledge of classes of objects is required for supervised learning.

Figure 3. Supervised learning: Classification

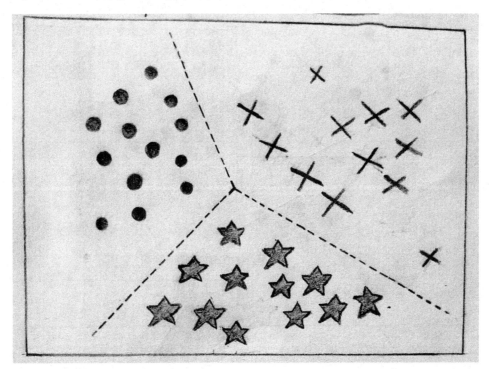

Unsupervised Learning

Unsupervised learning is a part of machine learning widely different from supervised learning as it doesn't include inputs and outputs for data training. Hence, this algorithm self-identity patterns from the given data. This is the same reason that it requires less time as well as less human involvement in training the data sets. It is used for three main tasks which are clustering, association, and dimensionality reduction. Unsupervised learning is many times revolves around clustering which is categorized into the following categories:

- Overlapping
- Hierarchical
- Exclusive
- Probabilistic

Another part of unsupervised learning than clustering is association. Association is used on variables to find the relationship in huge datasets. Association rule is mostly used in marketing.
Advantages:

Figure 4. Unsupervised learning: Clustering

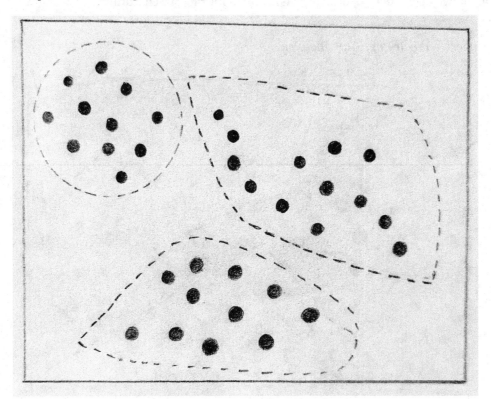

- For more complex tasks, unsupervised learning is preferred as compared to supervised learning because it doesn't need any labeled data as input.
- As this unlabeled data is easily available as compared to labeled data, Unsupervised learning is more preferred.

Disadvantages:

- It is harder as compared to supervised learning as it does not contain any matching output.
- Result of this algorithm can be less accurate because of unlabeled data input.

Classification

The classification method of supervised learning is used by investigators to predict the areas with a chance of crime occurrence. The algorithm classifies collected information into different classes which are called categories or labels or targets. The output of the Classification algorithm is a category not a value like regression. Some methods of classification include Logistic Regression, K-Nearest Neighbors (Sarker,2021), Decision tree classification, Random Forest Classification. Let's discuss some of them in detail:

Figure 5. Formula for Bayes' Rule

$$P(A|B) = \frac{P(B|A)P(A)}{P(B)}$$

- Naïve Bayes' Classification. (Sarker,2021)

This method is used in recognition of crimes such as robbery, rape, murder, sex abuse, vandalism, etc. It uses Bayes' Theorem also known as Bayes' Law or Bayes' Rule, therefore its decisions are based on predictions. It is considered in the simplest and highly effective algorithms. Quick decisions making machines are made in less time using this same classification. Famous examples of this classification include spam filter and article classification. It is classified into 3 different types namely Gaussian, Multinomial, and Bernoulli.

$P(A|B) = \{P(B|A)P(A)\} / P(B)$

- A is the event of which we will find the probability.
- B is related to A in some way and is considered as new evidence.
- P(A|B) is the probability of A over B and is known as posterior.
- P(B|A) is the probability of B over A and is known as likelihood.
- P(A) is probability before observing the evidence and is known as the prior probability.
- P(B) is the probability of evidence and Is known as Marginal probability.

The Only Disadvantage of Naïve Bayes Classification is:

- It is unable to learn the relationship of features as it assumes that of them are unrelated or independent.

Naïve Bayes Classification Advantages:

- It takes less time for training and predictions. Hence, it is considered as the fast algorithm of ML.
- It can be used for multi-class classification and also for Binary classification.
- For text classification problems, it is one of the best picks as well as most popular. O If compared to other algorithms in Multi-class predictions, it performs better.
  - *Apriori Algorithm.*

Apriori Algorithm is an approach of unsupervised learning. It was first introduced in 1994 by R. Agrawal and Srikant. It can determine the strength or weakness of connection between two different objects. Datasets which includes transactions are the ideal datasets for this algorithm as it is specially designed for the same. It can identify crime patterns that occur repeatedly. It is popularly known as data mining's classical algorithm. Association that is relevant and repetitive item sets can be mined using this algorithm.

Data mining:

It is a computer science subfield. In this process larger datasets are analyzed, using AI and ML to discover patterns. The information is extracted from data sets and is converted to an understandable structure.

Types of data that can be mined:

- Warehouse data.
- Database data.
- Transactional data.
- Other types of data.

Techniques:

- Clustering.
- Association.
- Classification.
- Prediction.
- Sequential patterns.

Apriori Algorithm Advantages:

- Apriori Algorithm is easily understandable.
- This algorithm can be used on huge databases without any difficulty.
- Resulting rules of this algorithm are intuitive and be easily communicated to the user.

Apriori Algorithm Disadvantages:

- The working of this algorithm is slower if compared with other algorithms.
- The algorithm scans the database repeatedly.

- *Random Forest Algorithm. (Sarker,2021)*

This algorithm is a part of supervised learning. Both ML problems like classification and regression using this algorithm. This algorithm includes an average of various decision trees with large subsets of data available which increases the accuracy. It can be used for crime recognition as it can analyze large sets of data and provide close to accurate results.

Random Forest Advantages:

Figure 6. Data mining approach using Apriori Algorithm

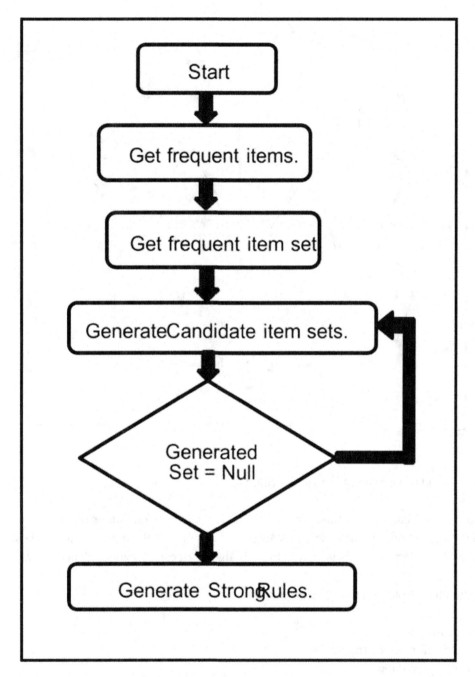

- It can perform both regression and classification tasks.
- Huge datasets with high dimensionality can be handled with this algorithm.
- Accuracy can be increased with this algorithm.

Figure 7. Random forest algorithm

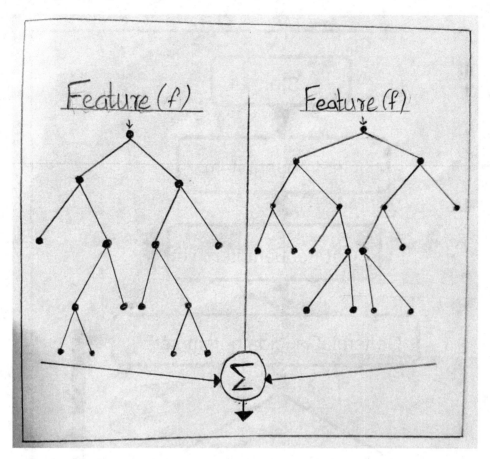

Why one should use a random Forest algorithm?

- This algorithm requires less time for training as compared to other algorithms.
- Even if large datasets are provided, this algorithm can predict the output of the highest accuracy.
- Even if a large part of data is not available this algorithm can provide high accuracy.

Implementation of random forest algorithm:

- Pre-processing data.
- Fitting algorithm in the training set.
- Test results prediction.
- Checking accuracy of results by creating a confusion matrix.
- Visualizing with the help of a graph.

- *Support vector machine learning algorithm. (SVM) (Sarker,2021)*

SVM is also used for both regression as well as classification problems and is a part of the supervised learning ML algorithm. It is one of the most popular algorithms. SVM algorithm provides us with the best differentiation or the correct decision line that can separate n-dimensional spaces. Hence, making it easy for us to put new data points incorrect groups. This division line is called a hyperplane. To create this hyperplane, SVM uses extreme vectors. This algorithm is categorized into two different types namely linear SVM and Non-linear SVM.

Advantages:

- When classes are separated clearly, it works well.
- If a higher number of dimensions are provided as compared to samples, SVM works more effectively.
- It generally saves memory.

Disadvantages:

- It does not work well with huge data sets.
- If classes are not separated, SVM cannot work well.
- It does not perform well if the number of features is more than the number of samples.

Implementation of SVM:

- Pre-processing data.
- Fitting in the training set.
- Predicting results of the test.
- Confusion matrix creation.
- Visualizing.

BlackWidow

BlackWidow is an application made for monitoring the DW services. This application creates a single analytics structure by collecting the data. It uses microservice architecture which is Docker-based. It can be used for a large amount of information collection and can examine a huge amount of formless data. In a case study conducted, it managed to collect years of pertinent information related to frauds and cyber security. (Schäfer et al., 2019)

Clustering

Very similar to classification, Clustering consists of only major differences which are, data classes information is unknown in clustering. As one can not tell whether the data can be classified or not, it is considered under Unsupervised learning. Clustering is more used in works like forensic analysis or behavior analytics but using it for crime recognition can help to some extent. Like group individuals or groups into different categories to differentiate values for risks can be done with the help of cluster-

Figure 8. Support vector machines learning algorithm (SVM)

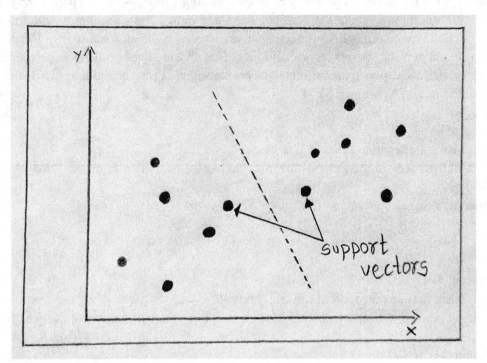

ing. Some ML applications of clustering include Knearest neighbors (KNN), Gaussian Mixture Model, Mean-shift, Agglomerative, DBSCn, K- means, etc. Let's discuss some of them in detail.

- *K-means clustering.*

k-means clustering aims to observations and separations into k clusters in which clusters with nearest means provide each observation. As a result, data spaces are separated into Voronoi cells. It uses signal processing from the method of vector quantization. It is often confused with K-nearest neighbors classifier, which is a famous Ml Method and uses a supervised learning algorithm whereas kmeans clustering uses an unsupervised learning algorithm. This algorithm performance mainly two activities:

- Determining value for centroids or k center points.
- Clustering each data point to its closest k center.

Advantages:

- Easy implementation.
- Computation is faster even if a large number of variables are available.
- Tight clusters are produced in k-means clustering as compared to hierarchical clustering.

Disadvantages:

- Number of clusters is hard to predict.
- Final result is impacted by initial seeds.

- Final result is also impacted by the order in which data is.
- If scales are rescaled the result can change completely. Hence, it is scale sensitive.

Implementation of k-means clustering:

o Pre-processing data.

o With the help of the elbow method, find the right number of clusters.

o K-means algorithm training.

o Visualizing.

• Agglomerative clustering.

It is one type of hierarchical clustering. This clustering groups objects based on the similarity between objects. This grouping is also known as Agglomerative Nesting (AGNES). One can perform Agglomerative clustering with R software by below steps:

- Prepare the data.
- Determining information of every pair of an object based on their dissimilarity in the data set.
- Based on information in step 1, group the objects in a hierarchical cluster tree by using the linkage function.
- To separate the data, decide where to cut the hierarchical tree into different clusters.

Regression

When the output is continuous or real value, it is a regression problem. It is a predictive algorithm that is used for analyzing variables. It is further divided into various methods like polynomial regression, Support Vector Regression (SVR), Decision tree, etc. Let's discuss some of them in detail:

• Linear regression.

As compared to other methods of regression, linear regression is considered one of the most easiest and popular ones. It shows a linear relationship between two or more variables. Hence, it is known as linear regression. It can be further classified into two different types namely simple linear regression and multiple linear regression.

Linear Regression Line

The line representing the relationship of independent and dependent variables is known as the linear regression line. It can be further classified into two different relationships namely positive linear relationship (PLR) and negative linear relationship (NLR).

$Y=A+Bx$

$Y=-A+Bx.$

Above are the mathematical representation for PLR and NLR respectively.

Techniques of estimation for linear regression:

Figure 9. Agglomerative clustering

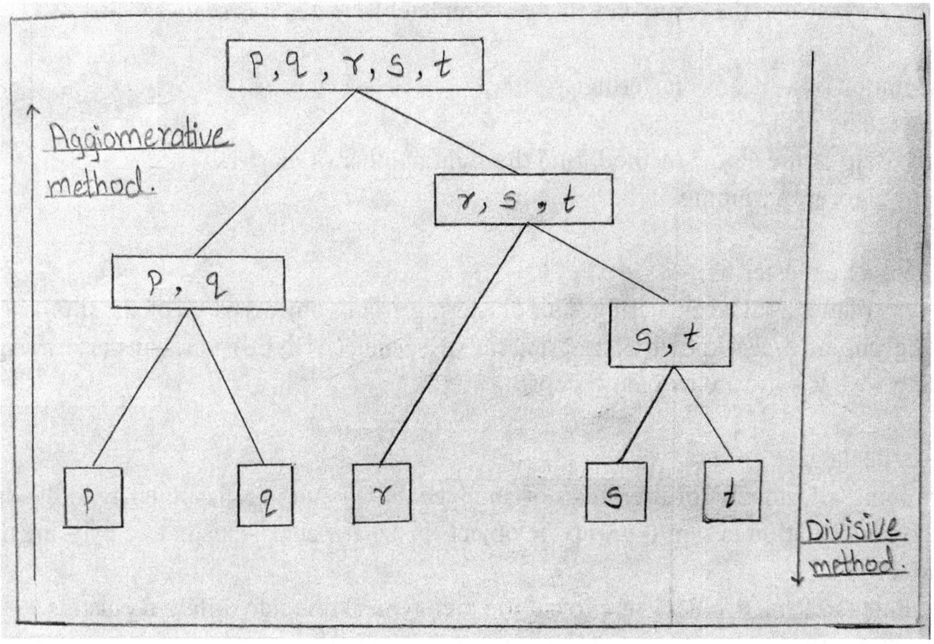

- Estimation of least-squares.
- Estimation of maximum likelihood.
- Least absolute deviation.
- Adaptive estimation.
- Mixed models.

- *Ridge Regression.*

To increase the accuracy of predictions and to decrease the errors in crime recognition, ridge regression is of great help. (Aldossari et al.,2020) The Ridge Regression method can be very useful in the case of data with multicollinearity. This regression method is mainly used when less than one lakh samples are available or when you have fewer samples than parameters. The basic regression equation used by this algorithm is

Y= XB+e .

Here, Y = dependent variable,
X = independent variable, B = coefficient of regression, E = errors.
Advantages:

- Overfitting problem can be solved with this algorithm.
- It can be a bit biased, to be more accurate.

Figure 10. Linear and nonlinear regression

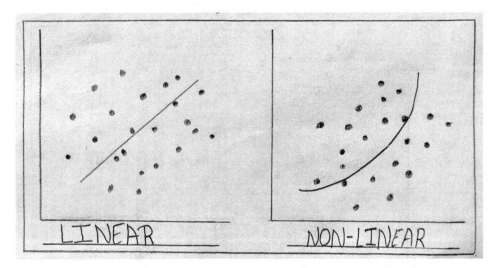

- Even if there are more features than training examples, this algorithm is more accurate compared to others.

Disadvantages:

- Unlike some methods select that only a few and important inputs, this algorithm goes through all the inputs to increase accuracy.
- If the feature is not important, this algorithm rather than marking it as a zero it just reduces theta coefficient to fewer values.

WAIKATO ENVIRONMENT FOR KNOWLEDGE ANALYSIS (WEKA)

WEKA is one of the ML applications written in JAVA and was first introduced by the University of Waikato, which is situated in New Zealand. It contains a huge collection of algorithms and visualization tools that is used for predicting and analyzing data. This application can be very useful for predicting crimes on the dark web as its features are easy to access and the app is great at predicting and analyzing.

WEKA advantages:

- It is available free of cost under GNU General public license.
- It can be used on any modern computing platform as it is implemented and written in JAVA.
- It consists graphical user interface making it easier to use for the user.

Disadvantages:

- It cannot handle larger datasets that are larger than a few megabytes.

Figure 11. Ridge regression

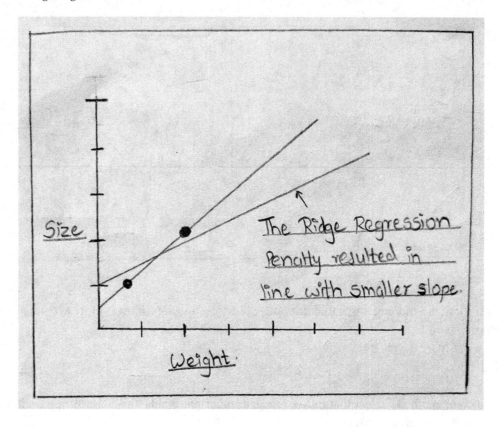

XVIGIL

CloudSEK is a service based on AI which helps the user to make the exact analysis of risks and threats with the least human involvement. It is an alert system that is reliable for detection, rapid in work and analysis. It was founded in 2015 by Rahul Sasi. It can identify how severe the threat is by using machine learning. The main and the latest product of CloudSEK is X-Vigil which is based on SaaS and provide timely warnings and can secure the user against thefts, cyber threats, and even data leak. It gathers information from online sources and then uses AI to remove false data and noise. Then based on this data, threats are recognized. (CloudSEK,2021)

ADVANTAGES AND RISKS OF USING ML AND AI APPLICATIONS FOR CRIME RECOGNITION.

Advantages

- Large-scale data can be easily analyzed and investigated with the help of these applications.
- AI and ML applications can detect the perpetrator's next step even before conducting the crime based on the previous data.

- These applications can be of greater help as perpetrators can be controlled if the right information is collected, categorized, and provided to the investigators.
- This application can trace those patterns which sometimes can get missed by human eyes. Hence, provide high chances of crime recognition.
- This application can store data and analyze a large amount of data in seconds which sometimes can be a hard task for humans to do.
- Human errors can be eliminated once these AI and ML applications are trained and are ready to work without any human involvement.
- Using this application requires less time as well as provides high accuracy.

Disadvantages

- As AI and ML algorithms are unable to differentiate between the factors like the relationship between two objects, age, gender, etc. Hence, sometimes it can draw biased conclusions.
- AI and ML applications should not be used in isolation. (Quest et al.)
- Access to these applications should be limited and taken care that it doesn't fall into any wrong hands to avoid risks. (Quest et al.)
- Sometimes some tasks can be categorized as illegal even though being legal. For example, if a large amount of money transfers discussion is done on DW to hide the process from the public, this application can still categorize it in the fraud or blackmailing category if correct instructions and training are not provided. (Quest et al.)
- Some hackers can use ML applications for their illegal activities.
- As these tools are based on data and patterns sometimes collection of this data can be and failure to recognizing these applications can be a disadvantage.

FUTURE OF AI AND ML APPLICATIONS IN DW CRIME RECOGNITION

AI and ML applications are already of great benefit in detecting crimes on Dark Web. But as mentioned above there are still some drawbacks which can be improved. Various researches are being conducted to develop and improve this application. One can think about a future with a system or machine that contains AI that can think like humans, feel or have emotions like humans. Or even a step further these machines would have consciousness of human level. This will not only decrease the errors but also increase the accuracy level and will be of great help to investors as more investigation can be done in less time. Many researchers and individuals are working towards achieving this and if it continues we will soon be able to witness the great revolution in the field of DW and crime recognition. These applications came up as solutions to investigators for the recognition of DW crimes. With this application continuously learning, these algorithms one day will also be able to predict the crimes even before the perpetrator thinks about it with the help of proper data and analyses. These algorithms collecting data over the period can also someday introduce us to the new side of the Dark Web which is still untouched by humans. To conclude in short, even though these algorithms contain some amount of drawbacks which are generally due to less data or less improvement, these algorithms are of huge benefit especially for investigators, and also can be of immense benefit for humans to know the DW well.

CONCLUSION

AI and ML have been of ocean help to the tech industry as well as investigators using it. Even though DW comes with both advantages and disadvantages, there's a realization that it was and still is important for investigators to recognize the crimes conducted on DW and take action against them. AI and ML applications came into the frame for crime recognition at the exact time and not only helped to reduce the time of recognizing crime but also helped to get a recognizable control over the crimes conducted on DW. The dark web is a huge mysterious ocean to be understood and so as the crimes there. The perpetrators are benefited from DW by completely hiding their self-identity. But applications of AI and ML are the light of hope, which can track such miscellaneous and illegal activities being conducted. If more studies are conducted and more work is exhorted on updating the existing application and creating new advanced applications it will definitely lead us towards a future with strong control over DW crimes. Also, to get ahead of perpetrators, focusing on security frameworks depending on new technologies like AI and ML will be no less than a great idea.

REFERENCES

Aldossari, S., Alqahtani, F., Alshahrani, N., Alhammam, M., Alzamanan, R., Aslam, N., & Irfanullah. (2020). *A Comparative Study of Decision Tree and Naïve Bayes Machine Learning Model for Crime Category Prediction in Chicago*. doi:10.1145/3379247.3379279

Algorithmia. (2021, May 17). *How machine learning works*. Algorithmia Blog. https://algorithmia.com/blog/how-machine-learning-works#how-does-machine-learning-work

Builtin. (n.d.). *What is artificial intelligence? How does AI work?* https://builtin.com/artificial-intelligence

Cloud, S. E. K. (2021, August 30). *XVigil – Artificial intelligence based digital risk monitoring – CloudSEK*. CloudSEK – Digital Risk Management Enterprise. https://cloudsek.com/campaigns/xvigil/

Das, T. A., & Gosavi, M. S. S. (2019). *Artificial intelligence and machine learning as a double-edge sword in cyber world*. Academic Press.

Findlaw. (2021, December 21). *Dark web crimes*. https://www.findlaw.com/criminal/criminal-charges/dark-web-crimes.html

innefuLabs. (n.d.). *How artificial intelligence in policing helps crime detection*. Innefu.Com.

O'hare, J. (2020). *Machine learning and artificial intelligence for online investigations*. Read.Nxtbook. Com. https://read.nxtbook.com/wordsmith/evidence_technology/april_2020/machine_learning_and_artifici.html

Quest, L., Charrie, A., & Roy, S. (n.d.). *The Risks And Benefits Of Using AI To Detect Crime*. Oliver Wyman. https://www.oliverwyman.com/our-expertise/insights/2018/dec/risk-journal-vol-8/rethinking-tactics/the-risks-and-benefits-of-using-ai-to-detect-crime.html

Sarker, I. H. (2021). Machine Learning: Algorithms, Real-World Applications and Research Directions. *SN Comput. Sci., 2*, 160. doi:10.1007/s42979-021-00592-x

Schäfer, M., Fuchs, M., Strohmeier, M., Engel, M., Liechti, M., & Lenders, V. (2019). BlackWidow: Monitoring the Dark Web for Cyber Security Information. *2019 11ᵗʰ International Conference on Cyber Conflict (CyCon),* 1-21. doi: 10.23919/CYCON.2019.8756845

Chapter 8

Detection of Cyber Crime Based on Facial Pattern Enhancement Using Machine Learning and Image Processing Techniques

RamaDevi Jujjuri

(iD) https://orcid.org/0000-0002-0480-882X

PVP Siddhartha Institute of Technology, India

Sankararao Majji

Gokaraju Rangaraju Institute of Engineering and Technology, India

Arun Kumar Tripathi

(iD) https://orcid.org/0000-0001-5138-2190

KIET Group of Institutions, Delhi, India

Boppuru Rudra Prathap

(iD) https://orcid.org/0000-0002-5161-4972

Christ University, India

Chandrika V. S.

KPR Institute of Engineering and Technology, India

Tulasi Radhika Patnala

GITAM University, India

ABSTRACT

Cybercrime has several antecedents, including the rapid expansion of the internet and the wide variety of users around the world. It is now possible to use this data for a variety of purposes, whether for profit, non-profit, or purely for the benefit of the individual. As a result, tracing and detecting online acts of terrorism requires the development of a sound technique. Detection and prevention of cybercrime has been the subject of numerous studies and investigations throughout the years. An effective criminal detection system based on face recognition has been developed to prevent this from happening. Principle component analysis (PCA) and linear discriminant analysis (LDA) algorithms can be used to identify criminals based on facial recognition data. Quality, illumination, and vision are all factors that affect the efficiency of the system. The goal of this chapter is to improve accuracy in the facial recognition process for criminal identification over currently used conventional methods. Using proposed hybrid model, we can get the accuracy of 99.9.5%

DOI: 10.4018/978-1-6684-6444-1.ch008

INTRODUCTION

Using computers or other communication technologies to terrorise or harm others or damage, hurt, or destroy property is what we mean when we say "cybercrime." Cybercrimes that are computer-assisted as well as computer-focused can be divided into two groups. Cyber stalking and child pornography are instances of computer-assisted crimes; phishing and hacking are examples of computer-focused offences. For a variety of factors, such as the culture in which the crime was committed, its severity, and occurrences that were not reported because of ignorance or social restraints, it is difficult to get accurate and official statistics on cybercrime. The involvement of law enforcement in circumstances like this is critical because it regulates the level of detail given. In the 1960s, the first cybercrime involving the duplication of computer programming occurred (Al-Khater, 2020). There were numerous fraud and forgery charges brought against Union Dime Savings Bank in New York in 1970 after a bank clerk embezzled $1.5 million from client accounts. Imperial Chemical Industries (ICI) employees stole hundreds of computers and their backups in the early 1970s and sought 275,000 pounds sterling in ransom. A computer worm was created in 1988 by Robert T. Morris at MIT in Cambridge, Massachusetts (MIT).

A phishing attempt was made for the first time in 1995The Electronic Disturbance Theatre was established in 1997 with the mission of creating electronic counterparts to the site-in tools protesters employ. The president of Mexico's website was attacked with a denial-of-service attack in 1998 using a tool called FloodNet (Sivakumar, 2021).

This was done in January 1998, when a coal-fired power station's emergency mode was activated and the SCADA system software was uninstalled. In 2005, a hacker attack on the bank's air conditioning systems resulted in the bank's computer systems being shut down because of the rising temperature in its computer room. The Russian Business Network (RB) was founded in 2006 and is based in New York City (Kester et al., 2021). This unlawful company has committed numerous cybercrimes and provided a wide range of Trojans, spam, and phishing-related tools and services. Its main business is the resale of stolen personal information. A webpage on how to construct bombs was replaced with a page on how to make cupcakes by British security agencies in 2011.

Several sorts of studies were examined in the review of the literature for this paper in order to establish approaches for the identification and prevention of cybercrime. It is through the use of statistical methods that we can better understand the nature of cybercrime and develop effective methods for identifying it. Approaches that focus on predicting outputs from data input include machine learning techniques. Cybercrime detection technologies now in use have been subjected to several reviews and surveys (Rawat et al.,2021). Existing review studies, on the other hand, only concentrated on analysing the detection methods that are limited to one or a few cybercrimes, such as cyber bullying or botnets.

A machine learning technique allows computers to learn and even improve themselves without being explicitly programmed, according to Arthur Samuel. It is possible for software systems to improve their accuracy at predicting outcomes without explicitly programming them through the use of machine learning (ML). When constructing an algorithm for machine learning, the primary concept is to employ statistical analysis to anticipate an output while also changing results in response to new data being available. The research of making computers capable of self-learning is known as machine learning. In my opinion, ML is one of the most intriguing technologies I've ever encountered (Nicholls et al., 2021). To put it plainly, the term reveals that it offers the computer the power to learn. It's possible that machine learning is now being applied in more places than you think.

Using PCA, we may reduce the amount of data without sacrificing any of its usefulness. There are numerous linear combinations of primary variables used to explain the variance composition and covariance composition without omitting crucial information. What we're trying to do here is find an orthogonal axis with the most variance in our dataset. Its primary goal is to overcome the problem's dimensionality. Dimensionality reduction should be done in such a way that the amount of data lost when decreasing higher dimensions is kept to a minimum. Main components may indicate links between variables that aren't obvious at first glance (Rawat et al., 2021). Data distribution can be explained in terms of the variables that cause the distribution.

One of the most often used dimensionality reduction techniques for supervised classification is Linear or Normal Discriminant Analysis, Discriminant Function Analysis, or Discriminant Linearity Analysis (Shaukat et al., 2020). It is employed to represent distinctions between groups, i.e. to distinguish between two or more categories. Features in higher dimension space are projected into a lower dimension space using it. Dimensionality can be reduced using LDA, or Linear Discriminant Analysis. As a preprocessing step, it is used in Machine Learning and pattern categorization applications. To avoid the curse of dimensionality and save resources and dimensional costs, LDA aims to project higher-dimensional features onto a lower-dimensional domain.

Ronald A. Fisher first devised linear discriminant analysis (also known as Fisher's Discriminant Analysis) in 1936. Originally, a two-class linear discriminant approach was all that Linear Discriminant was characterised as. C.R. Rao later generalised multi-class analysis as Multi-Discriminant Analysis. The generic term for all of them is Linear Discriminant Analysis (LDA).

Competitive machine learning models use LDA as a supervised classification algorithm. Image recognition and predictive analysis in marketing are two examples of applications that make use of this type of dimensionality reduction.

Dark Web

The Dark Web is a reality that has existed since the birth of the internet. While there is a load of material indexed on the web, widely available by anybody with internet connectivity irrespective of region, there is even more information and data that do not come to notice since it is hidden and requires specific credentials to access. This unchartered area of the web is called Dark Web.

Regulations and content policies don't apply to information on the dark web. In addition, because they are hidden and not indexed, pages delivering information on the dark web do not appear in SERP like those from Google and Bing. As a result, information on the dark web can only be accessed by a select group of people. In addition, browsers have flagged as hazardous the web pages delivering information on the dark web, so they cannot be accessed.

Because of abundant unlawful content, the Dark Web has received a terrible name. It is home to various kinds of information, but it has been tarnished by the predominance of illegal content, including illicit pornography and the selling of illegal narcotics (Rawat et al., 2021). The availability of unlawful content on the dark web makes it a good area for criminals to operate. If you're a journalist, you can use it to acquire information from sources without exposing your identity, and whistleblowers can use it to expose corporate and government malfeasance, etc.

This chapter explains about how we can detect cybercrime based on facial enhancement techniques using the machine learning algorithms. Section1 explains about the introduction of cyber crime and dark web, in second section we tried to explain about types of cyber crimes exist. The third section gives brief information about the related work to complete this work, in section 4 proposed methodology of our work and in section5 workflow of proposed cybercrime detection model. Results are discussed in the section6 and finally concluded the work.

CYBERCRIME TYPES

There are various types of cybercrime. Subsections in this section identify and explain each category.

Cyber Terrorism

Unlawful acts of violence against persons and property are at the heart of what is known as cyber terrorism. Racial or ideological motivations are not uncommon when it comes to politics. Due to the potential for fear, anxiety, and aggressiveness, this type of cybercrime has the potential to disrupt and devastate property. In the event of cyber-terrorism, data integrity and accessibility may be jeopardised (Yar et al., 2019). Terrorists utilise the Internet to spread propaganda, recruit new members, influence public opinion, and disrupt national infrastructure. phishing email was the starting point of a December 2015 Ukrainian power grid attack, which can be seen as an act of cyber-terrorism. Speculation about the safety of citizens is disrupted by some sequences of cyber terrorism (Rawat et al., 2021). In politics, this type of sequence can affect policy decisions. Cyber terrorism can cause death and disrupt society's cohesion through stealing money, destroying property, and inciting violence.

Cyber Warfare

The term "cyberwarfare" refers to a style of conflict fought without the use of physical weapons. Without approval from the government, it can be carried out by organisations or gangs of hackers. This may cause political tensions between countries. To this day, the most common form of conflict is cyberwarfare and cyber attack. In the previous two decades, there have been numerous cyber wars. Georgian government websites were targeted by SQL injection, denial-of-service attacks and cross site scripting during a 2008 cyber conflict between Russia and Georgia (Jain et al., 2020). In their cyber war, both Israeli and Arab hackers have committed numerous cyber wars. "Time is running out" was the Arabic subtitle for the cartoon movie of Hamas' leader being assassinated that Israel bombed in December 2008 to broadcast Al-transmission Aqua's of the movie. Several Estonian government websites were attacked by hackers in 2007. The attacks were attributed by the Estonian government to Russia.

When another Ukrainian power plant was attacked one year later, the national train system and several government departments were left without electricity. There were no survivors, therefore they were forced to work in constrained conditions and make manual efforts to heal themselves. The attackers, on the other hand, used strategies to impede and ultimately halt the healing process (Rawat et al., 2021). Uninterruptible power supply systems can be disconnected remotely. Also, the passwords of legitimate users have been changed by the attackers (Rawat et al., 2021). This meant that they couldn't access the system while it was being repaired. It took six months for the power plants to fully recover from the attack. The gateways were rendered unrecoverable by the attackers, who replaced the genuine software with malicious firmware.

Cyber Espionage

Spying on rival corporations or foreign governments and stealing their confidential information is what we mean when we say we are committing acts of espionage. Computers are used in cyber espionage missions. Cyber espionage assaults by Chinese entities affected more than 300 British businesses in December 2007. There were also numerous coordinated attacks by China on the US military's computers and networks throughout a period from 2003 to 2006. "Titan Rain" was the codename given to this coordinated assault.

Child Pornography

Pornographic images, films, and recordings depicting children in undignified or sexually suggestive poses, such as those shown in child pornography, are known as child pornography. In an effort to reduce the incidence of child pornography, numerous researches have been done. Children's pornography is typically distributed for profit or non-profit objectives. Many websites are selling child pornography for profit (Rawat et al., 2021). P2P networks can be used to share and disseminate child pornographic materials for non-profit causes.

It was illegal to produce, own, or distribute any digital content containing child pornography in any form (Thiyagarajan,2020). Self-esteem, trust in others, and sexual development are all included in this category. Yet this crime's long-term consequences for the child's mental health are severely devastating. Cyber-criminals who target children for sexual motives will be more likely to prey on youngsters who have access to digital content on the Internet, leading to more serious consequences and issues.

Cyber Bullying

People of all ages and genders are more prone to engage in bullying due of the widespread use of social media and technology. If you've ever been bullied, you know that it's one of the most harrowing situations a person can go through. Bullying is more common among children, adolescents, and women. A person's personality can change as a result of being bullied. Twitter, Facebook, and other social media can be used to harass and threaten the lives of victims of cyberbullying (Mahor et al., 2021). Many sorts of cybercrime can hurt a victim, including theft of personal information, credit card fraud, stalking, and psychological manipulation.

Phishing

As a result of its close association with the end user, phishing is one of the most widely used attacks. Such attacks involve the attacker fooling the end user into disclosing personal information. Social engineering and spoofing are both used in phishing. Attackers use emails to solicit personal information, warn their victims of an imminent attack, and persuade them to download and install malicious software (Mercaldo et al., 2020). Additionally, an email may include the URL of an imposter website. Avoiding clicking on links in questionable emails is a crucial part of your defence strategy. Avoiding phishing attacks can also be as simple as just visiting secure websites, such as those that begin with 'https,' and installing anti-virus software, firewalls, and anti-phishing toolbars on your browser.

Denial-of-Service Attack

A major online threat is the compromise of service availability by a denial-of-service (DoS) assault. As a result of ICMP and SYN floods, systems that have been penetrated get "crashed," causing the intended service to be interrupted. When an attacker takes control of numerous channels in a network, he or she can use each victim as a zombie to attack another system, much like the way a computer virus spreads through a network.

SQL Injection Attack

It is possible for an attacker to get access to databases by executing SQL queries. Prior to making any changes or deletions, the attacker can view the database and obtain its contents. If all users are required to have a username and password, this type of attack can be prevented.

Futuristic in Cyber Attacks

Hackers can now take advantage of a wide range of modern and futuristic devices and technologies to launch devastating cyber attacks. There is a great risk that these new technology may be targeted by hackers (Rawat et al., 2011). Wi-Fi technology is used by a wide range of people and businesses, which can put their security at risk.

RELATED WORK

Dinakar et al. used a support vector machine using JRip, J48, and a support vector classifier to identify YouTube comments including cyber bullying. As part of the investigation, the binary classifier was pitted against a more complex multi-classifier. Al-garadi et al., on the other hand, provided a method for detecting cyberbullying in tweets with an algorithm. In order to build a classifier that might detect cyberbullying, they retrieved various information from each tweet. Classifiers like KNN, decision trees, and support vector machines were tested to find which one was the most effective. Naive Bayes was shown to be the most effective and robust algorithm.

Text classification was used by Uzel et al. to identify acts of cyber terrorism and extremism (CTE). Textual language related with CTE was identified by applying numerical weights to specific phrases. A vector was created from the document. The researchers utilised four alternative weighting approaches to computerise the vector: binary weighting based on term frequency, term frequency weighting based on document frequency inverse. Classifiers for detecting CTE included SVM and a nave Bayes multinomial. They've also incorporated data on antisocial conduct into their study. The fuzzy set-based weighting technique with SVM had an accuracy of up to 99.5 percent.

It was suggested by Benferhat and coworkers that the naive Bayes approach should be used to investigate alarm correlations and to watch the attack plan. In order to successfully complete an attack, an attacker must follow a set of steps. The attack plan can be detected utilising the history of observations that have already been made. Researchers discovered that their approach reduced the number of false reports of assaults and did not require the involvement of an attack scenario or an expert.

Table 1. Summary of previous works done for Cybercrime detection using ML methods

Authors	Objective	Used Dataset	Methodology	Findings
Nandhini and Sheeba	Detect cyberbullying	FormSpring.me, MySpace.com	Naïve Bayes classifier and Levenshtein distance algorithm	95 percent of the time.
Reynolds et al.	Detect cyberbullying	FormSpring.me	instance-based learner and C4.5 decision tree	Both learners scored a 78.5 percent success rate.
Al-garadi et al.	Detect cyberbullying	Twitter	naïve Bayes, decision trees, KNN and SVM	It was the naive Bayes model that performed the best.
Ofoghi et al.	Detect phishing	emails Nazario datasets,phishig emails from 2004 to 2007, Spam Assassin	machine learning, Feature vector generator, feature evaluation, method selection inductor	The instrument had a 97% success rate.
Vijayanand et al.	A wireless mesh network IDS should be developed.	Network Simulator 3 was used to simulate a wireless mesh network.	Selection of features via genetic algorithm and classification by SVM	The system got 95.5% accuracy.
Nath	Recognize recurring themes in criminal activity	A sheriff's office.	An method called K-means is used to cluster and weight cybercrime attributes.	When mapping cybercrime regions, geospatial data was employed.
Al-diabat	Phishing assaults should be examined.	Information from the Phishtank website and the Yahoo! Directory.	In order to choose the best features for classification, the C4.5 and IREP algorithms are used.	C4.5 achieved a 96 percent accuracy rate, whereas the IREP algorithm achieved a 95 percent accuracy rate.
Darus et al.	Detect cybercrimes on the Android platform	APK files	KNN, decision tree, RF	RF out performed KNN and decision trees in terms of accuracy.

Cyberbullying in social media interactions may now be detected systematically by Hee et al. For the first time, researchers have developed a system that can detect not only harsh language but also implicit content like curses, defamation, and encouragement that they describe as tough because there are so many varieties of implicit cyber bullying. Support vector machine classifiers of the binary and linear variety were employed in this approach. A dataset of 113,698 ASKfm postings in both English and Dutch was used to test their hypothesis. The LIBLINEAR package in Python was used to create an SVM classifier because of its ability to execute huge linear classifications. After optimization, the new model's maximum F1 scores for Dutch and English were 58.72 and 64.32 percent.

PROPOSED FRAMEWORK FOR CYBERCRIME DETECTION

The proposed methodology explains how the cyber crime can be detected using the facial pattern enhancement using machine learning. In this process there are three steps involved. The first step is to find the IP address of the cyber criminal and the second step is involved by gathering facial features from the devices connected to detected IP address using image processing in first step and finally these features

Figure 1. Steps involved in cybercrime detection

are applied to the machine learning algorithms to find the cybercriminal and these images are applied to the access vector then these are compared with the criminal behaviour finally when the detector detects the criminal the alarm will sounds.

Finding IP Address

An IP address search is your first step in investigating an internet-related case. An IP address is a collection of numbers and letters that identifies a device on the internet. Some Internet Service Providers (ISPs) require a subpoena, warrant, or court order in order to obtain an IP address.

What an IP address is made up of:

- Whose network address is this?
- A domain name or computer name that is related to
- Geo-location,
- Inboxes and email addresses
- An identifier for a local service provider.

Everything a subscriber does on the internet is recorded by the ISPs, which are based on subscriptions. Because Internet service providers (ISPs) keep user data for varying lengths of time, this investigation must move rapidly. A formal request can be made to the Internet service provider (ISP) to preserve the data in question while a warrant, subpoena, or court order is issued. This letter does not compel ISPs to keep the data for law enforcement, even if they have received it. The facial images are collected from the devices which are connected to the above detected ISP.

Facial Recognition

A one-to-many matching process is used to identify a face from a database of previously saved photos by comparing the face image with the database's previously stored images of faces.

- *Face Detection:* Face localization (also known as face detection) is the process of locating a person's face in a photograph. The image is free of unwanted noise. Using a simple edge detection technique is sufficient if the image was taken in a controlled environment. Image processing began by converting the image into grayscale, but today facial recognition is also being improved by analysing skin colour patterns. Face detection is simple if the image of the face is captured in

Figure 2. Feature extraction for face recognition

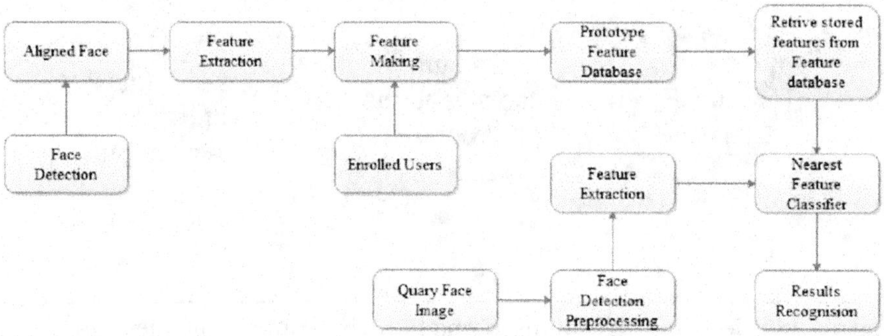

a controlled background with appropriate illumination and attitude. Image processing begins with the detection of a face in the image.

1. A gray-scale image is created by converting a colour digital camera image to a monochrome one.
2. The image is free of unwanted noise.
3. The image is resized to fit the dimensions of the database's image files, and then cropped accordingly.

*   *Feature Extraction:* We do feature extraction. We lower the image's dimensions before comparing it to the database instead than immediately comparing the query face with the database's images of faces. It gets rid of information that isn't needed. Moreover, it reduces the complexity and processing power of the system. PCA, LDA, or a mixture of both can be used to do the analysis. When utilising PCA for face identification, Eigen faces are the most common type of face to employ. To reduce the dimensionality even further, LDA is used after PCA.
*   *Face Classification:* To find a match for the query image of a face, classification is performed as the last step. It is compared to other faces registered in the database to see how it compares. The result of this phase is the face that matches the query face. The system's efficiency is determined by the classification algorithm employed in the last stage.

Face recognition is most commonly implemented using pre-processing, principal component analysis, and linear discriminant analysis. A pre-processing step is carried out in two ways:

*   A reduction in unwanted system noise and muddled effects
*   In order to make it easier to classify the image, it is necessary to move it to a new location.

Steps taken by the algorithm to detect a person's face:

*   Step1: Face image pre-processing
*   Step2: PCA for dimension reduction.
*   Step3: LDA-based feature extraction.
*   Step4: Neural network classification.

We next check this information against our database of vehicle registrations and criminal records to complete the process. Both methods will employ a comprehensive strategy to catching criminals.

WORK FLOW OF PROPOSED SYSTEM

A Java API for machine learning, WEKA, was used to implement three of the IDS framework's major functions. IDS queries are made using a pre-processing approach like attribute selection, attribute filtering or instance filtering. Two other components of the system, the PCA classification model and the Inference analyzer, are used to classify the network data and predict incoming traffic for testing purposes respectively.

Pre-processing: For the PCA model learning process, pre-processing is responsible for preparing the data for use. A dataset feature will be examined in this part based on an attack type and other domain expertise. It has been utilised with various pre-processing techniques such as attribute selection, discretization and filling missing instances in WEKA's attribute filter, Because the KDD dataset contains information on cyberattacks, a Bayesian network based on the types of attacks DDoS, R2L, U2R, and Probes was able to identify.

Input to the Vector Generator module, which generates vectors of weighted terms from the gathered pages (each page is converted to one vector). Vector of Cyber criminal transactions DB stores the vectors for processing. Input to the clustering module yielded n clusters representing the typical topics seen by cybercriminals, which were then unsupervised clustered. Using the cybercriminal Represent or module, a centroid vector is computed for each cluster that represents a topic of interest to cyber criminals. The Vector-Generator in the detection model's Monitoring module creates a 'access vector' from the content of each page a user accesses.

In order to identify criminal groups, the Detector analyses the access vector and criminal behaviour. This is accomplished by comparing the access vector to all of the criminal behaviour's centroid vectors. The similarity is calculated using the cosine measure. When the proximity of the access vector to the nearest centroid exceeds a certain threshold, the detector sounds an alarm.

RESULTS

Here we detect cybercrime based on facial Pattern enhancement technique using machine learning models. For feature classification we use a hybrid model that combines the PCA, LDA and Neural networks. Here we find out the accuracy of the system which is equal to 99.95%. The below table give the comparison of existing results with proposed model.

Proposed Hybrid Algorithm

Step1: Convert image of training set to image vector (Training set contains N images each of size i x i)
Step2: Normalise the face vector(Calculate the avg face vector and subtract from each face vector to get normalised face vector)
Step3: Calculate eigen vectors (To calculate eigen vector we need to find covariance vector)
Step4: If eigen vector value is less than no of images then reduce the dimensionality

Figure 3. Workflow of proposed model

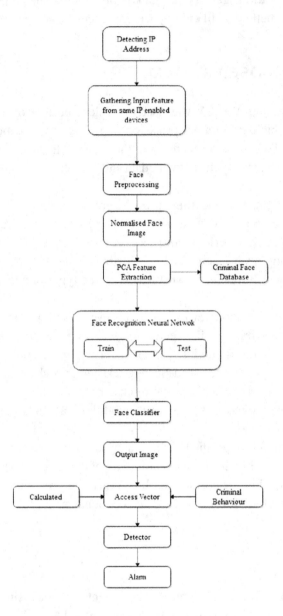

Step5: Using the eigenvalues to sort the eigenvectors, we can find the smallest eigenvalue first. For example, the first K-eigenvectors are utilised to create a two-dimensional space.

Step6: Eigen vectors can be sorted in decreasing order and the first K low-dimensional ones selected.

Step7: Use LDA's lower dimensional space to project all of the original samples.

Step8: Apply the same method to compute the feature vector of the test image as well.

Step9: Test feature vectors and all of the training feature vectors should be averaged to get the average distance (the Euclidean distance). To determine how similar two images are, the Euclidean distance between their weight vectors can be used.

Step10: Facial resemblance between test image and face class with smallest Euclidian distance is shown.

Step11: Classify the faces using Neural networks methods

Table 2. Performance comparison of existing and proposed methodology

Model	Accuracy	Precision	Recall
Naïve Bayes	95%	94.4%	94.2%
Decision tree and instance-based learner	78.5%	81.5%	80.5%
Feature vector generator	97%	92.5%	94.2%
Genetic algorithm for feature selection and SVM	95.5%	94.6%	93.9%
Proposed Hybrid Model (PCA+LDA+NN)	99.95%	98.5%	98.1%

Figure 4. Comparison of existing methods with proposed hybrid model

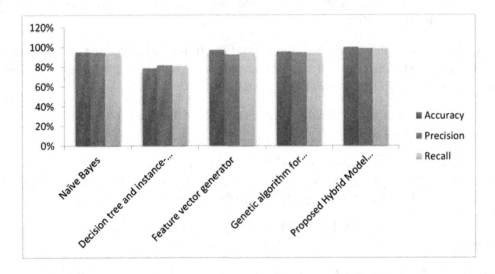

CONCLUSION

Most of our day-to-day interactions and transactions take place through the Internet, whether it's for work or play. On the other hand, it spawned complex problems like cybercrime. AI and data mining tools are already being used to fight cybercrime, according to academic resources. This paper has briefly discussed the current state of cybercrime prevention approaches and models, as well as their strengths and weaknesses. As cybercrime continues to rise on a daily basis, more strong detection and prevention strategies are needed.

REFERENCES

Al-Khater, W. A., Al-Maadeed, S., Ahmed, A. A., Sadiq, A. S., & Khan, M. K. (2020). Comprehensive Review of Cybercrime Detection Techniques. *IEEE Access: Practical Innovations, Open Solutions, 8,* 137293–137311. doi:10.1109/ACCESS.2020.3011259

Aldweesh, Derhab, & Emam. (2019). Deep learning approaches for anomaly-based intrusion detection systems: A survey, taxonomy, and open issues. Academic Press.

Almiani, AbuGhazleh, Al-Rahayfeh, & Atiewi. (2019). *Deep recurrent neural network for IoT intrusion detection system.* Academic Press.

Alurkar, A. A. (2019). *A Comparative Analysis and Discussion of Email Spam Classification Methods Using Machine Learning Techniques.* Applied Machine Learning for Smart Data Analysis. doi:10.1201/9780429440953-10

Amir, N., Latif, R., Shafqat, N., & Latif, S. (2020). Crowdsourcing Cybercrimes through Online Resources. *2020 13th International Conference on Developments in eSystems Engineering (DeSE),* 158-163. 10.1109/DeSE51703.2020.9450747

Andleeb, S., Ahmed, R., Ahmed, Z., & Kanwal, M. (2019). Identification and Classification of Cybercrimes using Text Mining Technique. *2019 International Conference on Frontiers of Information Technology (FIT),* 227-2275. 10.1109/FIT47737.2019.00050

Ani, L. (2015). Cyber Crime and National Security: The Role of the Penal and Procedural Law. Nigerian Institute of Advanced Legal Studies.

Bhalerao, R., Aliapoulios, M., Shumailov, I., Afroz, S., & McCoy, D. (2019). Mapping the Underground: Supervised Discovery of Cybercrime Supply Chains. *2019 APWG Symposium on Electronic Crime Research (eCrime),* 1-16. 10.1109/eCrime47957.2019.9037582

BinJubier, Ahmed, Ismail, Sadiq, & Khan. (2019). *Comprehensive Survey on Big Data Privacy Protection.* Academic Press.

Birkinshaw, C., Rouka, E., & Vassilakis, V. (2019). Implementing an intrusion detection and prevention system using software-defined networking: Defending against port-scanning and denialof-service attacks. Academic Press.

Cheng, L., Li, J., Silva, Y. N., Hall, D. L., & Liu, H. (2019). Xbully: Cyberbullying detection within a multi-modal context. In *Proceedings of the Twelfth ACM International Conference on Web Search and Data Mining* (pp. 339-347). ACM. 10.1145/3289600.3291037

Geluvaraj, B., Satwik, P., & Kumar, T. A. (2019). The future of cybersecurity: Major role of artificial intelligence machine learning and deep learning in cyberspace. *International Conference on Computer Networks and Communication Technologies,* 739-747. 10.1007/978-981-10-8681-6_67

Jain, A. K., Goel, D., Agarwal, S., Singh, Y., & Bajaj, G. (2020). Predicting Spam Messages Using Back Propagation Neural Network. *Wireless Personal Communications, 110*(1), 403–422. doi:10.100711277-019-06734-y

Jump, M. (2019). Fighting Cyberthreats with Technology Solutions. *Biomedical Instrumentation & Technology, 53*(1), 38–43. doi:10.2345/0899-8205-53.1.38 PMID:30702913

Karie, N. M., Kebande, V. R., & Venter, H. (2019). Diverging deep learning cognitive computing techniques into cyber forensics. Academic Press.

Kasongo & Sun. (2019). *A Deep Long Short-Term Memory based classifier for Wireless Intrusion Detection System.* Academic Press.

Kester, Q.-A., & Afoma, E. J. (2021). Crime Predictive Model in Cybercrime based on Social and Economic Factors Using the Bayesian and Markov Theories. *2021 International Conference on Computing, Computational Modelling and Applications (ICCMA),* 165-170. 10.1109/ICCMA53594.2021.00034

Liang, J., Ma, M., Sadiq, M., & Yeung, K.-H. J. K.-B. S. (2019). A filter model for intrusion detection system in Vehicle Ad Hoc Networks: A hidden Markov methodology (Vol. 163). Academic Press.

Lim, M., Abdullah, A., Jhanjhi, N., Khan, M. K., & Supramaniam, M. (2019). *Link Prediction in Time-Evolving Criminal Network With Deep Reinforcement Learning Technique.* Academic Press.

Lim, Abdullah, Jhanjhi, & Khan. (2019). *Situation-Aware Deep Reinforcement Learning Link Prediction Model for Evolving Criminal Networks.* Academic Press.

Mahor, V., Rawat, R., Kumar, A., Chouhan, M., Shaw, R. N., & Ghosh, A. (2021, September). Cyber Warfare Threat Categorization on CPS by Dark Web Terrorist. In *2021 IEEE 4th International Conference on Computing, Power and Communication Technologies (GUCON)* (pp. 1-6). IEEE. doi:10.1201/9781003140023-6

Mahor, V., Rawat, R., Telang, S., Garg, B., Mukhopadhyay, D., & Palimkar, P. (2021, September). Machine Learning based Detection of Cyber Crime Hub Analysis using Twitter Data. In *2021 IEEE 4th International Conference on Computing, Power and Communication Technologies (GUCON)* (pp. 1-5). IEEE.

Manyumwa, T., Chapita, P. F., Wu, H., & Ji, S. (2020). Towards Fighting Cybercrime: Malicious URL Attack Type Detection using Multiclass Classification. *2020 IEEE International Conference on Big Data (Big Data),* 1813-1822. 10.1109/BigData50022.2020.9378029

Mercaldo & Santone. (2020). Deep learning for image-based mobile malware detection. *Journal of Computer Virology and Hacking Techniques,* 1-15.

Nicholls, J., Kuppa, A., & Le-Khac, N.-A. (2021). Financial Cybercrime: A Comprehensive Survey of Deep Learning Approaches to Tackle the Evolving Financial Crime Landscape. *IEEE Access: Practical Innovations, Open Solutions, 9,* 163965–163986. doi:10.1109/ACCESS.2021.3134076

Rajawat, A.S., Rawat, R., Barhanpurkar, K., Shaw, R.N., & Ghosh,A.(2021). Vulnerability Analysis at Industrial Internet of Things Platform on Dark Web Network Using Computational Intelligence. *Computationally Intelligent Systems and their Applications,* 39-51.

Rajawat, A. S., Rawat, R., Barhanpurkar, K., Shaw, R. N., & Ghosh, A. (2021). Blockchain-Based Model for Expanding IoT Device Data Security. *Advances in Applications of Data-Driven Computing,* 61.

Rajawat, A. S., Rawat, R., Mahor, V., Shaw, R. N., & Ghosh, A. (2021). Suspicious Big Text Data Analysis for Prediction—On Darkweb User Activity Using Computational Intelligence Model. In *Innovations in Electrical and Electronic Engineering* (pp. 735–751). Springer. doi:10.1007/978-981-16-0749-3_58

Rajawat, A. S., Rawat, R., Shaw, R. N., & Ghosh, A. (2021). Cyber Physical System Fraud Analysis by Mobile Robot. In *Machine Learning for Robotics Applications* (pp. 47–61). Springer. doi:10.1007/978-981-16-0598-7_4

Rawat, R., Dangi, C. S., & Patil, J. (2011). Safe Guard Anomalies against SQL Injection Attacks. *International Journal of Computers and Applications*, 22(2), 11–14. doi:10.5120/2558-3511

Rawat, R., Garg, B., Mahor, V., Chouhan, M., Pachlasiya, K., & Telang, S. Cyber Threat Exploitation and Growth during COVID-19 Times. In *Advanced Smart Computing Technologies in Cybersecurity and Forensics* (pp. 85–101). CRC Press.

Rawat, R., Mahor, V., Chirgaiya, S., & Garg, B. (2021). Artificial Cyber Espionage Based Protection of Technological Enabled Automated Cities Infrastructure by Dark Web Cyber Offender. In *Intelligence of Things: AI-IoT Based Critical-Applications and Innovations* (pp. 167–188). Springer. doi:10.1007/978-3-030-82800-4_7

Rawat, R., Mahor, V., Chirgaiya, S., & Rathore, A. S. (2021). Applications of Social Network Analysis to Managing the Investigation of Suspicious Activities in Social Media Platforms. In *Advances in Cybersecurity Management* (pp. 315–335). Springer. doi:10.1007/978-3-030-71381-2_15

Rawat, R., Mahor, V., Chirgaiya, S., Shaw, R. N., & Ghosh, A. (2021). Sentiment Analysis at Online Social Network for Cyber-Malicious Post Reviews Using Machine Learning Techniques. *Computationally Intelligent Systems and their Applications*, 113-130.

Rawat, R., Mahor, V., Chirgaiya, S., Shaw, R. N., & Ghosh, A. (2021). Analysis of Darknet Traffic for Criminal Activities Detection Using TF-IDF and Light Gradient Boosted Machine Learning Algorithm. In *Innovations in Electrical and Electronic Engineering* (pp. 671–681). Springer. doi:10.1007/978-981-16-0749-3_53

Rawat, R., Mahor, V., Rawat, A., Garg, B., & Telang, S. (2021). Digital Transformation of Cyber Crime for Chip-Enabled Hacking. In *Handbook of Research on Advancing Cybersecurity for Digital Transformation* (pp. 227–243). IGI Global. doi:10.4018/978-1-7998-6975-7.ch012

Rawat, R., Rajawat, A. S., Mahor, V., Shaw, R. N., & Ghosh, A. (2021). Dark Web—Onion Hidden Service Discovery and Crawling for Profiling Morphing, Unstructured Crime and Vulnerabilities Prediction. In *Innovations in Electrical and Electronic Engineering* (pp. 717–734). Springer. doi:10.1007/978-981-16-0749-3_57

Rawat, R., Rajawat, A. S., Mahor, V., Shaw, R. N., & Ghosh, A. (2021). Surveillance Robot in Cyber Intelligence for Vulnerability Detection. In *Machine Learning for Robotics Applications* (pp. 107–123). Springer. doi:10.1007/978-981-16-0598-7_9

Shaukat, K., Luo, S., Chen, S., & Liu, D. (2020). Cyber Threat Detection Using Machine Learning Techniques: A Performance Evaluation Perspective. *2020 International Conference on Cyber Warfare and Security (ICCWS)*, 1-6. 10.1109/ICCWS48432.2020.9292388

Shaukat, K., Rubab, A., Shehzadi, I., & Iqbal, R. (2017). A Socio-Technological analysis of Cyber Crime and Cyber Security in Pakistan. *Transylvanian Review*, *1*(3).

Sinaeepourfard, A., Sengupta, S., Krogstie, J., & Delgado, R. R. (2019). Cybersecurity in Large-Scale Smart Cities: Novel Proposals for Anomaly Detection from Edge to Cloud. *2019 International Conference on Internet of Things, Embedded Systems and Communications (IINTEC)*, 130-135. 10.1109/IINTEC48298.2019.9112114

Sivakumar, P. (2021). Real Time Crime Detection Using Deep Learning Algorithm. *2021 International Conference on System, Computation, Automation and Networking (ICSCAN)*, 1-5. 10.1109/ICSCAN53069.2021.9526393

Thiyagarajan, P. (2020). A Review on Cyber Security Mechanisms Using Machine and Deep Learning Algorithms. In *Handbook of Research on Machine and Deep Learning Applications for Cyber Security* (pp. 23–41). IGI Global. doi:10.4018/978-1-5225-9611-0.ch002

Yar, M., & Steinmetz, K. F. (2019). *Cybercrime and society*. SAGE Publications Limited.

Yu, X. (2020). Design of Cross-border Network Crime Detection System Based on PSE and Big Data Analysis. *2020 IEEE International Conference on Power, Intelligent Computing and Systems (ICPICS)*, 480-483. 10.1109/ICPICS50287.2020.9202004

Chapter 9
Anomaly Detection in Biometric Authentication Dataset Using Recurrent Neural Networks

Chitra R.
Karunya Institute of Technology and Sciences, India

Anusha Bamini A. M.
Karunya Institute of Technology and Sciences, India

Chenthil Jegan T. M.
St. Xavier's Catholic College of Engineering, India

Padmaveni K.
Hindustan Institute of Technology and Science, India

ABSTRACT

In the biometric authentication, the stored data is used for the verification of used identity. The unique biological traits commonly used for biological authentication are facial characteristics, fingerprints, and retinas. It also offers superior fraud detection and customer satisfaction, compared to all other traditional multi factor authentication. Deep learning algorithms plays a major role in anomaly detection and fraud identification in various real-time applications. RNNs have proven that they work well in analysing and detecting anomalies in time series data. RNNs have the unique ability for each cell to have its own memory of all the previous cells before it. This allows for RNNs to process sequential data in time steps which other machine learning models cannot do. RNNs can also be found sorting through your emails to sort out spam and phishing emails from friendly emails. This chapter reviews the methodologies, purposes, results, and the benefits of RNNs in anomaly detection in biometric authentication.

INTRODUCTION

The dark web refers the collection of hidden information in the internet which can be used for both illegal

DOI: 10.4018/978-1-6684-6444-1.ch009

and legal applications. Dark Web Pattern Recognition and Crime Analysis Using Machine Intelligence is one of the emerging fields to discriminate the illegal activities of dark web. One key technique used for this analysis is to authenticate the user with proper validation methods. The process of validating the user identity before enabling access to the system or network is known as authentication. During authentication process, the user credentials are compared with the stored credentials to establish secured connection. If the user credential in the server is matched with the credential entered by the user, hen only the user is allowed to use resources (Chauhan et al., 2015, Goodfellow et al., 2014). The resources include software, hardware components, and the allocated time slot to use the resources for the particular user and so on (Patel et al., 2018). The traditional type of authentication used is a two-piece authentication with user name and password. This technique uses the password file where the user ID's are stored with the hash function of the password associated with it. Each login attempt, the password entered by the user is hashed and compared with the value stored in the password file (Li et al., 2019). If both hash functions match, the used is identified as the authenticated user and permission is granted to use the resources. Nowadays biometric authentication is used in many applications to improve the security. Fingerprint scans, facial or retina scan and voice recognition are the commonly used biometric authentication (Zhou et al., 2017).

An anomaly is a situation where the value is deviated from the normal form. The process of finding an outlier in the dataset is called as anomaly detection. This value deviated from the stored data objects in the normal dataset. Anomaly detection is one of the data science applications which includes the task classification, clustering and regression (Chalapathy et all., 2019). The outlier of the dataset is identified by one of the mentioned technologies. Finding anomaly in the stored biometric dataset is a challenging task for the researchers too. Anomaly may occur due to some critical incidents, technical fault or change in user behaviour. Statistical and Regression analysis are used to detect animalities. Machine learning especially deep learning algorithms plays a vital role in the detection of animalities in biometric dataset.

DARK WEB CRIME ANALYSIS

With the speedy growth of hacking methods and tools, it has become a crucial want for different organizations to take required mechanism against cyberattacks and cybercriminals. Dark web plays a vital role in the identification of crimes. Detecting, preventing and recovering cyber-attacks are significance in dark web (Tounsi et al., 2019). It is important to discover the features of cybercriminals' networks to analyse Dark Web forums for understanding the factors that affects the groups (Leukfeldt et al., 2017). Dark web increases the crime especially in the field of drug and terrorism. Silk Road was one of the examples in Dark Web marketplace that sold the drug over a billion dollar and posted drugs by DHL or drop shipping (Barratt et al., 2016, Maddox et al., 2016). Automated Dark Web marketplace is also one of the rubbing methodologies which was employed in various studies. The analysis of the scraped data could provide the basis for a subsequent investigation of suspected criminals and crimes (Celestini et al., 2017). A machine learning technique plays a major role in the analysis of crimes in dark web (Montasar et al., 2021). Intelligent algorithms like deep learning algorithms are used to identify the anomalies in dark web pattern now a day (Shakarian et al., 2018). Unauthorized accessing of system increases the activities of hackers in dark web pages. To prevent the system from unauthorized user, the secured authentication is required in local and remote systems. Biometric authentication is identified as a safe and secure tool for protecting the systems from anomaly entries.

Biometric Authentication

In biometric authentication the physical part of the body is used for security. A fingerprint, an iris scan, a retina scan, or some other physical characteristic which is unique for the individual is generally used in biometric authentication (Pandeeswari et al., 2016). A single or multi characteristics are used for authentication based on the security level required. Here instead of hash function in password, the physical characteristics are mapped with the user's name in the database. The user characteristics are scanned by the sensor and it is compared with the copy of the feature data stored in the database. That is suppose for fingerprint system, the output obtained from the finger print sensor is matched with the image stored in the database, if both a match then the authentication is successful. The suitable infrastructure is required to implement the same. Biometrics is combined with smartcard for high security applications. One of the major applications of biometric is network login. The biometric authentication is classified into many categories and it's shown in Fig 1.

Based on the characteristics Biometrics is classified into Physiological and Behavioural biometrics. In Physiological biometrics physical features are used for identification and it can be used for all sort of users (Kim et al., 2020). Mostly it is used to verify whether the person is physically present in the environment or not. It also uses the sensor output as traits for comparing with the dataset. The commonly used physiological biometrics is fingerprint, iris, face, hand and DNA (Vaughan et al., 2019). In behavioural biometric the common pattern or the behaviour of the human is considered for verification. In this technique the human computer interaction is considered as the key element for authentication (Channe et al., 2009). Behavioural produce better results in fraud detection of online banking and trading. Keystroke, signature and voice are some of the behavioural biometric features used in real life. The most popular biometric authentication techniques are

Fingerprint

Initially the authenticated user finger prints are scanned and stored in a file directly by user or by another agent. During the registration process the fingerprint is scanned repeatedly by placing the finger of the user on the finger print reader (Rawat et al.,2011). Multiple images are stored and analysed to identify and fix the point pattern of the user fingerprint. Once a consistent pattern is obtained it is stored in the database for future comparison. This authentication technique is used in many applications such as portable computers, mobile phones, voting, puncing in institutions and software industries etc.

Face

It is a type of biometric security. In this biometric dataset the facial geometry is used for authentication. The facial identity is recognized and verified by the facial pattern recognition devices. The face image of the person attempted to login is scanned and it is compared with the image already stored in biometric database. Hence the system determines if the two images are of the same person or not. Initially camera detects the face and then I is captured and analysed. Most of the facial recognition system 2D images rather than 3D images. The facial landmarks with distinguish features are extracted, it's converted into numerical code called as faceprint. Each person having his unique faceprint. This faceprint is further used for facial recognition.

Figure 1. Biometric classification

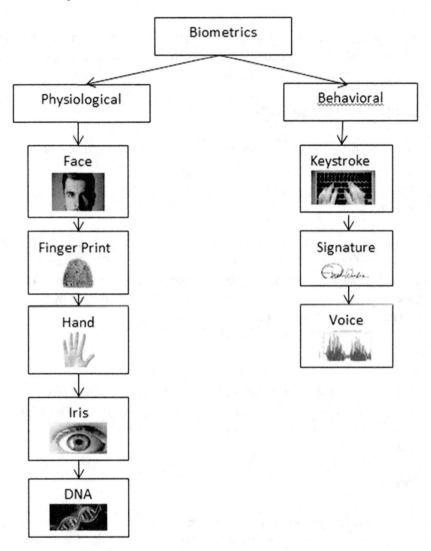

Iris and Retina

In Iris based authentication, the trabecular meshwork tissue in the iris is scanned by iris scanner and it is used for verification. The mathematical pattern recognition on video images of single or both iris is compared with the stored pattern. The iris patterns are unique and stable for individuals. The retina is a tissue located in the eye which contain complex capillaries, every human has unique pattern of retinal capillaries. If a low energy infra-red beam is passed through person's eye, the reflected wave is detected. The variance of code is generated by each person and it is stored in the database for further verification. This one of the most accurate technology with less than 0.0001% false prediction rate.

Hand

As like fingerprint, the handprint is also unique for a person. In this biometric the user is identified from the shape of their hands. In this technique the geometry like length, deviation, width and angle are calculated from the palm and fingers and it's stored in the database for verification.

Benefits of Biometric Authentication

In digital era, the biometric authentication used in many digital applications and it has a number of advantages.

Improved Security

Increase level of assurance is provided by the biometrics because a person is verified by his own trait itself. Data beach is one of the most security issues in passwords and PINs, it can be avoided in biometrics (Wan et al.,2016). The fraudsters may identify the password set by the user but can't use the face or finger of the user (Janjic et al.,2011). In biometrics the traits are provided by the living humans and hence it is not imitated by even Robots too.

Fast and User Convenient

In user point of view, the biometric authentication is easy, convenient and produces quick response. Unlocking the account simply by scanning the face or fingerprint is much easier than typing the multi-character password. Similarly major issue in the password verification is the chance to forget password and it can be avoided in biometrics.

Null Replication

The biometrics iris, retina, fingerprint, hand and face are impossible to replicate with current technology. Hence the 100-percentage security is obtained if the account is protected by biometric security.

Challenges in Biometric Authentication

Biometrics are used worldwide in many organizations and companies. The major challenge to implement this biometric authentication is the hardware cost. The special hardware is required for each biometrics and it must be installed and configured in all systems where log in is required (Han et al., 2018). Its impossible to use all the systems for authentication purpose. Similarly remote login policy is also difficult in this technology (Rajawat et al., 2021). The initial cost of the biometric authentication is high compared to all other techniques. In addition to initial cost the upgradation and maintenance cost of the biometric hardware is also high. Setting of the sensitivity level for the sample is also a potential issue in the biometric security. If the sensitivity level is too low there is a possibility to match more images in the recorded sample. If the sensitivity level is too high, the person who is legally authorized to access the system may also blocked. In some cases, in addition to finger print, the temperature level is also recorded to improve security; hence this biometric authentication is not used in internet-based applications.

The biometric data must be handled with increased security and caution because biometric data is irreplaceable and it's expensive and technically difficult in order to stay ahead of fraud advancements. If the password or PIN is stolen then there is a chance to change it but the biometric data cannot be modify by the used to protect it from hackers because it is the biological or behavioural characteristics of the human (Rajawat et al., 2021). The use of biometric authentication systems like facial recognition technology and other biometric security measures increases worldwide, the privacy of used should also take into consideration. If the biometric of the user is saved in the organization database, the used permanently placing their identity there and it will affect the privacy of the person after they left from the organization also. It can also be used to track the person with and without knowledge. Many biometric authentication methods trust on partial information to authenticate a user's identity. For example, a mobile biometric device will scan an entire fingerprint during the enrolment phase, and convert it into data. However, future biometric authentication of the fingerprint will only use parts of the prints to verify identity so it's faster and quicker. Hence there is a possibility of false prediction if more images are stored in the same database.

ANOMALY DETECTION IN BIOMETRIC DATASET

Anomaly detection is the process of finding outliers in a given dataset. Outliers are the data objects that stand out amongst other objects in the dataset and do not conform to the normal behaviour in a dataset. It's difficult to identify the anomaly in the biomedical dataset because the classification of normal and abnormal requires additional knowledge. The anomalies are rarely occurred in biometrics and it couldn't be identified in that particular instance. Statical and intelligent techniques can be used to identify the anomalies in the dataset. Anomaly may occur due to the fault in input scanners, storage interpretation or by intruders. These detections techniques are vey popular in real world situation and it is mainly used in networks, fabrications, saving card fraud detection and fabrications. Anomalies are also the unusual entries identified in the data set due to noise or inference, The supervised, unsupervised and semi supervised the common categories of the anomaly detection.

Anomaly Detection Terminology

In biometric dataset the patterns are generated by a sequence of datapoints. The datapoints are generated by some mathematical calculations. These datapoints underlies some statical methods and some statical model is used for the generation of datapoint. The parametric or non-parametric statical inference tests are required to analyse the anomaly in the biometric dataset. If the underlying distribution is known and the data is estimated based on certain parameters then it is called as parametric method. The Gaussian model and Regression model are the commonly known parametric models. If the parameters of the distributions are calculated from the existing data, its termed as nonparametric method. The methods include kernel function and histogram are example for non-parametric statistical methods. Sometimes semi parametric technique known as proximity-based techniques can also used to identify anomalies in the dataset. Statistical techniques have the advantage of being explainable as well as interpretable, especially when the distribution of the underlying data is known. In addition, some of these techniques, such as histogram-based or those which model single exponential distributions, can be easy to implement, or computationally efficient. However, kernel-based techniques and models with complex distribution

Figure 2. Normal distribution plot for Gaussian model

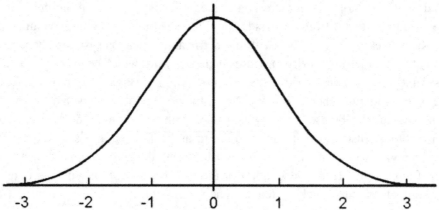

induce a higher computational complexity. A limitation of the statistical approaches is that testing for outliers assumes that a specific distribution characterizes the recorded data points. This turns out not to be the case for most of the high dimensional data. Another challenge is that it may not be straightforward to choose the best statistics test for detecting the anomalies. Furthermore, histogram-based techniques are not suited for multivariate data, as they do not take into account the interaction between the attributes of the data.Gaussian based anomaly detection is one of the simplest statistical methods used in biometric authentication dataset. In this terminology the entire algorithm works towards normal distribution. A Gaussian or a Normal Distribution is a form of continuous probability distribution for a real-valued random variable. The probability function is calculated using expression 1. μ is the mean and σ^2 is the variance.

$$\mathcal{N}(x \; ; \; \mu, \sigma) = \frac{1}{\sqrt{2\pi\sigma^2}} \exp \left[-\frac{1}{2}(x - \mu)^2 / \sigma^2 \right]$$

(1)

The probability distribution is symmetric about its mean and non-zero over the entire real line. The normal distribution is sometimes called the bell curve because the density graph looks like a bell. The normal distribution plot is shown in Figure 2.

To detect anomaly the probability function and the threshold is calculated and plotted, the data points far away from that threshold are considered anomalies. The probability function and its threshold mapping for the statistical data is shown in Figure 3. In figure 3 p(x) is the probability function and ε is the threshold value. The data points are represented by the crosses.

In the basic anomaly detection algorithm, we assume that each feature is distributed according to its own Gaussian Distribution with some set of means and variances. So using the training dataset, we fit a set of parameters $\mu_1, \mu_2, ..., \mu_n$ and $\sigma_1^2, \sigma_2^2, ..., \sigma_n^2$ with respect to features $x_1, x_2, ..., x_n$. Then the probability function p(x) is calculated as the probability of x1 times the probability of x2 times

Figure 3. Distribution of datapoints

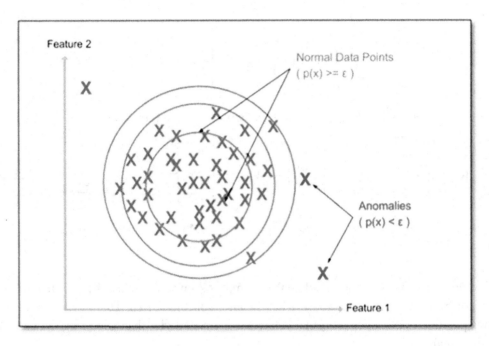

the probability of x3 and so on up to the probability of xn. When a new data point comes in, we simply calculate the probability p(x) and flag it as an anomaly if the probability is less than ε. This scenario is adopted in machine learning based anomaly detection of biometric dataset. Optimization algorithms are incorporated with machine learning algorithms for identifying the value of ε.

Supervised versus Unsupervised Anomaly Detection

Supervised learning algorithms has been proven as the key technology for many web based applications including healthcare, IoT and cloud applications (Chitra etal.,2015, Seenivasagam et al., 2016). Today many popular libraries like scikit-learn (for python) are used to implement the anomaly detection algorithms. Some of the well-known anomaly detection algorithms are Density-based techniques, Cluster analysis-based techniques, Bayesian Networks, Neural networks, autoencoders, LSTM networks, Support vector machines, Hidden Markov models and Fuzzy logic-based outlier detection. The unsupervised approach is the most common version of anomaly detection in biometric authentication dataset. Here a machine-learning model is trained to fit to the normal behaviour using an unlabelled dataset (Mahor et al.,2021). In this technique it is assumed that most of the data in the training set are normal and only few anomalous data points examples are identified among them. The data item differ from normal behaviour is flagged as an anomaly. In biometric dataset there is a possibility of small portion anomalies and thus unsupervised anomaly detections are well suited for it.

Typical classification technique is used in supervised anomaly detection. A classifier will be trained using a normal and abnormal dataset. Number of positive and negative examples are needed in supervised anomaly detection methodology (Rawat et al.,2021). Obtaining such a dataset will be very difficult since anomalous examples are rare. However, there are many different types of anomalies in any domain and

Figure 4. RNN architecture

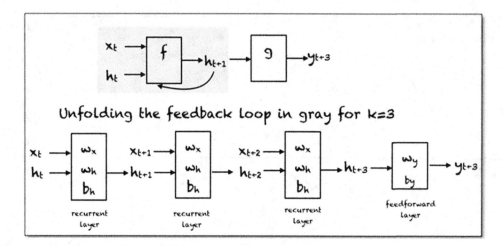

also future anomalies may look nothing like the examples seen so far. It will be very hard for any algorithm to learn from anomalous examples; what the anomalies look like. That is why the unsupervised approach is popular. Capturing the normal behaviour is much easier than capturing the many different types of abnormalities.

The accurate prediction anomaly detection in streaming data and real-time systems has an increasing demand. Deep learning algorithms play a vital role in anomaly detection in huge amount of data. In offline processing the complete

RECURRENT NEURAL NETWORK

General feed forward neural networks are well suited for data points independent to each other. But in biometric dataset the pattern is obtained from related datapoint, such that one datapoint depends on the previous once. Hence the modified structure of the neural network is required for processing the biometric dataset. The A recurrent neural network (RNN) is a special type of neural network in which the memory is incorporated to store the previous information for current processing.

The architecture of the RNN is shown in Figure 4.

Long short-term memory (LSTM): This is a popular RNN architecture, which was introduced by Sepp Hochreiter and Juergen Schmidhuber as a solution to vanishing gradient problem. The RNN model may not be able to accurately predict the current state and it can be overcome by LSTM. The LSTM networks are a sub-type of the more general recurrent neural networks (RNN). A key attribute of recurrent neural networks is their ability to persist information, or cell state, for use later in the network. Generally a cumulative sum method is used to identify the anomalies in a cyberphysical system. For biometric dataset the LSTM first used to design a predictive model of the required system. The Gaussian distribution of the dataset is used to find whether the given input is normal or abnormal. In LSTM no pre-processing is required. Selective read, write and forget technology is used LSTM. Figure 5 shows the selective write strategy.

Figure 5. LSTM selective write

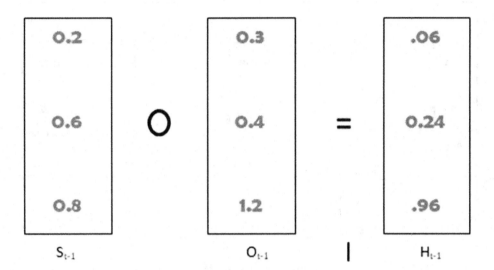

In RNN, S_{t-1} is fed along with x_t to a cell whereas in LSTM S_{t-1} is transformed to h_{t-1} using another vector O_{t-1}. This process is called selective write. The steps required for selective write is given in equation 2.

$$O_{t-1} = \sigma \left(U_0 x_{t-1} + W_0 h_{t-2} + b_0 \right)$$
$$h_{t-1} = S_{t-1} \circ O_{t-1}$$
$$O_t = \text{ output gate}$$

(2)

The example of selective Read operation is shown in Figure 6.

h_{t-1} is added with x_t to produce s_t. Then Hadamard product of and it is made to obtain s_t. This is called an input gate. In st only selective information goes and this process is called selective read. Mathematically, equations for selective read are as below

The concept of selective forget network is shown in Figure 7.

s_{t-1} is hadamard product with f_t and is called selective forget. Overall s_t is obtained from the addition of selective read and selective forget. The equation for elective forget is given as

To avoid anomalies the LSTM based authentication system is proposed for biometric systems.

$$i_t = \sigma \left(U_i x_t + W_i h_{t-1} + b_i \right)$$
$$\text{selective read } = \overline{s_t} \cdot oi_t$$

Figure 6. LSTM selective read

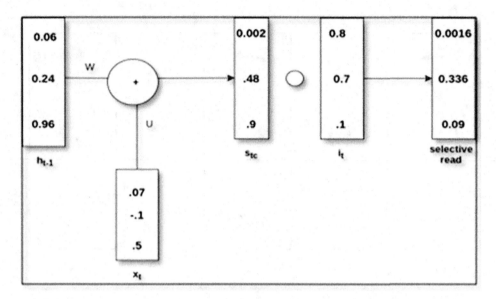

Figure 7. LSTM selective forget

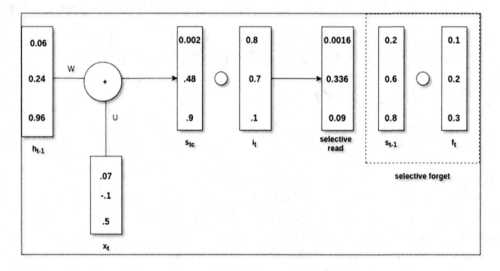

ANOMALY DETECTION USING LSTM

Dense neural network is used in LSTM for anomaly detection. The dataset obtained from multiple log entry is given as the input to detect and predict the outliers in the biometric images. When the raw data is processed, the generalized detection and diagnosis based on LSTM is adopted. The log data, uses the stacked LSTM, the output of each LSTM will be fed as an input to the next layer. The dataset is pre-processed initially for better performance. The LSTM network maps the input sequence $x_{(1:T)}, t = 1$ to T. Unique embedded vectors for each element in the log data are then mapped to a sequence of hidden vectors $h_{(1:T)}$ (1) as follows: where h at time t is a summary of the input sequence $x_{(1:T)}$; for the given hidden state at time $t-1$, the weight W and the bias-vector-calculated $p(t)$ is the probability distribution over sequence at time t.

$$LSTM(x_{(i:T)}) = h_{(i:T)}$$

$$p(t) = softmax(h_{(t-1)}W+b)$$

The network is trained and tested with known dataset. The dataset can be downloaded from http://www.cs.ucr.edu/~eamonn/discords/

Anomaly detection aims to determine patterns in the data that do not conform to expected normal behavior. One of the important issues for anomaly detection techniques is the availability of labeled data for model training / validation. A hyper approach centred on short-term and long-term memory (the LSTM autoencoder) and the one class carrier vector machine (OCSVM) are used to detect anomaly-based attacks in an unbalanced dataset, models training using only normal class examples. The LSTM automatic encoder is trained to learn the normal traffic model and to learn the compressed illustration of the input data, then feed it into an OCSVM approach. The hybrid model overcomes the shortcomings of the separate OCSVM, in which its poor ability to operate with massive and large data sets. Additionally, the experiment is performed using the latest Intrusion Detection Systems (IDS) (InSDN) dataset for SDN environments. This model offers a higher detection rate and considerably reduces the processing time. Therefore, our method offers great security in protecting SDN networks against malicious traffic.

CONCLUSION

The proposed a novel LSTM based DRNN architecture for ECG classification and performed experimental evaluation of our model on prescribed datasets. The results confirm that the proposed model outperforms various conventional methods and establishes a higher efficiency. This enhancement can be attributed to the ability of the model to extract more features of ECG using the deep layers of DRNN. The model can further control the temporal dependencies within the ECG signals. Furthermore the effect of the input sequence length and found the relationship between the hidden unit and hidden layer. Segmentation and grouping of ECGs using the preprocessing procedure can effectively impact a real-time system in the classification and authentication processes. The proposed model offers better performance with shorter sequences than advanced methods. This feature is useful in real-time personal ECG identification systems that require rapid results. The study confirms that the LSTM-based bidirectional DRNN proposal holds promise for real-time ECG-based biometric identification applications. Our experiments did not have the scale of the samples and the results were affected by the material environments. In the future, a large-scale experimental study with normal human ECG signals will be conducted: calm, eat, sleep, run, walk, etc. In addition, our LSTM-based bidirectional DRNN proposal will be extensively evaluated with other ECG signals obtained from individuals of different age groups. Future large research studies will aim to demonstrate the robustness and efficiency of the model.

REFERENCES

Barratt, M. J., Ferris, J. A., & Winstock, A. R. (2016). Safer scoring? Cryptomarkets, social supply and drug market violence. *The International Journal on Drug Policy*, *35*, 24–31. doi:10.1016/j.drugpo.2016.04.019 PMID:27241015

Billel, A., & Faycal, H. (2017). On Markov-switching periodic ARMA models. *Communications in Statistics*, *47*(2), 344–364.

Celestini, G. M., & Mignone, M. (2017). Tor marketplaces exploratory data analysis: The drugs case. *Int. Conf. Global Secur., Saf., Sustainability*.

Chalapathy & Chawla. (2019). *Deep learning for anomaly detection: A survey*. arXiv preprint:1901.03407.

Channe, S., Paul, J., & Wei, J. (2009). The future gamma-ray burst mission SVOM. *Proceedings of Science*.

Chauhan, S., & Vig, L. (2015). Anomaly detection in ECG time signals via deep long short-term memory networks. *IEEE International Conference on Data Science and Advanced Analytics (DSAA)*, 1–7. 10.1109/DSAA.2015.7344872

Chitra, R., & Seenivasagam, V. (2015). Heart Disease Prediction System Using Intelligent Network. *Power Electronics and Renewable Energy Systems*, *326*(134), 1377–1384.

Fei, H., Dong, H., & Wang, Z. (2018). Improved Tobit Kalman filtering for systems withcrandom parameters via conditional expectation. *Signal Processing*, *147*, 35–45. doi:10.1016/j.sigpro.2018.01.015

Goodfellow, Pouget-Abadie, Mirza, Xu, Warde-Farley, Ozair, Courville, &. Bengio. (2014). Generative adversarial nets. Advances in Neural Information Processing Systems, 27.

Kim, B.-H., & Pyun, J.-Y. (2020). ECG identification for personal authentication using LSTM-based deep recurrent neural networks. *Sensors (Basel)*, *20*(11), 3069. doi:10.339020113069 PMID:32485827

Leukfeldt, R., Kleemans, E. R., & Stol, W. P. (2017). Cybercriminal networks, social ties and online forums: Social ties versus digital ties within phishing and malware networks. *British Journal of Criminology*, *57*(3), 704–722.

Li, Chen, Jin, Shi, Goh, & Ng. (2019). Mad-gan: Multivariate anomaly detection for time series data with generative adversarial networks. In *International Conference on Artificial Neural Networks*. Springer. 10.1007/978-3-030-30490-4_56

Maddox, M. J., Barratt, M. J., Allen, M., & Lenton, S. (2016). Constructive activism in the dark Web: Cryptomarkets and illicit drugs in the digital demimonde. *Information Communication and Society*, *19*(1), 111–126. doi:10.1080/1369118X.2015.1093531

Mahor, V., Rawat, R., Kumar, A., Chouhan, M., Shaw, R. N., & Ghosh, A. (2021, September). Cyber Warfare Threat Categorization on CPS by Dark Web Terrorist. In *2021 IEEE 4th International Conference on Computing, Power and Communication Technologies (GUCON)* (pp. 1-6). IEEE. 10.1109/GUCON50781.2021.9573994

Meng. (2016). *Column store for gwac: a High-cadence, High-density, Large-scale astronomical light curve pipeline and distributed Shared-nothing database.* Astronomical Society of the Pacific.

Meng, W., Chao, W., & Zhang, Y. (2016). A Pre-research on GWAC Massive Catalog Data Storage and Processing System. *Tianwen Yanjiu Yu Jishu,* (3), 373–381.

Pandeeswari, N., & Kumar, G. (2016). Anomaly detection system in cloud environment using fuzzy clustering based ANN. *Mobile Networks and Applications, 21*(3), 494–505. doi:10.100711036-015-0644-x

Pankaj, Lovekesh, & Gautam. (2015). Long Short Term Memory networks for anomaly detection in time series. *European Symposium on Artificial Neural Networks,* 89-94.

Patel, N., Saridena, A. N., Choromanska, A., Krishnamurthy, P., & Khorrami, F. (2018). Adversarial learning-based on-line anomaly monitoring for assured autonomy. *IEEE/RSJ International Conference on Intelligent Robots and Systems (IROS),* 6149–6154. 10.1109/IROS.2018.8593375

Rajawat, A. S., Rawat, R., Barhanpurkar, K., Shaw, R. N., & Ghosh, A. (2021). Vulnerability Analysis at Industrial Internet of Things Platform on Dark Web Network Using Computational Intelligence. *Computationally Intelligent Systems and their Applications,* 39-51.

Rajawat, A. S., Rawat, R., Mahor, V., Shaw, R. N., & Ghosh, A. (2021). Suspicious Big Text Data Analysis for Prediction—On Darkweb User Activity Using Computational Intelligence Model. In *Innovations in Electrical and Electronic Engineering* (pp. 735–751). Springer. doi:10.1007/978-981-16-0749-3_58

Rawat, R., Dangi, C. S., & Patil, J. (2011). Safe Guard Anomalies against SQL Injection Attacks. *International Journal of Computer Applications, 22*(2), 11-14.

Rawat, R., Mahor, V., Chirgaiya, S., & Rathore, A. S. (2021). Applications of Social Network Analysis to Managing the Investigation of Suspicious Activities in Social Media Platforms. In *Advances in Cybersecurity Management* (pp. 315–335). Springer. doi:10.1007/978-3-030-71381-2_15

Rawat, R., Rajawat, A. S., Mahor, V., Shaw, R. N., & Ghosh, A. (2021). Dark Web—Onion Hidden Service Discovery and Crawling for Profiling Morphing, Unstructured Crime and Vulnerabilities Prediction. In *Innovations in Electrical and Electronic Engineering* (pp. 717–734). Springer. doi:10.1007/978-981-16-0749-3_57

Seenivasagam, V., & Chitra, R. (2016). Myocardial Infarction Detection Using Intelligent Algorithms. *Neural Network World, 26*(1), 91–110. doi:10.14311/NNW.2016.26.005

Tijana, J., & Lars, N. (2011). On domain localization in ensemble-based Kalman filter algoithms. *Monthly Weather Review, 139*(7), 2046–2060.

Tounsi, W. (2019). *What is cyber threat intelligence and how is it evolving? In Cyber-Vigilance and Digital Trust: Cyber Security in the Era of Cloud Computing and IoT.* ISTE Ltd.

Vaughan, S. (2020). Random time series in astronomy. Philosophical Transactions of the Royal Society of London, 371(1984).

Zhou & Paffenroth. (2017). Anomaly detection with robust deep autoencoders. *Proceedings of the 23rd ACM SIGKDD International Conference on Knowledge Discovery and Data Mining,* 665–674.

Section 4
Content Labeling for Hidden Services Using Keyword Extraction

Chapter 10
Content Labelling of Hidden Services With Keyword Extraction Using the Graph Decomposition Method

Ashwini Dalvi
Veermata Jijabai Technological Institute, India

Dhairya Rajendra Bhuta
Veermata Jijabai Technological Institute, India

Saurabh Mahesh Raut
Veermata Jijabai Technological Institute, India

Saikumar Nalla
Veermata Jijabai Technological Institute, India

Nirmit Joshi
Veermata Jijabai Technological Institute, India

S. G. Bhirud
Veermata Jijabai Technological Institute, India

ABSTRACT

The data investigation of hidden services on the dark web is gaining attention from the research community and law enforcement agencies. However, the anonymity feature of hidden services makes it difficult to index the hidden services for investigation. Therefore, one of the primary focuses of dark web data investigation research is labelling the hidden services so that the labelled services can be classified or indexed further. The methodology deployed in the proposed work is based on keyword extraction using the graph degeneracy method. The proposed work analyzes the text data by extracting keywords from each hidden service document. The accuracy of the proposed method is validated by LDA-based topic modelling approach. The document labelling obtained by the keyword extraction method and LDA model matched with the accuracy of 78. The main intuition behind the keywords extraction method is that central nodes make good keywords. This is because central nodes with high centrality in the GoW of a document correspond to the document's keywords, which are well-understood by humans.

DOI: 10.4018/978-1-6684-6444-1.ch010

INTRODUCTION

The usefulness of dark web content investigation has been established over the years. The discussed work is one of the leading examples of how researchers attempt to identify the suitability of dark web content (Samtani, S. et al., 2021).

The researchers have attempted machine learning based approaches to investigate crimes on the dark web. Researchers investigate the individual use cases to comprehend the dark web crime pattern. For example, researchers tried to analyse the lives of drug users using a website based in Finland (Haasio, A. et al.,2020). Nine thousand three hundred posts from the site were analysed to get insights into the socio-economic conditions of the users. This analysis involved using usernames and forum posts to find the representation of a user's way of life and their association with drugs. A user's identity can be determined based on the language they choose for their name. In the Sipulitori sample, usernames were mainly in Finnish, accounting for 57% of the total usernames, followed by English which accounted for 20%, and then 5% usernames were in other languages. For the remaining 17% usernames, the language could not be identified. This suggests that users would not opt for a global identity but prefer an identity that indicates they belong to the local community since there are notions that certain ethnicities are not reliable for doing business. Names based on drugs are relatively low. Usernames spanned a wide area of topics such as personal names, made-up words, names related to places, and names of fictional characters. This suggests that most users are hobbyists, not people involved in serious criminal activities. From the analysis of several messages, it could be figured out that the users' habitus was a learned way of keeping one's lifestyle in check without breaking social ethics.

The discussed work gave an overview of the Canadian illegal medicate advertisement (Broséus, J. et al., 2016). The work used information collected on eight crypto markets to understand the structure and organisation of dispersion systems existing online. It depicts how the investigation of information accessible online may inspire information on criminal activities.

The research investigated the hypothesis - the interactions in the dark web violate financial service regulation Todorof, M. (2019). For example, the personal data breach threatens investors' identity. The author proposed that the dark web would disrupt the traditional financial sector. The primary reason behind such disruption is the prevalence of bitcoin as a currency on the dark web. On similar premises, the research outlined those technologies like blockchain, cryptocurrencies, dark web make cyber security challenging (Diodati, J., et al., 2021). Further, researchers presented a review on blooming identity theft and fraud driven by the financial motive on the dark web (Szakonyi, A., et al., 2021).

The dark web research presented the hypothesis of crypto currency abused (Lee, S., et.al., 2019). The authors mentioned the framework MFScope which analysed about 27 million dark web pages. 10 million dark web pages were inspected to analyse crypto currency transactions on the dark web. The work concluded traces of Bitcoin, Ethereum, Monaro on dark web crypto currency economy. The dark web crypto currency economy is estimated to be around 180 million US dollars. The investigation also resulted in providing traces of Bitcoin transactions by transacting two real world illicit services.

Researchers employed a machine learning based approach to investigate data breaches and data related to stolen identities, particularly for Small and Medium Enterprises (SMEs) (Pantelis, G., et.al 2021). Thus, literature shows that researchers have explored diverse dark web crime patterns.

The surface web is easy to access and can be navigated through regular browsers like Chrome, Edge and many more. But when it comes to the dark web, one needs a particular type of browser called Tor (The Onion Router). Other browsers cannot access this network due to the unique and specific requirements that it needs. The web service host on the Tor network, leading to the dark web, hides its IP address from the internet to become unnoticeable. Websites hosted on the Tor network end with suffix .onion instead of standard internet, which is .com or .org. These websites can only be opened through the Tor browser and referred to as Hidden Services (HS).

The major challenge with dark web hidden service (HS) is identifying the content present on HS without opening it. The researchers attempted labelling of hidden service content with the help of experts, and researchers prepared a customised dataset. The content labelling with the experts required experts with domain-specific knowledge. For example, hidden services analysed for hacking forums and experts from cyber security domains must attest to the hidden service hosting related data. Another approach relies on creating a dataset that will serve the purpose of labelling the hidden service. Some research uses programming language-based topic modelling packages like MALLET (MAchine Learning for LanguagE Toolkit) to label the hidden service content (McCallum, A. K., 2002).

The Tor hidden service content labelling is driven by individual research groups' attempts to crawl the Tor dark web with existing crawlers or improvised crawler implementation. The crawled hidden service data is unlabelled. Some research attempts are made to label each hidden service with variants of text feature classification algorithms. However, the observations from research in dark web content identifications are available hidden service datasets are mostly related to dark web market listings, and no standard labelled hidden services dataset is available. Thus, researchers improvised to label the hidden service data with existing text feature classification approaches or other forms like keyword extractions.

The overall attempt is made to label the dark web hidden services by considering crawled hidden service pages in the form of documents to apply various machine learning based approaches to label the document. Different representation models have been developed in machine learning-based research to extract valuable information from the document vocabulary. There are two types of embeddings on a comprehensive level, namely word and graph. Word embeddings are further divided into two kinds: Frequency-based and Prediction based.

The proposed chapter extends the scope of content labelling of hidden services. The objectives of the proposed work are as follows:

- Label the individual hidden service by keyword extraction
- Apply graph degeneracy method to extract the keyword
- Evaluation of the results produced by keyword extraction method by comparing it with the results generated by the Latent Dirichlet allocation (LDA) on the same data

The main intuition behind the keywords extraction method is that central nodes make good keywords. This is because central nodes with high centrality in the Graph of Words (GoW) of a document correspond to the keywords for the document, which are well-understood by humans. Thus, such keywords are used to label the hidden service in the proposed work and eliminate the dependency of manual labelling of dark web hidden services.

The proposed approach aims to label hidden content service content from various domains, including cybercrime prevention, customer care service, fraud detection through claims investigation, social media data analysis and business intelligence.

The following chapter outlined section two to include background work involved in content labelling of hidden services. Then, the chapter contains a detailed discussion of the proposed work's dataset and methodologies. Next, the chapter includes the results generated by two approaches (Graph of Words and Bag of Words) and a description of the lemma confirmed from the implementation.

BACKGROUND

The most lucrative aspect of the dark web is the anonymity it offers its users, making it a haven for criminal activities. Some of the tools which provide these features are Tor, Freenet, I2P, etc., out of which Tor is the most widely used tool. The technological advancements required for accessing the darknet require crawling schemes that are more specialised, sophisticated, and more focused than the surface net.

The dark web content is research with reference to various approaches like drug market analysis and hacker forums. For example, the dark web marketplace Agora was researched (Baravalle, A., et.al., 2016). It was also found that Agora used techniques for several authentications and discouragement web scraping. Also, the total market for drugs was huge in all possible ways, such as total items on sale, total sellers offering drug-related services. Researchers even studied the marketplaces on the dark web passively. In work (Meland, P. H., et.al., 2019), researchers manually studied dark web marketplace to address research questions like types of cyberattacks available for sale and which attacks are more sellable.

The dark web crawled data need to be categorised depending upon respective domains, which is one of the most significant challenge researchers has faced. The literature discusses the different approaches for dark web content identification and classification. For example, the authors employed MapReduce based techniques to classify attack patterns of cybercriminals from the dark web data (Rajawat, A. S., et al., 2021). The Name entity Recognition (NER) based approach is discussed to identify names, locations, products, corporations from Tor dark web data (Al-Nabki, et al., 2019).

The primary literature approach is focused on inferring text data present on crawled hidden service web pages with the help of text classification. In one attempt, text summarisation algorithms are applied to the content extracted from the dark web. The work of (Joshi, A., Fidalgo et al., 2018) has compared common and reputed text summarisation methodologies to determine which algorithms give the best result. As per their results, TextRank is the best summarisation algorithm on average.

The proposed work is focused on labelling the Tor hidden service. Thus, the literature review is carried out to comprehend dark web content identification attempts.

Challenges of Content Labelling of Hidden Services

The literature review concerning labelling the Tor hidden service content resulted in two challenges: Manual labelling of Hidden Services and limited open source labelled dark web data sets.

In (Ghosh, S., et.al., 2017) the researcher discussed ATOL, which stands for Automatic Tool for Onion Labelling. Authors have used a two-phase methodology to accomplish their strategy. Firstly, their tool learns concise and biased keywords for various categories. In the second phase, these terms will map each onion page's content to a collection of thematic labels. The approach categorises the data in various types like categorisation based on their thematic labels (category of content), functional roles (like if seller hosts a site) and even content type (like blogs, etc.). The initial category-keywords listed is a manually curated list by domain experts (analysts). These pre-learned keywords associated with a category are further expanded per the onion category. This expanded list of category keywords will train a classifier categorising each onion page into thematic labels. This extraction process is done using

Natural Language Processing (NLP) since the label to the website is known. Thus, increasing the tool's list of words enables better classification further on. Now, for the web page, TFICF (Term Frequency Inverse Class Frequency) is used. TFICF is different from TFIDF (Term Frequency Inverse Document Frequency).

Requirement for a large dataset for training and manual labelling of dark web content are considered challenges in dark web content classification. To overcome the said challenges in work (He, S., et.al.,. (2019), authors referred selected set of rules related to pre-selected types of content such as pornography, hacker, drugs. The work used legal documents to pick up relevant terms to train the supervised learning models. The customised crawled Tor hidden services pages were collected and processed to feed the model. The model was a combination of TF-IDF and Naive Bayes algorithms. The discussed model offered advantages by using a limited dataset for training and no manual intervention required to label the data.

But the proposed approach was limited in categorising a limited set of illegal activities on the dark web. The idea of creating a training model based on authorised regulations for pre-selected categories is further exercised in (Mahor, V., et al., 2021). The authors manually tagged 5379 hidden services in Espionage, Sabotage, Electrical power grid, propaganda, economic disputation. The work was limited to English content. The legitimate text document database was referred to create feature selections for selected categories. Further, with TF IDF and ML-based classifiers like Ada boost, decision tree and SVM, the crawled data was classified. Thus, the researchers attempt a limited set of categories to train the supervised model with legitimate text features for illegal content or activities classification.

A manually labelled dataset drove the work of content classification to categorise the hidden services. In work (Sabbah, T., et.al., 2014), the authors applied a modified frequency-based term weight scheme on the dark web forum dataset. The said dataset was manually labelled. The SVM classifier was used for content classification. The limitations of the scope of discussed work were that the content classification is done on the existing dataset, and manual data labelling was used to train the model.

In (Khare, A., et al., 2020), the authors created a labelled dataset for nine domains by scraping content from related hidden services listed on Hidden wiki pages. The labelled data is trained Naïve Bayes, SVM, logistic regression and logistic regression with Keras model, which accepted text features by Bag of Words and TF-IDF based approaches. The better classification accuracy was achieved with the logistics regression model with Keras. The work discussed in (Dalins, J., et.al., 2018) proposed TMM Tor use Motivation Model to classify Tor dark web content used by law and enforcement agencies. The authors crawled around 1155549 Tor web pages from different 49 domains, and 4000 Tor pages were manually labelled to train the model.

In (Avarikioti, G., et al., 2018), manual labelling was done on collected crawled data samples to train an SVM-based supervised learning model. The authors crawled 17 dark web marketplaces to collect information or product offerings on malwares, exploits. The manual labelling is done on collected samples to apply unsupervised clustering (Marin, E., et al., 2016).

The work in (Faizan, M., et.al., 2019) explored and analysed the dark web by collecting the dataset using a customised Python crawler. The data were classified into 31 categories to examine and explore the content available on the dark web. The dark web consists of hidden services, and these services have their IP addresses hidden from the outside world. The discussed research is one of the few papers focusing on English and Non-English content. It was discovered that the second most used language on the dark web was Russian after English. In work (Yang, L., et al., G. 2019) contrast to traditional text feature classification algorithms, authors discussed deep learning based model for short text classification. The model categorises different products available in the dark web marketplace. The crawler developed by the authors collected the data.

In work (Spitters, M., et al., 2014), researchers applied the LDA model to investigate the organisation of hidden services. A dark web crawler implemented by researchers collected the hidden services under consideration. The work attempted the labelling of hidden services with three tasks. The first task was to estimate the model. In the discussion, the LDA model was implemented by Mallet implementation. Then, the 250 topics were estimated, and manual annotation was done to list the words under these categories. Further, the topic aggregation was done at the hidden service level. Finally, the work presented a topic model-based approach to label the unseen hidden service and presented linguistic diversity in collected hidden service data. But the future scope of work promised to look into a topic assignment in detail.

The framework 'BlackWidow' was designed to monitor deep and dark web content, which used LDA for topic classification on the dark web groups (M., Fuchs, et al., V. 2019). In (Dong, F., et al., 2018), researchers discovered 35 new cyber threats by analysing crawled data from the dark web. In addition, the work mentioned labelling manually 8000 samples to train the supervised learning models.

The alternate approach to manually label hidden service content is training classification models on open source/publicly available datasets. The alternate approach to manually label hidden service content is training classification models on open source/publicly available datasets.

In work (Heistracher, C., et al., 2020), publicly available 13 dark web marketplace datasets which had numerous product listings were evaluated against different text feature classification approaches along with machine learning based algorithms. The objective was to study to train the classification model to identify advertisements present on dark web marketplace hidden services related to weapons.

The very nature of the dark web allows the volatility of hosted links. In other words, links found on the dark web during crawling may not always be active. Moreover, the dark web links tend to be on-off, and so does the availability and unavailability of the content offer on these links. Therefore, it is essential to have a dedicated module to monitor the liveliness status of websites on the dark web. The shot-live nature of dark web hidden services motivated researchers to accomplish content classification at the edge level. In work (Yang, L., et al., 2019), the authors emphasised having an edge-based content classification mechanism for the dark web. The work collected hidden service addresses from the Tor directory service or open-source dataset named "Darknet Usage Text Addresses" (DUTA)". The crawler was designed to crawl to selected hidden services to collect text content of respective hidden services.

The researchers are attempting to create and contribute existing open-source datasets, which would be beneficial in hidden service content labelling. For example, in work (Al-Nabki, M. et al., 2020), authors mentioned adding 851mannualy labelled samples to W-NUT-2017 dataset. The W-NUT-2017 dataset is referred for Name Entity Recognition for Tor hidden services.

Also, researchers have always pointed out limitations of dark web data classification due to lack of labelling. But research community explored independent approaches for labelling. In (Takaaki, S., et.al., 2019), the authors have identified the zero-frequency problem with dark web data while applying the Naive Bayes algorithm. In general, a zero-frequency problem with the Naive Bayes algorithm is resolved by Laplace smoothing, but with discussed hidden services data in work, that approach was eliminated. Moreover, the test data was treated as teacher data to train the model. But still, in conclusion, researchers mentioned the limitation of the implemented approach.

Thus, improvised approaches adopted in research to label the dark web content motivated authors of the proposed work to attempt a graph of word (GoW) based hidden service content labelling. In (Samtani, S., et.al., 2020), the Graph of Words representation of the forum text enabled preserving the semantic relationships amongst the words and used several other graph-related measures to find deeper insights about the words used in the context of hacker forums. Unsupervised graph embedding methods helped create low dimensional embedding by preserving node proximities at several levels. Although graph embeddings are promising, they fail to capture evolution/shifts in the words used on the forum and the context in which they are used. The Diachronic Word Embeddings overcome the limitation of capturing changes in words used in the forum.

Graph of Words

In Graph of Words, nodes are words. Edges represent whether two words appear in a specified text unit. If the edges are weighted, weights represent the frequency of co-occurrences such as network density, clustering coefficient, etc. Graph of Words (GoWs) is gaining significant attention within the NLP community because they can capture and reveal relationships, patterns, and regularities.

Graph of Words (GoWs) captures term dependence and order (via directed edges). Also, GoWs encodes the strength of the dependence as edge weights. The proposed work is inspired by the application of GoW on single-document keyword extraction (Rousseau, F., et al., 2015).

The following section of the chapter follows the implementation of the proposed work, including a detailed discussion on the dataset, implementation approaches and results.

DARK WEB DATA COLLECTION

The dark web dataset was made available using a custom dark web crawler for the proposed work. The Python scripted dark web crawler crawled the Tor hidden services with the help of certain seed links. The seed links were provided to the crawler from the hidden wiki page. The hidden wiki page served the purpose of the Tor directory service. The seed link formed the crawler's starting point, and further links were explored as the crawler encountered them. In this way, the data was collected by crawling the dark web. It is important to note that the hidden service web pages collected belong to only one particular time frame.

Dataset Properties:

The collected data had the following properties:

1.   Large size of crawled data:

The dataset obtained comprised 50000 dark web hidden service pages, which accounted for 12.2 GB of data. Due to the large dataset, a lot of diversity was found in the languages of the hidden service pages. The different languages observed in these hidden service pages included English, Russian, Chinese, French, Spanish, etc.

The dataset included different file format structures, including .html, .php files, all of which had the HTML code of the crawled hidden service pages. Therefore, the large dataset size is attributed to the raw nature of the data, i.e., HTML code of all the hidden service pages. For example, suppose a particular hidden service page has text content equivalent to 100 words. In that case, the corresponding HTML code and the CSS styling and JavaScript can increase the file size by a significant amount.

The primary data cleaning steps were performed because of two features of the dataset, removing non-English web pages, and removing the HTML tags, JavaScript from the crawled hidden service files.

2.   Unlabelled data

The crawled dataset was entirely unlabelled. No manual labelling was performed, and there was no available information using which the topic of a particular hidden service page could be labelled. The unlabelled hidden service data restricted the analysis to unsupervised machine learning algorithms. The supervised machine learning algorithms require some form of labelling attached to the data.

Data Pre-Processing:

The data pre-processing part involved the following three steps:

1.   Removing HTML tags:

The hidden service web page is cleaned by removing HTML tags and JavaScript code from the documents. The Beautiful Soup library helped pull data from HTML, XML and other markup languages. For the proposed work, Python's HTML. parser was used. Figure 1 refers to a sample document from the dataset.

Figure 1. Hidden service Document before cleaning

```
<html>
    <head>
        <title>Buy Paypal accounts</title>
    </head>
    <body>
        <h1>Reliable and Secure</h1>
        <p>Best place to buy PayPal accounts with balance $100, $1000, etc</p>
        <h2>Click here to know more</h2>
    </body>
</html>
```

Figure 2 refers to the same document after cleaning it, i.e., after running the Python program to remove the HTML tags.

2.   Removing Non-English hidden service pages:

The following data pre-processing step was to remove all the hidden service pages, not English. The language processing was achieved with the help of the langdetect library in python. The mentioned library provides support for 55 different languages. Depending on the computations performed by the detect function available with the library, it returns the ISO 639-1 code for the language the text could belong

Figure 2. Hidden service Document after cleaning

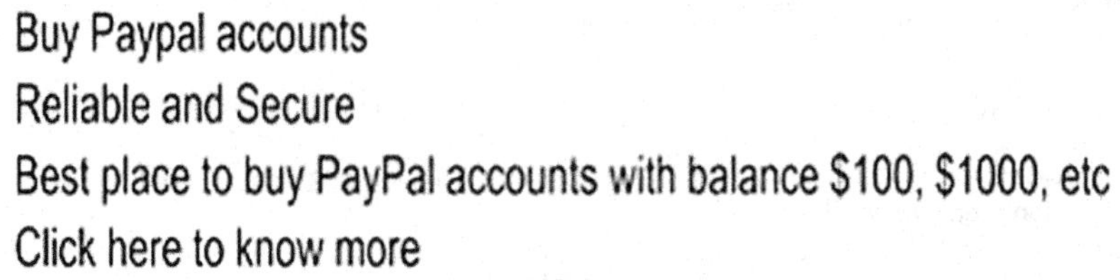

Buy Paypal accounts
Reliable and Secure
Best place to buy PayPal accounts with balance $100, $1000, etc
Click here to know more

to. So, for example, if the function finds that the input text is English content, it returns 'en'. After the Non-English webpages were removed, approximately 22,000 hidden service pages.

3.   Removing Facebook-related deep web pages:

On further analysing the reduced set of 22,000 hidden service pages, it was found that many of these were Facebook deep web pages, which mainly comprised of posts having personal opinions, status updates, descriptions of vacations. Thus, these wouldn't contribute much to labelling the dark web hidden service. On the contrary, these could have potentially distorted the dataset, and therefore Facebook posts were removed. This step was performed by removing the folders having "Facebook" as the substring in their names. There were around 89 such folders of the total 533 folders. The data pre-processing steps were concluded, and finally, a dataset comprising 2660 hidden service pages was used for labelling the hidden service content.

Dataset Properties and their Implications:

Mentioned properties of the dataset had the following effect on the model selection.

The large size of crawled dataset:

One of the key properties of the dataset was that each document contains many words.

Effect:

The large dataset volume forced only the selection of those methods, which were computationally efficient. Any algorithm having a higher degree of polynomial runtime (in terms of the input processing) was computationally intractable. However, the authors proposed some alternative approaches that one may adopt in the future when computational power may increase.

Unlabelled:

The dataset in hand is entirely unlabelled, not having any labels or information about a hidden service that allowed to infer the content of the hidden service.

Effect:

A vital conclusion derived that the mentioned property restricted implementation to unsupervised learning methods to a small family of machine learning methods. The absence of labels made it impossible to provide any supervised approach to crawled data.

Static:

Figure 3. GoW construction algorithm

GoW construction algorithm:

```
Input: Document D
Output: Graph of words G
Procedure:
        wordList = D.split()                        //Store the words present in the document into a list
        for word in wordList:
                if len(word) >= 3:                  //Remove words having length less than 3
                        don't remove word
        endfor
        G = DiGraph()                               //Initialise the graph
        for word in wordList:
                G.addNode(word)
                G.addEdge(word, nextWord)
        endfor
        Remove all nodes (words) that occur less than 2 times in G and also the corresponding edges
```

The dataset had states of the hidden service pages at a fixed instance. However, the information on a dark web hidden service page is generally evolving, which provides some critical insights about that hidden service page's nature.

Effect:

The static nature of the dataset removes the possibility of any temporal analysis of the dark web hidden service pages that could have been performed. For example, the methods like Samtani, et al., that used the Diachronic framework are not suitable for the dataset used in the proposed method.

PROPOSED APPROACH TO LABEL DARK WEB HIDDEN SERVICE

The proposed chapter discussed the methodology deployed to label the Tor hidden services. The analysis of hidden service data is performed by extracting keywords from each hidden service document and then evaluating the results produced by the keyword extraction method by comparing it with the results generated by the Latent Dirichlet allocation (LDA) on the same data. The keywords extraction uses each document's Graph of Words (GoW) representation, whereas the LDA model uses the documents' Bag of Words (BoW) representation.

Graph of Word

A very primitive algorithm, as shown in figure 3, for constructing GoWs was implemented in the initial stage of the proposed work. The GoW algorithm would consider all the words present in the document. As a result, the output GoWs was very dense with lots of edges and nodes. To improve the GoW approach, authors thought of including only those words in the GoWs that were more important than other words. This was done by counting the occurrences of all the words in the document and the words having a count greater than or equal to 2 were used for GoW construction.

Figure 4 shows GoW for a web page related to selling bitcoins (marketplace), and the same can be understood by analysing the graph.

Figure 4. Sample GoW of document

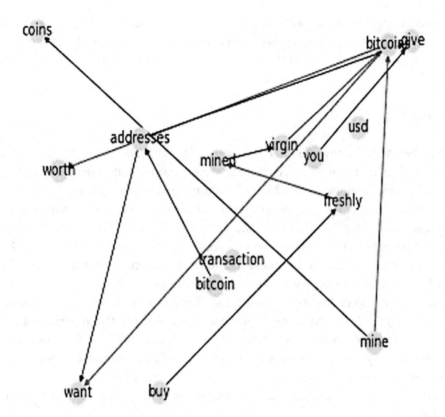

Note: The red edges represent that these pair of words occur more than once in the document together and are thus of more importance than other edges.

Figure 5. Comparing GoWs and word clouds

Further, to confirm the occurrence of words in the selected document, the authors prepared the word cloud of the same document, as shown in figure 5.

Due to the complex structure of the GoWs and a large number of such graphs, it wouldn't be feasible to manually analyse all the GoWs. Thus, it was essential to develop an automated mechanism that would help extract meaningful information from the graphs, so the next step performed was extracting key phrases from GoWs.

Keyword Extraction

The main intuition behind the keyword extraction method is that central nodes make good keywords; nodes with high centrality in the GoW of a document usually correspond to the document's keywords, which are well-understood by humans. So, by constructing GoWs for respective hidden services, the manual labelling could be eliminated, or knowledgeable assistance is offered for manual labelling.

Graph theory has various graph centrality measures, such as closeness, betweenness, clustering coefficients, eigenvector centrality, etc. Each one captures some specific aspects of the graph. However, the algorithmic implementations of calculating these measures require more than linear time (in terms of the input size) which may be possible for standard graphs. But the GoWs of the documents are large, and thus it is impossible to calculate these measures for all nodes in the GoW of a document.

The graph degeneracy method decomposed a graph into its cores such that it preserved a community of words that were good candidates to be the keywords for the document. After the core decomposition, a smaller subgraph with only a constant number of nodes was left as a potential candidate for keywords. Further, the closeness centrality measure of only a constant number of nodes in the residual subgraph was computed. Finally, the set of the best four possible words as the potential keywords for the document was picked up.

But a naive implementation of even this algorithm was computationally inefficient. So an improvised implementation was used that used a binsort algorithm to achieve O (n + m) runtime, i.e. a linear time complexity in terms of the input size. In the proposed work, k-core decomposition of the graph for a suitable value of k is done.

K-Core Decomposition of the Graph

A k-core of a graph is defined as:

A subgraph H = (VH, EH), induced by the subset of vertices VH ⊆ V, is called a k-core or a core of order k if and only if ∀ v ∈ VH, deg H(v) ≥ k and H is the maximal subgraph with this property. i.e., it cannot be augmented without losing this property.

Figure 6 shows the k- decomposition of a graph for three different values of k. First, a core decomposition of a GoW is attained for the smallest value of k such that for fewer than 30 nodes in its k-core. After this step, the best four words that have the highest closeness centrality measure were found. Note that any other centrality measure such as betweenness could also be used.

The approach of first decomposing a graph into its k-core and then finding the keywords in the smaller subgraph is termed graph degeneracy. The primary purpose here was to achieve computational efficiency to restrict the search of keywords to only a small community of closely related words.

Figure 7 shows the learning algorithm used to extract keywords from the documents of the dataset.

Figure 6. k-core of a graph for k = 0,1, 2,3

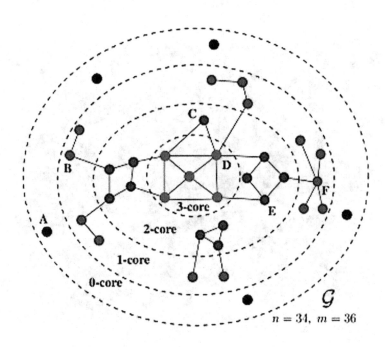

Figure 7. Algorithm to extract keywords from hidden service document

Algorithm	Keyword-Extractor from a document doc

Require: Text document doc after pre-processing steps(may be of any language)
Ensure: Set of keywords for doc and associated probability prob for each word

$G(V, E) \leftarrow$ gow_construction(doc)
$k \leftarrow 0$
while $|V| > 30$ **do**
    $G(V, E) \leftarrow$ k_core(G)
    $k \leftarrow k + 1$
end while

for all $v \in V$ **do**
    $C_C(v) \leftarrow \frac{1}{\sum_{u \neq v} d(u,v)}$
end for

prob $\leftarrow$ softmax(C_C)
keywords $\leftarrow$ the best four words with minimum closeness measure
Return (keywords, prob)

The mentioned algorithm ran on each document of the collected dataset to extract keywords for all the documents. The purpose is to find out the content of these pages. To understand the algorithm intuitively,

Figure 8. GoW for a document

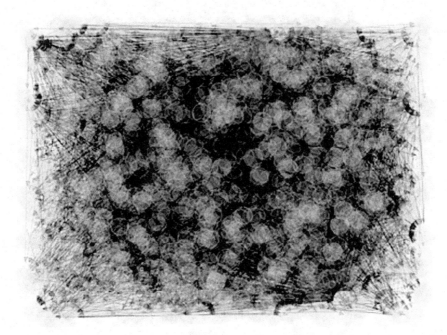

figure 8 shows an example of the algorithm's execution on a document containing pornographic content in the dataset. The generation of a GoW for the document generated the following massive graph. The words associated with the nodes in the graph are not displayed for better visualisation. Thus, the graph degeneracy method is applied to construct a degenerated subgraph by decomposing it into its core with fewer than 30 nodes. For example, figure 9 shows the degenerated graph.

After this, the closeness centrality measure for each node in the degenerated graph is computed. Then, the nodes with the least closeness measures as the keywords for the document is returned. For example, the circled nodes have high closeness measures. Thus, they form a set of keywords.

Topic Modelling with LDA Algorithm

To analyse the accuracy of the result obtained with the keyword extraction method, the authors implemented topic modelling with LDA. The keywords retrieved with the graph degeneracy method are compared with LDA topics.

Non-parametric Bayesian models use Dirichlet processes as stochastic processes models. Dirichlet processes result in discrete distributions for each draw. Dirichlet distributions are required for random distributions whose marginal distributions are finite-dimensional.

Let H be a distribution over theta and alpha be a positive real number. G is a Dirichlet process with base distribution H and concentration parameter alpha if for every finite, measurable partition A1, . . ., Ar of theta to have:

G(A1), . . ., G(Ar) ~ Dirich ($\propto$ H(A1), . . ., $\propto$ H(Ar))

where Dirich is a Dirichlet distribution, shown in figure 10, defined as:

Figure 9. Degenerated graph node with captions

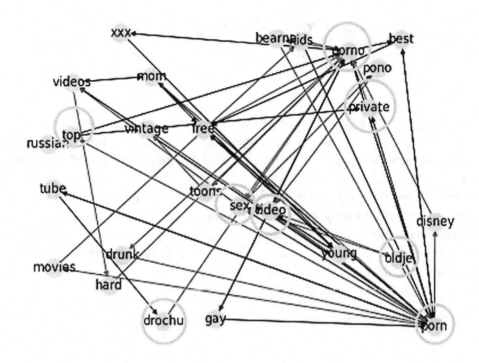

Figure 10. Dirichlet distribution

$$p(x_1, \ldots, x_k) = \frac{\Gamma\left(\sum_k \alpha_k\right)}{\prod_k \Gamma(\alpha_k)} \prod_{k=1}^{K} x_k^{\alpha_k - 1}$$

Latent Dirichlet Allocation (LDA)

Consider a dataset of observations x, where each data point is a group of observations $x_i = \{x_{i1}, x_{i2}, \ldots\ldots x_{im}\}$.

As a running example, the dataset is a corpus of documents, and each document is a collection of observed words.

The mixed-membership model draws each data point from its mixture model.

The mixture components are $\beta = \{\beta_1 \ldots\ldots \beta_k\}$ they are shared across the data.

The mixture proportions are $\theta = \{\theta_1 \ldots\ldots \theta_n\}$ they vary from data point to data point.

Figure 11. Corresponding joint distribution

$$p(\beta, \theta, x) = \prod_{k=1}^{K} p(\beta_k) \prod_{i=1}^{n} \left(p(\theta_i) \prod_{j=1}^{m} \left(p(z_{ij} \mid \theta_i) p(x_{ij} \mid z_{ij}, \beta) \right) \right)$$

The mixture assignments z is one-per-observation; the variable z_{ij} assigns observation x_{ij}s to one of the components. Each data point xi uses all the components β, but its proportions θ_i vary how

much it expresses each one. (When θ_i is sparse, different data points express different subsets of the components.)

Thus, a mixed-membership model captures both homogeneities. All the data share the same collection of components, and heterogeneity, in that each datapoint expresses those components to a different degree. The corresponding joint distribution, shown in figure 11, is

As for the mixture, the likelihood uses the assignment variable zij to select the component for observation x_{ij}, shown in figure 12

Figure 12. Likelihood for the observation

$$p(x_{ij} \mid \beta, z_{ij}) = \prod_{k=1}^{K} f(x_{ij}; \beta_k)^{z_{ij}^k}$$

The LDA begins with removing the punctuation marks from pre-processed documents. Then an array of the documents is created with each document as an element, and the next step is Lemmatization. A further step is the creation of a dictionary and document term matrix (bag of words).

An LDA model requires determining how many topics should be generated. By understanding the data and trying different values, the proposed work set the topic value to 5. Figure 13 shows the visualisation of the LDA model.

The following topics are considered for labelling the documents:

Hidden Wiki: This comprises a significant portion of our dataset and is similar to the Wikipedia of the surface web as it acts as a storehouse for onion links of different services.

Marketplace: This consists of all web pages selling different products such as drugs, PayPal accounts, passports, unregistered guns, bitcoins, etc.

Porn: This includes different porn-related web pages

Software: This comprises blogs, articles, discussions related to security, software updates, etc

Others: This covers every other topic not included in the above categories.

Figure 13. Visualisation of the LDA model

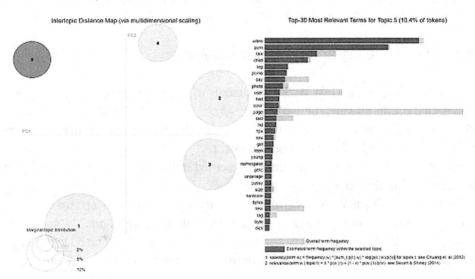

As discussed, the keyword extraction algorithm generates k keywords (in the proposed approach, k = 4) from the individual GoWs. Then, using these keywords, the authors manually assigned topic labels to all the documents.

Thus, the processing flow comprises converting documents to GoWs, extracting keywords from the GoWs generated, and finally manually assigning topic labels with the help of the keywords. Example in figure 14 represents document 58, for which keywords are obtained using the Keyword Extraction algorithm.

Figure 14. Example of document 58 labelled to marketplace topic

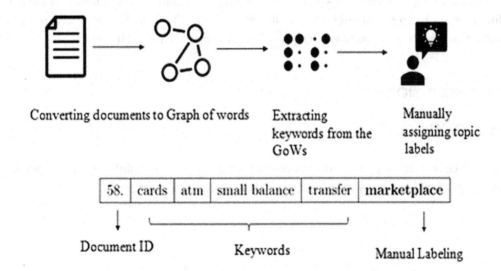

By analysing these keywords, namely cards, atm, small balance, transfer, it can be easily inferred that this document must belong to the "marketplace" category.

Trade-Off between the GoW and BoW Representations

The keywords extraction uses the GoW of the documents in the proposed work, whereas the LDA uses the BoW representation. Intuitively, the GoW representation seems to be more potent than the BoW representation, possibly because every information that can also be retrieved from the BoW representation can be retrieved from a GoW of the same document.

The formal notation of the above statement is presented in the following lemma and give an information-theoretic proof for the same.

Lemma: *For document D, there exists a Graph-of-Words representation G(D) that can entirely generate the Bag of Words B(D) by only looking at G(D), without needing the actual document D.*

Proof: Consider G(D), which has a node for each word in a document. The edges can be arbitrarily assigned with some meaning. The following procedure constructs the Bag-of-Words representation B(D) from G(D).

First, initialise B(D) to be a zero vector with the dimension of the size of the vocabulary. Then, for each node in the graph G(D), increase the frequency by incrementing the entry associated with the word by one. Repeating this procedure for all nodes in G(D) gives the correct B(D); this follows from the definition of the Bag-of-Words. Thus concludes the proof.

A natural question that may arise here is that if the LDA uses BoW representation, why did the proposed work choose LDA to compare it with the results generated by the keywords extraction method that enjoys richer representation power of GoW. The answer is a probabilistic machine learning (ML) method is a must to do the self-evaluation of the model.

But why didn't the proposed work evaluate against a probabilistic approach that uses the GoW? such as a method that assumes all the GoWs are sampled from some generative process with some hidden parameters over the space of random graphs.

The answer to this question lies in the computational limitations inherent to the selected data set. It is tough to model randomness over graphs using only a few hidden parameters. Estimating these parameters and finding their posterior distribution can be intractable. Thus, the BoW is used to compromise on the representation power but gain the advantage by achieving computational efficiency.

RESULT DISCUSSION

Results of GoW

Table 1 enlists keywords for two documents of each category. The probabilities with which keywords form part of a particular category are also specified along with the keywords.

Table 1. Keywords for two documents of each category

CATEGORY	KEYWORDS			
Wiki	Wiki (0.214)	account (0.200)	people (0.098)	pages (0.092)
	text page (0.217)	permission (0.182)	related logs (0.178)	title pages (0.143)
Marketplace	Cards (0.074)	atm (0.037)	small balance (0.034)	transfer (0.030)
	Caution (0.067)	scam (0.065)	credit cards (0.023)	paypal (0.021)
Porn	jasmine sex (0.080)	girls fun camera (0.072)	school (0.053)	adult (0.052)
	Glad (0.083)	lesbian (0.083)	groupsex (0.079)	zoo (0.078)
Software	mail service (0.132)	email provider (0.098)	privacy (0.085)	inbox (0.056)
	mb uploaded (0.11)	downloads (0.10)	party analytics cookies (0.058)	github (0.050)
Others	books (0.066)	libraries (0.059)	manga collection (0.036)	free ebooks (0.036)
	log type (0.11)	username (0.08)	case (0.07)	sensitive (0.07)

Results of LDA

The LDA model generates topic labelling for the documents. The LDA model assigns probabilities to the different topics a particular hidden service document can belong to and then assigns the label corresponding to the highest probability.

For example, if the LDA model generates an output of 90% for topic 0 and 10% for topic 1, the model would label the document to topic 0.

Figure 15. Distribution of keywords in Topic 1 (Wiki)

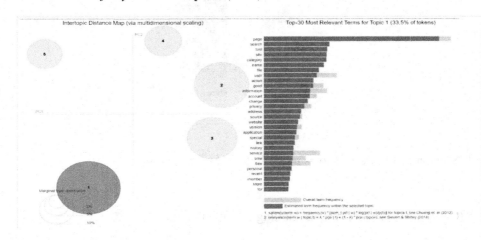

Figure 16. Distribution of keywords in Topic 2 (Marketplace)

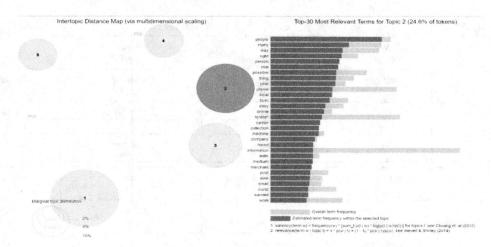

1. Topic 1(Wiki): Figure 15 shows modelling for Wiki topic.

2. Topic 2 (Marketplace): Figure 16 shows modelling for Marketplace topic.

3. Topic 3 (Porn): Figure 17 shows modelling for Porn topic.

Figure 17. Distribution of keywords in Topic 3 (Porn)

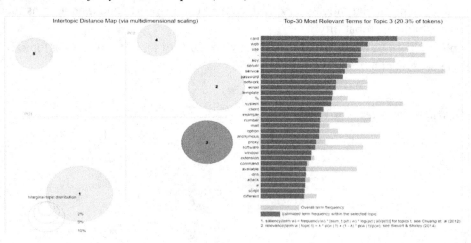

4. Topic 4 (Software): Figure 18 shows modelling for Software topic.

5. Topic 5 (Others): Figure 19 shows modelling for Others topic.

Figure 18. Distribution of keywords in Topic 4 (Software)

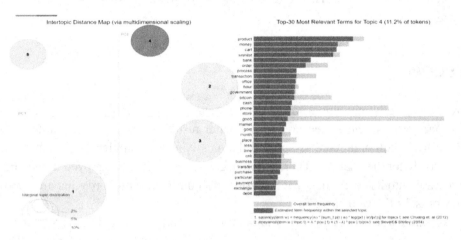

Figure 19. Distribution of keywords in Topic 5 (Others)

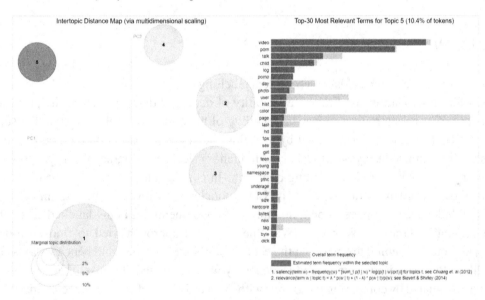

Result Analysis

The labels obtained from both the approaches are assembled into an excel sheet and find the total number of documents for which both results matches, let that be 'n'. The evaluation method adopted to confirm the consistency of both the results is accuracy. Thus, divide number 'n' by the total number of documents' N' to obtain the accuracy metric.

The accuracy of the model was calculated to be 78.05%. The percentage accuracy implies that out of the total 2660 documents, nearly 2100 documents have been labelled the same topic by both approaches. Since the GoW approach involves manually labelling the documents after observing the keywords, these labels can be considered the basis. Therefore, it is safe to conclude that the LDA model did a decent job by providing an accuracy of 78.05%.

FUTURE SCOPE

In the future, when the computation power may increase, potentially due to the arrival of quantum technologies, one may use these measures to get better results to find more accurate keywords for a webpage. But current computational setups and the massive GoWs hinder the possibility to use these measures effectively for the analysis. Thus, graph degeneracy methods employed in the proposed work decompose a graph into its cores such that it preserves a community of words that are good candidates to be the keywords for the web page.

The dark web hidden service pages are dynamic and constantly updated, but as previously mentioned, the dataset obtained comprises hidden service pages belonging to only a particular time. Thus the static nature of the dataset removed the possibility of any temporal analysis of the hidden service pages that could have been performed. But in the future scope of the proposed work, the discussed keyword extraction could be applied to regularly crawled data.

CONCLUSION

Two aspects drive the research on dark web content labelling – first, emphasise manual labelling of dark web content for classification and limited availability of dark web data sets. Thus, the proposed work is motivated to offer an alternative to manual labelling of the dark web content to train the supervised learning models. The objective is attained by applying the keyword extraction method on Tor hidden service and using extracted keywords to label the hidden service. The accuracy of the proposed method is validated by LDA based topic modelling approach. In conclusion, 78% of the document labelling obtained by the keyword extraction method and LDA model agree with each other. It implies that out of the total 2660 hidden service pages, approximately 2100 documents are being labelled correctly.

While generating Graph-of-Words (GoWs), the proposed approach tried to find intra-document structure. The intuition behind this was that the central words are essential, and hence various centrality measures like Closeness, Betweenness and Degeneracy were estimated. The usefulness of GoW representation was evaluated by comparing the graphs with the word cloud of the same documents. Keywords were extracted from GoWs to understand the topic of the documents.

Later, a completely different approach to topic modelling is applied to dive deeper into the data. LDA was used to make educated guesses about how words cohere by identifying patterns in how they co-occur in different documents. In other words, the proposed tried to find inter-document structure.

Thus, proposed work attempts to label the content of hidden services without or with minimum manual intervention.

REFERENCES

Al-Nabki, M. W., Fidalgo, E., & Mata, J. V. (2019). Darkner: A platform for named entity recognition in tor darknet. *Jornadas Nacionales de Investigación en Ciberseguridad*, *1*, 279-280.

Al-Nabki, M. W., Janez-Martino, F., Vasco-Carofilis, R. A., Fidalgo, E., & Velasco-Mata, J. (2020). Improving Named Entity Recognition in Tor Darknet with Local Distance Neighbour Feature. arXiv preprint arXiv:2005.08746

Avarikioti, G., Brunner, R., Kiayias, A., Wattenhofer, R., & Zindros, D. (2018). Structure and content of the visible Darknet. arXiv preprint arXiv:1811.01348

Baravalle, A., Lopez, M. S., & Lee, S. W. (2016, December). Mining the dark web: drugs and fake ids. In *2016 IEEE 16th International Conference on Data Mining Workshops (ICDMW)* (pp. 350-356). IEEE. 10.1109/ICDMW.2016.0056

Broséus, J., Rhumorbarbe, D., Mireault, C., Ouellette, V., Crispino, F., & Décary-Hétu, D. (2016). Studying illicit drug trafficking on Darknet markets: Structure and organisation from a Canadian perspective. *Forensic Science International*, *264*, 7–14. doi:10.1016/j.forsciint.2016.02.045 PMID:26978791

Dalins, J., Wilson, C., & Carman, M. (2018). Criminal motivation on the dark web: A categorisation model for law enforcement. *Digital Investigation*, *24*, 62–71. doi:10.1016/j.diin.2017.12.003

Diodati, J., & Winterdyk, J. (2021). Dark Web: The Digital World of Fraud and Rouge Activities. In Handbook of Research on Theory and Practice of Financial Crimes (pp. 477-505). IGI Global.

Dong, F., Yuan, S., Ou, H., & Liu, L. (2018, November). New cyber threat discovery from darknet marketplaces. In *2018 IEEE Conference on Big Data and Analytics (ICBDA)* (pp. 62-67). IEEE. 10.1109/ICBDAA.2018.8629658

Faizan, M., & Khan, R. A. (2019). Exploring and analysing the dark Web: A new alchemy. *First Monday*. Advance online publication. doi:10.5210/fm.v24i5.9473

Ghosh, S., Porras, P., Yegneswaran, V., Nitz, K., & Das, A. (2017, March). ATOL: A framework for automated analysis and categorisation of the Darkweb Ecosystem. *Workshops at the Thirty-First AAAI Conference on Artificial Intelligence.*

Haasio, A., Harviainen, J. T., & Savolainen, R. (2020). Information needs of drug users on a local dark Web marketplace. *Information Processing & Management*, *57*(2), 102080. doi:10.1016/j.ipm.2019.102080

He, S., He, Y., & Li, M. (2019, March). Classification of illegal activities on the dark web. In *Proceedings of the 2019 2nd International Conference on Information Science and Systems* (pp. 73-78). 10.1145/3322645.3322691

Heistracher, C., Mignet, F., & Schlarb, S. (2020). Machine Learning Techniques for the Classification of Product Descriptions from Darknet Marketplaces. In *International Conference on Applied Informatics* (pp. 128-137). Academic Press.

Joshi, A., Fidalgo, E., Alegre, E., & Al Nabki, M. W. (2018). Extractive text summarisation in dark web: A preliminary study. *International Conference of Applications of Intelligent Systems.*

Khare, A., Dalvi, A., & Kazi, F. (2020, July). Smart Crawler for Harvesting Deep web with multi-Classification. In *2020 11th International Conference on Computing, Communication and Networking Technologies (ICCCNT)* (pp. 1-5). IEEE. 10.1109/ICCCNT49239.2020.9225369

Lee, S., Yoon, C., Kang, H., Kim, Y., Kim, Y., Han, D., . . . Shin, S. (2019, February). Cybercriminal minds: an investigative study of cryptocurrency abuses in the dark web. In *26th Annual Network and Distributed System Security Symposium (NDSS 2019)* (pp. 1-15). Internet Society. 10.14722/ndss.2019.23055

Mahor, V., Rawat, R., Kumar, A., Chouhan, M., Shaw, R. N., & Ghosh, A. (2021, September). Cyber Warfare Threat Categorization on CPS by Dark Web Terrorist. In *2021 IEEE 4th International Conference on Computing, Power and Communication Technologies (GUCON)* (pp. 1-6). IEEE. 10.1109/GUCON50781.2021.9573994

Marin, E., Diab, A., & Shakarian, P. (2016, September). Product offerings in malicious hacker markets. In *2016 IEEE conference on Intelligence and Security Informatics (ISI)* (pp. 187-189). IEEE.

McCallum, A. K. (2002). *Mallet: A machine learning for language toolkit.* http://mallet. cs. umass.edu

Meland, P. H., & Sindre, G. (2019, December). Cyber-attacks for sale. In *2019 International Conference on Computational Science and Computational Intelligence (CSCI)* (pp. 54-59). IEEE. 10.1109/CSCI49370.2019.00016

Pantelis, G., Petrou, P., Karagiorgou, S., & Alexandrou, D. (2021, August). On Strengthening SMEs and MEs Threat Intelligence and Awareness by Identifying Data Breaches, Stolen Credentials and Illegal Activities on the Dark Web. In *The 16th International Conference on Availability, Reliability and Security* (pp. 1-7). Academic Press.

Rajawat, A. S., Rawat, R., Mahor, V., Shaw, R. N., & Ghosh, A. (2021). Suspicious Big Text Data Analysis for Prediction—On Darkweb User Activity Using Computational Intelligence Model. In *Innovations in Electrical and Electronic Engineering* (pp. 735–751). Springer. doi:10.1007/978-981-16-0749-3_58

Rousseau, F., Kiagias, E., & Vazirgiannis, M. (2015, July). Text categorisation as a graph classification problem. In *Proceedings of the 53rd Annual Meeting of the Association for Computational Linguistics and the 7th International Joint Conference on Natural Language Processing (Volume 1: Long Papers)* (pp. 1702-1712). Academic Press.

Sabbah, T., & Selamat, A. (2014, December). Modified frequency-based term weighting scheme for accurate dark web content classification. In *Asia Information Retrieval Symposium* (pp. 184-196). Springer. 10.1007/978-3-319-12844-3_16

Samtani, S., Li, W., Benjamin, V., & Chen, H. (2021). Informing Cyber Threat Intelligence through Dark Web Situational Awareness: The AZSecure Hacker Assets Portal. *Digital Threats: Research and Practice*, 2(4), 1–10. doi:10.1145/3450972

Samtani, S., Zhu, H., & Chen, H. (2020). Proactively identifying emerging hacker threats from the dark web: A diachronic graph embedding framework (d-gef). *ACM Transactions on Privacy and Security*, 23(4), 1–33. doi:10.1145/3409289

Schäfer, M., Fuchs, M., Strohmeier, M., Engel, M., Liechti, M., & Lenders, V. (2019, May). BlackWidow: Monitoring the dark web for cyber security information. In *2019 11th International Conference on Cyber Conflict (CyCon)* (Vol. 900, pp. 1-21). IEEE.

Spitters, M., Verbruggen, S., & Van Staalduinen, M. (2014, September). Towards a comprehensive insight into the thematic organisation of the tor hidden services. In *2014 IEEE Joint Intelligence and Security Informatics Conference* (pp. 220-223). IEEE.

Szakonyi, A., Leonard, B., & Dawson, M. (2021). Dark Web: A Breeding Ground for ID Theft and Financial Crimes. In Handbook of Research on Theory and Practice of Financial Crimes (pp. 506-524). IGI Global. doi:10.4018/978-1-7998-5567-5.ch025

Takaaki, S., & Atsuo, I. (2019, March). Dark web content analysis and visualisation. In *Proceedings of the ACM International Workshop on Security and Privacy Analytics* (pp. 53-59). ACM.

Todorof, M. (2019, July). FinTech on the dark web: The rise of cryptos. In *Era Forum* (Vol. 20, No. 1, pp. 1-20). Springer Berlin Heidelberg.

Yang, L., Yang, Y., Yu, H., & Zhu, G. (2019, December). Anonymous market product classification based on deep learning. In *Proceedings of the International Conference on Artificial Intelligence, Information Processing and Cloud Computing* (pp. 1-5). 10.1145/3371425.3371467

Yang, L., Yang, Y., Yu, H., & Zhu, G. (2019, December). Edge-Based Detection and Classification of Malicious Contents in Tor Darknet Using Machine Learning. *Mobile Information Systems*.

Chapter 11
Tapering Malicious Language for Identifying Fake Web Content

Shyamala Devi N.

iD https://orcid.org/0000-0003-4413-4775

Vels Institute of Science, Technology, and Advanced Studies, Chennai, India

Sharmila K.

Vels Institute of Science, Technology, and Advanced Studies, Chennai, India

ABSTRACT

The neoteric occurrence, the pandemic, and global crisis entails the extensive use of web portals to unfurl information. While this has built the cognizance of the common man, the infinitely unnoticed enumeration of malicious content on the web has escalated copiously. Spurious data and fake information has done more harm than what is actually unraveled to the public; however, scrupulously meticulous measures to agonize their source and delve into mitigating these data has become quite a challenge. This indignation delves into step-wise analysis of identifying the hoax through systematically programmed algorithms using natural language processing.

INTRODUCTION

The proposed methodology for identifying the malicious fake web content comprises of text mining from the malicious web site .The tools and techniques of Natural language processing and the deep learning techniques are applied in the methodology to detect the Malicious web content and the framework is represented in the below figure 1. Classify the Malicious fake Web content

Text analysis and the process of detecting fake content require an elaborate approach due to the intricacies it involves. The initial process incorporates the potently anatomized data to be obtained. This datasets holds a commingled data of authentic and spurious content for further processing. This datasets necessitates the method of web scrapping method that is explicated for extracting the appropriate data

DOI: 10.4018/978-1-6684-6444-1.ch011

Figure 1.

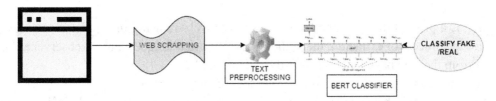

from the gargantuan web content that is available. The next phase of processing incorporates the scrapped texts which are a single clustered large embodiment of text to be separated into individual tokens. This process is effectively implemented using lexical parsing which scans the text clusters to effectively transform them into sequence of tokens. The next step is stop word removal in order to spurious over the spurious content and it is effectuated. Now that the content holds adequate correlation, a certain amount of pre-processing done through normalization is to scale the data is implemented. This process of normalization is utilized through the method of stemming and lemmatization that help in obtaining relevant content for Part of Speech(POS) tagging. Then the Subsequent approach of vectorization of text is words Vectorization in order to construct the environment ready for effective detection of anomalies. The final approach is to identify and extract this malicious content is executed through the method of BERT (Bidirectional encoder from transformer) in order to procure the associative correlation between the words and render an augmented precision of the web hoax that is disseminated. Thus the relationship behaviours between a text thereby evincing the malicious entailed web content through the series of we processing simulated using python programming.

PLATFORM USED FOR IDENTIFYING THE FAKE WEB CONTENT

Spyder (Python 3.6)

Spyder, the Scientific Python Development Environment, is a open itegerated development environment (IDE) that is incorporated with Anaconda. It incorporates altering, intelligent testing, troubleshooting, and reflection highlights. After you have introduced Anaconda, start Spyder on Windows, macOS, or Linux by running the spyder. Spyder is additionally pre-introduced in Anaconda Navigator, which is remembered for Anaconda. On the Navigator Home tab, click the Spyder symbol.

Jupyter Notebook

The Jupyter Notebook is an open source web application that you can use to make and share archives that contain live code, conditions, perceptions, and text. Jupyter Notebook is kept up with by individuals at Project Jupyter.

Jupyter Notebooks are a side project from the IPython project, which used to have an IPython Notebook project itself. The name, Jupyter, comes from the center upheld programming dialects that it upholds: Julia, Python, and R. Jupyter ships with the IPython part, which permits you to compose your projects in Python.

WEBSITE SCRAPPING

Web scraping is a process of collecting the data from the website using the application programming interface. For the process of extraction the python code is written for querying a webserver and requesting the data from the web page which extract the data needed.

Initial steps to install the python beautiful soup for scraping the website

Beautiful Soup is a Python library for hauling information out of HTML and XML documents. It works with your cherished parser to give informal methods of exploring, looking, and altering the parse tree. It regularly saves developers hours or long stretches of work

1.   Building the web scrapper

    ◦   Installing the beautiful soup
        Beautiful soup is a python library used for web scrapping.
        The basic method for installing in Linux platform
        $ sudo apt-get install python-bs4
        For the Macs
        $ sudo easy_install pip beautifulsoup

This installs the Python package manager pip. Then run the following to install the library:
$ pip install beautifulsoup4

The news website https://www.politifact.com/factchecks/list/ is scrapped with the help of the beautiful soup and the data from the website is copied in the csv file.

Request library in python Solicitations permits you to send HTTP/1.1 demands very without any problem. There's no compelling reason to physically add inquiry strings to your URLs, or to frame encode your POST information. Keep-alive and HTTP association pooling are 100% programmed, because of urllib3.

Pandas is an open source Python bundle that is most generally utilized for information science/information investigation and AI assignments. It is based on top of another bundle named Numpy, which offers help for multi-dimensional exhibits

After executing the above code the dataset from the news website data is stored in the .csv file which is give below

Pre-Processing of Text Data

The process of pre-processing the text is meant by normalizing the text for analysis. The data cleaning and text normalization involved the steps for data cleaning are Stop word removal, Removing the regular expression (Rajawat et al 2021). In text normalization it involves Tokenization, Stemming and lemmatization.

Figure 2. Code for web scrapping

```
Created on Wed Nov 10 20:35:04 2021

@author: HP
"""

import urllib.request,sys,time
from bs4 import BeautifulSoup
import requests
import pandas as pd

pagesToGet= 1

upperframe=[]
for page in range(1,pagesToGet+1):
    print('processing page :', page)
    url = 'https://www.politifact.com/factchecks/list/?page='+str(page)
    print(url)

    #an exception might be thrown, so the code should be in a try-except block
    try:
        #use the browser to get the url. This is suspicious command that might blow up.
        page=requests.get(url)                          # this might throw an exception if

    except Exception as e:                              # this describes what to do if an
        error_type, error_obj, error_info = sys.exc_info()      # get the exception information
        print ('ERROR FOR LINK:',url)                   #print the link that cause the
        print (error_type, 'Line:', error_info.tb_lineno)   #print error info and line that
        continue                                        #ignore this page. Abandon this
    time.sleep(2)
    soup=BeautifulSoup(page.text,'html.parser')
    frame=[]
    links=soup.find_all('li',attrs={'class':'class= RegularArticleLayout__content-container
                                    __10ugl-'})
    print(len(links))
    filename="NEWS4.csv"
    f=open(filename,"w", encoding = 'utf-8')
    headers="Statement,Link,Date, Source, Label\n"
    f.write(headers)

    for j in links:
        Statement = j.find("div",attrs={'class':'m-statement__quote'}).text.strip()
        Link = "https://www.politifact.com"
        Link += j.find("div",attrs={'class':'m-statement__quote'}).find('a')['href'].strip()
        Date = j.find('div',attrs={'class':'m-statement__body'}).find('footer')
        .text[-14:-1].strip()
        Source = j.find('div', attrs={'class':'m-statement__meta'}).find('a').text.strip()
        Label = j.find('div', attrs={'class':'m-statement__content'}).find('img',
                    attrs={'class':'c-image__original'}).get('alt').strip()
        frame.append((Statement,Link,Date,Source,Label))
        f.write(Statement.replace(",","^")+","+Link+","+Date.replace(",","^")+",
            "+Source.replace(",","^")+","+Label.replace(",","^")+"\n")
    upperframe.extend(frame)
f.close()
data=pd.DataFrame(upperframe, columns=['Statement','Link','Date','Source','Label'])
data.head()
```

Figure 3. Variables for web scrapping

Name	Type	Size	Value
data	DataFrame	(0, 5)	Column names: Statement, Link, Date, Source, Label
filename	str	1	NEWS4.csv
frame	list	0	[]
headers	str	1	Statement,Link,Date, Source, Label
links	element.ResultSet	0	ResultSet object of bs4.element module
pagesToGet	int	1	1
upperframe	list	0	[]
url	str	1	https://www.politifact.com/factchecks/list/?page=1

Figure 4. Output of web scrapped data

1	Statemen	Link	Date	Source	Label
2	President	https://w	ember 9^	Facebook	FALSE
3	â€œMore	https://w	ember 9^	Bloggers	barely-true
4	Merriam-\	https://w	mber 9^ 2	Facebook	barely-true
5	â€œFUN F	https://w	ember 9^	David Gur	TRUE
6	The death	https://w	ember 9^	Facebook	pants-fire
7	â€œAustr	https://w	ember 9^	Bloggers	FALSE
8	The Biden	https://w	ember 9^	Rebecca K	FALSE
9	In the infr	https://w	ember 8^	Lisa McCla	pants-fire
10	â€œFox N	https://w	ember 8^	Tweets	FALSE
11	Atheists	https://w	ember 8^	Bloggers	FALSE
12	This idea t	https://w	ember 8^	Aaron Roc	FALSE
13	Says N.C. ,	https://w	ember 8^	Mark Robi	barely-true
14	The Astro	https://w	ember 8^	Facebook	FALSE

Data Cleaning

Stop Word Removal

The words which are for the most part sifted through prior to handling a characteristic language are called stop words. These are really the most well-known words in any language (like articles, relational words, pronouns, conjunctions, and so forth) and doesn't add a lot of data to the text. Instances of a couple of stop words in English are "the", "a", "an", "so", "what".

In Python we have library to remove the stop word

Word Tokenization

In Python tokenization essentially alludes to separating a bigger group of message into more modest lines, words or in any event, making words for a non-English language. The different tokenization works in-incorporated into the nltk module itself and can be utilized in programs as displayed in the Figure 6.

Word Normalization

Stemming and Lemmatization

Stemming and Lemmatization are Text Normalization (or here and there called Word Normalization) methods in the field of Natural Language Processing that are utilized to get ready text, words, and reports for additional handling. Stemming and Lemmatization have been considered, and calculations have been created in Computer Science since the 1960's. In this instructional exercise you will find out with regards to Stemming and Lemmatization in a viable methodology covering the foundation, some popular calculations, utilizations of Stemming and Lemmatization, and how to stem and lemmatize words, sentences and reports utilizing the Python nltk bundle which is the Natural Language Tool Kit bundle gave by Python to Natural Language Processing assignments. The stemming and lemmatization is done in the dataset and displayed in the below Figure 7.

Word Vectorization

TF-IDF represents term recurrence reverse record recurrence. It is a traditional strategy for weighting the word esteem rather than basically counting it. It is utilized to decide how significant a word is to a text inside an assortment archives. TF-IDF is a sack of-words (BoW) portrayal of the text that depicts the event of words inside a text corpus (Rawat, R et al 2021)

TF represents Term Frequency. It tends to be perceived as a standardized recurrence score. It is determined through the accompanying recipe:

$$TF = \frac{FREQUENCY\ OF\ WORD\ IN\ A\ DOCUMENT}{TOTAL\ NUMBER\ OF\ WORDS\ IN\ THAT\ DOCUMENT}$$

So one can envision that this number will consistently remain ≤ 1, hence we currently judge how incessant a word is with regards to each of the words in a report.

DF represents Inverse Document Frequency, however before we go into IDF, we should figure out DF – Document Frequency. It's given by the accompanying equation:

$$DF = \frac{DOCUMENT\ CONTAINING\ WORD\ W}{TOTAL\ NUMBER\ OF\ DOCUMENTS}$$

DF informs us concerning the extent of archives that contain a specific word.

It's the complementary of the Document Frequency, and the last IDF score emerges from the accompanying equation:

$$IDF = LOG\left(\frac{TOTAL\ NUMBER\ OF\ DOCUMENTS}{DOCUMENTS\ CONTAINING\ WORD\ W}\right)$$

Similarly as we talked about over, the instinct behind it is that the more normal a word is across all reports, the lesser its significance is for the current archive.

A logarithm is produced to hose the results of IDF in the last computation.

$$TF - IDF = TF * IDF$$

The last TF-IDF score comes out to be given in the Figure 8 below

Figure 5. Data cleaning

```
import pandas as pd
#reading the data
data = pd.read_csv("News1.csv",encoding="ISO-8859-1")
data.head()
```

	Statement	Link	Date	Source	Label
0	President Joe Biden threatened to â swoop down with Special Forces folks and gather up every gun in America.â	https://www.politifact.com/factchecks/2021/nov/09/facebook-posts/biden-was-describing-misinformation-about-gun-cont/	ember 9^ 2021	Facebook posts	FALSE
	... ...				

```
pd.set_option('display.max_colwidth', -1)
data= data [['Statement']]
data.head()
```

```
C:\Users\HP\Anaconda3\lib\site-packages\ipykernel_launcher.py:1: FutureWarning:
Passing a negative integer is deprecated in version 1.0 and will not be support
ed in future version. Instead, use None to not limit the column width.
  """Entry point for launching an IPython kernel.
```

	Statement
0	President Joe Biden threatened to â swoop down with Special Forces folks and gather up every gun in America.â
1	More fraud in New Jerseyâs election uncovered voting machines would not allow citizens to vote for Republican governor candidate

```
import string
string.punctuation
def remove_punctuation(text):
    punctuationfree="".join([i for i in text if i not in string.punctuation])
    return punctuationfree
#storing the puntuation free text
data['clean_msg']= data['Statement'].apply(lambda x:remove_punctuation(x))
data.head()
```

	Statement	clean_msg
0	President Joe Biden threatened to â swoop down with Special Forces folks and gather up every gun in America.â	President Joe Biden threatened to â swoop down with Special Forces folks and gather up every gun in Americaâ
1	More fraud in New Jerseyâs election uncovered voting machines would not allow citizens to vote for Republican governor candidate	More fraud in New Jerseyâs election uncovered voting machines would not allow citizens to vote for Republican governor candidate
2	Merriam-Webster recently changed its definition of the word â vaccineâ and removed the immunity	MerriamWebster recently changed its definition of the

BERT CLASSIFIER

BERT and other Transformer encoder designs have been ridiculously fruitful on an assortment of assignments in NLP (regular language handling). They register vector-space portrayals of normal language that

Figure 6. Word tokenization

```
#applying the function
data['no_stopwords']= data['msg_tokenied'].apply(lambda x:remove_stopwords(x))

data['msg_tokenied']

0    [president joe biden threatened to â swoop down with special forces folks
and gather up every gun in americaâ]
1    [more fraud in new jerseyâs election uncovered  voting machines would not
allow citizens to vote for republican governor candidate]
2    [merriamwebster recently changed its definition of the word â vaccineâ  a
nd removed the immunity portion]
3    [fun fact west virginia is home to zero billionaires]
4    [the deaths at the astroworld festival were part of a satanic ritual]
5    [â  australian military being trained to force vaccinate in doortodoor at
58]:
```

	Statement	Link	Date	Source	Label	clean_msg	msg_lower	msg_tokenied	no_stopwords
0	President Joe Biden threatened to â swoop down...	https://www.politifact.com/factchecks/2021/nov...	ember 9^ 2021	Facebook posts	FALSE	President Joe Biden threatened to â swoop down	president joe biden threatened to â swoop down	[president joe biden threatened to â swoop dow...	[president joe biden threatened to â swoop dow...
1	More fraud in New Jerseyâs election uncovered...	https://www.politifact.com/factchecks/2021/nov...	ember 9^ 2021	Bloggers	barely-true	More fraud in New Jerseyâs election uncovered	more fraud in new jerseyâs election uncovered	[more fraud in new jerseyâs election uncovered...	[more fraud in new jerseyâs election uncovered...

Figure 7. Stemming and lemmatization

```
In [53]:  #importing the Stemming function from nltk library
          from nltk.stem.porter import PorterStemmer
          #defining the object for stemming
          porter_stemmer = PorterStemmer()

In [54]:  #defining a function for stemming
          def stemming(text):
              stem_text = [porter_stemmer.stem(word) for word in text]
              return stem_text
          data['msg_stemmed']=data['clean_msg'].apply(lambda x: stemming(x))

In [55]:  from nltk.stem import WordNetLemmatizer
          #defining the object for Lemmatization
          wordnet_lemmatizer = WordNetLemmatizer()

In [56]:  #defining the function for lemmatization
          def lemmatizer(text):
              lemm_text = [wordnet_lemmatizer.lemmatize(word) for word in text]
              return lemm_text
          data['msg_lemmatized']=data['no_stopwords'].apply(lambda x:lemmatizer(x))
```

Figure 8. Text vectorization

```
In [61]:  from sklearn.feature_extraction.text import TfidfVectorizer

In [62]:  tfidf = TfidfVectorizer()

In [70]:  data['transformed'] = tfidf.fit_transform(data['msg_tokenied'])

In [71]:  data.head()
```

	Link	Date	Source	Label	clean_msg	msg_lower	msg_tokenied	no_stopwords	transformed
	//www.politifact.com/factchecks/2021/nov .	ember 9^ 2021	Facebook posts	FALSE	President Joe Biden threatened to â swoop down...	president joe biden threatened to â swoop down...	[president joe biden threatened to â swoop dow...	[president joe biden threatened to â swoop dow...	(0, 22)\t0.26146429092234075\n (0. 165)\t0....
	//www.politifact.com/factchecks/2021/nov .	ember 9^ 2021	Bloggers	barely-true	More fraud in New Jerseyâs election uncovered ...	more fraud in new jerseyâs election uncovered ...	[more fraud in new jerseyâs election uncovered...	[more fraud in new jerseyâs election uncovered...	(0, 22)\t0.26146429092234075\n (0. 165)\t0....

Figure 9. Bert classifier

```
: from sklearn.model_selection import train_test_split

  # split into training and validation sets
  X_tr, X_val, y_tr, y_val = train_test_split(train.msg_tokenied, train.Label, test_size=0.25, random_state=42)

  print('X_tr shape:',X_tr.shape)

: from bert_serving.client import BertClient

  # make a connection with the BERT server using it's ip address
  bc = BertClient(ip="YOUR_SERVER_IP")
  # get the embedding for train and val sets
  X_tr_bert = bc.encode(X_tr.tolist())
  X_val_bert = bc.encode(X_val.tolist())

: from sklearn.linear_model import LogisticRegression

  # LR model
  model_bert = LogisticRegression()
  # train
  model_bert = model_bert.fit(X_tr_bert, y_tr)
  # predict
  pred_bert = model_bert.predict(X_val_bert)

: from sklearn.metrics import accuracy_score

  print(accuracy_score(y_val, pred_bert))
```

are appropriate for use in profound learning models. The BERT group of models utilizes the Transformer encoder engineering to deal with every badge of information message in the full setting of all tokens previously, then after the fact, thus the name: Bidirectional Encoder Representations from Transformers. BERT models are normally pre-prepared on a huge corpus of text, then, at that point, calibrated for explicit assignments (Rafael Prieto Curiel at al 2020).

The Bert classifier is used to detect the fake web content in the website .It is pre trained with millions of corpus from Wikipedia and from book corpus (Mahor et al 2021),.

The sentence from the file is cleaned with the NLP technique and tools is stored in the data frame.

The sklearn library in the scikit_learn is already pre-processed with train_test_split variable of x and y values for training the model.

The BertClient is imported from the ber_serving.client for encoding the input sequence .

The logistic regression is used from the sklearn linear model for the prediction of the fake web content from the website. The accuracy of the model is calculated from sklearn metrics with 95% accuracy. The code for BERT model is given below in the figure 9.

CONCLUSION

In this chapter the identification of malicious web content is carried out with the help of natural language processing tools and technique from the news website. The model proposed which works on deep learning BERT classifier to identify the malicious fake content on the web it provides the accuracy of 95%.The future work will be based on detection of Bimodal Malicious web content using fake image and text data.

REFERENCES

Curiel, R. P., Cresci, S., Muntean, C. I., & Bishop, S. R. (2020). Crime and its fear in social media. *Palgrave Communications*, *6*(1), 57. Advance online publication. doi:10.105741599-020-0430-7

Mahor, V., Rawat, R., Kumar, A., Chouhan, M., Shaw, R. N., & Ghosh, A. (2021, September). Cyber Warfare Threat Categorization on CPS by Dark Web Terrorist. In *2021 IEEE 4th International Conference on Computing, Power and Communication Technologies (GUCON)* (pp. 1-6). 10.1109/GUCON50781.2021.9573994

Mahor, V., Rawat, R., Telang, S., Garg, B., Mukhopadhyay, D., & Palimkar, P. (2021, September). Machine Learning based Detection of Cyber Crime Hub Analysis using Twitter Data. In *2021 IEEE 4th International Conference on Computing, Power and Communication Technologies (GUCON)* (pp. 1-5). 10.1109/GUCON50781.2021.9573736

Rajawat, A. S., Rawat, R., Barhanpurkar, K., Shaw, R. N., & Ghosh, A. (2021). Vulnerability Analysis at Industrial Internet of Things Platform on Dark Web Network Using Computational Intelligence. *Computationally Intelligent Systems and their Applications*, 39-51.

Rajawat, A. S., Rawat, R., Mahor, V., Shaw, R. N., & Ghosh, A. (2021). Suspicious Big Text Data Analysis for Prediction—On Darkweb User Activity Using Computational Intelligence Model. In *Innovations in Electrical and Electronic Engineering*. Springer.

Rajawat, A. S., Rawat, R., Shaw, R. N., & Ghosh, A. (2021). Cyber Physical System Fraud Analysis by Mobile Robot. In *Machine Learning for Robotics Applications*. Springer.

Rawat, R., Dangi, C. S., & Patil, J. (2011). Safe Guard Anomalies against SQL Injection Attacks. *International Journal of Computers and Applications*, *22*(2), 11–14. doi:10.5120/2558-3511

Rawat, R., Garg, B., Mahor, V., Chouhan, M., Pachlasiya, K., & Telang, S. Cyber Threat Exploitation and Growth during COVID-19 Times. In Advanced Smart Computing Technologies in Cybersecurity and Forensics. CRC Press.

Rawat, R., Mahor, V., Chirgaiya, S., & Garg, B. (2021). Artificial Cyber Espionage Based Protection of Technological Enabled Automated Cities Infrastructure by Dark Web Cyber Offender. In Intelligence of Things: AI-IoT Based Critical-Applications and Innovations. Springer. doi:10.1007/978-3-030-82800-4_7

Rawat, R., Mahor, V., Chirgaiya, S., & Rathore, A. S. (2021). Applications of Social Network Analysis to Managing the Investigation of Suspicious Activities in Social Media Platforms. In Advances in Cybersecurity Management. Springer. doi:10.1007/978-3-030-71381-2_15

Rawat, R., Mahor, V., Chirgaiya, S., Shaw, R. N., & Ghosh, A. (2021). Sentiment Analysis at Online Social Network for Cyber-Malicious Post Reviews Using Machine Learning Techniques. *Computationally Intelligent Systems and their Applications*, 113-130.

Rawat, R., Mahor, V., Chirgaiya, S., Shaw, R. N., & Ghosh, A. (2021). Analysis of Darknet Traffic for Criminal Activities Detection Using TF-IDF and Light Gradient Boosted Machine Learning Algorithm. In *Innovations in Electrical and Electronic Engineering* (pp. 671–681). Springer. doi:10.1007/978-981-16-0749-3_53

Rawat, R., Mahor, V., Rawat, A., Garg, B., & Telang, S. (2021). Digital Transformation of Cyber Crime for Chip-Enabled Hacking. In *Handbook of Research on Advancing Cybersecurity for Digital Transformation* (pp. 227–243). IGI Global. doi:10.4018/978-1-7998-6975-7.ch012

Rawat, R., Rajawat, A. S., Mahor, V., Shaw, R. N., & Ghosh, A. (2021). Dark Web—Onion Hidden Service Discovery and Crawling for Profiling Morphing, Unstructured Crime and Vulnerabilities Prediction. In *Innovations in Electrical and Electronic Engineering*. Springer.

Chapter 12
Cyber Security Event Sentence Detection From News Articles Based on Trigger and Argument

Nikhil Chaturvedi
Shri Vaishnav Vidyapeeth Vishwavidyalaya, India

Jigyasu Dubey
Shri Vaishnav Vidyapeeth Vishwavidyalaya, India

ABSTRACT

Events are critical for comprehending the things that occur in the actual world. The term "events" is frequently used to describe the numerous relationships between people, places, activities, and things. Events-centered modelling entails the representation of several facets of an event in addition to the semantic representation of event facts. Detecting cybersecurity occurrences is important to keep us aware of the rapidly increasing number of such incidents reported via text. The authors focus on cyber security event detection task in this study, specifically on identifying event trigger words and arguments in the cybersecurity area. For this study, they use the CASIE dataset. They propose a system that involves the events identification, event triggers identification, and event arguments extraction. In this section, they divide the cyber security event sentence classification model into two steps: event trigger and argument identification, and cyber security event sentence classification using the training corpus.

INTRODUCTION

The internet is a necessary aspect of our life. It enables us to obtain real-time information from any location with a network connection. The procedure for acquiring Real-time or historical data has evolved and gotten much easier with the emergence of online newspapers. Numerous news agencies compete with one another to deliver a superior service to attract consumers, which benefits the customers by obtaining more accurate and useful information.

DOI: 10.4018/978-1-6684-6444-1.ch012

Cyber thieves, terrorists, and state-sponsored spies use the Dark Web (Ji and Grishman 2008) to achieve their illicit goals because it is one of the most difficult and untraceable mediums. Cybercrime on the Dark Web is similar to criminality in the real world. The sheer breadth, unpredictable environment, and anonymity given by Dark Web sites, on the other hand, are crucial battlegrounds in tracing criminals. Evaluating the various Dark Web crime threats is a vital step in discovering potential remedies to cyber-crime.

Cyber-attacks and cybercrime are widespread in the modern period, and their frequency and severity are expected to grow. Additionally, they are being created to capitalise on emerging threats and surroundings, such as the IOT and cyber systems. People and systems will be better equipped to defend themselves against assaults if we can stay current on trends and vulnerabilities.

We have proposed a methodology for extracting cyber security events from online news articles. The task of detecting instances of certain events in text and extracting pertinent information from them has been researched extensively over a long period of time yet continues to be a difficult one. The task was established at the second Message Understanding Conference in 1989 and has been used in a range of formation extraction tasks ever since; for a history of MUC, see (Grishman and Sundheim 1996). Efforts to improve event detection performance have often focused on increasing additional features or optimizing pattern matching algorithms (Li, Ji, and Huang 2013) or on building neural networks that better capture in formation, such as dependency tree based CNNs (Nguyen and Grishman 2018). Multiple sources of external knowledge have been leveraged to overcome the data scarcity of labelled data, including semantic frame analyses (Liu et al. 2016 and Li et al. 2019), (Chen et al. 2017), consistent along with complementary information for disambiguation from multilingual data (Liu et al. 2018), and expert-level patterns from an open-source pattern-based event extraction system called TABARI (Cao et al. 2018).

The majority of earlier research on event detection has been conducted on frequent occurrences in a person's life, such as those described by ACE (Walker et al. 2006) or the TAC Knowledge Base Population (Mitamura et al.,2015). These life events include "birth," "marriage," "beginning a career," and "being charged with a crime." One critical distinction between extracting life events and cybersecurity events is the domain-specific skills required. We have the same issue when obtaining information about other domains, such as biological events. The creation of these extensive event extraction datasets and tasks has aided in the advancement of BioNLP (Kim et al. 2009).

The intrinsic complexity of cyber security events is a second distinction between extracting life events and cyber security events. A cyber-attack event might consist of a series of attempted or accomplished activities. Each of these activities might be regarded as a distinct cyber security event description, increasing the number of possible cyber security event references. In comparison to real-world events, the difficulty lies in determining the homonym and synonym sets associated with an event mention.

In our work, we use the CASIE dataset (Satyapanich et al. 2019), this is already trained corpus of one thousand English online news articles published between 2017 to 2019 were includes event-based annotations on cyber-attack and vulnerability-related incidents They identify and specify five cyber security events, as well as their semantic roles, as well as twenty-four sorts of arguments that could be used as role-fillers. They propose a novel, difficult corpus of news stories that are annotated with information about cyber security.

While earlier research on cyber attack event analysis has been conducted (Qiu et al., 2016)(Khandpur et al. 2017), this research, to our knowledge, includes the broadest variety and complexity of cyber security incidents. We begin by providing definitions of cyber security events and common terminology utilized in our event detection job. Then we define our model's overall design and each of its components. After that, we present our assessment and experimental findings, as well as our current and future research.

This article is broken down into several sections. The following section discusses prior studies undertaken on this issue by various researchers. The third portion discussed the methods utilised to perform this research, which involves the examination of the data used, text preparation, and identification of cyber-attack triggers and argument categorization using the BiLSTM and CNN with self-attention models. Finally, in the final section, preliminary results will be presented, and a conclusion drawn.

RELATED WORK

-Numerous academics have made significant contributions to the field of event extraction and analysis by developing numerous approaches for extracting events from news stories. Numerous efforts have been made to analyse the narratives in internet news items.

Chen et al. (2015) offered a model of a typical neural network that incorporates dynamic multi-pooling (DMCNN). To gather additional information, this makes use of dynamic multi-pooling based on the event trigger and argument.

Tillo et al. (2015) suggested developing a web-based event extraction system in which recommendations are examined automatically and the exploration process exposes how users are related.

Yagung et al. (2017) Based on their database, they displayed a timeline of significant events connected to the query word, which can assist users in learning about pertinent subjects. When clustering phrases based on their events dates, researchers evaluated the importance of inaccuracies in event sentences. Since each event date right now has a single date vector, they can extract only the most critical information from each date vector. It is possible that the same type of event occurred on many occasions on the same date.

Liu et al., (2017) illustrate how to use supervised approaches to extract explicit argument information for event detection. Researchers study the proposed model using a systematic method and a range of attention strategies in this model.

Namazifar et al. (2018) suggested a method for identifying and classifying named entity in text. The suggested Named Entity Recognition method is applicable to the extraction of named entities from Tweets. According to the researcher, the suggested method is also used for the text of internet news stories.

Jacoab et al. (2018) classifier and dataset for detecting company-specific economic events in English news stories are suggested. Thus, further other resources and annotated data are required to better clarify the confusing event sentences in this model.

Hamborg et al. (2018) presented an open-source system for retrieving answers to when, why, who, where, what, and how questions in online published news items on major occurrences.

Yang et al. (2018) introduced an unsupervised learning method for automatically extracting event profiles. Their framework proposal is based on event profiling. Numerous difficulties arise during the implementation of work, such as determining the event types of previously unknown events for users or determining the event kinds of previously defined schemas in the model. As a result, classifying events according to their type continues to be a challenge in information and event extraction.

Ding et al.(2019) proposed system for categorising human needs based on words and circumstances. They devise a system for associating words with relevant concepts throughout the classification process. The researchers are constructing a supervised model for classifying words according to their semantic concepts to categorise information about human wants. They classify semantic concepts into ten unique groups in their work.

Walker et al. (2018) created new model centred on GRU integrates information about the mechanism's temporal and syntactic structure. When applied to the ACE dataset split, the outcome reveals that it is comparable to other cutting-edge methodologies, such as neural network construction. They imply that events can be classified according to their categories.

Yang et al. (2019)developed a robust collapsed Gibbs sampling technique for determining news facts and user credibility in the absence of labelled data. The researcher demonstrates in this model that it outperforms the other evaluated methods through experiment findings on two separate data sets.

Yang et al. (2019) introduce TOR, the current mainstream dark network communication system, and develop a visual dark web forum post association analysis system to graphically display the relationship between various forum messages and posters, allowing analysts to explore deeper levels of the dark web.

The researchers (Wang et al. 2019) suggested a novel approach based on adversarial training for extracting structured presentations of events from online literature. The study compared the proposed model to numerous state-of-the-art approaches and discovered that AEM greatly improved extraction performance, particularly for longer texts.

METHODOLOGY

-The cyber security event detection system architecture, as illustrated in Figure 1, consists of five steps: word embedding, event trigger detection, event argument detection, concatenation of event trigger and argument features, classification, and finally news articles classify into the event sentences and no-event sentences. We focus on the first three steps in this work, formalizing each as a binary classification task and using them as event coreference task for future work.

Word Embeddings:-There are already numerous words embedding techniques that are constructed from collections of varying sizes and genres. We investigated four different forms of embeddings: Transfer-Word2vec, Domain-Word2vec, Cyber-Word2vec, and Pre-built BERT. These four techniques are classified as context-independent embeddingse.g., Word2vec (Mikolov et al. 2013) or context-independent embeddings.

We trained two alternative Word2vec embeddings for the context-free embeddings: Transfer-Word2vec and Domain-Word2vec.

The non-contextual embedding types were trained on a dataset of 5,000 cybersecurity news stories and varied in terms of initialization and dimension. There are 2,531,577 tokens in the 5,000 articles (separated by spaces). TransferWord2vec was initialized using the publicly available Google-News-vectors-negative300 model in 300 dimensions (Mikolov et al. 2013). Following training, 14,960 additional phrases were added. Domain-Word2vec made use of 100-dimensional randomly initialised vectors and demanded that each word appear at least twice in the corpus. The Domain-word2vec embedding had a vocabulary of 28,283 words. Padia et al. (2018) created the Cyber-Word2vec embeddings. It has a hundred-dimensional structure and was trained on a corpus of around one million cybersecurity-related webpages. CyberWord2vec has a total of 6,417,554 vocabularies.

We generated context-dependent embeddings using the pretrained "BERT-Base Uncased" model (Devlin et al. 2018), fine-tuning our neural networks in the process. This model is a 12-layer, 12-attention brain network that generates a context-dependent embedding in the 768 dimensions for each word

Figure 1. Model overview of Cyber Security Event Sentence Detection from News Articles based on trigger and argument

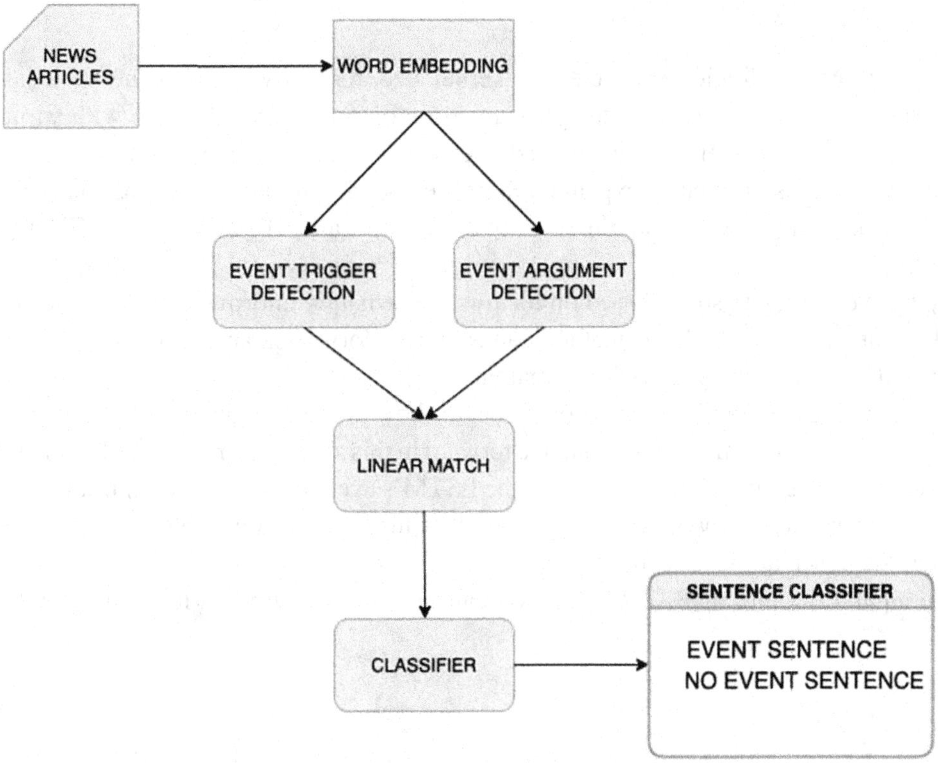

token. Due to the context-dependent nature of BERT, the same word in multiple phrases generates distinct vectors. BERT employed Word Piece tokenization, which divides words into constituents and generates embeddings for each constituent. We used the mean of the embeddings for the components of a word as its embedding; this is referred to as "Pre-built BERT." We retained all word embeddings as input and discovered experimentally that the fourth-to-last hidden layer provided the best development performance.

Event Trigger Detection: -In this part, we will demonstrate how to extract event triggers in detail.To begin; we extract event triggers using a convolutional neural network (Krizhevsky, A. el. al 2012) with a self-attention mechanism. In this case, CNN and self-attention can catch both local and global aspects. These properties are quite useful for intuitively identifying event triggers.

CNN with Self-Attention: -In this research proposal, we used the CNN model to analyse the importance of local range semantic information for event trigger extraction (Feng X. et al. 2015).Here study, we use CNN to obtain semantic information at the local level, circumventing the limitations associated with feature-based techniques. Additionally, we believe that semantic information in the local range resolves lexical ambiguity difficulties in text.

In our proposed method we encoded the embedding sequence using CNN. Given an input embedding sequence e $= (e_1, e_2,..,e_i,.., e_n)$the convolutional operation formula is as follows:

$$c_i^k = \text{conv}^{\left(e_{i-\lfloor \frac{k \cdot d}{2} \rfloor}, \ldots, e_i, \ldots, e_{i+\lfloor \frac{k \cdot d}{2} \rfloor}\right)}$$

whered and k are the dilation coefficientandkernel size, respectively. We generate local-range semantic information in this study by employing a variety of convolutional filters with variable kernel sizes. Multiple convolutional filters can be used to extract semantic information from a local region at various granularities. As previously explained, here we encoded semantic information obtained using two convolutional filters with two and three widths.(Liao T. et al. 2016). As a result, CNN's output isc $= (c_1, c_2 \ldots c_i, c_n)$.

Identifying event triggers solely based on local-range semantic information is insufficient. Because the self-attention (Lin. Z. el. al 2017) method can capture information about long-range dependencies, we apply it in this work to generate richer semantic information.

Event Argument Detection: - This section discusses how to label arguments in depth.

Bi-LSTM: -We feed the embedding sequence forward in this study. The reverse order is feed by LSTM in both positive and negative directions.Due to the LSTM's aversion to contextual information, we can augment the current moment with knowledge about its history and future by treating the embedding chronological sequence in two directions.

Give the input text x into theBiLSTM has an input of e_t and an output of h_t at time step t:

$$\overrightarrow{h}_t = \text{lstm}\left(e_t, \overrightarrow{h}_{t-1}\right)$$

$$\overleftarrow{h}_t = \text{lstm}(e_t, \overleftarrow{h}_{t+1})$$

$$h_t = [h_t \oplus h_t]$$

As a result of this procedure, we have a list of hidden states like $h = (h_1, h_2 \ldots, h_i \ldots, h_n)$.

Table 1. Number of cyber event instances in CASIE corpus, and the average number of annotated roles per event

Event Type	Events	Event Trigger	Role/Event
Attack.Databreach	916	1780	2.90
Attack.Phishing	955	1564	2.34
Attack.Ransom	944	1585	2.23
Discover.Vulnerability	560	2122	2.93
Patch.Vulnerability	528	1419	2.79

CRF for Labeling: -Bi-LSTM cannot construct an ideal label sequence because it does not capture information about the dependencies between neighbouring labels.This limitation is addressed in this work by utilising CRF.

Match and Sentence Classification: -After identifying the cyber security event trigger and argument present in the sentence, we corelate these arguments with the event triggers using a simple linear matching strategy. And finally, we used the CRF classifier for the binary sentence classification of cyber security events.

EXPERIMENTS

This section primarily introduces the CASIE Corpus and experimental results in depth. To begin, we

Table 2. Summarises the model's overall performance metrics on the CASIE dataset

Metrics	Precision (P)	Recall (R)	F1 metrics
Trigger identification	79.6	74.6	78.6
Argument identification	72.22	76.74	74.66
Classification	77.59	77.7	77.65

describe the CASIE Corpus and experimental conditions in detail: Finally, we present the overall results, followed by a quick analysis.

CASIE Dataset: -They collected approximately 5,000 cyber security news articles for this CASIE dataset (Satyapanich, T., 2019). These news articles were originally published between 2017 and 2019. Around 1,000 of them contain references to our five events, which were annotated by three expert computer scientists, who picked the final annotations by majority vote. Multiple cyber security events were nearly always included in each article, as were multiple event kinds. For event sentence or no event sentence classification in this corpus, we added another label. Table 1 contains summary data on the corpus.

Experiment Details: - For the above experiment, we used trainable parameters that were initialised with values from 0 to 1, and other hyperparameters were set based on the performance of the validation test. In our experiment, we set the threshold value at 0.6. Other values, we set both λ_1 and λ_2 to 1.

Other parameters for the model: Bi-LSTM and CNN hidden sizes are set to 256; 200 is the embedding size; the rate of learning is set at 0.001; and the batch size is 32. To avoid over-fitting, we used dropout during training and rectified linear units to improve network training.In our model firstly we train the event argument and trigger modules independently, after that we train the classifier model and finally evaluate its precision, recall, and F1 score matrices.

Results: -The work of cyber security event sentence classification entails identifying triggers, identifying arguments, and classifying sentences according to them.Our study utilised measures created for the TAC Event Task (NIST 2015) to determine the optimal mapping between the output of our model with the proper labels.For that, we used 8-fold cross validation of 900 articles from the training data set, using 100 articles for testing. We tested our sub-systems by averaging scores for five runs. Because all the experiments were conducted using Google Colab, the results may vary in some ranges.

CONCLUSION

In the given article, we try to provide an excellent neural network model for the classification of cyber event sentences from the news articles dataset. To be more precise, we extract event triggers using CNN and self-awareness. We next provide arguments for event triggers based on the binary classification's essence. In comparison to pipelined approaches, our methodology can mitigate error propagation. We presented a novel task for the extraction of cyber security event sentences and outlined five distinct event categories, their semantic implications, and the alternative argument types used to fill them. Our methods focus on the different tasks required of an event detection system, like recognising event triggers and arguments and anticipating binary event sentence classification using results metrics. In the future, we will focus on detecting event phrases that are contextually connected.

REFERENCES

Alsaedi, N., & Burnap, P. (2015, August). Feature extraction and analysis for identifying disruptive events from social media. In *Proceedings of the 2015 IEEE/ACM International Conference on Advances in Social Networks Analysis and Mining 2015* (pp. 1495-1502). 10.1145/2808797.2808867

Anam, M., Shafiq, B., Shamail, S., Chun, S. A., & Adam, N. (2019, June).Discovering Events from Social Media for Emergency Planning. In *Proceedings of the 20th Annual International Conference on Digital Government Research* (pp. 109-116). 10.1145/3325112.3325213

Can, F., Kocberber, S., Baglioglu, O., Kardas, S., Ocalan, H. C., & Uyar, E. (2010). New event detection and topic tracking in Turkish. *Journal of the American Society for Information Science and Technology*, *61*(4), 802–819. doi:10.1002/asi.21264

Cao, K., Li, X., Ma, W., & Grishman, R. (2018). Including new patterns to improve event extraction systems. In *Florida AI Conference*. AAAI.

Chen, Y., Liu, S., Zhang, X., Liu, K., & Zhao, J. 2017.Automatically labelled data generation for large scale event extraction. In *Proceedings of the 55th Annual Meeting of the Association for Computational Linguistics (Volume 1: Long Papers)* (pp. 409–419). 10.18653/v1/P17-1038

Chen, Y., Xu, L., Liu, K., Zeng, D., & Zhao, J. (2015, July).Event extraction via dynamic multi-pooling convolutional neural networks. In *Proceedings of the 53rd Annual Meeting of the Association for Computational Linguistics and the 7th International Joint Conference on Natural Language Processing (Volume 1: Long Papers)* (pp. 167-176). 10.3115/v1/P15-1017

Chen, Z., & Ji, H. (2009, June). Language specific issue and feature exploration in Chinese event extraction. In *Proceedings of Human Language Technologies: The 2009 Annual Conference of the North American Chapter of the Association for Computational Linguistics, Companion Volume: Short Papers* (pp. 209-212). 10.3115/1620853.1620910

Devlin, J., Chang, M., Lee, K., & Toutanova, K. (2018). *BERT: Pre-training of deep bidirectional transformers for language understanding.* CoRR abs/1810.04805.

Ding, H., Jiang, T., & Riloff, E. (2018, June). Why is an event affective? Classifying affective events based on human needs. *Workshops at the Thirty-Second AAAI Conference on Artificial Intelligence.*

Ding, H., & Riloff, E. (2018, June). Human needs categorization of affective events using labeled and unlabeled data. In *Proceedings of the 2018 Conference of the North American Chapter of the Association for Computational Linguistics: Human Language Technologies*, Volume 1 *(Long Papers)* (pp. 1919-1929). 10.18653/v1/N18-1174

Ding, H., Riloff, E., & Feng, Z. (2019, June). Improving Human Needs Categorization of Events with Semantic Classification. In *Proceedings of the Eighth Joint Conference on Lexical and Computational Semantics (* SEM 2019)* (pp. 198-204). 10.18653/v1/S19-1022

Feng, Huang, Tang, Ji, Qin, & Liu. (2016). A languageindependent neural network for event detection. *Proceedings of the 54th Annual Meeting of the Association for Computational Linguistics*, 66–71.

Grishman, R., & Sundheim, B. (1996). Message understanding conference 6: A brief history. *16th International Conference on Computational Linguistics.*

Hamborg, F., Breitinger, C., Schubotz, M., Lachnit, S., & Gipp, B. (2018, May). Extraction of main event descriptors from news articles by answering the journalistic five W and one H questions. In *Proceedings of the 18th ACM/IEEE on Joint Conference on Digital Libraries* (pp. 339-340). 10.1145/3197026.3203899

Hamborg, F., Donnay, K., & Gipp, B. (2019). Automated identification of media bias in news articles: An interdisciplinary literature review. *International Journal on Digital Libraries*, *20*(4), 391–415. doi:10.100700799-018-0261-y

Hamborg, F., Lachnit, S., Schubotz, M., Hepp, T., & Gipp, B. (2018, March). Giveme5W: main event retrieval from news articles by extraction of the five journalistic w questions. In *International conference on information* (pp. 356-366). Springer. 10.1007/978-3-319-78105-1_39

Hinton, G. E., Srivastava, N., Krizhevsky, A., Sutskever, I., & Salakhutdinov, R. R. (2012). *Improving neural networks by preventing co-adaptation of feature detectors.* arXiv preprint arXiv:1207.0580.

Jacobs, G., Lefever, E., & Hoste, V. (2018, July). Economic event detection in company-specific news text. In *Proceedings of the First Workshop on Economics and Natural Language Processing* (pp. 1-10). 10.18653/v1/W18-3101

Ji, H., & Grishman, R. (2008). Refining event extraction through cross-document inference. *Proceedings of the 46th Annual Meeting of the Association for Computational Linguistics*, 254–262.

Kamel, M., Keyvani, N., & Yazdi, H. S. (2018). Sentimental content analysis and knowledge extraction from news articles. arXiv preprint arXiv:1808.03027

Keshavarz, S., Saleemi, I., & Atia, G. (2017, September). Exploiting probabilistic relationships between action concepts for complex event classification. In *2017 IEEE International Conference on Image Processing (ICIP)* (pp. 1572-1576). IEEE. 10.1109/ICIP.2017.8296546

Khandpur, R. P., Ji, T., Jan, S., Wang, G., Lu, C. T., & Ramakrishnan, N. (2017, November). Crowd-sourcing cybersecurity: Cyber attack detection using social media. In *Proceedings of the 2017 ACM on Conference on Information and Knowledge Management* (pp. 1049-1057). 10.1145/3132847.3132866

Kim, J. D., Ohta, T., Pyysalo, S., Kano, Y., & Tsujii, J. I. (2009, June). Overview of BioNLP'09 shared task on event extraction. In *Proceedings of the BioNLP 2009 workshop companion volume for shared task* (pp. 1-9). 10.3115/1572340.1572342

Krizhevsky, A., Sutskever, I., & Hinton, G. E. (2012). Imagenet classification with deep convolutional neural networks. *Advances in Neural Information Processing Systems, 25*, 1097–1105.

Lafferty, J., McCallum, A., Pereira, F., & Duh, K. (2002). Probabilistic models for segmenting and labeling sequence data. *International Conference on Machine Learning*.

Lin, Z., Feng, M., Santos, C. N. D., Yu, M., Xiang, B., Zhou, B., & Bengio, Y. (2017). *A structured self-attentive sentence embedding.* arXiv preprint arXiv:1703.03130.

Liu, J., Chen, Y., Liu, K., & Zhao, J. (2018). Event detection via gated multilingual attention mechanism. *ThirtySecond AAAI Conference on Artificial Intelligence*.

Liu, S., Chen, Y., He, S., Liu, K., & Zhao, J. (2016). Leveraging Frame net to improve automatic event detection. In *Proceedings of the 54th Annual Meeting of the Association for Computational Linguistics (Volume 1: Long Papers)* (pp. 2134–2143). 10.18653/v1/P16-1201

Liu, S., Chen, Y., Liu, K., & Zhao, J. (2017, July).Exploiting argument information to improve event detection via supervised attention mechanisms. In *Proceedings of the 55th Annual Meeting of the Association for Computational Linguistics (Volume 1: Long Papers)* (pp. 1789-1798). 10.18653/v1/P17-1164

Michael, T., & Akbik, A. (2015, July). SCHNÄPPER: A Web Toolkit for Exploratory Relation Extraction. In *Proceedings of ACL-IJCNLP 2015 System Demonstrations* (pp. 67-72). 10.3115/v1/P15-4012

Mikolov, T., Chen, K., Corrado, G., & Dean, J. (2013). *Efficient estimation of word representations in vector space.* arXiv preprint arXiv:1301.3781.

Mitamura, T., Liu, Z., & Hovy, E. H. (2015). Overview of TAC KBP 2015 event nugget track. In *Text Analysis Conference*. National Institute of Standards and Technology.

Nair, V., & Hinton, G. E. (2010, January). Rectified linear units improve restricted boltzmann machines. ICML.

Namazifar, M. (2017). *Named Entity Sequence Classification.* arXiv preprint arXiv:1712.02316.

Nguyen, T. H., Fu, L., Cho, K., & Grishman, R. (2016, August).A two-stage approach for extending event detection to new types via neural networks. In *Proceedings of the 1st Workshop on Representation Learning for NLP* (pp. 158-165). 10.18653/v1/W16-1618

Nguyen, T. H., & Grishman, R. (2016). Modelling skip grams for event detection with convolutional neural networks. *Conference on Empirical Methods in Natural Language Processing*, 886–891.

NIST. (2015). *TAC KBP event track*. http://tac.nist.gov/- 2015/KBP/Event/

Padia, A., Roy, A., Satyapanich, T. W., Ferraro, F., Pan, S., Park, Y., & Finin, T. (2018). *UMBC at SemEval-2018 Task 8: Understanding text about malware*. UMBC Computer Science and Electrical Engineering Department.

Qiu, X., Lin, X., & Qiu, L. (2016, October). Feature representation models for cyber attack event extraction. In *2016 IEEE/WIC/ACM International Conference on Web Intelligence Workshops (WIW)* (pp. 29-32). IEEE. 10.1109/WIW.2016.020

Rao, B. T., Patibandla, R. L., & Murty, M. R. (2020). A comparative study on effective approaches for unsupervised statistical machine translation. In *Embedded Systems and Artificial Intelligence* (pp. 895–905). Springer.

Sarma, P. K., Liang, Y., & Sethares, W. A. (2018). Domain adapted word embeddings for improved sentiment classification. arXiv preprint arXiv:1805.04576. doi:10.18653/v1/P18-2007

Satyapanich, T., Finin, T., & Ferraro, F. (2019). Extracting rich semantic information about cybersecurity events. *Second Workshop on Big Data for CyberSecurity*. 10.1109/BigData47090.2019.9006444

Singh, S. (2018). *Natural language processing for information extraction*. arXiv preprint arXiv:1807.02383.

Suchanek, F. (2007). a core of semantic knowledge. *Proceedings of the 16th international conference on World Wide Web ACM*, 697–706. 10.1145/1242572.1242667

Walker, C., Strassel, S., Medero, J., & Maeda, K. (2006). *ACE 2005 multilingual training corpus.Technical report*. Linguistic Data Consortium.

Walker Orr, J., Tadepalli, P., & Fern, X. (2018). *Event Detection with Neural Networks: A Rigorous Empirical Evaluation*. arXiv e-prints, arXiv-1808.

Wang, R., Zhou, D., & He, Y. (2019). Open event extraction from online text using a generative adversarial network. arXiv preprint arXiv:1908.09246. doi:10.18653/v1/D19-1027

Wang, W. (2012, April). Chinese news event 5W1H semantic elements extraction for event ontology population. In *Proceedings of the 21st International Conference on World Wide Web* (pp. 197-202). 10.1145/2187980.2188008

Wu, Y., Sun, H., & Yan, C. (2017, March). An event timeline extraction method based on news corpus. In *2017 IEEE 2nd International Conference on Big Data Analysis (ICBDA)* (pp. 697-702). IEEE. 10.1109/ICBDA.2017.8078725

Yang, Q. (2018). *Open schema event profiling for massive news corpus. CIKM'18*.

Yang, S., Shu, K., Wang, S., Gu, R., Wu, F., & Liu, H. (2019, July). Unsupervised fake news detection on social media: A generative approach. *Proceedings of the AAAI Conference on Artificial Intelligence, 33*(01), 5644–5651. doi:10.1609/aaai.v33i01.33015644

Yang, Y., Yang, L., Yang, M., Yu, H., Zhu, G., Chen, Z., & Chen, L. (2019, May). Dark web forum correlation analysis research. In *2019 IEEE 8th Joint International Information Technology and Artificial Intelligence Conference (ITAIC)* (pp. 1216-1220). IEEE. 10.1109/ITAIC.2019.8785760

Yarrabelly, N., & Karlapalem, K. (2018, June). Extracting predictive statements with their scope from news articles. *Twelfth International AAAI conference on web and social media.*

Section 5
Assessment of Dark Web Threat Evolution

Chapter 13
Systematic Approach for Detection and Assessment of Dark Web Threat Evolution

P. William

ⓘ https://orcid.org/0000-0002-0610-0390

Sanjivani College of Engineering, Savitribai Phule Pune University, India

M. A. Jawale

Sanjivani College of Engineering, Savitribai Phule Pune University, India

A. B. Pawar

Sanjivani College of Engineering, Savitribai Phule Pune University, India

Rahul R. Bibave

Sanjivani College of Engineering, Savitribai Phule Pune University, India

Priyanka Narode

Sanjivani Jr. College, India

ABSTRACT

Cyber thieves and terrorists use the dark web as one of the most difficult channels to achieve their nefarious goals. There are many similarities between cyber-crimes and real-world crimes taking place on the dark web. However, the dark web's sheer breadth and anonymity are key to tracing the offenders. The first step in finding effective solutions to cybercrime is to assess the different dark web criminal hazards. The investigation of the dark web includes a review of crimes to minimize crime issues. To assist cyber security specialists, the authors used the systematic literature review approach and extracted data from 65 publications from the most relevant internet resources to meet research aims. As a result of an exhaustive investigation, systematic literature review is able to provide a clear picture of how criminal activity on the dark web is expanding and examine the strengths and weaknesses of existing methods for tracking down criminals. This study has showed, to aid law enforcement in the apprehension of criminals, digital evidence must be analyzed as per established standards.

DOI: 10.4018/978-1-6684-6444-1.ch013

INTRODUCTION

In spite of its complexity, the World Wide Web (WWW) holds an unimaginable amount of digital information. Search engines like Google and Yahoo make it easier to find information on the Internet's most common topics. However, there are enormous swaths of the Internet that are not indexed by the major search engines. The Deep Web, a hidden portion of the Internet, is thought to account for 96% of all WWW content (Holgado and Peñalvo,2018). The Dark Web or Dark Net is a subclass of the Deep Web that is mostly utilised for unlawful purposes (Nabki et al.,2017). A whopping 57% of the Dark Web's traffic is comprised of criminal activity or unlawful material. Illegal narcotics, weapons trafficking, child pornography, stolen financial information, illegal talks, false money, and terrorist communication are just a few of the more prevalent ones (Chertoff and Simon,2015).

In 2013, the FBI took down Silk Road, the most notorious marketplace on the Dark Web, and these illicit actions were brought to the public's notice. The Dark Web's harmful intentions and unlawful material may be found through hidden wiki and deep search engines. Many further Deep Web connections may be found using these portals (Holgado and Peñalvo,2018). Forensic analysts researching criminal activity on the Dark Web have a significant problem because of the anonymity afforded by Dark Web services. Use of the Dark Web's content and services is common among anonymity services such as Tor, Freenet.

In contrast to a centralised computer server, the most widely used Dark Web service is the TOR network, which enables users to transmit information covertly and anonymously through peer-to-peer connections. Naval Research Laboratory developed this service in 2002 to overcome censorship and protect critical communications (Dredge,2013). The anonymity of the TOR network makes it difficult to monitor the Dark Web. Criminals use the Onion Router (TOR) to access the Dark Web because it is untraceable and tough to shut down. Thus, security and law enforcement are under tremendous pressure to monitor and track the activities of people on the Dark Web.

The TOR is often used by criminals to hide their activity on the Dark Web behind a relay station. This means that when police trace an IP address to a crime committed using the TOR browser, they can only discover one TOR exit relay. Various tactics and approaches have been developed by researchers to keep track of and catch criminals on the Deep Web. Memex is a successful Dark Web data mining tool developed and used by the United States Defense Advanced Research Projects Agency (DARPA) (William et al.,2021). Findings from a research study included mapping and monitoring of hidden service directories; monitoring social media; customer data monitoring; semantic analysis; and market profiling (Ciancaglini et al.,2013). Additionally, law enforcement has used numerous tactics to discover offenders, such as social media, IP addresses, monitoring user activity, and monitoring Bitcoin accounts.

There are several advantages to doing a comprehensive evaluation of scientific literature in order to discover the research issues and the rationale for further investigation in any given field . An SLR is a methodical review of the literature aimed at discovering relevant works in a certain field by following a series of research stages and procedures. To our knowledge, no comprehensive literature study on the evaluation of the Dark Web as a threat assessment has been done, which has prompted us to offer this survey. These crimes include drug trades, terrorism, human trafficking, and marketplaces for cybercrime tools. This research examines the effects of these crimes, as well as their accompanying crime-monitoring technology. To do this, we have methodically identified and examined 65 papers that are related to our study objective. As a result, the paper's contributions include:

- Conducting a study of new crimes on the Dark Web.
- The repercussions of the crimes on society, the economy, and the ethics.
- Difficulties and obstacles in tracing down offenders.
- Techniques and tactics for apprehending criminals and committing crimes, as well as their limits.

The remainder of this article will be organised in the following manner: Section II contains a description of the research methodologies that were employed. Section III summarises our results, while Section IV gives information on the selected works to serve as examples. Section V depicts the architectures of the selected publications, and Section VI concludes our work by discussing the research's future directions.

RESEARCH METHODOLOGY

This section outlines the process for doing this study, which is a Systematic Literature Review (SLR). In addition, we looked at other recent studies that used the SLR technique (Ghappour,2017). In SLR, the research subject is defined, the literature is searched, the results are screened and selected, and data is extracted from the selected findings to be qualitative or quantitatively analysed and synthesised. Data extraction, data analysis, and synthesis are all steps in the process that begin with formulating the research question(s), followed by identifying the most relevant data sources and search methods.

Research Questions

It is the major goal of this work to summarise the most recent Dark Web crimes, their consequences, and the most effective defence techniques. Consequently, the following questions and reasons are provided:

RQ1: What new threats do criminals on the Dark Web face?

Researching the Dark Web's many different forms of threats may help demonstrate how illegal information and services are accessible and their consequences. Developing more effective methods for catching criminals is vital, and this shows the difficulty and importance of doing so.

RQ2: What methods are used in the hunt for criminals operating on the Dark Web?

There are a wide range of technologies that may be used by law enforcement agencies to trace illegal activity on dark web sites. Using cutting-edge technology and law enforcement, it lays forth a future strategy for combating the goals of cybercriminals.

Search Strategy and Selection

We adhered to the search strategy guidelines outlined in (Erb,2019) and (Gai et al.,2016), which are detailed below. IEEE Xplore, ScienceDirect, Springer, Scopus, the ACM Digital Library, and Google Scholar were used to acquire data for the review articles.

In our search term, we included the Dark Web offences specified in (Chen,2011) and (Dolliver and Kenney,2016). Keywords from our research questions were used in Section II of our paper. A. A Boolean search employing ANDS and ORs has been created for particular phrases. Table 1 shows the search terms that were used to find our relevant articles. So that it's clear several search terms were used to find related articles. Using the references found in the relevant publications, a search for other papers was done.

Table 1. Selection of literatures based on search term

Sl	Search Term
1	"Dark Web" AND " crimes" OR "Dark Net" AND "cyber security"
2	"Dark Web" AND "threats" OR "attack" AND "crime rates"
3	"crypto markets" OR "Dark Net marketplaces" OR "bit coin" OR "silk road" OR "TOR"
4	"illicit" OR " illicit Products" AND "Dark Net"
5	"techniques" AND " Dark Web" OR "strategies" AND "Dark Web"
6	"law enforcement" OR "darpa" OR "memex" AND "challenges" AND "Dark Web"
7	"drugs" OR "human trafficking" OR "fraud" OR "prostitution" OR "terrorism" Or "data breach" AND "Dark Web"

Table 2. Selection of literatures based on inclusion criteria

IC#	Description
IC1	A study that is focused on Dark Web related crimes and demonstrates the crimes, consequences and assess techniques
IC2	A study that is based on the tracing techniques and technologies for locating the criminals in the Dark Web for cyber security
IC3	The search term keywords in Tab.I applies the operators of search syntax OR, AND. AND operator signifies that both keywords must be present in the search queries and OR means that at least one keyword must be present in the queries searched
IC4	Studies published in English language
IC5	Include data from journals, conferences and web articles published between the year 2003 to 2019
IC6	Include abstract based and full-text studies

EC#	Description
EC1	Exclude the duplicate articles obtained by authors and/or different libraries
EC2	Exclude articles those specifies Dark Web but do not include crime threats or crime locating techniques
EC3	Exclude cyber security defense articles not related to Dark Web

Figure 1. Methodology of applied SLR

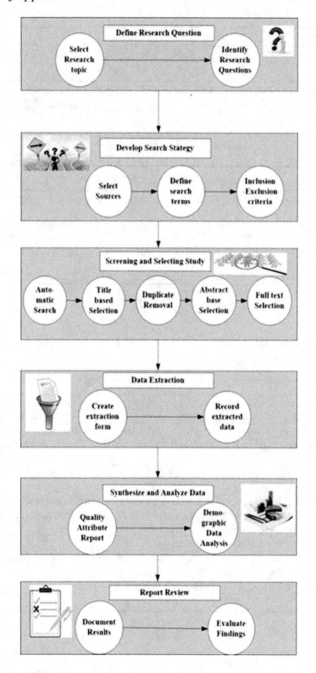

Search phrases in digital libraries, with the exception of the Springer library, are matched to particular portions of papers based on the title, abstract, and keywords of those papers. We filtered and screened articles using the following criteria in order to select the most relevant papers. Tables 2 and 3 detail the survey's inclusion and exclusion criteria. The 65 publications that met the inclusion and exclusion criteria were selected for this review.

Table 4. Data extraction form

SL	Data Item	Description
1	Year	Publication year of the article
2	Authors	Authors of the article
3	Source	Source of the publication article(e.g., google scholar)
4	Title	Title of the article
5	Type	Type of the publication article(e.g., journal)
6	Criteria	Selected criteria of the articles (e.g., cryptomarkets)
7	RQ1	Emerging threats in the Dark Web crime
8	RQ2	Techniques applied to locate the criminals in Dark Web

After applying both inclusive and exclusive criteria to our screening process, we came up with 65 papers. Figure 1 depicts our whole procedure for choosing SLR papers for publishing in our survey. As an example, consider the following selection strategies:

- Automated search:We were able to find a total of 1920 articles using the search parameters from the six databases listed above.
- Title-based choice:The implementation of a title-based selection system made it easier to choose articles. Articles are selected for our SLR based on their titles. The final tally now stands at 581 documents.
  - Paper recycling:Since some of the papers' database indexes may be found in other databases, we were able to delete any duplicates. After removing duplicates, the total number of articles was reduced to 393.
- Selection on the basis of abstracts:The abstracts of the 372 articles we picked were examined to see whether they were relevant to our SLR. One hundred articles were whittled down from the thousands of abstracts at this point.
- Full-text selection:Each of the 100 submissions was carefully reviewed before 65 were finally picked.

IEEE Xplore provided 18 articles, Google Scholar provided 22, ScienceDirect provided 6, Springer provided 9, Scopus provided 5, and ACM Digital Library provided the last 5 publications for a total of 65 publications.

Data Extraction and Synthesis

Data extraction and analysis from the filtered papers are discussed in this part in order to answer our research questions. Table 4 shows the data extraction form that was used to get the filtered articles' data. Using Microsoft Excel, the obtained information was inputted.

To answer our study objectives, we used a number of procedures to synthesise the data we collected. Descriptive statistics were used to examine the demographics of the submitted manuscripts.

Table 5. The QARS of this SLR

QAR#	Description
QAR1	Are the objectives of the research articles clearly defined?
QAR2	Are the Dark Web crime backgrounds addresses properly?
QAR3	Are the Dark Web crimes tracing techniques used clearly defined?
QAR4	Are the articles comprehensive and take into consideration past and current literature?
QAR5	Are the methods used to analyze the results appropriately?
QAR6	Do the articles identify the gap of knowledge?

Section IV discusses and illustrates the demographic information analysis results. Section V discusses and illustrates the structures of the literatures discovered throughout the data analysis process.

Figure 2 summarises the data analysis procedure for our RQs. We began by identifying the articles' quality qualities using the selection criteria for each RQ. Motives were collected and themes were discovered via thematic analysis (Cruzes and Dyba,2011) of articles based on the RQ.

RQ1: Using quality indicators and selection criteria, we first culled out the motivations from the literature and then identified the different architectures applied within. After that, we conducted a thematic analysis to identify the study's major topics. After that, we carried out qualitative data analysis based on the topics that had been gathered. In this part, we'll take a look at the literary frameworks. According to Appendix A Table 11, ID 10, ID 26, and ID 40 are themed as 'Terrorist and ISIS' study based on the motives for these studies, since terrorism is one of the most hazardous crimes related with the Dark Web, as shown by the reasons for these studies. Identifiers 7 through 56 are classified as 'Drug transactions' studies because their primary goal is to conduct Deep Web research for terrorist organisations. Various architectural frameworks gathered in the RQ1 block are sent into the RQ2 block as input. This means that RQ1 provides RQ2 with crucial information.

RQ2: Our RQ2 data analysis is based on the output of RQ1, which assists in organising the architecture of various literatures depending on the results of the study, as seen in Figure 2. We began by extracting motives from the architectures summary in order to discover the features of the models employed in the designs' various frameworks. These features include the amount of data utilised, its practical use, and the model's performance. Then, using theme analysis, we were able to obtain generalised models. This stage establishes the context and rationale for our architectural examination.

To evaluate the effectiveness of techniques used in models inside frameworks, we examined the experimental findings and implications of the methods and then conducted thematic analysis to get the

final outcomes and constraints resulting from the applied methods. As a consequence, we obtained the outcome and constraints for our architectural study. We may describe the collected analysis findings as follows from the RQ2.

Method:Hash value analysis, sock puppet attacks, key informant and TOR assaults, exit node analysis, network traffic monitoring, network traffic categorization, marketplace scarping and Dark Web monitoring are among the nine regularly utilised crime and criminal detection tactics on the Dark Web.

Figure 2. Data analysis process

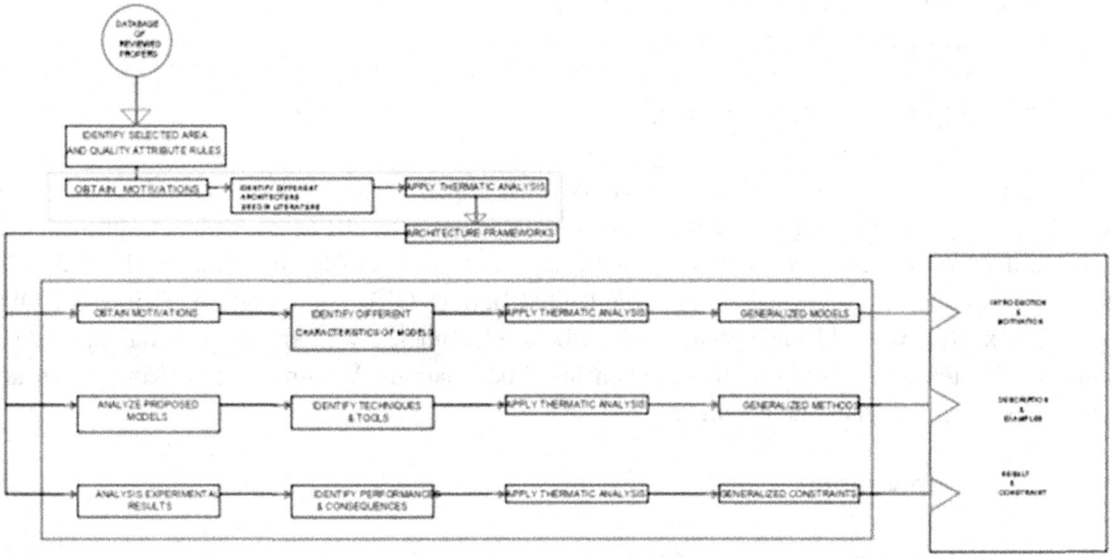

Tools:MLAT, DARPA, Bit coin flow, and social media were all found to be frequently utilised by law enforcement in our investigation of Dark Web criminal forensics.

RESULTS AND COMMENTS

In this section, we will answer the two research questions and evaluate the results of our comprehensive literature study. In the first research question (RQ1), we are interested in determining the increasing dangers of Dark Web illegal activities. Subsection A will deal with this topic. Subsections III.A.1 to III.A.8 of this section summarise the risks on the Dark Web as a consequence of illicit conduct relevant to our RQ1. Examining the different strategies used to hunt down offenders on Dark Web is our second research topic (RQ2). In subsection B, we dealt with this issue and discussed it in detail. Our RQ2's Subsection III.B.1.a to III.B.2.i examines the strategies and tactics used to combat these dangers. Next, we provide the third paragraph III.C, which summarises the content and contributions of the 65 retrieved papers.

Criminal Activity Threats in the Darkweb(Rq1)

Based on the articles we selected, found eight major criminal threats on the Dark Web, which answers our RQ1. Listed below are the various threats that have been made:

- Sex Trafficking
- Industry of Pornography
- Assassinations and its marketing
- Drug transactions
- Child Pornography

- Terrorism
- Markets for Cybercrime Tools and Stolen Data
- DarkNet currency exchange using bitcoin

Sex Trafficking and Human Trafficking

Online forums, chat services, and the anonymity of the Deep Web have led to an increase in human trafficking and sex trafficking in recent years (Hétu and Giommoni,2017). As a human rights violation, human trafficking is widely considered. Modern-day slavery is estimated to affect roughly 2.5 million individuals around the globe, according to the United Nations Office on Drugs and Crime (UNODC). Beggars, sex workers, child soldiers, industrial labourers, domestic workers, and workers in a range of commercial enterprises are just a few of the enslaved occupations. Victims of trafficking are attracted to traffickers via dialogues and contracts.

Industry of Pornography

The pornography industry's primary victims are women involved in human trafficking and sex trafficking . Once male-female partners sign an agreement to do the actions, traffickers coerce victims into pornography creation out of fear of murder. Without the victims' permission, the sex trafficker captures footage and distributes it to interested parties through the pornography business. Additionally, traffickers upload recordings and photographs on their websites (Eyes,2011).

Dark Web has a large number of sexually explicit websites. Traffickers in pornography use similar methods to those used by human and sexual traffickers to find victims, then kidnap them while keeping their identities secret(Clawson and Dutch,2008). Online prostitution videos and photographs include new types of illegal conduct as well as excessive degrees of violence (William and Badholia,2021).

Assassins and Marketing

The Dark Web is used by criminals to sell their assassination skills. Recruiting fees of $10,000 in the US and $12,000 in Europe were mentioned on the websites MailOnline, White Wolves, and C'thuthlu in advertisements for criminals (Chertoff and Simon,2015). When it comes to high-ranking politicians, the price ranges from $40,000 to $1.5 million. The most popular means for researching the Deep Web are the Hidden Wiki and Deep search engines, which provide hundreds of links to illegal onion sites (Holgado and Peñalvo,2018).

Drug Transactions

On the Deep Web, there are often two types of drug markets. Markets where just one kind of drug is sold, such as heroin. As a result of the vendor-customer relationship and the product expertise, they are quite popular. For the general buyer, the second kind of drug market is the general buyer market that offers unlawful products such as stolen jewellery and black-market cigarettes. A vast range of pharmaceuticals, as well as drug hardware and manufacturing materials, are among the most common products (Christin,2013).

The Deep Web's anonymity has facilitated a significant increase in drug transactions, resulting in the establishment of a digital black market for drugs. Due to the fact that drug trading does not need face-to-face contact, illegal sellers purchase and sell narcotics over the Dark Web. Silk Road was one of the Dark Web marketplaces that sold narcotics worth more than a billion dollars and sent them by DHL or drop shipping (Aldridge and Hétu,2016), (Aldridge and Hétu,2014), (Barratt et al.,2016).

Abuse of Child

Children may chat anonymously on websites like Omegle and Ask.fm, as well as other social media platforms (Cranford,2015). These applications are being used by paedophiles to communicate with children. The Dark Web is used extensively by paedophiles and other criminals for child pornography, photo sharing, and pons, among other things. Freedom hosting provided space on 550 servers throughout Europe for anybody who wanted to submit pornographic material directed towards kids.

Terrorism

There is a serious danger to national security on the Deep Web, where terrorists and terrorist organisations are active. In order to achieve their harmful aims and transmit propaganda (Bates,2016), (Fanusie and Robinson,2018), terrorist organisations such as al-Qaeda and ISIS have benefitted from the Dark Web's advantages.

Uses the Dark Web to gather donations, promote their cause, as well as communicate information during leadership transitions. ISIS or ISIS-supported organisations are using the Dark Web for purposes other than spreading propaganda and self-aggrandizement, according to a Defence One technology editor. Bitcoins are used by ISIS to pay for services on the Dark Web. As a result, law enforcement and the military have been unable to monitor the Dark Web without violating people's privacy rights (Hétu and Giommoni,2017).

Markets for Stolen Data and Cybercrime Tools

Cyber criminals rely on the Dark Web's anonymous marketplaces to buy and sell cybercrime tools and stolen or leaked data. Three of the most well-known and fast expanding Dark Net markets have subsequently been shut down: Black Market Reloaded, Sheep Market, and the Silk Road (William and Badholia,2020).

In the wake of the legendary Silk Road, a number of bitcoin exchanges have emerged. From 2013 to 2015, (Ciancaglini et al.,2013) explored an important part of these market-place ecosystems. This includes Agora and Atlantis; Black Flag; Tor Bazaar; Cloud 9; Evolution; Hydra; The Marketplace; Pandora; Sheep Marketplace; Silk Road 2.0; Silk Road; and Utopia. More than a few are under investigation or have been shut down by the government for alleged fraud. Internet marketplaces like these anonymous ones are a main source for the sale of stolen or leaked information such as credit card numbers, bank statements, cloned credentials, and sensitive data, in addition to the selling of those items.

Exchange of Dark Net Currencies with Bitcoin

Using Bit coin, Dark Net market participants may transact anonymously (William and Patil,2016). Bit coin is sometimes the only form of payment accepted by dark net marketplaces. About US$1.2 billion was made on Silk Road, one of the most successful underground markets. As a currency that increases and masks money-laundering, Bitcoin has been much contested (Bryans,2014).

Methods for Identifying Criminals on the Dark Web (rq2)

Even though cybercrime on the Dark Web is quite comparable to regular crime, it's difficult for law enforcement to follow virtual crimes on the Dark Web. Certain forensic analysts may run into difficulties researching illicit activity because of the anonymity provided by Dark Web sites. In the end, forensic inquiry into criminal activity suffers as a direct consequence of this policy. The Dark Web has been the subject of a great deal of criminal detection research. There are sub-sections on law enforcement and detecting methods where we'll look at how these approaches are used and started. To our RQ2, we've included this section.

Law Enforcements

Increasingly sophisticated cybercriminals have made it more difficult for smaller law enforcement agencies to tackle some crimes. Laws governing illicit, civil, and regulatory activity on the Dark Web all apply to criminal activity. Criminal law deals with offences committed at the local, state, and federal levels of government. A fine or perhaps life in prison is possible as a penalty. According to the state where the offence occurred, there may be a possibility of the death sentence being applied.

Socialmedia

Illegal conduct on the Dark Web may be detected using social media and the Deep Web together. Twitter, YouTube, and Facebook are all used to identify suspects (Cranford,2015). It has been shown that the majority of fraudsters rely on social media networks like Facebook and Snapchat to sell stolen identities, credit card data, and other valuable information (Brown,2019).

These networks are popular among cyber criminals because of the ease with which anything, including malware, can be shared and distributed through social media. Adverts, sharing buttons, and plug-ins are common scamming tactics on these platforms compared to others. Hackers may spread malware more quickly because of the hundreds of thousands of people connected to these networks (Bleau,2019).

Memex And DARPA

The Defense Advanced Research Projects Agency (DARPA) has compiled a list of items that law enforcement agencies may utilise to help them track down criminals on the Dark Web. The Metasploit Decloaking Engine was previously used by the FBI to aid in their investigation of the Dark Web. US law enforcement organisations employ the Metasploit Decloaking Engine and Memex technologies to intelligently analyse Deep Web pages in order to identify criminals, notably human traffickers Memex, a set of technologies developed by DARPA (Defense Advanced Research Projects Agency), makes it easier for law enforcement to track down offenders on the Dark Web (Ehney and Shorter,2016), (Erb,2019) There are various institutions involved in the development of this software, which is mostly developed in Python.

Bitcoinflow

Transacting on the Deep Web requires the usage of bit coins, a kind of virtual cash (Lindsey,2019). Law enforcement and police agencies use the BitCoin movement on the Dark Web to track down criminals. Bit coin flow may be used by law enforcement to trace criminal activity. Criminals may be caught on the Deep Web using tools like the Silk Road server. Based on the volume of bitcoin transactions, the FBI pinpointed the server's location in Iceland's data centre. Due to a mistake on Silk Road's login page, which provided information about the server's IP addresses and physical location, the site was recognised as TOR, an anonymous network.

MLAT

Mutual Legal Assistance Treaty (MLAT) helps law enforcement conduct investigations more successfully. To help law enforcement, the United States undertakes a joint investigation that allows for the involvement of more than one countries in the criminal probe. Analysts may launch an official event by informing the Office of International Affairs (OIA) and initiating the generation of MLAT protocols (Lightfoot and Pospisil,2017).

MLAT is a well-established technique for law enforcement agencies to share information across national boundaries. If a state wishes to get access to digital evidence located beyond its borders, it must submit a formal request. The purpose of MLAT is to safeguard the legal rights of individuals suspected of offshore offences. However, the MLAT process is lengthy, sometimes taking months, the structure is opaque, and the procedure is cumbersome owing to the high volume of petitions (William and Badholia,2021).

Detection of Crime

Identifying the perpetrators and related crimes on the Dark Web is essential to halting the spread of criminal activity. Understanding cyber criminals' opaque networks may be a challenging task, but numerous methods and techniques have been developed that can be put to good use.

Hash value analysis

Because computer-based technologies are used to perpetrate cybercrime, locating and apprehending those responsible requires a lot of digital evidence collection and identification. Because hash functions may be used to authenticate the validity of any evidence revealed during an investigation, they are very valuable in cryptography. Hash functions generate hash values that accurately describe the message from which they were generated (Damgård,1989). MD5,SHA-1,SHA-256, and SHA-512 are all prominent hash algorithms.

While the internal nodes and hash value calculations of TOR's complex structure are untraceable, the exit node can be studied. (AlQahtani and El-Alfy,2015) and (Dingledine et al.,2004) The connected server's final resting place can be discovered through onion routing's exit node layer hash value analysis (AlQahtani and El-Alfy,2015), (Bauer et al.,2007). Using hash value analysis as a tool for criminal detection and digital forensics, several research have been carried out.

Information analysis And sockpuppets

When an individual uses many internet IDs to communicate, they are known as a sock puppet. (Breitinger et al.,2013) Because of this, cyber criminals utilise this tactic to steal identities, sell counterfeit goods, and carry out terroristic activities on the Dark Web. In order to do forensic accounting, extrapolate information about criminals, monitor conversations, and screen the Dark Web for terrorist monitoring, identifying sock puppets is essential in cyber intelligence operations.

Network analysis methodologies

Cybercriminal and terrorist networks may be more effectively hindered if the structure of these networks can be better understood and studied. There has been network analysis of terrorist and extremist organisations on the Dark Web (Caiani and Parenti,2009), (Chen et al.,2008) in order to discover criminal threats. Analysis of Dark web portals employing a topic-based methodology has been applied in research on intrinsic themes (Buxton and Bingham,2015).

Market place scraping

One of the key ways that cyber criminals spread and carry out their illicit actions is via the use of dark web marketplaces. As a result, scraping data from these marketplaces may help identify and capture criminals. An article by Alan Travis claims that anonymous marketplaces and forums for the selling of financial data have revealed 5.1 million incidents of online fraud in England and Wales.

Researchers have developed and tested an automated Dark Web marketplace scraping method. The scraped data analysis might serve as the foundation for a further examination of suspected criminals and crimes. Researchers have investigated deals in anonymous marketplaces or cryptocurrency markets in order to determine the implications and remedies for Dark Web marketplace-related crimes (Bancroft and Scott Reid,2017), (Baravalle et al.,2016).

Observing the dark web

Due to the Dark Web's untraceable and anonymous architecture, monitoring it is very difficult. Numerous tools and procedures have been developed by researchers to monitor the Deep Web. Several strategies for monitoring the Internet's secret areas were described (Ciancaglini et al.,2013). Monitoring the Dark Web may benefit crime analysts since it allows for the creation of a conspicuous database containing critical information about a secret site, which can aid in tracking future illicit activity and offenders.

Numerous academics have embraced the monitoring of extremist and hate organisations in order to analyse the use and content of Dark Web data (Chen,2011). Numerous studies have been presented to track hostile activity and dangers on the Dark Web (Bailey et al.,2006).

Honeypot deployment

Attacking the network server is a common tactic used by cybercriminals to spread dangerous malware or gain access to a computer system. On the TOR network, network traffic monitoring is another efficient way for discovering unlawful behaviour (Fan et al.,2018). The use of honeypots has been proposed in various studies to detect cyber-attacks and criminal behaviour in network traffic (Catakoglu et al.,2017).

Ransomware has been detected using honeypots (Armstrong et al.,2011). An attacker may be deceived because the honeypot pretends to be a decoy machine in order to detect illegal access. Detecting compromised secure socket connections may help avoid DoS attacks, SSH port scanning, SSH brute-force attacks, and phishing attacks. To identify SSH with malicious activities, a detection technique based on honeypots and machine learning was created (Chang et al.,2019).

Implementing tripwire

Site penetration and organisational exploit may be enabled by credential theft and the convenience of password reusing. Monitoring systems like Tripwire, another detecting device, may help identify any suspicious behaviour that might lead to the theft of sensitive information. Many studies have utilised this strategy to uncover system-wide dangers that might indicate attacks or hacking. ' (Agraotis et al.,2016),(DeBlasio et al.,2017).

Method of anomaly detection

Anomaly detection may be used to avert security breaches and cyber assaults. (Chen and Ghorbani,2019) discusses several user profiling approaches for creating security profiles in anomaly detection. Numerous research (Ahmed et al.,2016), have used anomaly detection methods to identify cyber-incidents.

Intrusion detection techniques

Intrusion detection is crucial in recognising potential dangers and attacks because it examines system records and network traffic. In order to have a better understanding of the approaches, the study examined numerous intrusion detection methods with attack detection capabilities (Aldridge and Hétu,2018).

They discussed network-based, host-based, signature-based and other anomaly-based techniques to intrusion detection, as well as physical intrusion detection. A flow-based intrusion detection model was developed utilising statistical and machine learning methodologies (Dingledine et al,2004).

INFORMATION ABOUT DEMOGRAPHY

According to search criteria, we've segmented the distribution of peer-reviewed papers by publication type, year, and number of publications. On top of that, we looked at the most often used terms in the articles we examined. We'll also talk about the publications' most common writers and publishers. We analysed the nations of origin of the most referenced journals, conferences, and books.

Publication Type

The type of publications chosen for our SLR is depicted in Figure 3(a). For our evaluation, we consulted three categories of articles: journals, conference proceedings, and books. According to the statistic, 37 citations and 57 percent of the 65 selected publications are journal articles, followed by 25 conferences with 38 percent, three books with 5 percent, and two other publications with 2 percent.

Figure 3. a) Category based on Number of Papers and b) Criteria based on Number of Papers

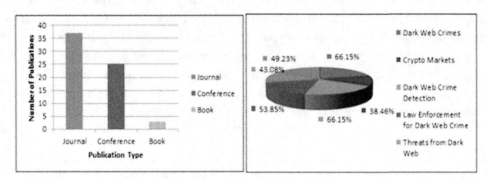

Linear View

Studies in this study were published between 2005 and 2019, as shown in Figure 4. It is part of our search strategy for relevant articles to include papers published before to July 2019. The number of Dark Web publications is rising, as seen in the graph.

Publication Criteria and Representative Authors

The distribution of the reviewed articles according to their selection criteria is shown in Figure 3(b). Criterion is used in the majority of articles to answer our two main RQs. Our RQs value other factors as well. The following are the requirements for a research paper: Cybercrimes, Cryptocurrencies, Criminal Intelligence on the Dark Web, Criminal Law Enforcement on the Dark Web, and Cybercrime Dangers on the Dark Web.

Table 6. Most representative authors

ID	No of Citations	Authors
1	672	Nicolas Christin
20	444	Reuben Grinberg
11	324	Kyle Soska & Nicolas Christin
18	230	Thomas J Holt & Eric Lampke
54	209	Judith Aldridge & David Décary-Hétu
55	208	James Martin
52	208	Nathan S. Evans, Roger Dingledine & Christian Grothoff
26	197	Yilu Zhou , Edna Reid, Jialun Qin, Hsinchun Chen & Guanpi Lai
3	163	Daniel Moore & Thomas Rid
50	120	Masoud Akhoondi , Curtis Yu & Harsha V. Madhyastha

Based on the number of citations their articles received in the field of study, we selected the most representative authors. We looked at the ten most cited articles from the 65 selected for this study. Nicolas Christin has the most referenced publication in this area of research, according to our analysis [ID 1, ID 11]. Although some writers have written in a variety of fields of research, we determined their popularity based on the number of citations in our area of study. The most typical writers are included in Table 6.

Widespread Databases

According to the statistics gathered by extracting articles from the six databases listed in paragraph II.B, Google Scholar has the most easily available resources for the study, followed by IEEE Xplore and the National Library of Medicine. Articles from Google Scholar, IEEE Xplore, ScienceDirect, Springer, Scopus, and the ACM Digital Library databases were used to compile this collection, which totals 22, 18, 6, 9, 5, and 5 articles.

Sources and Countries with the Most Publications

In order to establish the top 10 publishing sites, we analysed the 65 publications and counted the number of citations they received. The United States of America is the country that produces and hosts the greatest number of journals, conferences, and books which is shown in Table 7.

Table 7. Most published sources and countries

ID	Publication Source	Country of Publication
1	International Conference on World Wide Web	Rio de Janeiro, Brazil
20	Hastings Science and Technology Law Journal	California, USA
11	USENIX Security Symposium	Washington, D.C ,USA
18	Criminal Justice Studies: A Critical Journal of Crime, Law and Society	United Kingdom
54	Social Science Research Network(SSRN)	Mableton ,Georgia ,USA
55	Palgrave Macmillan	London ,United Kingdom
52	USENIX Security Symposium	California, USA
26	IEEE Intelligent Systems	USA
3	Survival: Global Politics and Strategy	United Kingdom
50	IEEE Symposium on Security and Privacy	San Francisco, CA ,USA

Figure 4. Number of selected publications per year

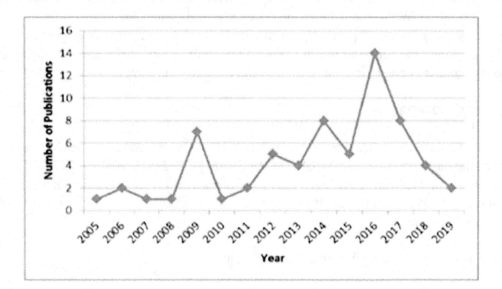

ARCHITECTURAL ANALYSIS

This section discusses the architectural frameworks for the chosen Dark Web articles. Figure 5 depicts the entire architectural perspective. It is worth noting that the structures' many components are not restricted to those shown in the illustration.

We discovered many architectural frameworks based on distinct criminal topic analyses in the evaluated literature. Section III discusses all of the specifics in depth. Figure 5 is an example of a publication's general structure for the purposes of this study. A wide range of themes, including drug trafficking, terrorists and ISIS, human trafficking, the pornography industry, and money laundering, have been studied extensively. These ideas have spawned a slew of architectural frameworks. Network analysis, hash value analysis, market monitoring, and scraping are examples of detection methods that fall under this framework category. Law enforcement tools like DARPA, MLAT, and others fall under this framework category.

The procedures and outcomes of the architectural framework analysis are shown in Figure 6. To conduct an analysis of the current models derived from research The generalised procedures utilised in the models applied to various designs are shown in Figure 6. the models in Appendix A have implemented designs drawn from those in the publications listed therein. This graphic assists in comprehending each critical component of a model, as well as their instances and significance. Additionally, this relates to the results of each stage in order to have a better understanding of the essential criteria's. The next section discusses the generalised elements.

Gathering of Information: Using this component, you may determine which data sets are available for use in your models, how large they are, and where they came from. Depending on the researcher and the firm, several types of data are acquired. Data from publicly available internet databases has been utilised in many research, many of which rely on data from onion sites.

Preparation of Data: In the data processing process, this is a crucial step to do. The key components of this process are feature selection, filtering, extraction, and noise reduction. This step is usually followed by the requirement to feed the model, which arises in the majority of studies.

Figure 5. Architectural analysis overview

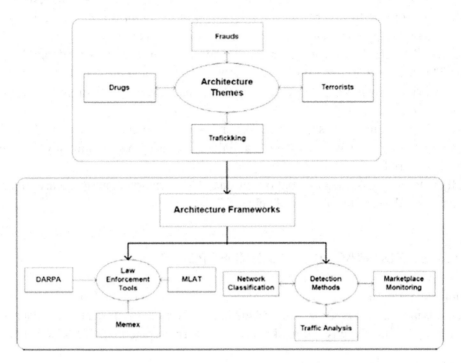

Figure 6. Architectural framework analysis overview

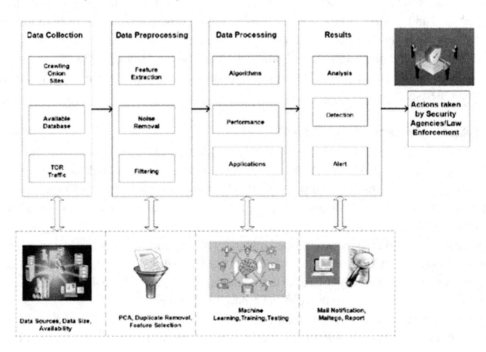

Processing of data: The implementation of algorithms such as machine learning, data classifications such as clustering or labelling, performance assessment of the algorithms using training and test data, and application of the approaches to their respective domains make this the essential step of any model.

Outcomes: The outputs, depending on the model, are what the framework-building process was aiming for. This leads to the detection of crimes, their location, and the distribution of system alerts to hazardous behaviour through email or mobile applications, as well as the study of crimes using accessible software such as Maltego.

The model's output may be used by security or law enforcement agencies to take action, which is the ultimate goal of all frameworks. Figure 6 and the accompanying text are only a few instances and ways that may be used.

We will analyse many strategies from our evaluated publications that make use of various models and tools based on the architectures listed below.

TECHNIQUES FOR MACHINE LEARNING [ID 13]

Introduction and Purpose: Machine learning techniques have the potential to be very useful in monitoring and identifying harmful activity. Researchers have devised a way for gathering data from Dark Net and Deep Net discussion forums and marketplaces concerning potentially hazardous hacking products and services.

For their trial, they looked at information from 10 marketplaces and two online forums. Data from the marketplace and forums was first sifted through, followed by a categorization analysis that enabled them to isolate certain forum topics and marketplace commodities as being linked to malicious hacking. supervised and unsupervised machine learning methods were employed for both marketplaces and forums. Co-training and label propagation were utilised as well as supervised methods such as Naive Bayes (NB), Random Forests (RF), SVM, and Logistic Regression (LOG-REG).

Constraints and Result: Each week, the proposed system accumulates an average of 305 high-quality cyber threat alerts.

Affect Analysis Technique [Id 24]

Introduction and Purpose: Affect analysis of extremist organisations on Dark Web forums results in the propagation of violence, hatred, and propaganda. To collect emotion-related material about extremist organisations from Dark Web forums, this research created an affect lexicon using a probabilistic disambiguation approach.

In order to conduct their experiment, the University of Arizona collected data from extremist forums, including postings from 16 American and Middle Eastern sites. Lexicon creation and analysis were the two halves of the system. Affected lexicon database was created by gathering messages and using probabilistic disambiguation to remove effect ambiguity from a word list.

As a result of these limitations, In addition to hate and violence, they found racism in US forums, but in the Middle East forums, hatred and violence are rampant. Forum posts were not included in the research, despite the fact that they provide a plethora of information for these kinds of analysis.

Technique of Fingerprinting [Id 28]

An Overview of the Project and Its Purpose: Website fingerprinting attacks are essential for gathering data on encrypted communications and anonymous connections. For the sake of obtaining hidden service connections and determining which hidden services have been accessed, this research will use fingerprinting attacks against TOR as part of its methodology.

For four months, they searched all known hidden service search engines every day using an automated algorithm to accumulate a total of 13,243 unique addresses. Onion addresses were also collected from the TOR network directly by leveraging the protocols' secret service directory. Tor's hidden services and regular websites were accessed via TBB. For data extraction and processing, they integrated numerous pages to avoid subpages with blank pages or little information. Two categorization processes are included in the recommended fingerprinting method. Client interactions with hidden services are initially tracked, and the content accessed by the client is determined in the second phase.

As a result of these limitations, In order to detect content that isn't scalable by the methods currently in use, their dataset displays the potential of connecting to a hidden service.

Technique of Authorship Analysis [Id 32]

Introduction and Purpose: Forensic examination of the Dark Web is crucial to identifying offenders who utilise anonymity services such as TOR authorship detection. Alias classification and author attribution are two essential goals for user identification in the drug trafficking section of the Dark Web that this study addressed.

We got our experimental data from Black Market Reloaded, a forum on the dark web (BMR). A total of 8,348 unique contributors contributed 92,333 posts throughout 12,923 different talks, all in a variety of languages. During the data filtering stage, English language threads, those with more than 250 posts, and those with less than 50 posts were removed. They began the alias categorization process by using stylometric analysis. Stylometric analysis focused on topic-independent traits, and character n-grams as a user profile feature was also studied utilising forum posts with time-based features. To figure out who wrote what, a multiclass categorization system was used. A user's writing style was captured by combining many posts selected at random into a single post, which was then ignored in favour of more regular or instructive ones. The data was classified using a support vector machine (SVM).

As a result of these limitations, Alias categorization, which assesses whether two user accounts are aliases, attained an accuracy of 91% with a recall of 25% for 177 users, but only 25% for 25 of them achieved the same level of accuracy with a recall of 45%. As the number of readers grows, the findings of authorship attribution become more variable. Using SVM, classification accuracy was 88% for 177 users, but may be as high as 94% for a smaller number of individuals. If different users write in a different manner in different postings, this technique becomes skewed by the stylometric analysis, and hence other characteristics other than character n-grams and time are necessary.

Technique of Dark Web Scrapping [id 17]

Introduction and Purpose: Scraping Dark Web markets and forums may provide valuable information that can aid law enforcement and security organisations in their investigations and forensic investiga-

Table 8. Primary reviewed articles

ID	Title	Year
1	SilkRoad Traveling: Analysis of a large anonymous online market place	2013
2	Cybercrime and Deepweb	2013
3	The Darknet and Crypto politik	2016
4	Addressing the needs of victims of human trafficking: Challenges, barriers, and promising practices	2008
5	Deviant Men, Prostitution, and the Internet: Qualitative analysis of Men who killed Prostitutes whom they met online	2012
6	Tor market place sex exploratory data analysis: the drugs case	2017
7	Buying drugs on a Darknet market: A better deal? Studying the online illicit drug market through the analysis of digital, physical and chemical data	2016
8	Webcamchild prostitution: An exploration of current and futuristic methods of detection	2017
9	LikeWar: The Weaponization of social media	2018
10	Going dark: Terrorism on the darkweb	2016
11	Measuringthelongitudinalevolutionoftheonlineanonymousmarketplaceecosystem	2015
12	Dark-Net Ecosystem Cyber-Threat Intelligence (CTI) Tool	2019
13	Darknetanddeepnetminingforproactivecybersecuritythreatintelligence	2016
14	Darknet mining and game theory for enhanced Cyber threat intelligence	2016
15	Exploring malicious hacker forums	2016
16	Identifyingtopsellersinundergroundeconomyusingdeeplearning-basedsentimentanalysis	2014
17	A Framework for More Effective Dark Web Marketplace Investigations	2018
18	Exploring stolen data markets online: products and market forces	2010
19	Exploring and estimating there venues and profits of Participants in stolen data markets	2016
20	Bitcoin: An innovative alternative digital currency	2012
21	Bitcoin, silk road, and the need for a new approach to virtual currency regulation	2013
22	Intrusion detection techniques in cloud environment: A survey	2017
23	Large-Scale Monitoring for Cyber Attacks by Using Cluster Information on Darknet Traffic Features	2015
24	Affect intensity analysis of dark web forums	2007
25	Automatic detection of cyber-recruitment by violent Extremists	2014
26	US domestic extremist groups on the Web: link and content analysis	2005
27	Anonymity services Tor, I2P, JonDonym: classifying in the dark	2017
28	Analysis of fingerprinting techniques for tor hidden Services	2017
29	Anonymous connections based on onion routing: A review and a visualization tool	2015
30	Fraud and financial crime detection model using malware forensics	2014
31	A sock puppet detection algorithm on virtual spaces	2013
32	Authorship analysis on dark marketplace forums	2015
33	Sockpuppet gang detection on social media sites	2016
34	An army of me: Sockpuppets in online discussion Communities	2017
35	Multiple account identity deception detection in social media using nonverbal behavior	2014
36	Searching Places Unknown: Law Enforcement Jurisdiction on the Dark Web	2017
37	The dark side of the web: Italian right-wing extremist groups and the Internet	2009
38	Dark web forums portal: searching and analyzing jihadist forums	2009
39	Surfacing collaborated networks in dark web to find illicit and criminal content	2016
40	On the topology of the dark web of terrorist groups	2006
41	Topic-based social network analysis for virtual communities of interests in the dark web	2011
42	Dark web portal overlapping community detection based on topic models	2012
43	Discovering topics from dark websites	2009
44	Attacks landscape in the dark side of the web	2017
45	Honeypots deployment for the analysis and visualization of malware activity and malicious connections	2014
46	Detecting Ransomware with Honeypot techniques	2016
47	Detecting DDoS attacks against data center with correlation analysis	2015
48	Correlation-based traffic analysis attacks on anonymity networks	2009

continued on following page

Table 8. Continued

ID	Title	Year
49	Locating network domain entry and exit point/path for DDoS attack traffic	2009
50	LASTor: A low-latency AS-aware Tor client	2012
51	A new cell-counting-based attack against Tor	2012
52	A Practical Congestion Attack on Tor Using Long Paths	2009
53	Safer scoring? Crypto markets, social supply anddrug market violence	2016
54	Not an 'Ebay for Drugs". The Crypto market 'SilkRoad' as a Paradigm Shifting Criminal Innovation	2014
55	Drugs on the dark net: How crypto markets are transforming the global trade in illicit drugs	2014
56	Constructive activism in the dark web: crypto markets and illicit drugs in the digital demimonde'	2016
57	Hidden wholesale: The drug diffusing capacity of online drug crypto markets	2016
58	Analysis of Hacking Related Trade in the Darkweb	2018
59	Do Police Crackdowns Disrupt Drug Crypto markets? A Longitudinal Analysis Of The Effects Of Operation Onymous	2017
60	Comparing crypto markets for drugs. A characterisation of sellers and buyers over time	2018
61	Challenging the cryptomarket users using techno politics	2016
62	Mining the darkweb: fake ids and drugs	2016
63	Scraping Cryptomarkets on Tor by Python Scrapers	2019
64	Analysis of practical correlation between scan and malware profiles	2009
65	Drakweb, Deepweb, Invisible Web and the post ISIS World	2016

tions. The author constructed an automated scraping framework and analysed the scraped Dark Web markets using free technologies.

To compile a list of the onion URLs for the major marketplaces on Reddit and DeepDotWeb. They have suggested an Apple script-based web crawler. Only new accounts that were not detected during the crawling process will be added to the list. After scraping the marketplace websites, the Maltego programme was utilised to identify probable suppliers on the Dark Web's main drug marketplace using scraping findings. They personally analysed the marketplace and its approximately 3000 individual suppliers.

Results and Constraints: Maltego was found to be used by four of the most active dealers, whose origins were traced back to the Web crawler's account information on over 3000 drug market merchants. It raised doubts about the merchants' authenticity because they did not interact with any sellers and did not purchase anything from the marketplace. Additionally, manual data input into the Maltego programme is inaccurate and time consuming.

CONCLUSION

To be more specific, this SLR includes a full discussion of Dark Net crime risks, technological and forensic issues associated with anonymous network topologies, and detection methodologies, algorithms, tools, and tactics used to locate crimes and offenders on the Dark Web. Cyber thieves are getting more cunning in their resistance to the enforcing tactics used to discover them within the Dark Web. As a consequence, difficulties increase. International border control is one of the most difficult tasks for law enforcement and security authorities. The sheer size of the Dark Web necessitates the development of increasingly effective defences against its potential threats. Technology must be used to trace the black market and its transactions in order to catch the criminals. Crimes on the Dark Web are harder to find because of its unindexed, fragmented, and multi-layered nature. Due to the very unpredictable nature of the Dark Web ecosystem, where old sites disappear daily and new ones develop, powerful digital evidences are essential for forensic law enforcement organisations to guarantee they overcome barriers in apprehending and punishing the perpetrators.

REFERENCES

Abbasi, A., & Chen, H. (2007). Affect intensity analysis of dark Web forums. *Security Informatics*.

Açar, K. V. (2017). Webcam child prostitution: An exploration of current and futuristic methods of detection. *International Journal of Cyber Criminology, 11*(1), 98-109.

Agra, Erola, Goldsmith, & Creese. (2016). *A tripwire grammar for insider threat detection*. Presented at the *Int. Workshop Manag.Insider Secur. Threats (MIST)*.

Ahmed, M., Mahmood, A. N., & Islam, M. R. (2016). A survey of anomaly detection techniques in financial domain. *Future Generation Computer Systems, 55*, 278–288. doi:10.1016/j.future.2015.01.001

Akhoondi, M., Yu, C., & Madhyastha, H. V. (2012). LASTor: A low-latency AS-aware tor client. *IEEE/ACM Transactions on Networking, 22*(6), 1742–1755. doi:10.1109/SP.2012.35

Al Nabki, M. W., Fidalgo, E., Alegre, E., & de Paz, I. (2017). Classifying illegal activities on tor network based on Web textual contents. *Computational Linguistics*, ●●●, 1.

AldridgeJ.Décary-HétuD. (2014). 'Not an Ebay for Drugs': The cryptomarket silk road as a paradigm shifting criminal innovation. *Social Sci. Res. Netw*. doi:10.2139/ssrn.2436643

Aldridge, J., & Décary-Hétu, D. (2016). Hidden wholesale: The drug diffusing capacity of online drug crypto markets. *International Journal of Drug Policy, 35*, 7–15. doi:10.1016/j.drugpo.2016.04.020

AlQahtani, A. A., & El-Alfy, E. M. (2015). Anonymous connections based on onion routing: A review and a visualization tool. *Procedia Computer Science, 52*, 121–128. doi:10.1016/j.procs.2015.05.040

Armstrong, R., Hall, B. J., Doyle, J., & Waters, E. (2011). Scoping the scope of a cochrane review. *Journal of Public Health, 33*(1), 147–150. doi:10.1093/pubmed/fdr015

Arnold, N., Ebrahimi, M., Zhang, N., Lazarine, B., Patton, M., Chen, H., & Samtani, S. (2019). Dark-net ecosystem cyber-threat intelligence (CTI) tool. In *IEEE international conference Intellettuale Security Informat*. Intercollegiate Studies Institute.

Backman, B. (2013). *Follow the white rabbit: An ethnographic exploration nto the drug culture concealed within the deep web*. Universidad Nebraska Omaha, Tech. Rep. UMI 1551711.

Bailey, M., Cooke, E., Jahanian, F., Myrick, A., & Sinha, S. (2006). Practicaldarknet measurement. *40th Annu. Conf. Inf. Sci. Syst.*

Bancroft, A., & Scott Reid, P. S. (2017). Challenging the techno-politics of anonymity: The case of cryptomarket users. *Information, Communication and Society, 20*(4), 497–512. doi:10.1080/1369118X.2016.1187643

Baravalle, A., Lopez, M. S., & Lee, S. W. (2016). *Mining the dark Web:drugs and fake IDS*. Presented at the IEEE 16th Int. Conf. Data Mining Workshops (ICDMW).

Barratt, M. J., Ferris, J. A., & Winstock, A. R. (2016). Safer scoring? Cryptomarkets,social supply and drug market violence. *International Journal of Drug Policy, 35*, 24–31. doi:10.1016/j.drugpo.2016.04.019

Bates, R. (2016). Tracking lone wolf terrorists. *The Journal of Public and Professional Sociology, 8*(1), 6.

Bauer, K., McCoy, D., Grunwald, D., Kohno, T., & Sicker, D. (2007). *Low resource outing attacks against tor.* Presented at the *ACM Workshop Privacy Electron.*

Beckham, K., & Prohaska, A. (2012). Deviant men, prostitution, and the Internet: A qualitative analysis of men who killed prostitutes whom they met online. *International Journal of Criminal Justice Sciences, 7*(2), 635-648.

Bleau, H. (2019). *Social media and the digital transformation of Cybercrime.* https://www.rsa.com/enus/blog/2019-04/social-media-and-the-digital-transformation-ofcybercrime

Breitinger, F., Astebol, K. P., Baier, H., & Busch, C. (2013). MvHash-B_A new approach for similarity preserving hashing. Presented at the *7th Int. Conf. It Secur. Incident Management It Forensics.*

Breitinger, F., & Baier, H. (2012). Similarity preserving hashing: Eligible properties and a new algorithm MRSH-v2. Presented at the *Int. Conf. Digit. Forensics Cyber Crime.*

Brown, S. (2019). *Cybercriminals ramping up fraud attacks on social media, says report.* CNET. https://www.cnet.com/news/cybercriminals-are-ramping-up-fraudattacks-on-social-media-says-report/

Bryans, D. (2014). Bitcoin and money laundering: Mining for an effective solution. *Industrial Law Journal, 89*(1), 441.

Bu, Z., Xia, Z., & Wang, J. (2013). A sock puppet detection algorithm on virtual spaces. *Knowledge-Based Systems, 37*, 366–377. doi:10.1016/j.knosys.2012.08.016

Buxton, J., & Bingham, T. (2015). The rise and challenge of dark net drug markets. *Policy Brief, 7*, 1-24.

Caiani, M., & Parenti, L. (2009). The dark side of the Web: Italian right-wingextremist groups and the Internet. *South European Society and Politics, 14*(3), 273–294. doi:10.1080/13608740903342491

Catakoglu, O., Balduzzi, M., & Balzarotti, D. (2017). Attacks landscape in the dark side of the Web. Presented at the Symp. Appl. Comput. SAC.

Celestini, A., Me, G., & Mignone, M. (2017). *Tor marketplaces exploratory data analysis: The drugs case.* Presented at the Int. Conf. Global Secur., Saf. Sustainability.

Chang, D., Ghosh, M., Sanadhya, S. K., Singh, M., & White, D. R. (2019). FbHash: A new similarity hashing scheme for digital forensics. *Digital Investigation, 29*, S113–S123. doi:10.1016/j.diin.2019.04.006

Chaudhari, R. R., & Patil, S. P. (2017). Intrusion detection system: Classification,techniques and datasets to implement. *International Research Journal of Engineering and Technology, 4*(2).

Chen, H. (2011). *Dark web: Exploring and data mining the dark side of the Web, 30.* Springer.

Chen, H., Chung, W., Qin, J., Reid, E., Sageman, M., & Weimann, G. (2008, June). Uncovering the dark Web: A case study of jihad on the Web. *Journal of the American Society for Information Science and Technology, 59*(8), 1347–1359. doi:10.1002/asi.20838

Chen, M., & Ghorbani, A. A. (2019). A survey on user pro_ling model foranomaly detection in cyber-space. *J. Cyber Secur. Mobility, 8*(1), 75-112.

Cherqi, O., Mezzour, G., Ghogho, M., & El Koutbi, M. (2018). *Analysis of hacking related trade in the darkweb*. Presented at the IEEE Int. Conf. Intell. Security Informatics (ISI).

Chertoff, M., & Simon, T. (2015). *The impact of the darkWeb on Internet governanceand cyber security*. Centre Int. Governance Innovation (CIGI), Waterloo, ON, Canada, Tech. Rep. 6.

Christin, N. (2013). *Traveling the silk road: A measurement analysis of a large anonymous online marketplace*. Presented at the 22nd Int. Conf. World Wide Web. 10.1145/2488388.2488408

Ciancaglini, V., Balduzzi, M., Goncharov, M., & McArdle, R. (2013). *Deep web and cybercrime*. Trend Micro Rep. 9.

Clawson, H. J., & Dutch, N. (2008). *Addressing the needs of victims of human trafficking: Challenges, barriers, and promising practices. Department of Health and Human Services, Office of the Assistant Secretary*.

Convenant Eyes. (2011). *The connections Between Pornography and sex Trafficking*. https://www.covenanteyes.com/2011/09/07/the-connections-between-pornographyand-sex-traf_cking/

Cranford, C. (2015). *Dangerous apps on Your Teen's mobile device*. https://www.cybersafetycop.com/dangerous-apps-on-your-teens-mobile-device/

Cruzes, D. S., & Dyba, T. (2011). *Recommended steps for thematic synthesis insoftware engineering*. Presented at the Int. Symp. Empirical Software Engineering Meas.

Cuellar, M.-F. (2002). The tenuous relationship between thought against money laundering and the disruption of criminal finance. *The Journal of Criminal Law & Criminology, 93*(2), 311.

Damgård, I. B. (1989). *A design principle for hash functions*. Presented at the Conf. Theory Appl. Cryptol.

DeBlasio, J., Savage, S., Voelker, G. M., & Snoeren, A. C. (2017). *Tripwire: Inferring Internet site compromise*. Presented at the *Internet Meas. Conf.*

Décary-Hétu, D., & Giommoni, L. (2017). Do police crackdowns disrupt drugcryptomarkets? A longitudinal analysis of the effects of operation onymous. *Crime, Law and Social Change, 67*(1), 55–75. doi:10.1007/s10611-016-9644-4

DeepDotWeb. (2015). *Mr. Nice Guy. Marketadmin. Tells His Story*. https://gir.pub/deepdotweb/2015/06/03/interview-with-mr-niceguy-market-admin/

Dingledine, R., Mathewson, N., & Syverson, P. (2004). *Tor: The second generation onion router*. Naval Research Laboratory, Tech. Rep.

DNStats. (2019). *Dark Net STATS*. https://dnstats.net/

Dolliver, D. S., & Kenney, J. L. (2016). Characteristics of drug vendors on thetor network: A cryptomarket comparison. *Victims and Offenders, 11*(4), 600–620. doi:10.1080/15564886.2016.1173158

Dredge, S. (2013). *What is tor? A Beginner's Guide to the Privacy Tool*. https://www.theguardian.com/technology/2013/nov/05/tor-beginnersguide-

Dughi, P. (2016). *17 Times social media helped police track downthieves, murderers, and gang criminals.* Medium. https://medium.com/the-mission/17-times-social-media-helped-policetrack-down-thieves-murderers-and-gang-criminals-a814b6c40fb

Ehney, R., & Shorter, J. D. (2016). Deep Web, dark Web, invisible Web and the post isis world. *Information Systems, 17*(4), 36-41.

Erb, K. P. (2019). IRS followed bitcoin transactions, resulting in takedown of the largest child exploitation site on the Web. *Forbes.* https://www.forbes.com/sites/kellyphillipserb/2019/10/16/irs-followed-bitcoin-transactionsresulting-in-takedown-of-the-largest-child-exploitation-site-on-theweb/#327343231ed0

Evans, N. S., Dingledine, R., & Grothoff, C. (2009). *A practical congestion attack on tor using long paths.* Presented at the USENIX Secur. Symp.

Fan, W., Du, Z., Fernandez, D., & Villagra, V. A. (2018). Enabling an an atomic view to investigate honeypot systems: A survey. *IEEE Systems Journal, 12*(4), 3906–3919. doi:10.1109/JSYST.2017.2762161

Fanusie, Y., & Robinson, T. (2018). Bitcoin laundering: An analysis of illicit *flows into digital currency services.* Center Sanctions Illicit Finance Memorandum.

Fernquist, J., Kaati, L., & Schroeder, R. (2018). *Political bots and the Swedishgeneral election.* Presented at the IEEE Int. Conf. Intell. Security Informatics (ISI).

Finklea. (2015). Dark Web. *Proc. Congressional Res. Service*, 1-16.

Gai, K., Qiu, M., Tao, L., & Zhu, Y. (2016). Intrusion detection techniques formobile cloud computing in heterogeneous 5G. *Security and Communication Networks, 9*(16), 3049–3058. doi:10.1002/sec.1224

García-Holgado, A., & García-Peñalvo, F. J. (2018). *Mapping the systematicliterature studies about software ecosystems.* Presented at the 6th Int. Conf. Technol. Ecosystems Enhancing Multiculturality (TEEM). 10.1145/3284179.3284330

Ghappour, A. (2017). Searching places unknown: Law enforcement jurisdiction on the dark Web. *Stanford Law Review*, *69*(4), 1075.

Li, W., & Chen, H. (2014). *Identifying top sellers in underground economyusing deep learning-based sentiment analysis.* Presented at the IEEE Joint Intell. Security Informatica Conference.

Lightfoot, S., & Pospisil, F. (2017). *Surveillance and privacy on the deepWeb.* ResearchGate.

Lindsey, N. (2019). Cyber criminals have turned social mediacyber crime into a $3 billion business. *CPO Magazine.* https://www.cpomagazine.com/cyber-security/cyber-criminalshave-turned-social-media-cyber-crime-into-a-3-billion-business/

Lipoaie & Shortis. (n.d.). *From dealer to doorstep-How drugs are sold on the dark net.* GDPO Situation Anal. Swansea University, Global DrugsPolicy Observatory.

William, P., & Badholia, A. (2021). Analysis of personality traits from text based answers using HEXACO model. In *International Conference on Innovative Computing, Intelligent Communication and Smart Electrical Systems (ICSES), 2021* (pp. 1–10). 10.1109/ICSES52305.2021.9633794

William, P., & Dr Badholia, A. (2020). Evaluating efficacy of classification algorithms on personality prediction dataset. *Elementary Education Online, 19*(4), 3400–3413. doi:10.17051/ilkonline.2020.04.764728

William, P., & Dr Badholia, A. (2021, July). Assessment of Personality from Interview Answers using Machine Learning Approach. *IJAST, 29*(08), 6301–6312.

William, P., & Dr Badholia, A. (2021). A review on prediction of personality traits considering interview answers with personality models. *International Journal for Research in Applied Science and Engineering Technology, 9*(5), 1611–1616. doi:10.22214/ijraset.2021.34613

William, P., Kumar, P., Chhabra, G. S., & Vengatesan, K. (2021). Task allocation in distributed agile software development using machine learning approach. In *International Conference on Disruptive Technologies for Multi-Disciplinary Research and Applications (CENTCON), 2021* (pp. 168–172). 10.1109/CENTCON52345.2021.9688114

William, P., & Patil, V. S. (2016). Architectural challenges of cloud computing and its security issues with solutions. *International Journal for Scientific Research and Development, 4*(8), 265–268.

Chapter 14
Enthusiastic Cyber Surveillance for Intimidation Comprehension on the Dark Web and the Deep Web

Vinod Mahor
(iD) https://orcid.org/0000-0002-2187-6920
IES College of Technology, Bhopal, India

Sadhna Bijrothiya
(iD) https://orcid.org/0000-0002-8913-7753
Maulana Azad National Institute of Technology, Bhopal, India

Rakesh Kumar Bhujade
Information Technology, Government Polytechnic, Daman, India

Jasvant Mandloi
Government Polytechnic, Daman, India

Harshita Mandloi
Shri Vaishnav Vidyapeeth Vishwavidyalaya, India

Stuti Asthana
UT Administration of Dadra and Nagar Haveli and Daman and Diu, India

ABSTRACT

The authors offer an operational method for obtaining cyber intimidation intelligence from diverse social platforms on the internet, notably dark-web and deep-web sites with Tor, in this study. They concentrate their efforts on gathering information from hacker forums and marketplaces that sell harmful hacking-related items and services. They've established an operational mechanism for gathering information from these sites. This system now collects 400 high-quality cyber-intimidation notifications every week on average. These danger alerts provide details on newly generated malware and exploits that have yet to be used in a cyber-attack. This is a valuable service for cyber-surveillance. Various machine learning approaches are used to dramatically improve the system. They can recall 93% of items in marketplaces and 85% of comments on forums about harmful hacking with great precision using machine learning models. They do preliminary analysis on the data gathered, illustrating how it might be used to assist a security professional in improved intimidation analysis.

DOI: 10.4018/978-1-6684-6444-1.ch014

Table 1. Give a specific example and current database status

S.N.	Stages	Proceedings
1.	Jan –June 2015	"Microsoft has identified the remote code execution vulnerability MS15-010/CVE 2015-0057 in Windows. At the time the vulnerability was disclosed, there was no publicly known exploit".
2.	July –Dec 2015	"On a darknet market, an exploit for MS15-010/CVE 2015-0057 was uncovered and sold for 48 BTC ("about $10,000-15,000 USD")".
3.	Jan –June 2016	"The Dyre Banking Trojan, which was meant to collect credit card numbers, actually exploited this vulnerability, according to FireEye".
4.	July –Dec 2016	"At the time the vulnerability was disclosed, there was no publicly known exploit".

INTRODUCTION

Pre-reconnaissance cyber intimidation info is info received before an adverse entity engages with the protected personal computer. Table 1 provides an illustration of the relevance of cyber intimidation intelligence. In February of 2015 and 2016, Microsoft Windows vulnerability was discovered. The vulnerability's disclosure was basically Microsoft's way of alerting users to a surveillance problem. It's worth noting that there was no publicly known technique of exploiting this issue in a cyber-intrusion at the time (i.e. an available exploit). However, a month later, an exploit was discovered for sale on the dark-web market and deep-web market. A large cyber surveillance firm, (V. Benjamin, W. Li, 2015) discovered that the "Dyre Banking Trojan", which was meant to "steal credit cards, exploited this flaw - the first time an intrusion had been revealed". This vignette shows how danger alerts gleaned from the dark-web may be extremely useful to surveillance experts. The "Dyre Banking Trojan", together with another banking virus called Dridex1, had a global average exposure of 57.3 percent. It indicates that approximately six out of ten companies throughout the world have been impacted, which is a disproportionately large figure on a global scale (T. Fu, A. Abbasi, and H. Chen., 2010).

In this study, we look at how such intelligence might be obtained and evaluated on the Internet's many social stages, notably on the dark-web and deep-web (T. J. Holt and E. Lampke., 2010). We ran across a few issues while doing so, which we solved using a variety of data mining approaches. Our present system is up and running, gathering roughly 305 cyber intimidations every week.

The current database statistics are shown in Table 2. It displays the overall amount of data obtained as well as info on harmful hacking. Only those persons detected by the system as being involved in the

Table 2. The condition of the information environments

Markets	M1-Total Number	18
	M2-Total products	11981
	M3-Hacking related	1563
	M4-Vendors	453
Environments	E1-Total Number	22
	E2-Topics/Posts	22870/165897
	E3-Hacking related	4425/32115
	E4-Users	5549

chat or deal of harmful "hacking-related" content are included in the vendor and user statistics given. The info is gathered from two dark-web/deep-web sources: marketplaces and convention (T. J. Holt, D. Strumsky, O. Smirnova, and M. Kilger, 2015, D. Lacey and P. M. Salmon., 2015). We're offering this data to cyber surveillance specialists to help them with strategic cyber-defense planning, such as:

- Which suppliers and users are active in numerous dark-web/deep-web markets/convention?
- How nil exploits are nefarious crackers planning?
- Which vulnerabilities are the most recent intrusions aimed at?

This work makes the following contributions:

- An explanation of a method for collecting cyber surveillance intimidation infofrom several social media sites over internet access, so as deep-web and dark-web site.
- The development and testing of knowledge based representations to distinguish meaningful data from noise in data acquired after more internet websites.
- A collection of case studies exhibiting various results linked to hostile cyber-hacker activity gleaned from our operating system's data.

Circumstantial: Several of the people behindhand cyber actions, especially those that originate separate of govt. run laboratories or armed force headquarters, trust on a large communal of cyber-crackers (M. Motoyama, D. McCoy, K. Levchenko, S. Savage, 2011).

They communicate using a number of internet convention ("as a way to remain anonymous while also reaching out to geographically separated partners").

Web link on the Dark-web and Deep-web: "The Onion Router" is able s/w designed to protecting the confidentiality of its employers by disguising road "traffic analysis" as a kind of network monitoring (J. Robertson, V. Paliath, J. Shakarian, A. Thart, and P, 2016). It's a popular choice for clandestine communications. "The Onion Router's" network traffic is routed over a network of helper run guides (also known as "nodes"). Each network node encrypts the data it travels without noting where the traffic originated from or where it is going (J. Robertson, V. Paliath, J. Shakarian, A. Thart, and P, 2016), making it impossible to monitor. This effectively enables for both anonymised surfing ("the IP address exposed will only be that of the previous node") and censorship2 evasion. We will use the term "dark-web" to refer to the unidentified statement afforded by "crypto networks" similar "The Onion Router's" as opposed to "deep-web," it alludes to webpages that are hosted on the open Internet (the "Clear net") but not be indexed by search terms (S. Samtani, R. Chinn, and H., 2015).

Dark-web marketplaces provide a fresh perspective on the present condition of infosurveillance. In the fields of malicious hacking, drugs, pornography, guns, and software, the marketplaces supply goods and services. Only a tiny fraction of things (13%) are related to illegal crackers, so according our analysis. In order to bring attention to their goods or services, vendors routinely post adverts for respective items on communities (Müller, J.-W. 2014).

Conventions are user-driven stages that exist only to facilitate dialogue. It allows for the formation of a community of like-minded people, regardless of their geographical location. Administrators create dark-web conventions with communication surveillance in mind for their users. People who go to Dark-web conventions don't care about the same things as people who go to more well-known web conventions. Discussions about programming, hacking, and cyber surveillance may be found at conventions enthusiastic to malevolent crackers (Natale, S., & Ballatore, A., 2014). Outfits are enthusiastic to surveillance problems like confidentiality and online safety-themes that feedback addicted to and shape the stages' architecture and use.

SYSTEM OVERVIEW

The system is depicted in Figure 1 as a whole. Human analysts were able to locate convention and markets frequented by malevolent crackers using search engines and spider services on the Tor network. Other stages were uncovered through links posted on convention on the Tor or clear-net networks. The system is made up of three primary elements that were created separately before being combined. Currently, the system is completely integrated and gathering cyber risk cleverness system (Rawat, R., Rajawat, A. S., Mahor, V., Shaw, R. N., &Ghosh, A., 2021).

Dawdler: A dawdler is an s/w that dawdlers a website in order to retrieve HTML content. For targeted crawling, topic-based dawdlers have been employed to retrieve just websites of interest (Rawat, R., Mahor, V., Chirgaiya, S., & Garg, B., 2021)). Focused crawling was recently utilised to harvest forum talks from the dark-web.

Due to the structural differences and access control mechanisms for all stage, we created various dawdlers for different stages ("markets/convention") specified by specialists. To acquire infoabout items from markets and discussions on convention, we handle design difficulties like as accessibility, unresponsive servers, and repeated links forming a loop, and so on in our dawdler.

Pursuer: We created a pursuer to extract particular data from marketplaces ("such as those selling worm/exploits") and hacker convention ("discussion regarding services and intimidations").

A relational database is used to store this well-structured data. We have two databases: one for markets and the other for discussion boards (Rawat, R., Garg, B., Mahor, V., Chouhan, M., Pachlasiya, K., & Telang, S. Cyber, 2022). Each stage, like the dawdler, has its own pursuer. The pursuer also talks with the dawdler on a regular basis in order to collect temporal data. The dawdler receives a list of appropriate URLs from the pursuer, which are then scanned again to obtain time-varying data. The following critical product fields are collected.

Markets: Items names, explanations, vendor names, delivery details, product ratings, products sold, CVE, things left, transaction records, and ratings are all included. We collect data on-topic content, posting substance, theme writer, posting writer, writer position, repute, and theme awareness (Owenson, G., Cortes, S., & Lewman, A. 2018).

Classifier: To recognise appropriate items and subjects from the marketplaces and conventions outlined in this section, we use a machine learning approach based on an expert-labeled dataset. The classifications are comprised of addicted the pursuer to filter out items and subjects that aren't related to harmful hacking, such as drugs and weapons (Owenson, G., Cortes, S., & Lewman, A. 2018).

EVALUATION

In this work, we look at the categorization of detecting appropriate products in dark-web/deep-web markets and appropriate subjects on forum posts including harmful hacker communication. It's a binary

Figure 1. System architecture

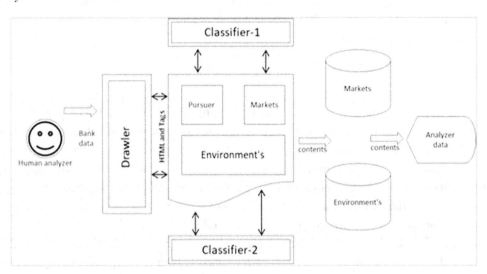

classification issue, in which the data sample ("in this case, products/forum topics") is either appropriate or not. To address the categorization or we look at together "supervised and semi-supervised algorithms".

Machine-Learning Methodologies

We use a combination of "supervised and semi-supervised algorithms in this study". The "well-known classification techniques of Naive Bayes (NB), Random Forest (RF), Support Vector Machine (SVM), and logistic regression are among the supervised approaches (LOG-REG)" (Oz, M., Zheng, P., & Chen, G. M. 2018). However, supervised procedures necessitated tagged data, which is costly and frequently necessitates expert expertise. Semi-supervised techniques use knowledge from unlabeled data to operate with limited labelled data. We go through some of the most prominent semi-supervised techniques that were employed in this study. Parser

Pursuer to discover the best settings for the learning approaches, we use a grid search. Propagation of labels (LP). For semi-supervised classification tasks, the label propagation strategy has been frequently employed (Salmon, P. M., Lane, B. R., Desmond, D., Cherney, A., Kulatilleke, G., Matthews, A., Lacey, D., & Stanton, N. A. 2019). This graphs Wavelet coefficients approach is used to compute the label values, where the concept is symbolized by weighted graph $G = (V, E)$ with V is denoted a vertices representative the illustrations and E denoting a weights denoting the relationship b/w opinions. Under the premise that the edges can represent the similarity b/w samples, a subsection of these "vertices" are labelled, and these "vertices" are then uses to estimate the labels of the other "vertices". As a result, the effectiveness of these strategies is determined by the similarity measure utilised. The "K-NN and Gaussian kernel" are two of the most often used similarity metrics (Venger, O. 2019).

Co-education (CT). Blum and Mitchell proposed the Co-training technique. The feature set is separated addicted two sets ("assumed to be self-governing ") in this technique and two classify are trained data using the restricted labelled set represented by L. The labels for the unlabeled opinions are then estimated using these trained classifiers. Classifier-1's high confidence label estimations are added to classifier-2's labelled set L, and vice versa. We've set the confidence level at 70% in the present configuration (Schmidt, H. C., 2015). The classifiers are retrained every time the labelled set L is updated. This technique is repeated until all of the spots that aren't identified have been labelled. It's as though two classifiers are training one other.

Investigates

Markets offer commodities and facilities that have nothing to do with harmful hacking, such as narcotics, pornography, firearms, and s/w services. Malicious hacking is only mentioned in a tiny percentage of items 15%). As a result, we'll need a classical that dismiss distinguish b/w appropriate and inappropriate products. Because the data acquired from marketplaces is noisy, it cannot be used as an input to a learning model directly. As a result, the raw data goes through a series of automatic data cleansing stages. We'll now go over the issues that came with the dataset and how we overcame them through data processing. We've seen that forum data presents comparable issues (Romil Rawat, Vinod Mahor, Bhagwati Garg, Shrikant Telang, Kiran Pachlasiya, Anil Kumar, Surendra Kumar Shukla & Megha Kuliha, 2021).

Cleaning up the text. On marketplaces, product titles and explanations typically have a lot of language that confuses the classifier (e.g. SALE). We initially eliminated To deal with any of these circumstances, remove any "non-alphanumeric chars from the product explanation". This, along with regular stop-word reduction, resulted in a significant improvement in classification performance (Rawat, R., Rajawat, A. S., Mahor, V., Shaw, R. N., &Ghosh, A., 2021).

Word Variations and Misspellings On convention and markets, misspellings are common, posing a challenge for the traditional bag-of-words categorization method. Furthermore, using the traditional bag-of-words method, variants of arguments are assessed self-governing ly ("e.g. hacker, hack, crackers, etc.").

The term of stemming helps to solve the problem of word variants, but it doesn't solve the problem of misspellings (Rawat, R., Mahor, V., Chirgaiya, S., &Rathore, A. S. 2021). We employ char N-gram charities to handle this. Consider the word "hacker" as an example of char N- gram features. The words "hacker" would generate the features "hac", "ack", "cke", and "ker" if we used tri-gram char charistics. The advantage is that variants or errors of the word in the systems "hack," "hackz," and "hackker" will all have certain features.

In our tests, we discovered that employing char N-grams in the b/w range (4, 6) overtook term stopping.

Sample feature area. The feature matrix grows increasingly huge as the number of words increases in the typical bag-of-words technique, as contrasted to the char N-grams approach (Rawat, R., Mahor, V., Rawat, A., Garg, B., &Telang, S. (2021). As the number of unique words increases, the performance of this bloated feature matrix degrades significantly. The introduction of N-grams features extends the feature matrix, which is already rather large. We utilised the sparse matrix data structure in the scipy3 package to tackle this issue, which takes use of the fact that most of the entries would be zero. The sparse matrix simply does not contain an entry for a word or N-grams characteristic that isn't present in a sample.

Keep the headline feature's context in mind. Because the title and explanation of the product are disjoint, we noticed that simply concatenating the explanation to the product title before extracting features resulted in sub-optimal classification results (Rawat, R., Rajawat, A. S., Mahor, V., Shaw, R. N., &Ghosh, A., 2021). We believe that by utilizing a simple concatenation, we were omitting important contextual information. Several features should be treated differently based on whether or not they exist in the title or explanations. We began with two classifiers: one for the title and another for the explanation (Rawat, R., Mahor, V., Chirgaiya, S., & Garg, B. 2021). Using this structure, we would send the title to the title classifier and the explanation to the explanation classifier when categorizing an unknown product. If

Table 3. Product collection by markets

M1	M2	M3	M4	M5	M6	M7	M8	M9	M10
440	1330	460	4080	869	497	195	754	2015	650

another classification generated a '+' classification, we would classify the product as '+'. However, we believe that this has once again resulted in the loss of key background info. To fix this, we isolate the char N-grams features from the product explanation.

As a consequence of this step, a title feature vector and an explanation extracted features are constructed. Then, for the product description, we concatenate these vectors horizontally to generate a single feature vector with distinct selected features.

Table 4. Product related information

S.N.	Title of Product	Related
1	"25+ Hacking Tools (Botnets Keyloggers Worms and More!)"	TRUE
2	"6 gm Colombian Cocaine"	FALSE

Results: We investigate 10 marketplaces in order to train and assess our learning model. The product collection by markets Table 3 and Table 4 is depicts an example of elements that have been evaluated as suitable or inappropriate. With the help of surveillance experts, we label 25% of the products in each marketplace (Rawat, R., Garg, B., Mahor, V., Chouhan, M., Pachlasiya, K., & Telang, S., 2022). The experimental setup is as follows. A cross-validation with one marketplace left out is done. To put it another way, we train on one and test on the other, given n markets. For each marketplace, the experiment is repeated. In the supervised experiment, just the 35% tagged data from each marketplace is utilised. Precision, recall, and unbiased F1 are the three key performance indicators. The proportion of suitable items that varied from those predicted is referred to as precision (Mahor, V., Rawat, R., Kumar, A., Chouhan, M., Shaw, R. N., & Ghosh, A. 2021). The proportion of suitable items that are recalled is known as the recall rate. F1 is the harmonic mean of accuracy and recall.

The results are averaged after being weighted by the number of samples in each market. We don't want to overlook anything vital, thus a high recall is preferable in this case (Mahor, V., Rawat, R., Telang, S Garg, B., Mukhopadhyay D., Palimkar P.,2021). Among the supervised approaches, SVM with linear kernel performed the best, remembering 87 percent of the right commodities while maintaining an accuracy of 85 percent (Fig. 2). SVM outperformed the others, most likely because it focuses on generality rather than precision.

As previously indicated, only 25% of the data is labelled, as labelling frequently necessitates specialist knowledge. However, by using a semisupervised strategy that uses unlabeled data to help with categorization, this large cost and time commitment can be avoided. A person can identify 5 marketplace goods or 2 forum posts as appropriate or not in around one minute, demonstrating the high cost of manual labelling.

Figure 2. Compare the result of SVM, RF, LOG and REG, NB

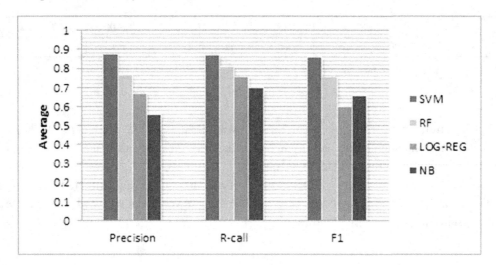

Its experimental design is the same as the supervised method, but this time we employ a large amount of "unlabeled data from each marketplace" (80%) for training.

Figure 3. Compare the result of CT-SVM, CT-RF, CT-LOG and REG, CT-NB and LP

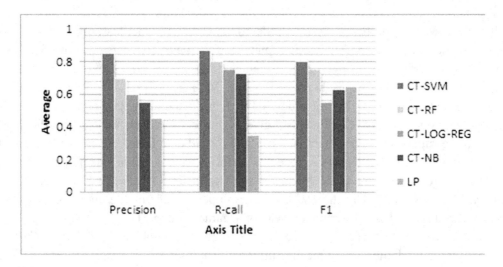

The performance comparison for semi-supervised techniques is shown in Figure 3. For the founder technique, we split the extracted features randomly into two pairs. Char N-gramss are utilised in each of the feature sets. The set of words from which char N-gramss are produced, on the other hand, is discontinuous b/w the two groups. The two matching ("feature vectors") can be viewed as self-governing of one additional in this fashion. As a result, we have two different perspectives on the same sample.

When compared to label propagation and other types of co-trainer, supervised learning as linear support vector machine can remember 90 percent of the appropriate products while keeping on 80 percent accuracy, which is ideal. The unlabeled data improved the categorization in this situation, increasing the recall to 90 percent without sacrificing precision.

Experiment using Convention as a Third Option

There are various dark-web convention where individuals discuss harmful hacking related issues, in addition to the dark-web/deep-web markets that we must previously described. Everywhere is also the issue that only a small percentage of the subjects with postings on these sites include info appropriate to harmful hacking or exploit trade. As a result, a classifier is required to classify appropriate subjects. This sorting problem is extremely similar to the product sorting problem we described earlier, and both have comparable problems.

We evaluated two of these English discussion boards. There were 781 topics in all, with 5373 posts. We label 25% of the topics and use "supervised algorithms" to do a 10-fold cross validation. The findings of the top two "supervised and semi-supervised algorithms" are shown. LOG-REG had the greatest results in the supervised situation, with an accuracy of 80% and a recall of 68%. (Fig. 4). Using unlabeled data in a "semi-supervised" method, on the other hand, enhanced recall while retaining precision. The 10-fold cross validation was conducted just on the designated opinions in this scenario. In the "semi-supervised domain", LOG-REG co-training increased recall to 80% and accuracy to 82 percent.

Figure 4. Compare the result of CT-SVM, CT-LOG and REG, SVM and LOG and REG

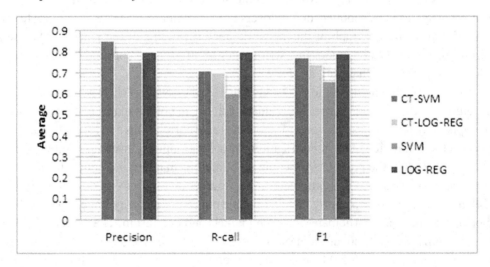

CASE STUDY

We examine the data in order to respond to the issues posed in Section. The following important surveillance phrases will be used. Vulnerability is a defect in s/w or an operating system this makes it possible for an intruder to cooperation it (Rawat, Romil and Kumar, Anil and TELANG, SHRIKANT and Pachlasiya, Kiran and Garg, Bhagwati and Mahor, Vinod and Chouhan, Mukesh, 2021). The exploitation is a piece of s/w that takes advantage of a defect in a piece of s/w or system s/w to undermine it. Patches are pieces of s/w that are used to improve the surveillance of existing s/w by correcting vulnerabilities. The following case studies are discussed.

Finding Zero-Day Exploits

We discovered "16 Zero (0)-Days" vulnerabilities in the marketplace data during a four-week timeframe. Zero-day exploits take use of vulnerabilities that the vendor is unaware. The Android WebView zero-day exploits a flaw in how websites are rendered on android machine. It is affected "android 4.3 Jelly Bean devices" and older versions of the OS. In 2015 and 16, this accounted for additional 60 percent of all Android smartphones. Following the first publication of this zero-day, a fix for "Android KitKat 4.4 and Lollipop 5.0 was provided, requiring users to upgrade their operating systems. Because not everyone has updated to the new OS", the exploit is still being offered for a premium price. Detecting zero (0)-day vulnerabilities early on can help businesses prevent or mitigate the impact of an intrusion on their systems. In this circumstance, for example, a company could opt to prioritise repairing, upgrading, or replacing particular Android-based systems (Rawat, Romil and Mahor, Vinod, 2021).

Users who Participate in Marketplaces or Convention

Previous dark-web crawling research has focused on a specific domain, mainly convention. We develop a social network that contains both markets and convention, which are the two sources of info examined in this research. As a result, we may investigate and discover previously unknown cross-site linkages. Using the "usernames" used by suppliers or employers in every domain, we were able to create this linked graph. Figure 5 depicts a "sub-graph of this network" featuring some of the persons who are concurrently retailing dangerous hacking goods and writing in hacking-related convention (Rawat, Romil and Chouhan, Mukesh and Garg, Bhagwati, 2015).

The vendors are usually attempting to A/D "advertises and discusses" their goods in the convention in order to demonstrate their competence. Individuals' activity in both domains may be seen using these integrated graphic representations, allowing for more accurate correlations and a better understanding of hostile hacker networks. It aids in the identification of social groupings inside user-interaction convention. A power rule governs the presence of people on numerous markets and convention. According to Figure 6, the majority of users only participate in one market or forum (Vinod Mahor; Romil Rawat; Shrikant Telang, 2021). It's worth noting that 751 people are active on many stages. One such user/vendor is depicted. The merchant participates in seven markets and one forum. The dealer sells 82 harmful hacking-related items and talks about them on the forum. With over 7000 completed transactions, the seller has an average rating of 4.8/5.0 from consumers on the flea market, reflecting the dependability of the items and the popularity of the vendor.

RELATED WORK

Website crawler is a popular technique for collecting large amounts of data from the Internet. Many academics are sensitive to particular disciplines because they may be used in a variety of situations. As a consequence, a targeted dawdler, also known as a topic-based dawdler, is necessary (Salmon, P. M., Lane, B. R., Desmond, D., Cherney, A., Kulatilleke, G., Matthews, A., Lacey, D., & Stanton, N. A.

Figure 5. Salesperson/user network in market and forum environments

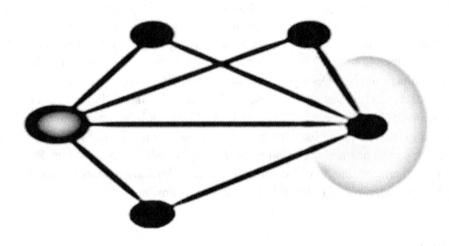

2019). The bulk of targeted dawdlers were designed to gather data from the surface web, with dark-web sites receiving less attention. Recently, a tailored dawdler concentrating on dark-web convention was constructed. This research focuses mostly on convention, collecting relevant data and then examining online groups using symbolic execution. Several data mining techniques for these conventions are also discussed in. We, but at the other hand, just shouldn't look at dark-web conventions; we also get information from marketplaces that offer a range of potentially dangerous hacking-related things. DARPA's Memex program4, which has specific aims from the work mentioned in this article, is exploring another method of leveraging dark-web info to fight human trafficking (Schmidt, H. C. 2015).

Previous research leveraged market information to build system settings that decrease the possible effect of a hostile cyber-attack using a game theoretic framework (Rawat, Romil and Chouhan, Mukesh, 2021). Outlines efforts to analyse hacker conventions for threats that pose a serious danger to people,

Figure 6. Centralized network of salesman in forum environments

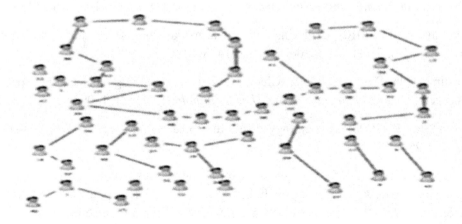

organisations, and the government. It continues, "Information is communicated by convention." People with just elementary abilities may be able to acquire enough by simply utilising these phases. By analysing these hacking communities, the social ties that bind them may be discovered. The dissemination of information among users in these groups is also depending on their skill level and reputation. These conventions are also used to sell malware and stolen personal information (Vinod Mahor; Romil Rawat; Shrikant Telang; Bhagwati Garg;Debajyoti Mukhopadhyay, 2021). Samtani et al. investigate hacker assets during an underground gathering. They discuss the characteristics and dynamics of tutorials, source code, and "attachments" (such as e-books, system surveillance tools, and hardware/software). The most common method of disseminating harmful intrusion materials appears to be through tutorials. These conventions' source code has nothing to do with specific assaults (Vinod Mahor; Romil Rawat; Anil Kumar, 2021). Furthermore, the dynamic trust relationships built by mutually suspicious parties have been explored using underground (non-malicious hacking) conventions.

CONCLUSION

In this research, we develop a method for acquiring intelligence about harmful hacking. Our system is up and running right now. This system is now being transitioned to a commercial partner. For data acquisition, we examine dark-web and deep-web social sites. Using data mining and machine learning approaches, we address several design difficulties in order to construct a focused dawdler. The info is made available to surveillance experts so that they may spot new cyber-intimidations and capabilities.

REFERENCES

Benjamin, V., Li, W., Holt, T., & Chen, H. (2015). Exploring threats and vulnerabilities in hacker web: Forums, irc and carding shops. In *Intelligence and Security Informatics (ISI), 2015 IEEE International Conference on* (pp. 85–90). IEEE.

Chakrabarti, S., Van den Berg, M., & Dom, B. (1999). Focused crawling: A new approach to topic-specific web resource discovery. *Computer Networks, 31*(11), 1623–1640. doi:10.1016/S1389-1286(99)00052-3

Fu, T., Abbasi, A., & Chen, H. (2010). A focused crawler for dark web forums. *Journal of the American Society for Information Science and Technology, 61*(6), 1213–1231. doi:10.1002/asi.21323

Holt, T. J., & Lampke, E. (2010). Exploring stolen data markets online: Products and market forces. *Criminal Justice Studies, 23*(1), 33–50. doi:10.1080/14786011003634415

Holt, T. J., Strumsky, D., Smirnova, O., & Kilger, M. (2012). Examining the social networks of worm writers and hackers. *International Journal of Cyber Criminology, 6*(1), 891–903.

Jordan, T., & Taylor, P. (1998). A sociology of hackers. *The Sociological Review, 46*(4), 757–780. doi:10.1111/1467-954X.00139

Lacey, D., & Salmon, P. M. (2015). It's dark in there: Using systems analysis to investigate trust and engagement in dark web forums. In D. Harris. In E. Psychology & C. Ergonomics (Eds.), *Lecture Notes in Computer Science* (Vol. 9174, pp. 117–128). Springer International Publishing.

Mahor, V., Rawat, R., Kumar, A., Chouhan, M., Shaw, R. N., & Ghosh, A. (2021, September). Cyber Warfare Threat Categorization on CPS by Dark Web Terrorist. In *2021 IEEE 4th International Conference on Computing, Power and Communication Technologies (GUCON)* (pp. 1-6). IEEE.

Mahor, V., Rawat, R., Kumar, A., Chouhan, M., Shaw, R. N., & Ghosh, A. (2021). Cyber Warfare Threat Categorization on CPS by Dark Web Terrorist. *IEEE 4th International Conference on Computing, Power and Communication Technologies (GUCON)*. DOI: 10.1109/GUCON50781.2021.9573994

Mahor, V., Rawat, R., Telang, S., Garg, B., Mukhopadhyay, D., & Palimkar P. (2021). Machine Learning based Detection of Cyber Crime Hub Analysis using Twitter Data. *IEEE 4th International Conference on Computing, Power and Communication Technologies (GUCON)*. DOI: 10.1109/GUCON50781.2021.9573736

Mahor, V., Rawat, R., Telang, S., Garg, B., Mukhopadhyay, D., & Palimkar, P. (2021). Machine Learning based Detection of Cyber Crime Hub Analysis using Twitter Data. *IEEE 4th International Conference on Computing, Power and Communication Technologies (GUCON)*. DOI: 10.1109/GUCON50781.2021.9573736

Motoyama, M., McCoy, D., Levchenko, K., Savage, S., & Voelker, G. M. (2011). An analysis of underground forums. In *Proceedings of the 2011 ACM SIGCOMM conference on Internet measurement conference* (pp. 71–80). ACM.

Müller, J.-W. (2014). On Conceptual History. In Rethinking Modern European Intellectual History. Oxford University Press. https://doi.org/10.1093/acprof:oso/9780199769230.003.0004.

Natale, S., & Ballatore, A. (2014). The web will kill them all: New media, digital utopia, and political struggle in the Italian 5-Star Movement. *Media Culture & Society*, *36*(1), 105–121. https://doi.org/10.1177/0163443713511902

Owenson, G., Cortes, S., & Lewman, A. (2018). The darknet's smaller than we thought: The life cycle of Tor Hidden Services. *Digital Investigation*, *27*, 17–22. https://doi.org/10.1016/j.diin.2018.09.005

Oz, M., Zheng, P., & Chen, G. M. (2018). Twitter versus Facebook: Comparing incivility, impoliteness, and deliberative attributes. *New Media & Society*, *20*(9), 3400–3419. https://doi.org/10.1177/1461444817749516

Rawat, R., Garg, B., Mahor, V., Chouhan, M., Pachlasiya, K., & Telang, S. Cyber Threat Exploitation and Growth during COVID-19 Times. In *Advanced Smart Computing Technologies in Cybersecurity and Forensics* (pp. 85–101). CRC Press.

Rawat, R., Garg, B., Mahor, V., Chouhan, M., Pachlasiya, K., & Telang, S. Cyber Threat Exploitation and Growth during COVID-19 Times. In *Advanced Smart Computing Technologies in Cybersecurity and Forensics* (pp. 85–101). CRC Press.

Rawat, R., Mahor, V., Chirgaiya, S., & Garg, B. (2021). Artificial Cyber Espionage Based Protection of Technological Enabled Automated Cities Infrastructure by Dark Web Cyber Offender. In *Intelligence of Things: AI-IoT Based Critical-Applications and Innovations* (pp. 167–188). Springer.

Rawat, R., Mahor, V., Chirgaiya, S., & Garg, B. (2021). Artificial Cyber Espionage Based Protection of Technological Enabled Automated Cities Infrastructure by Dark Web Cyber Offender. In *Intelligence of Things: AI-IoT Based Critical-Applications and Innovations* (pp. 167–188). Springer.

Rawat, R., Mahor, V., Chirgaiya, S., & Rathore, A. S. (2021). Applications of Social Network Analysis to Managing the Investigation of Suspicious Activities in Social Media Platforms. In *Advances in Cybersecurity Management* (pp. 315–335). Springer.

Rawat, R., Mahor, V., Garg, B., Telang, S., Pachlasiya, K., Kumar, A., Shukla, S. K., & Kuliha, M. (2021). Analyzing Newspaper Articles for Text-Related Data for Finding Vulnerable Posts Over the Internet That Are Linked to Terrorist Activities. International Journal of Information Security and Privacy, 16(1). DOI: doi:10.4018/IJISP.285581

Rawat, R., Mahor, V., Rawat, A., Garg, B., & Telang, S. (2021). Digital Transformation of Cyber Crime for Chip-Enabled Hacking. In Handbook of Research on Advancing Cybersecurity for Digital Transformation (pp. 227-243). IGI Global.

Rawat, R., Rajawat, A. S., Mahor, V., Shaw, R. N., & Ghosh, A. (2021). Dark Web— Onion Hidden Service Discovery and Crawling for Profiling Morphing, Unstructured Crime and Vulnerabilities Prediction. In *Innovations in Electrical and Electronic Engineering* (pp. 717–734). Springer.

Rawat, R., Rajawat, A. S., Mahor, V., Shaw, R. N., & Ghosh, A. (2021). Surveillance Robot in Cyber Intelligence for Vulnerability Detection. In *Machine Learning for Robotics Applications* (pp. 107–123). Springer.

Rawat, R., Rajawat, A. S., Mahor, V., Shaw, R. N., & Ghosh, A. (2021). Dark Web— Onion Hidden Service Discovery and Crawling for Profiling Morphing, Unstructured Crime and Vulnerabilities Prediction. In *Innovations in Electrical and Electronic Engineering* (pp. 717–734). Springer.

Rawat, Chouhan, Garg, Telang, Mahor, & Pachlasiya. (2021). *Malware Inputs Detection Approach (Tool) based on Machine Learning [MIDT-SVM].* Available at SSRN: https://ssrn.com/abstract=3915404

Rawat, Kumar, Telang, Pachlasiya, Garg, Mahor, & Chouhan. (2021). Drug Trafficking crime analysis using Systematic literature Review (SLR) within Darkweb. *AIBM - 2nd International Conference on "Methods and Applications of Artificial Intelligence and Machine Learning In Heterogeneous Brains".* Available at SSRN: https://ssrn.com/abstract=3903797

Rawat, Mahor, Pachlasiya, Garg, Telang, Chouhan, & Kumar. (2021). Twitter Crime analysis and categorization. *AIBM - 2nd International Conference on "Methods and Applications of Artificial Intelligence and Machine Learning In Heterogeneous Brains".* Available at SSRN: https://ssrn.com/abstract=3896252

Robertson, J., Paliath, V., Shakarian, J., Thart, A., & Shakarian, P. (2016). Data driven game theoretic cyber threat mitigation. IAAI.

Salmon, P. M., Lane, B. R., Desmond, D., Cherney, A., Kulatilleke, G., Matthews, A., Lacey, D., & Stanton, N. A. (2019). Breaking bad systems with Human Factors and Ergonomics: Using Work Domain Analysis to identify strategies to disrupt trading in dark net marketplaces. *Proceedings of the Human Factors and Ergonomics Society Annual Meeting*, 63(1), 458–462. https://doi.org/10.1177/1071181319631315

Samtani, S., Chinn, R., & Chen, H. (2015). Exploring hacker assets in underground forums. In *Intelligence and Security Informatics (ISI), 2015 IEEE International Conference on* (pp. 31–36). IEEE.

Schmidt, H. C. (2015). Student Newspapers Show Opinion Article Political Bias. *Newspaper Research Journal, 36*(1), 6–23.

Venger, O. (2019). The use of experts in journalistic accounts of media events: A comparative study of the 2005 London Bombings in British, American, and Russian newspapers. *Journalism, 20*(10), 1343–1359.

Chapter 15
Anonymous Trading on the Dark Online Marketplace:
An Exploratory Study

Piyush Vyas
Dakota State University, USA

Gitika Vyas
Independent Researcher, USA

Akhilesh Chauhan
Dakota State University, USA

Romil Rawat
Shri Vaishnav Vidyapeeth Vishwavidyalaya, India

Shrikant Telang
https://orcid.org/0000-0001-5477-865X
Shri Vaishnav Vidyapeeth Vishwavidyalaya, India

Madhu Gottumukkala
Dakota State University, USA

ABSTRACT

Advancement in technology provides numerous solutions to not only legitimate businesses but to illegal trades as well. Selling substances, drugs, and prohibited merchandise and goods on the internet comes under illegal trading. The internet we surf is merely a thin layer of this deeply rooted miraculous mechanism of connecting the world. The dark web is the part of the deep web that utilizes the internet to flourish the illicit intentions of trading illegal items, thereby fostering the ongoing societal devastation. This chapter is exploring anonymous trading on the dark online marketplace using the Silkroad 2.0 dataset. This work aims to analyze the various aspects of dark e-commerce trading and highlight different themes used for trading illicit drugs on Twitter by performing the thematic analysis using Latent Dirichlet Allocation unsupervised machine learning with a 0.44 coherence score. The findings have shown that developed countries are participating in illegal trading, and teenage schoolgoers can be victims of social media drug trading.

DOI: 10.4018/978-1-6684-6444-1.ch015

INTRODUCTION

The Deep Web is the portion of the Internet that holds the most sensitive information, such as bank accounts, government records, and private emails. The Surface Web is the main reference point for most people when it comes to the Internet. However, it only accounts for 5% of the web. Any activity you engage in on any online platform can be tracked(Hutcheon & Warren, 2021).Darknet markets are online platforms where cybercriminals can sell or steal data. Due to the nature of the marketplaces, it is difficult to predict when and how organized crimes will occur(Wang et al., 2018). Illegal merchandise such as drugs, weapons, child pornography, and hitman services are being sold through online black marketplaces, which are also known as crypto markets wherein buyers and sellers use different methods to hide their identities(Reksna, 2017).

The hidden service (HS) protocol in The Onion Router (Tor) allows web services to stay secret by distorting the IP addresses of network servers and passing them through various relays within Tor's overlay network utilizing onion routing. These concealed anonymous services are sometimes referred to as onion sites or just onions since they use the onion special top-level domain (TLD). Drug and weapon marketplaces (SilkRoad, Armory) engaged in illegal trade, hacker forums publishing details of victims' identities, terrorist forums attracting large donations, whistleblower sites (WikiLeaks), and fraudulent financial sites (EasyCoin, OnionWallet) engaged in monetary scams are just a few recent examples(Ghosh et al., 2017). Illegal trading on darknet platforms is one expression of serious and organized crime.Around two-thirds of darknet market activity is thought to be related to drugs. Almost every substance, even new psychoactive compounds, is available to customers with little technical knowledge with just a few keystrokes. This trend poses a substantial threat to the health and security of residents and communities(EMCDDA, 2017).

Cryptocurrencies are one of the world's largest unrestrained capitalisms. Approximately one-quarter of bitcoin users and half of the bitcoin transactions are linked to illegal conduct. Bitcoin is involved in over $72 billion in criminal activities each year, which is equivalent to illicit drug trading in the United States and Europe. With widespread interest in bitcoin and the emergence of more opaque cryptocurrencies, the unlawful share of bitcoin activity is decreasing. Cryptocurrencies are facilitating "black e-commerce," which alters the way the black market functions(Foley et al., 2019).

The anonymous sale of illicit commodities is orchestrated by darknet markets, the bulk of which are cannabis, ecstasy, and cocaine-related products (70 percent). Over the last few years, these internet marketplaces have become increasingly popular for selling and buying narcotics. The most famous market in 2013 was SilkRoad, which produced over 300,000 US dollars per day, whereas the most popular market in 2017 was Alphabay, which generated around 800,000 US dollars per day. This trend toward darknet sales might result in a disruptive shift away from traditional drug distribution routes, reducing governments' capacity to control the drug trade(Calis, 2018). SilkRoad2 was founded in November 2013 as the successor to the well-known market SilkRoad (shut down by the FBI in October 2013). SilkRoad2 soon became the largest darknet market in 2014 due to its brand recognition. SilkRoad2 was compromised in February 2014, resulting in the loss of 2.6 million dollars in bitcoins and a massive dent in the company's reputation. Authorities shut down SilkRoad2 on November 6, 2014, and its administrator was detained(Wang et al., 2018).

Exploration of Artificial intelligence strengthens the subordinate branches such as supervised and unsupervised machine intelligence. Where supervised machine intelligence required a guided approach by labeling the training data(Vyas, Liu, et al., 2021)and unsupervised machine intelligence work upon unlabeled datasets (Vyas, Reisslein, et al., 2021). Unsupervised techniques learn detecting, classifying, and extracting desired information/classes/labels as the training process progresses. Researchers such as (Garrahan, 2018)(Ghosh et al., 2017)(Zhang et al., 2020)(Foley et al., 2019)(Zhao et al., 2020) have used machine intelligence in the area of dark web crimes.Therefore, this work has utilized the thematic analysis approach by adopting LatentDirichlet Allocation (LDA) techniques to identify the Mephedrone (i.e., the psychostimulant drug known as 4-methylmethcathinone) related trading signs and communication. Mephedrone possesses various slang names such as M-CAT, White Magic, and Meow Meow; these words have been continuously spreading on the platforms like Twitter. Illegal trading is not only limited to the dark web marketplaces but also proliferated on social media and microblogging sites. Customers use this drug as an alternative to cocaine for euphoria, mood elevation, and mental stimulation functions. Hence, this work has used available Twitter data (Kolliakou et al., 2015).

This chapter is exploring anonymous trading on the dark online marketplace and the key terms used for trading illegal drugs on Twitter. The overarching goal of this work is to analyze the various aspects of dark e-commerce trading, such as the most common trading locations across the globe, common categories of sold items, Cryptocurrency rates, Customer satisfaction (by rating), and who sold the items. Moreover, this chapter will shed light upon the different used terms to buy/sell drugs on Twitter by performing the thematic analysis. The proposed work will contribute to the literature on cybercrime by highlighting the aforementioned analytical findings. Moreover, this work will help law and enforcement dignitaries to understand the interleaved behavior of such dark e-commerce markets.

LITERATURE REVIEW

The realm of dark web marketplacesbuilds upon interleaved components such as illicit trading by cryptocurrencies. Such currencies tend to have a pseudonymous nature, and Bitcoin is the crux. To operate any illegal or illegitimate activities, crypto turns out to be a feasible option over cash. Darknet markets are the prominent hub of all deals made for services like drugs and weapons. C. Janze(2017)reveals that growth in the number of goods and services offered on darknet markets is related to the growth in the number of transactions on the Bitcoin blockchain. Although, external shocks such as international law enforcement operations made it hard for darknet markets to survive, with the verge of them being closed or shut down. Despite these strict enforcements, these markets flourish due to the multiplicity of new crypto markets where many users tend to migrate. Norbutas et al.(2020) state that the trust between the buyers and sellers in the new marketplace is crucial as it can affect the reputation of the Illegal online marketplaces. Thus,reputation transferability is the focal point in these market trading's recovery after they face the sudden shutdowns and seizing.

Darknet behaves similar to the Internet but with the high anonymity and concealed identities of buyers and users. Users usually need to build an account to get access to the available products that are to be sold by the dealer on these darknet marketplaces. Due to the greater security, encrypted and decentralized nature of cryptocurrencies, Bitcoins are specifically the most widely used mode of transactions. With these benefits and security, dark online businesses permit sellers to spread globally. The international reach of these illicit marketplaces made it a compulsion to use the undetectable mode of communication and trading. PGP (Pretty Good Privacy) encryption is usually preferred for secure communication. Moreover, to avoid being grabbed by law agencies, customers are advised to reveal their real identities online while forming accounts(Foley et al., 2019). The implementation of hidden services within the illegal onion sites on the dark web aids to perfectly guard their location, making them unreachable and invulnerable to legal systems. It has become crucial to detect and supervise these sites for computer security and law enforcement sectors. For this purpose, Ghosh et al. (2017).created an automated system that stores bulk onion sites data after crawling and indexing them in the repository named LIGHTS. For thematic assessment of these stored onion sites data, an innovative, scalable analytical tool-Automated Tool for Onion Labeling (ATOL), is used in work by(Ghosh et al., 2017).

The illicit goods trading marketplace has virtually made it approachable for the users to the illegal stuff, but the core tension lies toward shipping these products within an international radius. Norbutas (2018) stated that the geographic constraint is a factor that can have implications for the buyers' behavior and eventually on the illegal online trades, but the impact is indescribable. Although it became evident that users got inclined towards localized trade rather than the cross boundaries trade because of fear of hidden and fake seller information as one of the many reasons(Norbutas, 2018).Darknet data that is the hub of illegal activities can propagate cybercrimes. For the supervision of darknet resources, their data are mined to alarm the network operators for the related cyber threats. As network operators often lack proper resources to search for the threats and resolve this difficulty, Lawrenceet al. (2017) presented a modular framework as a solution called a D-miner. The D-miner mines the darknet online data and convert it to JSON objects for searching, visualizations, and alerts. This medium is beneficial for network operators to monitor the threats associated with illegal data(Lawrence et al., 2017).

Apart from the dark web marketplaces, social media platforms are the instant disseminators of any information, which can be dangerous when related to illegal drugs. The ease of drug availability and their commercialization are the two significant factors that intensified the drug epidemic. Social media use is making a boom among grown-ups; there is enormous capacity for online advancement of illicit drugs with postponed or restricted prevention of such informing. Furthermore, general business deal applications shield exchanges; although, they don't segregate between legitimate and unlawful deal exchanges. These facilities over the online social platforms hinder the proper scrutiny of the drug markets and their involvement in drug abuse and related deaths due to their overdose(Zhao et al., 2020).Because of technical difficulties, identifying the involved dealers with illegalities has become a cumbersome task for many law enforcement authorities. Majorly the reasons around this are - first, due to privacy issues related to social media sites, there remains restricted data availability, and second, the drug traffickers have attained finesse in creating a pattern to deal with drugs thus, it forms an ambiguous environment to detect the unlawful drug dealers from regular legal customers(Hu et al., 2021).

Advancement in psychotropic substances and modifications in the old used drugs has made it challenging to ace the pace with the updated drugs and their related terms for the researchers and medical practitioners. The use of novel vocabulary on social media platforms indicates that the analyses of these platforms can alleviate this problem by unfolding new records and information related to drugs terminologies.Simpson et al.(2018)examined drug-related phrases in a sample of US tweets incorporating substance use epidemiologists and linguistic scientists who used natural language processing tools for the investigation. Young people involved in the distribution of illegal drugs are rising, which has become a concern for many places, especially England. The issues like consumer capitalism, drugs prevention, varied inequality, and problems related to social media have impacted the younger population to indulge in this vicious cycle of the drugs market. The UK government's insufficiency in the response indicated that the pressure on the children would continue. Additionally, adults would keep exploiting young people if the drugs were not made authorized and legalized, or a new surge of opportunities, standard

Table 1. Existing literature's approach and techniques

Authors	Focus	Data Source	Techniques
(C. Janze, 2017)	Usage of Cryptocurrency as a mode of payments	GRAMS--darknet markets search engine.	Rational Choice Theory - Autoregressive Distributed Lag (ADL) model.
(Garrahan, 2018)	authorship classification in dark web forum posts	SilkRoad Data	LSTM
(Ghosh et al., 2017)	Thematic assessment of Onion sites	LIGHTS repository	ATOL (Automated Tool for Onion Labeling) + Term Frequency Inverse Class Frequency (TFICF) + SVM, Naive Bayes, and Logistic Regression classifiers
(Zhang et al., 2020)	dSytle-GAN:a tool to analyze drug identification.	SilkRoad1, SilkRoad 2, SilkRoad 3, Agora, AlphaBay and Empire	generative adversarial network (GAN) + Attributed Heterogeneous Information Network (AHIN)
(Ladegaard, 2018)	Analyzing Drug dealer enticement	Agora	Regression Analyses
(Norbutas, 2018)	Analyze Buyer / Seller Interaction	Abraxas	descriptive analysis + Exponential Random Graph Models (ERGM)
(van der Sanden et al., 2021)	Identify the usage predictors of social media to purchase the illicit drug in New Zealand	Via New Zealand Drug Trends Survey (NZDTS)	Logistic regression models
(Norbutas et al., 2020)	analyzing cryptomarket sellers' reputation transferability	Abraxas, Agora, and AlphaBay.	Longitudinal Multi-Level Regression Model
(Foley et al., 2019)	characterize the illegal trade facilitated by bitcoin	Manually extracted bitcoin transactions	Smart Local Moving (SLM) algorithm
(Wang et al., 2018)	Detecting multiple vendor identities	Agora, Evolution, SilkRoad2	transfer learning + deep neural network
(Zhang et al., 2019)	Identifying drug trafficker	Valhalla, Dream Market, SilkRoad2 and Evolution.	uStyle-uID: attributed heterogeneous information network (AHIN) + Deep Neural Network (DNN)
(Zhao et al., 2020)	to identify illicit drug ads from social media	Google+, Flickr and Tumblr	support vector machine (SVM) + CNN + LSTM
(Simpson et al., 2018)	to uncover unknown drug terms on social media	Twitter data	Bag of words + vector space model (VSM)
(Hu et al., 2021)	to identify illicit drug dealers on Instagram.	Manually: Instagram data.	Bidirectional Encoder Representations from Transformers (BERT) + ResNet

living, good incomes, and status was to be encouraged compared to those offered by drugs dealers to the adults(Irwin-Rogers, 2019).

Moreover, machine learning techniques contributed to attaining distinctive objectives in the realm of the dark web. Such as machine learning has been used to detect the trading patterns on dark web marketplaces. Additionally, unsupervised and supervised machine learning techniques have been applied to identify different themes, dimensions, and clusters for various illicit product categories, that have been sold out across the globe. Researchers such as (Mahor, Rawat, Kumar, et al., 2021; Mahor, Rawat, Telang, et al., 2021; Rajawat, Rawat, Barhanpurkar, et al., 2021b, 2021a; Rajawat, Rawat, Mahor, et al.,

2021; Rajawat, Rawat, Shaw, et al., 2021; Rawat, Mahor, Chirgaiya, Shaw, et al., 2021a; Rawat, Mahor, Rawat, et al., 2021; Rawat, Rajawat, Mahor, Shaw, et al., 2021b, 2021a; Rawat et al., 2011; Rawat, Mahor, Chirgaiya, & Garg, 2021; Rawat, Mahor, Chirgaiya, & Rathore, 2021; Rawat, Mahor, Chirgaiya, Shaw, et al., 2021b) has been used machine learning techniques in their work and successfully demonstrate their approach by highlighting their findings.

The presented chaptercomplements the existing studies such as (C. Janze, 2017; Ghosh et al., 2017; Norbutas et al., 2020)by utilizing the available Silkroad2.0 dataset and extending the literature by performing the thematic analysis on the Twitter data set through LDA. Moreover, Table 1 summarizes the existing research approaches adopted by the researchers. Table 1 indicates the various available datasets, study focus, and adopted techniques.

METHODOLOGY

An adequatemethodologyis necessary to perform a suitable exploratory data analysis (EDA) and thematic analysis; therefore, as shown in figure 1,this work has introduced a framework that incorporates all the relevant steps, including data collection, data preprocessing, EDA, and topic extraction for thematic analysis.Figure 1 indicates the flow between all stages. First,this work has collected data for dark web e-commerce websitessuch as SilkRoad 2.0 and Mephedrone Drug Twitter data. Second,this work has performed extensive data preprocessing for each of the data set separately. Third, to get relevant insights into illegal trading on the dark web market, this work presents EDA for SilkRoad data.Fourth, to analyze terms that have been used on Twitter to buy, sell, and proliferate illegal drug information. This work has extracted those terms by utilizing the Latent Dirichlet Allocation (LDA) technique, wherein the essential information is extracted in the form of topics. Further subsections discuss all aforementioned steps in detail.

Data Collection

In this chapter,this work has used two distinct datasets. The first dataset belongs to the dark web e-commerce website SilkRoad 2.0 (data link: https://www.kaggle.com/dpet922/silk-road-2-listings)(Branwen et al., 2015), and the second dataset belongs to Mephedrone drug tweets(Kolliakou et al., 2015) (Datalink: https://figshare.com/articles/dataset/Mephedrone_annotations_for_Twitter/1613832). The Silkroad2.0 data consists of 618,860 records with the Product title, Seller_id, Price USD, Price BTC, Ratings,Review, Origin, Category, Subcategory, Market, and Date. Wherein Subcategory records are empty, reviews are in encrypted text, and Market records belong to a single entity, i.e., Silkroad2.The following Table 2 defines each of these entries,

The drug tweet data has been annotated by (Kolliakou et al., 2015). The data has a collection of 5000 tweets related to the trading of Mephedrone psychoactive substances.Figure 2 and Figure 3 show the example tweets that indicate the proliferation of the information related to buying/selling of illegal mephedrone drugs by using one of its slang names, i.e., Meow Meow.

Figure 1. A high-level diagram of the Implemented framework

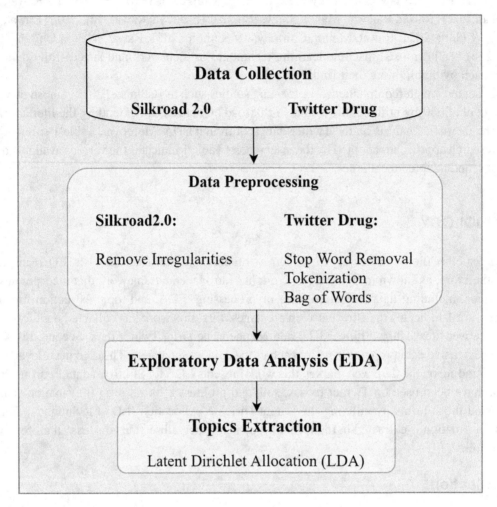

Data Preprocessing

This work has performed a data preprocessing task for each dataset. From the Silkroad dataset, this work has removed irregularities in terms of missing records such as subcategories, and this work has eliminated the customer review variable because of having encrypted text. Finally, this work has got 292,665 records from 618860. Moreover, from Mephedrone tweet data,this work has removed the stop words such as period signs ('.', '..') and non-English words. This work has not removed the repeated and incomplete words such as Meow-Meow, Meth, and so on. The reason being including such incomplete words and phrases is to extract such commonly used words in the trading of illegal substances on Twitter.This work has further lowercased all the words in the tweets that helped to perform tokenization. Tokenization is an essential step in natural language processing tasks such as topic extractions. It separates each word in terms of tokens. This work has not performed the stemming (i.e., the inclusion of root words, e.g., Studies will become studi) or lemmatization (i.e., the inclusion of the contextual word, e.g., Studies will become study) because this will potentially eliminate the slag words that are crucial for the topic extraction.

Table 2. SilkRoad variable definitions

Variables	Description
Product title	Product title comprises the information related to product categories such as drugs, goods, apparel, et cetera.
Seller_id	Seller ID indicates the information related to the seller account.
Price USD	Price USD variable consists ofthe information of associated price to every categorized item.
Price BTC	Price BTC variable consists of the converted price from Bitcoin (BTC) to USD.
Ratings	The rating variable has the rating for each categorized item ranges from0- 5.
Review	Review variable comprises all the actual encrypted information provided by the buyers of illegal substances on SilkRoad 2.0, which is complex to decrypt to include for analysis in this chapter.
Origin,	Origin variable consists of information related to those countries from where the illegal trading was initiated.
Category	The category column comprises the name of the main category of each illegal item.
Subcategory	The subcategory variable indicates the information related to a specific item for each category, such as theparticular name of an illegal drugassociated witha top category, i.e., drug substance.However, this information is not available in the data set and is further removed in the preprocessing step.
Market	The market variable indicates the information related to dark web e-commerce websites for illegal trading, which is SilkRoad in common for all the records.
Date	The date variable indicates the range of the period for which the data set has been collected.

Figure 2. Example tweets from the dataset: a) a tweet by a potential seller and b) a tweet by apotential buyer

Figure 3. Example tweets from the dataset: a tweet by a potential buyer

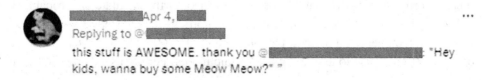

Doc2Vec

Document to vector (Doc2Vec)is a technique implemented by Le and Mikolov(Le & Mikolov, 2014) in 2014. Doc2Vec converts the words in textual data into vector representation of fixed length that is required to perform any machine learning-based tasks that include data in the form of text. Doc2Vec is an unsupervised machine learning technique that learns a continuous representation of the text.Such a technique ishelpful for any variable-length chunk of text such as tweets.

EDA

To understand the trends and trading on the dark web e-commerce website such as Silkroad, it is essential to perform an extensive exploratory data analysis. Therefore,this work has performed the multi-directional EDA. By utilizing various graphical and tabular representations,this work has disclosed various information in the data set. This work has presented the item's categories that have been sold, the trading information of buyer and seller, the customer feedback for each category of an illegal substance, the business transactions in terms of USD and BTC.Such identified information will help to understand the illegal trading across the globe, the most sold substances, customer satisfaction, and the seller's geographical locations.

Topic Extraction

Similar toclustering, topic modeling/thematic analysis is an unsupervised approach to identifying and classifying contextual info without having a prior understanding of data. The aim is to extract a collection of words to form an underlying topic and classify the text within those topics. The terms such as drugs and psychotics substance among the tweets can be grouped under generalized topic/theme such as Drugs—the whole process of categorizing the underlying topic in a generalized form often known as Thematic analysis.This study used the Latent Dirichlet Allocation (LDA) approach to extract topics from drug tweet data. The words are represented as Latent and Dirichlet represents the probability distribution. The goal of LDA is to look into various topics depending on the words in a textual document. LDA is an unsupervised learning approach in which each document is treated as a jumble of words. LDA begins by assuming themes in the same manner that a text document is formed, and then it links a collection of words with those supposed topics(Blei et al., 2003).

Figure 4 shows the interleaved components of the LDA, whereinthe presumed themes/topics denoted by K, topic distribution per document denoted by α, words per topic distribution denoted by β, topic distribution for a document denoted byθ, word distribution for a topic denoted by φ, N is the number of total words, M represents the number of documents, and z denotes the topic for the nth word. LDA performs the recursive processes to construct a topic: first, selection of the number of topics to be retrieved from the texts has been performed; second, parse through each document one by one to assign the specified topic to each word; third, calculation of probabilities such as p(topic | document) and p(word | topic) for each theme of each word in each document, has been performed, forth, calculate the probability p (topic | document) x p(word | topic) to allocate the new topic to a word. 5) Repeat steps 3–4 until LDA returns themes for words in a document that are comparable(Blei et al., 2003). The perplexity and coherence scores have been used as a metric to assess the LDA topic model. Perplexity is a metric that evaluates

Figure 4. LDA by (Blei et al., 2003).

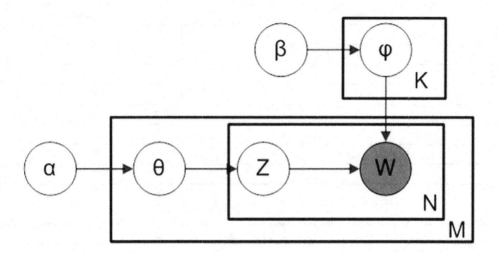

how effectively LDA predicts topics for an unknown dataset, such as test data that has been left out from the tweet data in part.

Moreover according to "Blei et al., (2003) the perplexity, used by convention in language modeling, is monotonically decreasing in the likelihood of the test data, and is algebraically equivalent to the inverse of the geometric mean per-word likelihood. More formally, for a test set of M documents, the perplexity is":

$$perplexity(D_{test}) = \exp\left\{-\left(\sum_{d=1}^{M} \log p(w_d) / \sum_{d=1}^{M} N_d\right)\right\}$$

Here D stands for a corpus of documents, w is the specific word and N is for a sequence of words. LDA performs better when the perplexity score is lower. Coherence, on the other hand, is a measure of resemblance between high-scoring terms in a topic. A higher coherence score indicates that the model is doing better.

RESULTS AND DISCUSSION

SilkRoad 2.0 EDA

This work has performed EDA on the SilkRoad dataset to analyze the underlying patterns and elements for illegal trading. This work has extracted numerous product categories and their quantities from the trading transactions, seller and recipient information, customer feedback ratings for sold items, transactions in united states dollars (USD), and Bitcoins (BTC). Table3 indicates the top 20 item categories that have been sold on the SilkRoad and their quantities. Here one can analyze that drug prescriptions have been sold many times in large quantities, i.e., 53,150. In contrast, electronics holds the twentieth

Table 3. Top 20 categories

Categories	Quantities
Prescription	53150
Psychedelics	38520
Stimulants	36868
Cannabis	33699
Ecstasy	25871
Steriodpeds	19710
Other	19476
Drugs	8827
Opiods	8634
Digital	6867
Drug	6203
Books	6088
Apparel	5782
Money	4312
Dissociatives	3635
Custom	3511
Services	3021
Forgeries	2888
Erotica	1220
Electronics	810

place with 810 quantities. Various categories have been sold on SilkRoad, such as stimulants, cannabis, steroid-peds, drugs, opioids, et cetera. Such item categories show that anonymous buyers use dark web e-commerce websites to buy illegal drugs. Thus, indicating a sign of societal devastation in part.

Table 4 shows customer satisfaction by providing appropriate ratings to the sold items. Here analyzed that majority of customers were happy with the items that had been sold to them. For example, 249,715 customers rated 4 to purchased items; this trend indicates the popularity of illicit items and encourages the high utilization of dark web e-commerce sites. Table5 and Table6 show the top 10 geographical locations of seller and buyer; here, can be analyzed that majority of transactions utilized the concept of

Table 4. Distribution of feedback ratings

Ratings	Quantity
0	7202
1	771
2	6050
3	28221
4	249715

Table 5. Top 10 seller

Seller Countries	Quantity	Percentage
Undeclared	47638	16.28%
USA	45648	15.60%
China	36062	12.32%
United Kingdom	35335	12.07%
Australia	20251	6.92%
Germany	19641	6.71%
Netherlands	18812	6.43%
India	15779	5.39%
Belgium	12199	4.17%
Canada	11655	3.98%

anonymity by not disclosing the specific country name, rather using generalized terms such as "undeclared" and "worldwide". A region like, the USA, Canada, the United Kingdom (UK), Australia, and

Table 6. Top 10 recipients

Recipient Countries	Quantity	Percentage
Worldwide	179540	61.35%
USA	33105	11.31%
Australia	18888	6.45%
Undeclared	18233	6.23%
European union	14646	5.00%
World wd. Expt. Australia	12313	4.21%
US and Canada	5589	1.91%
UK	4715	1.61%
Norway	1344	0.46%
Germany	1243	0.42%

Europe have majorly participated in the trade of illegal items. For example, the USA is leading in the realm of illicit deeds by holding 15.60% of the selling part and 11.31% of the total buying. All these regions are considered as developed economies hence have access to advanced technologies, but it is shocking to see the participation of developing countries like India in the trading; it is alarming that illegal trading on the darkweb is spreading among the large population in the world without using any significantly advanced technology.

Figure 5 shows the transaction history of sell on a specific day. The analysis shows that on an average of $8823.09 per day, USD transactions happened with a max of $13,685 and a min of $2,613. This trend of monetary transactions indicates the high probability of a rise in the daily sell/buy trading of

Figure 5. Day wise transaction in USD

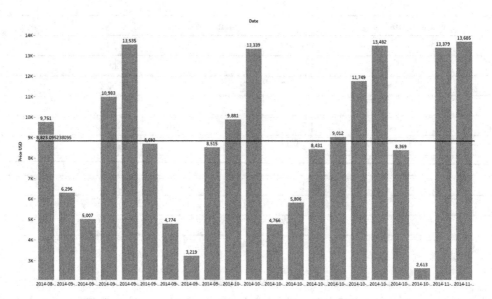

high amounts. Moreover, Figure 6 shows the transactions in BTC values converted to USD amount. Wherein on an average of $13,936.42 per day, BTC equivalent USD transactions have happened with a max of $20,845 and a min of $4,861. Here the assertion is that the cryptocurrency (bitcoin) has been used more than the usual currency, and customers preferred cryptos over USD. The reason behind using cryptos could be its global nature. In other words, cryptocurrencies hold the same monetary values across the world, hence, eliminating the process of currency exchange. Therefore, bitcoins are used more than USD in illicit trading.

Topic Extraction

To extract the various themes/topics from the Mephedrone illicit drug tweet dataset, this work has used a Gensim python-based open-source library. Gensim was developed by Rehurek& Sojka(2011) and provided a way of implementing the LDA algorithm. After performing the aforementioned (see Methodology) preprocessing task, to assign the word vectors for LDA, this work has used the pre-trained en_core_web_md - Spacy model (Honnibal & Montani, 2017) and GloVe vectors (Pennington et al., 2014). Further, to create a document term matrix for explaining the word frequency among tweets, this work has created a vocabulary of 2000 words and used the doc2vec () method. It is required to tune the parameters of LDA to get the optimum or best results. Therefore, this work has tuned the parameters such as number of topics, chunk size (number of tweets in a batch/iteration), number of passes and number of iterations, alpha (Document-Topic Density), and beta (Word-Topic Density~ beta) to attain the high coherence score. The final value set are - number of topics: 9, chunk size: 500, passes:50, iterations:50, 0.01 alpha and 0.9 beta. LDA model's perplexity and coherence scores on tweet data are -14.01 and 0.44 respectively, that are considered as good scores.

Table 7 shows the extracted top words from the tweets and their associated themes/ topics. After analyzing the identified words,this work has categorized them into five themes as "White magic", "Kitty cat love", "Death", "School Teenager," and "Buy-Sell drug chemical". Such themes indicate some alarming issues for the law and enforcement and society. For example, the school teenager theme suggests that school-goers can be the target or participate in illegal trading on social media. Moreover, apart from "Meow Meow", there is an upsurge of "kitty cat" and "white magic" slang to indicate drug availabili-

Figure 6. Day-wise transaction in BTC to USD

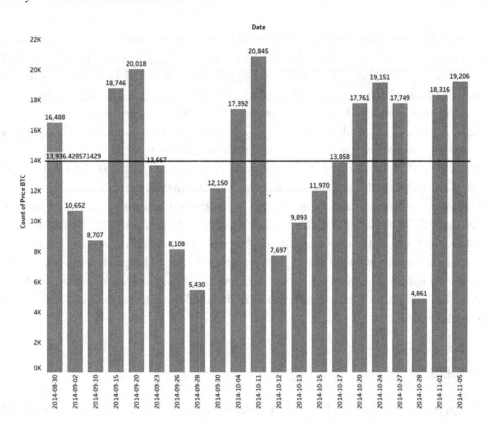

Table 7. Shows the extracted topics along with their associated words

Theme / Topics	Code	Top words
White magic (T1) Kitty Cat Love (T2, T9) Death (T3, T6) School Teenager (T4,T6) Buy-Sell drug chemical(T5, T7, T9)	T1	"dance" "white" "magic" "great" "spell" "money" "love" "help" "drug" "manual"
	T2	"cat" "kitty" "just" "so" "little" "know" "now" "love" "go" "be"
	T3	"old" "beat" "bad" "so" "death" "year" "die" "time" "just" "curse"
	T4	"costume" "most" "dangerous" "isn" "bark" "drug" "alcohol" "even" "school" "hat"
	T5	"buy" "friend" "only" "favorite" "ever" "surprise" "sale" "chance" "give" "take"
	T6	"drug" "ban" "say" "legal" "take" "death" "high" "teenager" "make" "why"
	T7	"other" "sale" "research" "quality" "chemical" "high" "sell" "grade" "buy" "plant"
	T8	"card" "art" "original" "mmccouk" "greeting" "www" "list" "just" "purchase" "item"
	T9	"cat" "go" "love" "want" "night" "kitty" "tonight" "get" "let" "now"

tydemand on social media. Since the tweet data concentrates on the mephedrone drug, therefore,this work has got the Buy-Sell drug chemical theme in the majority of tweets.The Twitter user also discussed possible "deaths" associated withan overdose of the Mephedrone drug. The aforementioned Table 7 indicates the ongoing illegal trading on the social media platforms like Twitter, right infront of our eyes.

CONCLUSION

The evolution of technologies acts as a double-sided coin. On the one side, one can experience the betterment of society, and on the other side, one can face the side-effects of such advancements. Illicit trading is not new to society, but it is strengthened by advanced techniques to remain hidden. Dark web and TOR networks complement each other to create the illicit trading e-commerce ecosystem. Due to anonymity on the dark web, the devastation continues by the time law and enforcement detain such illegal practices. This work has analyzed one of the popular dark-web e-commerce sites, SilkRoad2.0, to find out the possible monetary transactions, participations, and illegal item exchanges.

Moreover, this work has performed the thematic analysis on Twitter data to examine the possible open trading of well-known illicit drugs, i.e., Mephedrone. Our findings suggest that despite the detention of illicit marketplaces on the dark web, such services are migrating with their customer base on distinct platforms by using TOR services and keep on damaging societal values. The results of this work are limited to old records due to the unavailability of the latest data related to ongoing trading on the dark web but indicate a fair judgment for the ingrowing illicit market. The proposed work will contribute to the literature on cybercrime by highlighting the aforementioned analytical findings. Moreover, this work will help law and enforcement dignitaries to understand the interleaved behavior of such dark e-commerce markets.

REFERENCES

Blei, D. M., Ng, A. Y., & Jordan, M. I. (2003). Latent dirichlet allocation. *Journal of Machine Learning Research, 3*, 993–1022.

Branwen, G., Christin, N., Décary-Hétu, D., & Andersen, R. M. (2015). *Dark Net Market archives, 2011-2015.* https://www.gwern.net/DNM-archives

Calis, T. (2018). *Multi-homing sellers and loyal buyers on darknet markets* [Unpublished Masters Thesis]. Erasmus University, the Netherlands.

EMCDDA. (2017). *Drugs and the darknet. Perspectives for enforcement, research and policy.* doi:10.2810/834620

Foley, S., Karlsen, J. R., & Putniņš, T. J. (2019). Sex, drugs, and bitcoin: How much illegal activity is financed through cryptocurrencies? *Review of Financial Studies, 32*(5), 1798–1853. doi:10.1093/rfs/hhz015

Garrahan, J. (2018). *Authorship detection in dark web marketplaces using lstm and rnn neural networks.* Academic Press.

Ghosh, S., Das, A., Porras, P., Yegneswaran, V., & Gehani, A. (2017). Automated categorization of onion sites for analyzing the darkweb ecosystem. *Proceedings of the 23rd ACM SIGKDD International Conference on Knowledge Discovery and Data Mining*, 1793–1802. 10.1145/3097983.3098193

Honnibal, M., & Montani, I. (2017). spaCy 2: Natural language understanding with Bloom embeddings, convolutional neural networks and incremental parsing. *To Appear, 7*(1), 411–420.

Hu, C., Yin, M., Liu, B., Li, X., & Ye, Y. (2021). Identifying Illicit Drug Dealers on Instagram with Large-scale Multimodal Data Fusion. *ACM Transactions on Intelligent Systems and Technology, 12*(5), 1–23. doi:10.1145/3472713

Hutcheon, P. D., & Warren, R. (2021). *Under the Cover of Darkness: Insider Trading and the Dark Web.* https://www.natlawreview.com/article/under-cover-darkness-insider-trading-and-dark-web

Irwin-Rogers, K. (2019). Illicit drug markets, consumer capitalism and the rise of social media: A toxic trap for young people. *Critical Criminology, 27*(4), 591–610. doi:10.100710612-019-09476-2

Janze, C. (2017). Are cryptocurrencies criminals best friends? Examining the co-evolution of bitcoin and darknet markets. *Amer. Conf. Inf. Syst. (AMCIS)*. https://aisel.aisnet.org/amcis2017/InformationSystems/Presentations/2

Kolliakou, A., Ball, M., Derczynski, L., Chandran, D., & Stewart, R. (2015). *Mephedrone annotations for Twitter.* Figshare.

Ladegaard, I. (2018). Instantly hooked? freebies and samples of opioids, cannabis, MDMA, and other drugs in an illicit E-commerce market. *Journal of Drug Issues, 48*(2), 226–245. doi:10.1177/0022042617746975

Lawrence, H., Hughes, A., Tonic, R., & Zou, C. (2017). D-miner: A framework for mining, searching, visualizing, and alerting on darknet events. *2017 IEEE Conference on Communications and Network Security (CNS)*, 1–9. 10.1109/CNS.2017.8228628

Le, Q., & Mikolov, T. (2014). Distributed representations of sentences and documents. *International Conference on Machine Learning*, 1188–1196.

Mahor, V., Rawat, R., Kumar, A., Chouhan, M., Shaw, R. N., & Ghosh, A. (2021). Cyber Warfare Threat Categorization on CPS by Dark Web Terrorist. *2021 IEEE 4th International Conference on Computing, Power and Communication Technologies (GUCON)*, 1–6.

Mahor, V., Rawat, R., Telang, S., Garg, B., Mukhopadhyay, D., & Palimkar, P. (2021). Machine Learning based Detection of Cyber Crime Hub Analysis using Twitter Data. *2021 IEEE 4th International Conference on Computing, Power and Communication Technologies (GUCON)*, 1–5.

Norbutas, L. (2018). Offline constraints in online drug marketplaces: An exploratory analysis of a cryptomarket trade network. *The International Journal on Drug Policy, 56*, 92–100. doi:10.1016/j.drugpo.2018.03.016 PMID:29621742

Norbutas, L., Ruiter, S., & Corten, R. (2020). Reputation transferability across contexts: Maintaining cooperation among anonymous cryptomarket actors when moving between markets. *The International Journal on Drug Policy, 76*, 102635. doi:10.1016/j.drugpo.2019.102635 PMID:31972474

Pennington, J., Socher, R., & Manning, C. D. (2014). Glove: Global vectors for word representation. *Proceedings of the 2014 Conference on Empirical Methods in Natural Language Processing (EMNLP)*, 1532–1543. 10.3115/v1/D14-1162

Rajawat, A. S., Rawat, R., Barhanpurkar, K., Shaw, R. N., & Ghosh, A. (2021a). Blockchain-Based Model for Expanding IoT Device Data Security. *Advances in Applications of Data-Driven Computing*, 61.

Rajawat, A. S., Rawat, R., Barhanpurkar, K., Shaw, R. N., & Ghosh, A. (2021b). Vulnerability Analysis at Industrial Internet of Things Platform on Dark Web Network Using Computational Intelligence. *Computationally Intelligent Systems and Their Applications*, 39–51.

Rajawat, A. S., Rawat, R., Mahor, V., Shaw, R. N., & Ghosh, A. (2021). Suspicious Big Text Data Analysis for Prediction—On Darkweb User Activity Using Computational Intelligence Model. In *Innovations in Electrical and Electronic Engineering* (pp. 735–751). Springer. doi:10.1007/978-981-16-0749-3_58

Rajawat, A. S., Rawat, R., Shaw, R. N., & Ghosh, A. (2021). Cyber Physical System Fraud Analysis by Mobile Robot. In *Machine Learning for Robotics Applications* (pp. 47–61). Springer. doi:10.1007/978-981-16-0598-7_4

Rawat, R., Dangi, C. S., & Patil, J. (2011). Safe Guard Anomalies against SQL Injection Attacks. *International Journal of Computers and Applications*, 22(2), 11–14. doi:10.5120/2558-3511

Rawat, R., Mahor, V., Chirgaiya, S., & Garg, B. (2021). Artificial Cyber Espionage Based Protection of Technological Enabled Automated Cities Infrastructure by Dark Web Cyber Offender. In Intelligence of Things: AI-IoT Based Critical-Applications and Innovations (pp. 167–188). Springer. doi:10.1007/978-3-030-82800-4_7

Rawat, R., Mahor, V., Chirgaiya, S., & Rathore, A. S. (2021). Applications of Social Network Analysis to Managing the Investigation of Suspicious Activities in Social Media Platforms. In *Advances in Cybersecurity Management* (pp. 315–335). Springer. doi:10.1007/978-3-030-71381-2_15

Rawat, R., Mahor, V., Chirgaiya, S., Shaw, R. N., & Ghosh, A. (2021a). Analysis of Darknet Traffic for Criminal Activities Detection Using TF-IDF and Light Gradient Boosted Machine Learning Algorithm. In *Innovations in Electrical and Electronic Engineering* (pp. 671–681). Springer. doi:10.1007/978-981-16-0749-3_53

Rawat, R., Mahor, V., Chirgaiya, S., Shaw, R. N., & Ghosh, A. (2021b). Sentiment Analysis at Online Social Network for Cyber-Malicious Post Reviews Using Machine Learning Techniques. *Computationally Intelligent Systems and Their Applications*, 113–130.

Rawat, R., Mahor, V., Rawat, A., Garg, B., & Telang, S. (2021). Digital Transformation of Cyber Crime for Chip-Enabled Hacking. In *Handbook of Research on Advancing Cybersecurity for Digital Transformation* (pp. 227–243). IGI Global. doi:10.4018/978-1-7998-6975-7.ch012

Rawat, R., Rajawat, A. S., Mahor, V., Shaw, R. N., & Ghosh, A. (2021a). Dark Web—Onion Hidden Service Discovery and Crawling for Profiling Morphing, Unstructured Crime and Vulnerabilities Prediction. In *Innovations in Electrical and Electronic Engineering* (pp. 717–734). Springer. doi:10.1007/978-981-16-0749-3_57

Rawat, R., Rajawat, A. S., Mahor, V., Shaw, R. N., & Ghosh, A. (2021b). Surveillance Robot in Cyber Intelligence for Vulnerability Detection. In *Machine Learning for Robotics Applications* (pp. 107–123). Springer. doi:10.1007/978-981-16-0598-7_9

Rehurek, R., & Sojka, P. (2011). Gensim--python framework for vector space modelling. NLP Centre, Faculty of Informatics, Masaryk University.

Reksna, T. (2017). *Complex network analysis of Darknet black market forum structure*. Academic Press.

Simpson, S. S., Adams, N., Brugman, C. M., & Conners, T. J. (2018). Detecting novel and emerging drug terms using natural language processing: A social media corpus study. *JMIR Public Health and Surveillance*, *4*(1), e2. doi:10.2196/publichealth.7726 PMID:29311050

van der Sanden, R., Wilkins, C., Romeo, J. S., Rychert, M., & Barratt, M. J. (2021). Predictors of using social media to purchase drugs in New Zealand: Findings from a large-scale online survey. *The International Journal on Drug Policy*, *98*, 103430. doi:10.1016/j.drugpo.2021.103430 PMID:34487954

Vyas, P., Liu, J., & El-Gayar, O. (2021). Fake News Detection on the Web: An LSTM-based Approach. *AMCIS 2021 Proceedings*, 5. https://aisel.aisnet.org/amcis2021/virtual_communities/virtual_communities/5

Vyas, P., Reisslein, M., Rimal, B. P., Vyas, G., Basyal, G. P., & Muzumdar, P. (2021). Automated Classification of Societal Sentiments on Twitter with Machine Learning. *IEEE Transactions on Technology and Society*, 1–1. doi:10.1109/TTS.2021.3108963

Wang, X., Peng, P., Wang, C., & Wang, G. (2018). You are your photographs: Detecting multiple identities of vendors in the darknet marketplaces. *Proceedings of the 2018 on Asia Conference on Computer and Communications Security*, 431–442. 10.1145/3196494.3196529

Zhang, Y., Fan, Y., Song, W., Hou, S., Ye, Y., Li, X., Zhao, L., Shi, C., Wang, J., & Xiong, Q. (2019). Your style your identity: Leveraging writing and photography styles for drug trafficker identification in darknet markets over attributed heterogeneous information network. *The World Wide Web Conference*, 3448–3454. 10.1145/3308558.3313537

Zhang, Y., Qian, Y., Fan, Y., Ye, Y., Li, X., Xiong, Q., & Shao, F. (2020). dStyle-GAN: Generative Adversarial Network based on Writing and Photography Styles for Drug Identification in Darknet Markets. *Annual Computer Security Applications Conference*, 669–680. 10.1145/3427228.3427603

Zhao, F., Skums, P., Zelikovsky, A., Sevigny, E. L., Swahn, M. H., Strasser, S. M., Huang, Y., & Wu, Y. (2020). Computational approaches to detect illicit drug ads and find vendor communities within social media platforms. *IEEE/ACM Transactions on Computational Biology and Bioinformatics*. PMID:32149652

Compilation of References

Abbasi, A., & Chen, H. (2007). Affect intensity analysis of dark Web forums. *Security Informatics*.

Abbasi, M., Shahraki, A., & Taherkordi, A. (2021). Deep learning for network traffic monitoring and analysis (ntma): A survey. *Computer Communications*, *170*, 19–41. doi:10.1016/j.comcom.2021.01.021

Abrams, L. (2021). *HDDCryptor Ransomware Overwrites Your MBR Using Open Source Tools*. Retrieved 20 October 2021, from https://www.bleepingcomputer.com/news/security/hddcryptor-ransomware-overwrites-your-mbr-using-open-source-tools/

Aburomman, A. A., & Reaz, M. B. I. (2016). A novel SVM-kNN-PSO ensemble method for intrusion detection system. *Applied Soft Computing*, *38*, 360–372. doi:10.1016/j.asoc.2015.10.011

Açar, K. V. (2017). Webcam child prostitution: An exploration of current and futuristic methods of detection. *International Journal of Cyber Criminology, 11*(1), 98-109.

Aceto, G., Ciuonzo, D., Montieri, A., & Pescapé, A. (2019). Mobile encrypted traffic classification using deep learning: Experimental evaluation, lessons learned, and challenges. *IEEE eTransactions on Network and Service Management*, *16*(2), 445–458. doi:10.1109/TNSM.2019.2899085

Aceto, G., Ciuonzo, D., Montieri, A., & Pescapé, A. (2021). DISTILLER: Encrypted traffic classification via multimodal multitask deep learning. *Journal of Network and Computer Applications*, *183-184*, 102985. doi:10.1016/j.jnca.2021.102985

Agarap, A. F. M. (2018, February). A neural network architecture combining gated recurrent unit (GRU) and support vector machine (SVM) for intrusion detection in network traffic data. In *Proceedings of the 2018 10th International Conference on Machine Learning and Computing* (pp. 26-30). 10.1145/3195106.3195117

Agra, Erola, Goldsmith, & Creese. (2016). *A tripwire grammar for insider threat detection*. Presented at the *Int. Workshop Manag. Insider Secur. Threats (MIST)*.

Ahmad, M., Younis, T., Habib, M. A., Ashraf, R., & Ahmed, S. H. (2019). A review of current security issues in Internet of Things. *Recent trends and advances in wireless and IoT-enabled networks*, 11-23.

Ahmad, I., Basheri, M., Iqbal, M. J., & Rahim, A. (2018). Performance comparison of support vector machine, random forest, and extreme learning machine for intrusion detection. *IEEE Access: Practical Innovations, Open Solutions*, *6*, 33789–33795. doi:10.1109/ACCESS.2018.2841987

Ahmad, M., Abdullah, M., & Han, D. (2019). A novel encoding scheme for complex neural architecture search. *Proceedings of the 2019 34th International Technical Conference on Circuits/Systems, Computers and Communications (ITC-CSCC)*, 1–4.

Ahmad, M., Riaz, Q., Zeeshan, M., Tahir, H., Haider, S. A., & Khan, M. S. (2021). Intrusion detection in internet of things using supervised machine learning based on application and transport layer features using UNSW-NB15 dataset. *EURASIP Journal on Wireless Communications and Networking, 2021*(1), 1–23. doi:10.118613638-021-01893-8

Ahmed, M., Mahmood, A. N., & Islam, M. R. (2016). A survey of anomaly detection techniques in financial domain. *Future Generation Computer Systems, 55*, 278–288. doi:10.1016/j.future.2015.01.001

Ahmed, A. A., Jabbar, W. A., Sadiq, A. S., & Patel, H. (2020). Deep learning-based classification model for botnet attack detection. *Journal of Ambient Intelligence and Humanized Computing, 2020*, 1–10. doi:10.100712652-020-01848-9

Akhoondi, M., Yu, C., & Madhyastha, H. V. (2012). LASTor: A low-latency AS-aware tor client. *IEEE/ACM Transactions on Networking, 22*(6), 1742–1755. doi:10.1109/SP.2012.35

Al Nabki, M. W., Fidalgo, E., Alegre, E., & de Paz, I. (2017). Classifying illegal activities on tor network based on Web textual contents. *Computational Linguistics,* 1.

Aldossari, S., Alqahtani, F., Alshahrani, N., Alhammam, M., Alzamanan, R., Aslam, N., & Irfanullah. (2020). *A Comparative Study of Decision Tree and Naïve Bayes Machine Learning Model for Crime Category Prediction in Chicago.* doi:10.1145/3379247.3379279

Aldridge, J., & Décary-Hétu, D. (2016). Hidden wholesale: The drug diffusing capacity of online drug crypto markets. *International Journal of Drug Policy, 35*, 7–15. doi:10.1016/j.drugpo.2016.04.020

AldridgeJ.Décary-HétuD. (2014). 'Not an Ebay for Drugs': The cryptomarket silk road as a paradigm shifting criminal innovation. *Social Sci. Res. Netw.* doi:10.2139/ssrn.2436643

Aldweesh, Derhab, & Emam. (2019). Deep learning approaches for anomaly-based intrusion detection systems: A survey, taxonomy, and open issues. Academic Press.

Alenezi, M., Almustafa, K., & Meerja, K. A. (2019). Cloud based SDN and NFV architectures for IoT infrastructure. *Egypt Inform J., 20*(1), 1–10. doi:10.1016/j.eij.2018.03.004

Alghamdi, H., & Selamat, A. (2022). *Techniques to detect terrorists/extremists on the dark web: a review.* Data Technologies and Applications. doi:10.1108/DTA-07-2021-0177

Alghazo, J., Rathee, G., Gupta, S., Quasim, M. T., Murugan, S., Latif, G., & Dhasarathan, V. (2020). A Secure Multimedia Processing through Blockchain in Smart Healthcare Systems. *ACM Trans. Multimedia Comput. Commun. Appl.* . doi:10.1145/3396852

Algorithmia. (2021, May 17). *How machine learning works.* Algorithmia Blog. https://algorithmia.com/blog/how-machine-learning-works#how-does-machine-learning-work

Al-Khater, W. A., Al-Maadeed, S., Ahmed, A. A., Sadiq, A. S., & Khan, M. K. (2020). Comprehensive Review of Cybercrime Detection Techniques. *IEEE Access: Practical Innovations, Open Solutions, 8*, 137293–137311. doi:10.1109/ACCESS.2020.3011259

Almiani, AbuGhazleh, Al-Rahayfeh, & Atiewi. (2019). *Deep recurrent neural network for IoT intrusion detection system.* Academic Press.

Almuammar, M., & Fasli, M. (2019). Deep Learning for Non-stationary Multivariate Time Series Forecasting. *2019 IEEE International Conference on Big Data (Big Data)*, 2097–2106. 10.1109/BigData47090.2019.9006192

Almukaynizi, M., Grimm, A., Nunes, E., Shakarian, J., & Shakarian, P. (2017). Predicting cyber threats through hacker social networks in Darkweb and Deepweb forums. In *Proceedings of the 2017 International Conference of the Computational Social Science Society of the Americas (CSS 2017)*. Association for Computing Machinery.

Almukaynizi, M., Paliath, V., Shah, M., Shah, M., Shakarian, P., & Cryptocurrency, F. (2018). Attack indicators using temporal logic and Darkweb data. *Proceedings of the 2018 IEEE International Conference on Intelligence and Security Informatics (ISI)*, 91–93.

Al-Nabki, M. W., Fidalgo, E., & Mata, J. V. (2019). Darkner: A platform for named entity recognition in tor darknet. *Jornadas Nacionales de Investigación en Ciberseguridad*, *1*, 279-280.

Al-Nabki, M. W., Janez-Martino, F., Vasco-Carofilis, R. A., Fidalgo, E., & Velasco-Mata, J. (2020). Improving Named Entity Recognition in Tor Darknet with Local Distance Neighbour Feature. arXiv preprint arXiv:2005.08746

AlQahtani, A. A., & El-Alfy, E. M. (2015). Anonymous connections basedon onion routing: A review and a visualization tool. *Procedia Computer Science, 52*, 121–128. doi:10.1016/j.procs.2015.05.040

Al-Qatf, M., Lasheng, Y., Al-Habib, M., & Al-Sabahi, K. (2018). Deep learning approach combining sparse autoencoder with SVM for network intrusion detection. *IEEE Access: Practical Innovations, Open Solutions*, *6*, 52843–52856. doi:10.1109/ACCESS.2018.2869577

Alsaedi, N., & Burnap, P. (2015, August). Feature extraction and analysis for identifying disruptive events from social media. In *Proceedings of the 2015 IEEE/ACM International Conference on Advances in Social Networks Analysis and Mining 2015* (pp. 1495-1502). 10.1145/2808797.2808867

Alsaedi, N., Hashim, F., Sali, A., & Rokhani, F. Z. (2017). Detecting sybil attacks in clustered wireless sensor networks based on energy trust system (ETS). *Computer Communications*, *110*, 75–82. doi:10.1016/j.comcom.2017.05.006

Alurkar, A. A. (2019). *A Comparative Analysis and Discussion of Email Spam Classification Methods Using Machine Learning Techniques*. Applied Machine Learning for Smart Data Analysis. doi:10.1201/9780429440953-10

Amir, N., Latif, R., Shafqat, N., & Latif, S. (2020). Crowdsourcing Cybercrimes through Online Resources. *2020 13th International Conference on Developments in eSystems Engineering (DeSE)*, 158-163. 10.1109/DeSE51703.2020.9450747

Ampel, B., Samtani, S., Zhu, H., Ullman, S., & Chen, H. (2020). Labeling hacker exploits for proactive cyber threat intelligence: a deep transfer learning approach. *Proceedings of the 2020 IEEE International Conference on Intelligence and Security Informatics (ISI)*, 1–6. 10.1109/ISI49825.2020.9280548

Anam, M., Shafiq, B., Shamail, S., Chun, S. A., & Adam, N. (2019, June).Discovering Events from Social Media for Emergency Planning. In *Proceedings of the 20th Annual International Conference on Digital Government Research* (pp. 109-116). 10.1145/3325112.3325213

Andleeb, S., Ahmed, R., Ahmed, Z., & Kanwal, M. (2019). Identification and Classification of Cybercrimes using Text Mining Technique. *2019 International Conference on Frontiers of Information Technology (FIT)*, 227-2275. 10.1109/FIT47737.2019.00050

Andy Greenberg. (2017). *The Reaper IoT Botnet Has Already Infected a Million Networks*. https://www.wired.com/story/reaper-iot-botnetinfected-million-networks/

Ani, L. (2015). Cyber Crime and National Security: The Role of the Penal and Procedural Law. Nigerian Institute of Advanced Legal Studies.

Armstrong, R., Hall, B. J., Doyle, J., & Waters, E. (2011). Scoping the scope of a cochrane review. *Journal of Public Health, 33*(1), 147–150. doi:10.1093/pubmed/fdr015

Arnold, N., Ebrahimi, M., Zhang, N., Lazarine, B., Patton, M., Chen, H., & Samtani, S. (2019). Dark-net ecosystem cyber-threat intelligence (CTI) tool. In *IEEE international conference Intellettuale Security Informat*. Intercollegiate Studies Institute.

Asadi, M., Jamali, M. A. J., Parsa, S., & Majidnezhad, V. (2020). Detecting botnet by using particle swarm optimization algorithm based on voting system. *Future Generation Computer Systems, 107*, 95–111. doi:10.1016/j.future.2020.01.055

Associates, A. (2021). *Piping botnet: Researchers warns of possible cyberattacks against urban water services*. Retrieved 19 October 2021, from https://securityaffairs.co/wordpress/75389/hacking/piping-botnet-water-services.html

Austin, J., Kennedy, J., & Lees, K. (1995). A neural architecture for fast rule matching. *Proceedings of the Second New Zealand International Two-Stream Conference on Artificial Neural Networks and Expert Systems*, 255–260.

Avarikioti, G., Brunner, R., Kiayias, A., Wattenhofer, R., & Zindros, D. (2018). Structure and content of the visible Darknet. arXiv preprint arXiv:1811.01348

Backman, B. (2013). *Follow the white rabbit: An ethnographic exploration nto the drug culture concealed within the deep web*. Universidad Nebraska Omaha, Tech. Rep. UMI 1551711.

Bailey, M., Cooke, E., Jahanian, F., Myrick, A., & Sinha, S. (2006). Practicaldarknet measurement. *40th Annu. Conf. Inf. Sci. Syst.*

Bamakan, S. M. H., Wang, H., & Shi, Y. (2017). Ramp loss K-Support Vector Classification-Regression; a robust and sparse multi-class approach to the intrusion detection problem. *Knowledge-Based Systems, 126*, 113–126. doi:10.1016/j.knosys.2017.03.012

Bancroft, A., & Scott Reid, P. S. (2017). Challenging the techno-politics of anonymity: The case of cryptomarket users. *Information, Communication and Society, 20*(4), 497–512. doi:10.1080/1369118X.2016.1187643

Banerjee, U., Juvekar, C., Wright, A., & Chandrakasan, A. P. (2018, February). An energy-efficient reconfigurable DTLS cryptographic engine for End-to-End security in iot applications. In *2018 IEEE International Solid-State Circuits Conference-(ISSCC)* (pp. 42-44). IEEE. 10.1109/ISSCC.2018.8310174

Bannister, A. (2022). *New York Attorney General flags 1.1 million online accounts compromised by credential stuffing attacks* [Blog]. Retrieved 24 January 2022, from https://portswigger.net/daily-swig/new-york-attorney-general-flags-1-1-million-online-accounts-compromised-by-credential-stuffing-attacks

Bao, Z., Shi, W., He, D., & Chood, K. K. R. (2018). *Iotchain: A three-tier blockchain-based iot security architecture*. arXiv preprint arXiv:1806.02008.2018

Baravalle, A., Lopez, M. S., & Lee, S. W. (2016). *Mining the dark Web:drugs and fake IDS*. Presented at the IEEE 16th Int. Conf. Data Mining Workshops (ICDMW).

Baravalle, A., Lopez, M. S., & Lee, S. W. (2016, December). Mining the dark web: drugs and fake ids. In *2016 IEEE 16th International Conference on Data Mining Workshops (ICDMW)* (pp. 350-356). IEEE. 10.1109/ICDMW.2016.0056

Barratt, M. J., Ferris, J. A., & Winstock, A. R. (2016). Safer scoring? Cryptomarkets, social supply and drug market violence. *The International Journal on Drug Policy, 35*, 24–31. doi:10.1016/j.drugpo.2016.04.019 PMID:27241015

Barthe, G., Grégoire, B., & Laporte, V. (2018). Secure Compilation of Side-Channel Countermeasures: The Case of Cryptographic "Constant-Time". *2018 IEEE 31st Computer Security Foundations Symposium (CSF)*, 328-343. doi:10.1109/CSF.2018.00031

Bates, R. (2016). Tracking lone wolf terrorists. *The Journal of Public and Professional Sociology, 8*(1), 6.

Bauer, K., McCoy, D., Grunwald, D., Kohno, T., & Sicker, D. (2007). *Low resource outing attacks against tor.* Presented at the *ACM Workshop Privacy Electron.*

Baza, M. (n.d.). Detecting Sybil Attacks using Proofs of Work and Location in VANETs. *IEEE Transactions on Dependable and Secure Computing.* Advance online publication. doi:10.1109/TDSC.2020.2993769

Baza, M., Nabil, M., Mahmoud, M. M. E. A., Bewermeier, N., Fidan, K., Alasmary, W., & Abdallah, M. (2020). Detecting sybil attacks using proofs of work and location in vanets. *IEEE Transactions on Dependable and Secure Computing.*

BBC News. (2021). *Hacker tries to poison water supply of Florida city.* Retrieved from https://www.bbc.com/news/world-us-canada-55989843

Beckham, K., & Prohaska, A. (2012). Deviant men, prostitution, and the Internet: A qualitative analysis of men who killed prostitutes whom they met online. *International Journal of Criminal Justice Sciences, 7*(2), 635-648.

Benjamin, V., Li, W., Holt, T., & Chen, H. (2015). Exploring threats and vulnerabilities in hacker web: Forums, irc and carding shops. In *Intelligence and Security Informatics (ISI), 2015 IEEE International Conference on* (pp. 85–90). IEEE.

Beshiri, A. S., & Susuri, A. (2019). Dark web and its impact in online anonymity and privacy: A critical analysis and review. *Journal of Computer and Communications, 7*(03), 30–43. doi:10.4236/jcc.2019.73004

Bhagoji, A. N., Cullina, D., & Mittal, P. (2017). *Dimensionality reduction as a defense against evasion attacks on machine learning classifiers.* arXiv preprint arXiv:1704.02654

Bhalerao, R., Aliapoulios, M., Shumailov, I., Afroz, S., & McCoy, D. (2019). Mapping the Underground: Supervised Discovery of Cybercrime Supply Chains. *2019 APWG Symposium on Electronic Crime Research (eCrime),* 1-16. 10.1109/eCrime47957.2019.9037582

Bhardwaj, A., Mangat, V., & Vig, R. (2020). Hyperband Tuned deep neural network with well posed stacked sparse Auto-Encoder for detection of DDoS attacks in cloud. *IEEE Access: Practical Innovations, Open Solutions, 8,* 181916–181929. doi:10.1109/ACCESS.2020.3028690

Bhatia, V., Choudhary, S., & Ramkumar, K. R. (2020, June). A Comparative Study on Various Intrusion Detection Techniques Using Machine Learning and Neural Network. In *2020 8th International Conference on Reliability, Infocom Technologies and Optimization (Trends and Future Directions)(ICRITO)* (pp. 232-236). IEEE. 10.1109/ICRITO48877.2020.9198008

Bhattacharjya, A., Zhong, X., Wang, J., & Li, X. (2020). CoAP—application layer connection-less lightweight protocol for the Internet of Things (IoT) and CoAP-IPSEC Security with DTLS Supporting CoAP. In *Digital Twin Technologies and Smart Cities* (pp. 151–175). Springer. doi:10.1007/978-3-030-18732-3_9

Bilen, A., & Özer, A. B. (2021). Cyber-attack method and perpetrator prediction using machine learning algorithms. *PeerJ. Computer Science, 7,* e475. doi:10.7717/peerj-cs.475 PMID:33954249

Billel, A., & Faycal, H. (2017). On Markov-switching periodic ARMA models. *Communications in Statistics, 47*(2), 344–364.

BinJubier, Ahmed, Ismail, Sadiq, & Khan. (2019). *Comprehensive Survey on Big Data Privacy Protection.* Academic Press.

Birkinshaw, C., Rouka, E., & Vassilakis, V. (2019). Implementing an intrusion detection and prevention system using software-defined networking: Defending against port-scanning and denialof-service attacks. Academic Press.

Bleau, H. (2019). *Social media and the digital transformation of Cybercrime.* https://www.rsa.com/enus/blog/2019-04/social-media-and-the-digital-transformation-ofcybercrime

Blei, D. M., Ng, A. Y., & Jordan, M. I. (2003). Latent dirichlet allocation. *Journal of Machine Learning Research, 3*, 993–1022.

Bracci, A., Nadini, M., Aliapoulios, M., McCoy, D., Gray, I., Teytelboym, A., ... Baronchelli, A. (2008). *The COVID-19 online shadow economy*. Academic Press.

Branwen, G., Christin, N., Décary-Hétu, D., & Andersen, R. M. (2015). *Dark Net Market archives, 2011-2015*. https://www.gwern.net/DNM-archives

Breitinger, F., Astebol, K. P., Baier, H., & Busch, C. (2013). MvHash-B_A new approach for similarity preserving hashing. Presented at the *7th Int. Conf. It Secur. Incident Management It Forensics*.

Breitinger, F., & Baier, H. (2012). Similarity preserving hashing: Eligible properties and a new algorithm MRSH-v2. Presented at the *Int. Conf. Digit. Forensics Cyber Crime*.

BroadhurstR.LordD.MaximD.Woodford-SmithH.JohnstonC.ChungH. W.SabolB. (2018). *Malware trends on 'darknet' crypto-markets: Research review*. doi:10.2139/ssrn.3226758

Broséus, J., Rhumorbarbe, D., Mireault, C., Ouellette, V., Crispino, F., & Décary-Hétu, D. (2016). Studying illicit drug trafficking on Darknet markets: Structure and organisation from a Canadian perspective. *Forensic Science International, 264*, 7–14. doi:10.1016/j.forsciint.2016.02.045 PMID:26978791

Brown, S. (2019). *Cybercriminals ramping up fraud attacks on social media, says report*. CNET. https://www.cnet.com/news/cybercriminals-are-ramping-up-fraudattacks-on-social-media-says-report/

Bryans, D. (2014). Bitcoin and money laundering: Mining for an effective solution. *Industrial Law Journal, 89*(1), 441.

Bu, Z., Xia, Z., & Wang, J. (2013). A sock puppet detection algorithm on virtual spaces. *Knowledge-Based Systems, 37*, 366–377. doi:10.1016/j.knosys.2012.08.016

Bublea, A., & Caleanu, C. D. (n.d.). *Deep Learning based Eye Gaze Tracking for Automotive Applications: An Auto-Keras Approach*. Academic Press.

Buehner, M., & Young, P. (2006). A tighter bound for the echo state property. *IEEE Transactions on Neural Networks, 17*(3), 820–824. doi:10.1109/TNN.2006.872357 PMID:16722187

Builtin. (n.d.). *What is artificial intelligence? How does AI work?* https://builtin.com/artificial-intelligence

Burguera, I., Zurutuza, U., & Nadjm-Tehrani, S. (2011, October). Crowdroid: behavior-based malware detection system for android. In *Proceedings of the 1st ACM workshop on Security and privacy in smartphones and mobile devices* (pp. 15-26). 10.1145/2046614.2046619

Burhan, M., Rehman, R. A., Khan, B., & Kim, B. S. (2018). IoT elements, layered architectures and security issues: A comprehensive survey. *Sensors (Basel), 18*(9), 2796. doi:10.339018092796 PMID:30149582

Burhanuddin, M. A., Mohammed, A. A. J., Ismail, R., Hameed, M. E., Kareem, A. N., & Basiron, H. (2018). A review on security challenges and features in wireless sensor networks: IoT perspective. *Journal of Telecommunication, Electronic and Computer Engineering (JTEC), 10*(1-7), 17-21.

Buxton, J., & Bingham, T. (2015). The rise and challenge of dark net drug markets. *Policy Brief, 7*, 1-24.

Caiani, M., & Parenti, L. (2009). The dark side of the Web: Italian right-wingextremist groups and the Internet. *South European Society and Politics, 14*(3), 273–294. doi:10.1080/13608740903342491

Calis, T. (2018). *Multi-homing sellers and loyal buyers on darknet markets* [Unpublished Masters Thesis]. Erasmus University, the Netherlands.

Cam-Winget, N., Sadeghi, A. R., & Jin, Y. (2016, June). Can IoT be secured: Emerging challenges in connecting the unconnected. In *2016 53nd ACM/EDAC/IEEE Design Automation Conference (DAC)* (pp. 1-6). IEEE.

Can, F., Kocberber, S., Baglioglu, O., Kardas, S., Ocalan, H. C., & Uyar, E. (2010). New event detection and topic tracking in Turkish. *Journal of the American Society for Information Science and Technology, 61*(4), 802–819. doi:10.1002/asi.21264

Cao, K., Li, X., Ma, W., & Grishman, R. (2018). Including new patterns to improve event extraction systems. In *Florida AI Conference*. AAAI.

Casey, W., Kellner, A., Memarmoshrefi, P., Morales, J. A., & Mishra, B. (2018). Deception, identity, and security: The game theory of sybil attacks. *Communications of the ACM, 62*(1), 85–93. doi:10.1145/3190836

Catakoglu, O., Balduzzi, M., & Balzarotti, D. (2017). Attacks landscape in the dark side of the Web. Presented at the Symp. Appl. Comput. SAC.

Celestini, A., Me, G., & Mignone, M. (2017). *Tor marketplaces exploratory data analysis: The drugs case*. Presented at the Int. Conf. Global Secur., Saf. Sustainability.

Celestini, G. M., & Mignone, M. (2017). Tor marketplaces exploratory data analysis: The drugs case. *Int. Conf. Global Secur., Saf., Sustainability*.

Chakrabarti, S. (2001, April). Integrating the document object model with hyperlinks for enhanced topic distillation and information extraction. In *Proceedings of the 10th International Conference on World Wide Web* (pp. 211-220). 10.1145/371920.372054

Chakrabarti, S., Joshi, M., & Tawde, V. (2001, September). Enhanced topic distillation using text, markup tags, and hyperlinks. In *Proceedings of the 24th Annual International ACM SIGIR Conference on Research and Development in Information Retrieval* (pp. 208-216). 10.1145/383952.383990

Chakrabarti, S., Van den Berg, M., & Dom, B. (1999). Focused crawling: A new approach to topic-specific web resource discovery. *Computer Networks, 31*(11), 1623–1640. doi:10.1016/S1389-1286(99)00052-3

Chalapathy & Chawla. (2019). *Deep learning for anomaly detection: A survey*. arXiv preprint:1901.03407.

Chandre, P. R., Mahalle, P. N., & Shinde, G. R. (2018, November). Machine learning based novel approach for intrusion detection and prevention system: A tool based verification. In *2018 IEEE Global Conference on Wireless Computing and Networking (GCWCN)* (pp. 135-140). IEEE. 10.1109/GCWCN.2018.8668618

Chang, D., Ghosh, M., Sanadhya, S. K., Singh, M., & White, D. R. (2019). FbHash: A new similarity hashing scheme for digital forensics. *Digital Investigation, 29*, S113–S123. doi:10.1016/j.diin.2019.04.006

Channe, S., Paul, J., & Wei, J. (2009). The future gamma-ray burst mission SVOM. *Proceedings of Science*.

Chaudhari, R. R., & Patil, S. P. (2017). Intrusion detection system: Classification,techniques and datasets to implement. *International Research Journal of Engineering and Technology, 4*(2).

Chauhan, S., & Vig, L. (2015). Anomaly detection in ECG time signals via deep long short-term memory networks. *IEEE International Conference on Data Science and Advanced Analytics (DSAA)*, 1–7. 10.1109/DSAA.2015.7344872

Chen, H. (2008, June). Sentiment and affect analysis of dark web forums: Measuring radicalization on the internet. In *2008 IEEE International Conference on Intelligence and Security Informatics* (pp. 104-109). IEEE.

Chen, M., & Ghorbani, A. A. (2019). A survey on user pro_ling model foranomaly detection in cyberspace. *J. Cyber Secur. Mobility, 8*(1), 75-112.

Chen, Z., & Ji, H. (2009, June). Language specific issue and feature exploration in Chinese event extraction. In *Proceedings of Human Language Technologies: The 2009 Annual Conference of the North American Chapter of the Association for Computational Linguistics, Companion Volume: Short Papers* (pp. 209-212). 10.3115/1620853.1620910

Chen, C., Liu, B., Wan, S., Qiao, P., & Pei, Q. (2021). An edge traffic flow detection scheme based on deep learning in an intelligent transportation system. *IEEE Transactions on Intelligent Transportation Systems, 22*(3), 1840–1852. doi:10.1109/TITS.2020.3025687

Cheng, L., Li, J., Silva, Y. N., Hall, D. L., & Liu, H. (2019). Xbully: Cyberbullying detection within a multi-modal context. In *Proceedings of the Twelfth ACM International Conference on Web Search and Data Mining* (pp. 339-347). ACM. 10.1145/3289600.3291037

Cheng, M., Crow, M., & Erbacher, R. F. (2013). Vulnerability analysis of a smart grid with monitoring and control system. In *Proceedings of the Eighth Annual Cyber Security and Information Intelligence Research Workshop*. ACM. 10.1145/2459976.2460042

Chen, H. (2011). *Dark web: Exploring and data mining the dark side of the web* (Vol. 30). Springer Science & Business Media.

Chen, H. (2011). *Dark web: Exploring and data mining the dark side of the Web, 30*. Springer.

Chen, H., Chung, W., Qin, J., Reid, E., Sageman, M., & Weimann, G. (2008, June). Uncovering the dark Web: A case study of jihad on the Web. *Journal of the American Society for Information Science and Technology, 59*(8), 1347–1359. doi:10.1002/asi.20838

Chen, Y., Liu, S., Zhang, X., Liu, K., & Zhao, J. 2017.Automatically labelled data generation for large scale event extraction. In *Proceedings of the 55th Annual Meeting of the Association for Computational Linguistics (*Volume 1*: Long Papers)* (pp. 409–419). 10.18653/v1/P17-1038

Chen, Y., Xu, L., Liu, K., Zeng, D., & Zhao, J. (2015, July).Event extraction via dynamic multi-pooling convolutional neural networks. In *Proceedings of the 53rd Annual Meeting of the Association for Computational Linguistics and the 7th International Joint Conference on Natural Language Processing (*Volume 1*: Long Papers)* (pp. 167-176). 10.3115/v1/P15-1017

Cherqi, O., Mezzour, G., Ghogho, M., & El Koutbi, M. (2018). *Analysis of hacking related trade in the darkweb*. Presented at the IEEE Int. Conf. Intell. Security Informatics (ISI).

Cherqi, O., Mezzour, G., Ghogho, M., & el Koutbi, M. (2018). Analysis of hacking related trade in the Darkweb. *Proceedings of the 2018 IEEE International Conference on Intelligence and Security Informatics (ISI)*, 79–84.

Chertoff, M., & Simon, T. (2015). *The impact of the darkWeb on Internet governanceand cyber security*. Centre Int. Governance Innovation (CIGI), Waterloo, ON, Canada, Tech. Rep. 6.

Chitra, R., & Seenivasagam, V. (2015). Heart Disease Prediction System Using Intelligent Network. *Power Electronics and Renewable Energy Systems, 326*(134), 1377–1384.

Christin, N. (2013). *Traveling the silk road: A measurement analysis of a large anonymous online marketplace*. Presented at the 22nd Int. Conf. World Wide Web. 10.1145/2488388.2488408

Chun, S. A., Avinash Paturu, V., Yuan, S., Pathak, R., Atluri, V., & Adam, R., N. (2019). Crime Prediction Model using Deep Neural Networks. *Proceedings of the 20th Annual International Conference on Digital Government Research*, 512–514. 10.1145/3325112.3328221

Ciancaglini, V., Balduzzi, M., Goncharov, M., & McArdle, R. (2013). *Deep web and cybercrime.* Trend Micro Rep. 9.

Cil, A. E., Yildiz, K., & Buldu, A. (2021). Detection of DDoS attacks with feed forward based deep neural network model. *Expert Systems with Applications*, *169*, 114520–114530. doi:10.1016/j.eswa.2020.114520

Cimpanu. (2018). *Hide and Seek Becomes First IoT Botnet Capable of Surviving Device Reboots.* https://www.bleeping-computer.com/news/security/hide-and-seekbecomes-first-iot-botnet-capable-of-surviving-device-reboots/

Ciotti, M., Ciccozzi, M., Terrinoni, A., Jiang, W. C., Wang, C. B., & Bernardini, S. (2020). The COVID-19 pandemic. *Critical Reviews in Clinical Laboratory Sciences*, *57*(6), 365–388. doi:10.1080/10408363.2020.1783198 PMID:32645276

Claeys, T., Vučinić, M., Watteyne, T., Rousseau, F., & Tourancheau, B. (2021). Performance of the Transport Layer Security Handshake Over 6TiSCH. *Sensors (Basel)*, *21*(6), 2192. doi:10.339021062192 PMID:33801018

Clawson, H. J., & Dutch, N. (2008). *Addressing the needs of victims of human trafficking: Challenges, barriers, and promising practices. Department of Health and Human Services, Office of the Assistant Secretary.*

Cloud, S. E. K. (2021, August 30). *XVigil – Artificial intelligence based digital risk monitoring – CloudSEK.* CloudSEK – Digital Risk Management Enterprise. https://cloudsek.com/campaigns/xvigil/

Comar, P. M., Liu, L., Saha, S., Tan, P. N., & Nucci, A. (2013, April). *Combining supervised and unsupervised learning for zero-day malware detection. In 2013 Proceedings IEEE INFOCOM.* IEEE.

Constantinides, C., Shiaeles, S., Ghita, B., & Kolokotronis, N. (2019, June). A novel online incremental learning intrusion prevention system. In *2019 10th IFIP International Conference on New Technologies, Mobility and Security (NTMS)* (pp. 1-6). IEEE. 10.1109/NTMS.2019.8763842

Convenant Eyes. (2011). *The connections Between Pornography and sex Trafficking.* https://www.covenanteyes.com/2011/09/07/the-connections-between-pornographyand-sex-traf_cking/

Coulombe, J. C., York, M. C. A., & Sylvestre, J. (2017). Computing with networks of nonlinear mechanical oscillators. *PLoS One*, *12*(6), e0178663. doi:10.1371/journal.pone.0178663 PMID:28575018

Cranford, C. (2015). *Dangerous apps on Your Teen's mobile device.* https://www.cybersafetycop.com/dangerous-apps-on-your-teens-mobile-device/

Cruzes, D. S., & Dyba, T. (2011). *Recommended steps for thematic synthesis insoftware engineering.* Presented at the Int. Symp. Empirical Software Engineering Meas.

Cuellar, M.-F. (2002). The tenuous relationship between thought against money laundering and the disruption of criminal finance. *The Journal of Criminal Law & Criminology*, *93*(2), 311.

Curiel, R. P., Cresci, S., Muntean, C. I., & Bishop, S. R. (2020). Crime and its fear in social media. *Palgrave Communications*, *6*(1), 57. Advance online publication. doi:10.105741599-020-0430-7

Cutting-edge Tech Solutions for Seniors and Caregivers. (2021). Retrieved 27 November 2021, from https://zanthion.com/about-us/

Da Cruz, M. A., Rodrigues, J. J., Lorenz, P., Solic, P., Al-Muhtadi, J., & Albuquerque, V. H. C. (2019). A proposal for bridging application layer protocols to HTTP on IoT solutions. *Future Generation Computer Systems*, *97*, 145–152.

Dahal, B., & Kim, Y. (2019). AutoEncoded domains with mean activation for DGA botnet detection. *International Conference on Global Security, Safety and Sustainability IEEE*, 208-212. 10.1109/ICGS3.2019.8688037

Dale, M., Miller, J. F., Stepney, S., & Trefzer, M. A. (2016). Evolving carbon nanotube reservoir computers. *Lecture Notes in Computer Science*, 49–61. doi:10.1007/978-3-319-41312-9_5

Dalins, J., Wilson, C., & Carman, M. (2018). Criminal motivation on the dark web: A categorisation model for law enforcement. *Digital Investigation*, 24, 62–71. doi:10.1016/j.diin.2017.12.003

Dalvi, A., Paranjpe, S., Amale, R., Kurumkar, S., Kazi, F., & Bhirud, S. G. (2021, May). SpyDark: Surface and Dark Web Crawler. In *2021 2nd International Conference on Secure Cyber Computing and Communications (ICSCCC)* (pp. 45-49). IEEE.

Damgård, I. B. (1989). *A design principle for hash functions*. Presented at the Conf. Theory Appl. Cryptol.

Danial, J., Das, D., Ghosh, S., Raychowdhury, A., & Sen, S. (2020). SCNIFFER: Low-Cost, Automated, Efficient Electromagnetic Side-Channel Sniffing. *IEEE Access: Practical Innovations, Open Solutions*, 8, 173414–173427. doi:10.1109/ACCESS.2020.3025022

Das, T. A., & Gosavi, M. S. S. (2019). *Artificial intelligence and machine learning as a double-edge sword in cyber world*. Academic Press.

Das, K. C., Maden, A. D., Cangül, I. N., & Çevik, A. S. (2017). On average eccentricity of graphs. *Proceedings of the National Academy of Sciences. India. Section A, Physical Sciences*, 87(1), 23–30. doi:10.100740010-016-0315-8

DeBlasio, J., Savage, S., Voelker, G. M., & Snoeren, A. C. (2017). *Tripwire: Inferring Internet site compromise*. Presented at the *Internet Meas. Conf.*

Décary-Hétu, D., & Giommoni, L. (2017). Do police crackdowns disrupt drugcryptomarkets? A longitudinal analysis of the effects of operation onymous. *Crime, Law and Social Change, 67*(1), 55–75. doi:10.1007/s10611-016-9644-4

DeepDotWeb. (2015). *Mr. Nice Guy. Marketadmin. Tells His Story*. https://gir.pub/deepdotweb/2015/06/03/interview-with-mr-niceguy-market-admin/

Demertzis, K., & Iliadis, L. (2014). A hybrid network anomaly and intrusion detection approach based on evolving spiking neural network classification. *Communications in Computer and Information Science*, 11–23. doi:10.1007/978-3-319-11710-2_2

Demertzis, K., & Iliadis, L. (2014). Evolving computational intelligence system for Malware detection. In *Lecture Notes in Business Information Processing* (pp. 322–334). Springer. doi:10.1007/978-3-319-07869-4_30

Demertzis, K., & Iliadis, L. (2015). Evolving smart URL filter in a zone-based policy firewall for detecting algorithmically generated malicious domains. *Lecture Notes in Computer Science*, 223–233. doi:10.1007/978-3-319-17091-6_17

Demertzis, K., & Iliadis, L. (2020). GeoAI: A model-agnostic meta-ensemble zero-shot learning method for hyperspectral image analysis and classification. *Algorithms*, 13(3), 61. doi:10.3390/a13030061

Demertzis, K., Iliadis, L. S., & Anezakis, V.-D. (2018). Extreme deep learning in biosecurity: The case of machine hearing for marine species identification. *Journal of Information and Telecommunication*, 2(4), 492–510. doi:10.1080/24751839.2018.1501542

Demertzis, K., Iliadis, L., & Anezakis, V.-D. (2018). *A dynamic ensemble learning framework for data stream analysis and real-time threat detection*. In Lecture Notes in Computer Science. Springer. doi:10.1007/978-3-030-01418-6_66

Demertzis, K., Iliadis, L., & Bougoudis, I. (2020). Gryphon: A semi-supervised anomaly detection system based on one-class evolving spiking neural network. *Neural Computing & Applications, 32*(9), 4303–4314. doi:10.100700521-019-04363-x

Demertzis, K., Iliadis, L., Tziritas, N., & Kikiras, P. (2020). Anomaly detection via blockchained deep learning smart contracts in industry 4.0. *Neural Computing & Applications, 32*(23), 17361–17378. doi:10.100700521-020-05189-8

Department of Health. (2020). https://www.unb.ca/cic/datasets/dohbrw-2020.html

Deshmukh, S., & Sonavane, S. S. (2017, March). Security protocols for Internet of Things: A survey. In *2017 International conference on Nextgen electronic technologies: Silicon to software (ICNETS2)* (pp. 71-74). IEEE.

Devlin, J., Chang, M., Lee, K., & Toutanova, K. (2018). *BERT: Pre-training of deep bidirectional transformers for language understanding.* CoRR abs/1810.04805.

Dhanabal, L., & Shantharajah, D. S. P. (2015). A study on NSL-KDD dataset for intrusion detection system based on classification algorithms. *International Journal of Advanced Research in Computer and Communication Engineering, 4,* 7.

Dhanda, S. S., Singh, B., & Jindal, P. (2020). Lightweight cryptography: A solution to secure IoT. *Wireless Personal Communications, 112*(3), 1947–1980.

Dhote, Y., Agrawal, S., & Deen, A. J. (2015). A survey on feature selection techniques for Internet traffic classification. *Proceedings of the 2015 International Conference on Computational Intelligence and Communication Networks (CICN),* 1375–1380.

Ding, H., Jiang, T., & Riloff, E. (2018, June). Why is an event affective? Classifying affective events based on human needs. *Workshops at the Thirty-Second AAAI Conference on Artificial Intelligence.*

Ding, J., Guo, X., & Chen, Z. (2020). Big data analyses of ZeroNet sites for exploring the new generation DarkWeb. In *Proceedings of the 3rd International Conference on Software Engineering and Information Management (ICSIM2020)* (pp. 46–52). Association for Computing Machinery.

Ding, H., & Riloff, E. (2018, June). Human needs categorization of affective events using labeled and unlabeled data. In *Proceedings of the 2018 Conference of the North American Chapter of the Association for Computational Linguistics: Human Language Technologies,* Volume 1 *(Long Papers)* (pp. 1919-1929). 10.18653/v1/N18-1174

Ding, H., Riloff, E., & Feng, Z. (2019, June). Improving Human Needs Categorization of Events with Semantic Classification. In *Proceedings of the Eighth Joint Conference on Lexical and Computational Semantics (* SEM 2019)* (pp. 198-204). 10.18653/v1/S19-1022

Ding, J., Guo, X., & Chen, Z. (2020, January). Big data analyses of zeronet sites for exploring the new generation darkweb. In *Proceedings of the 3rd International Conference on Software Engineering and Information Management* (pp. 46-52). 10.1145/3378936.3378981

Dingledine, R., Mathewson, N., & Syverson, P. (2004). *Tor: The second generation onion router.* Naval Research Laboratory, Tech. Rep.

Diodati, J., & Winterdyk, J. (2021). Dark Web: The Digital World of Fraud and Rouge Activities. In Handbook of Research on Theory and Practice of Financial Crimes (pp. 477-505). IGI Global.

Dizdarevic, J., Carpio, F., Jukan, A., & Masip-Bruin, X. (2019). A survey of communication protocols for internet of things and related challenges of fog and cloud computing integration. *ACM Computing Surveys, 51*(6), 1–29,116.

DNStats. (2019). *Dark Net STATS.* https://dnstats.net/

Dolliver, D. S., & Kenney, J. L. (2016). Characteristics of drug vendors on thetor network: A cryptomarket comparison. *Victims and Offenders, 11*(4), 600–620. doi:10.1080/15564886.2016.1173158

Dong, F., Yuan, S., Ou, H., & Liu, L. (2018, November). New cyber threat discovery from darknet marketplaces. In *2018 IEEE Conference on Big Data and Analytics (ICBDA)* (pp. 62-67). IEEE. 10.1109/ICBDAA.2018.8629658

DouglasL. J.MontgomeryC.KulahciM. (2015). https://www.wiley.com/en-us/Introduction+to+Time+Series+Analysis+and+Forecasting%2C+2nd+Edition-p-9781118745113

Dredge, S. (2013). *What is tor? A Beginner's Guide to the Privacy Tool.* https://www.theguardian.com/technology/2013/nov/05/tor-beginnersguide-

Dughi, P. (2016). *17 Times social media helped police track downthieves, murderers, and gang criminals.* Medium. https://medium.com/the-mission/17-times-social-media-helped-policetrack-down-thieves-murderers-and-gang-criminals-a814b6c40fb

Dyrmishi, S., Elshawi, R., & Sakr, S. (2019). A decision support framework for AutoML systems: A meta-learning approach. *Proceedings of the 2019 International Conference on Data Mining Workshops (ICDMW)*, 97–106.

Ebrahimi, M., Nunamaker, J. F., & Chen, H. (2020). Semi-supervised cyber threat identification in dark net markets: A transductive and deep learning approach. *Journal of Management Information Systems, 37*(3), 694–722.

Ehney, R., & Shorter, J. D. (2016). Deep Web, dark Web, invisible Web and the post isis world. *Information Systems, 17*(4), 36-41.

Ek, B., Ver Schneider, C., & Narayan, D. A. (2015). Global efficiency of graphs. AKCE. *International Journal of Graphs and Combinatorics, 12*(1), 1–13. doi:10.1016/j.akcej.2015.06.001

Eliasi, M., Raeisi, G., & Taeri, B. (2012). Wiener index of some graph operations. *Discrete Applied Mathematics, 160*(9), 1333–1344. doi:10.1016/j.dam.2012.01.014

EMCDDA. (2017). *Drugs and the darknet. Perspectives for enforcement, research and policy.* doi:10.2810/834620

Erb, K. P. (2019). IRS followed bitcoin transactions, resulting in takedown of the largest child exploitation site on the Web. *Forbes.* https://www.forbes.com/sites/kellyphillipserb/2019/10/16/irs-followed-bitcoin-transactionsresulting-in-takedown-of-the-largest-child-exploitation-site-on-theweb/#327343231ed0

Erhan, D., & Anarim, E. (2020). Hybrid DDoS detection framework using matching pursuit algorithm. *IEEE Access: Practical Innovations, Open Solutions, 8*, 118912–118923. doi:10.1109/ACCESS.2020.3005781

Evans, N. S., Dingledine, R., & Grothoff, C. (2009). *A practical congestion attack on tor using long paths.* Presented at the USENIX Secur. Symp.

Faizan, M., & Khan, R. A. (2019). Exploring and analysing the dark Web: A new alchemy. *First Monday.* Advance online publication. doi:10.5210/fm.v24i5.9473

Faizan, M., & Khan, R. A. (2020). A Two-Step Dimensionality Reduction Scheme for Dark Web Text Classification. In *Ambient Communications and Computer Systems* (pp. 303–312). Springer. doi:10.1007/978-981-15-1518-7_25

Fan, W., Du, Z., Fernandez, D., & Villagra, V. A. (2018). Enabling an an atomic view to investigate honeypot systems: A survey. *IEEE Systems Journal, 12*(4), 3906–3919. doi:10.1109/JSYST.2017.2762161

Fang, W., Tan, X., & Wilbur, D. (2020). Application of intrusion detection technology in network safety based on machine learning. *Safety Science, 124*, 104604. doi:10.1016/j.ssci.2020.104604

Fanusie, Y., & Robinson, T. (2018). Bitcoin laundering: An analysis of illicit *flows into digital currency services*. Center Sanctions Illicit Finance Memorandum.

Faruki, P., Bharmal, A., Laxmi, V., Ganmoor, V., Gaur, M. S., Conti, M., & Rajarajan, M. (2014). Android security: A survey of issues, malware penetration, and defenses. *IEEE Communications Surveys and Tutorials*, *17*(2), 998–1022. doi:10.1109/COMST.2014.2386139

Fei, H., Dong, H., & Wang, Z. (2018). Improved Tobit Kalman filtering for systems withcrandom parameters via conditional expectation. *Signal Processing*, *147*, 35–45. doi:10.1016/j.sigpro.2018.01.015

Feng, Huang, Tang, Ji, Qin, & Liu. (2016). A languageindependent neural network for event detection. *Proceedings of the 54th Annual Meeting of the Association for Computational Linguistics*, 66–71.

Ferencz, Domokos, & Kovács. (2021). Review of Industry 4.0 Security Challenges. *2021 IEEE 15th International Symposium on Applied Computational Intelligence and Informatics (SACI)*, 245-248. doi: 10.1109/SACI51354.2021.9465613

Fernquist, J., Kaati, L., & Schroeder, R. (2018). *Political bots and the Swedishgeneral election.* Presented at the IEEE Int. Conf. Intell. Security Informatics (ISI).

Findlaw. (2021, December 21). *Dark web crimes.* https://www.findlaw.com/criminal/criminal-charges/dark-web-crimes.html

Finklea. (2015). Dark Web. *Proc. Congressional Res. Service*, 1-16.

Foley, S., Karlsen, J. R., & Putniņš, T. J. (2019). Sex, drugs, and bitcoin: How much illegal activity is financed through cryptocurrencies? *Review of Financial Studies*, *32*(5), 1798–1853. doi:10.1093/rfs/hhz015

Frustaci, M., Pace, P., Aloi, G., & Fortino, G. (2017). Evaluating critical security issues of the IoT world: Present and future challenges. *IEEE Internet of Things Journal, 5*(4), 2483-2495.

Fu, T., Abbasi, A., & Chen, H. (2010). A focused crawler for dark web forums. *Journal of the American Society for Information Science and Technology*, *61*(6), 1213–1231. doi:10.1002/asi.21323

Gaharwar, R. S., & Gupta, R. (2020). Review of cyber security threats and proposed trustworthy memory acquisition mechanism. *Journal of Discrete Mathematical Sciences and Cryptography*, *23*(1), 137–144. doi:10.1080/09720529.2020.1721877

Gaharwar, R. S., & Gupta, R. (2020). Vulnerability assessment of android instant messaging application and network intrusion detection prevention systems. *Journal of Statistics and Management Systems*, *23*(2), 399–406. doi:10.1080/09720510.2020.1744314

Gaharwar, R. S., & Gupta, R. (2020, February). Android data leakage and anomaly based Intrusion detection System. In *2nd International Conference on Data, Engineering and Applications (IDEA)* (pp. 1-5). IEEE. 10.1109/IDEA49133.2020.9170738

Gai, K., Qiu, M., Tao, L., & Zhu, Y. (2016). Intrusion detection techniques formobile cloud computing in heterogeneous 5G. *Security and Communication Networks, 9*(16), 3049–3058. doi:10.1002/sec.1224

Galushka, V., Marshakov, D., & Fathi, V. (2017). Dynamic document object model formation technique for corporate website protection against automatic coping of information. In *MATEC Web of Conferences* (Vol. 132, p. 05001). EDP Sciences. 10.1051/matecconf/201713205001

García-Holgado, A., & García-Peñalvo, F. J. (2018). *Mapping the systematicliterature studies about software ecosystems.* Presented at the 6th Int. Conf. Technol. Ecosystems Enhancing Multiculturality (TEEM). 10.1145/3284179.3284330

Garrahan, J. (2018). *Authorship detection in dark web marketplaces using lstm and rnn neural networks*. Academic Press.

Geluvaraj, B., Satwik, P., & Kumar, T. A. (2019). The future of cybersecurity: Major role of artificial intelligence machine learning and deep learning in cyberspace. *International Conference on Computer Networks and Communication Technologies*, 739-747. 10.1007/978-981-10-8681-6_67

Ghappour, A. (2017). Searching places unknown: Law enforcement jurisdiction on the dark Web. *Stanford Law Review*, *69*(4), 1075.

Ghosh, S., Das, A., Porras, P., Yegneswaran, V., & Gehani, A. (2017, August). Automated categorization of onion sites for analysing the darkweb ecosystem. In *Proceedings of the 23rd ACM SIGKDD International Conference on Knowledge Discovery and Data Mining* (pp. 1793-1802). ACM.

Ghosh, S., Porras, P., Yegneswaran, V., Nitz, K., & Das, A. (2017, March). ATOL: A framework for automated analysis and categorisation of the Darkweb Ecosystem. *Workshops at the Thirty-First AAAI Conference on Artificial Intelligence.*

Ghosh, S., Das, A., Porras, P., Yegneswaran, V., & Gehani, A. (2017). Automated categorization of onion sites for analyzing the darkweb ecosystem. *Proceedings of the 23rd ACM SIGKDD International Conference on Knowledge Discovery and Data Mining*, 1793–1802. 10.1145/3097983.3098193

Gonzalez-Amarillo, C., Cardenas-Garcia, C., Mendoza-Moreno, M., Ramirez-Gonzalez, G., & Corrales, J. C. (2021). Blockchain-IoT Sensor (BIoTS): A Solution to IoT-Ecosystems Security Issues. *Sensors (Basel)*, *21*(13), 4388.

Goodfellow, Pouget-Abadie, Mirza, Xu, Warde-Farley, Ozair, Courville, &. Bengio. (2014). Generative adversarial nets. Advances in Neural Information Processing Systems, 27.

Grishman, R., & Sundheim, B. (1996). Message understanding conference 6: A brief history. *16th International Conference on Computational Linguistics.*

Gunnarsson, M., Brorsson, J., Palombini, F., Seitz, L., & Tiloca, M. (2021). Evaluating the performance of the OSCORE security protocol in constrained IoT environments. *Internet of Things*, *13*, 100333.

Gupta, S., & Bhatia, K. K. (2017). Optimal query generation for hidden web extraction through response analysis. *The Dark Web: Breakthroughs in Research and Practice*, *2001*, 65–83. doi:10.4018/978-1-5225-3163-0.ch005

Haasio, A., Harviainen, J. T., & Savolainen, R. (2020). Information needs of drug users on a local dark Web marketplace. *Information Processing & Management*, *57*(2), 102080. doi:10.1016/j.ipm.2019.102080

HaddadPajouh, H., Dehghantanha, A., Khayami, R., & Choo, K.-K. R. (2018). A deep Recurrent Neural Network based approach for Internet of Things malware threat hunting. *Future Generation Computer Systems*, *85*, 88–96. doi:10.1016/j.future.2018.03.007

Hage, P., & Harary, F. (1995). Eccentricity and centrality in networks. *Social Networks*, *17*(1), 57–63. doi:10.1016/0378-8733(94)00248-9

Hamamreh, J. M., Furqan, H. M., & Arslan, H. (2018). Classifications and applications of physical layer security techniques for confidentiality: A comprehensive survey. *IEEE Communications Surveys and Tutorials*, *21*(2), 1773–1828.

Hamborg, F., Breitinger, C., Schubotz, M., Lachnit, S., & Gipp, B. (2018, May). Extraction of main event descriptors from news articles by answering the journalistic five W and one H questions. In *Proceedings of the 18th ACM/IEEE on Joint Conference on Digital Libraries* (pp. 339-340). 10.1145/3197026.3203899

Hamborg, F., Donnay, K., & Gipp, B. (2019). Automated identification of media bias in news articles: An interdisciplinary literature review. *International Journal on Digital Libraries*, *20*(4), 391–415. doi:10.100700799-018-0261-y

Hamborg, F., Lachnit, S., Schubotz, M., Hepp, T., & Gipp, B. (2018, March). Giveme5W: main event retrieval from news articles by extraction of the five journalistic w questions. In *International conference on information* (pp. 356-366). Springer. 10.1007/978-3-319-78105-1_39

Hamdan, S., Hudaib, A., & Awajan, A. (2021). Detecting Sybil attacks in vehicular ad hoc networks. *International Journal of Parallel, Emergent and Distributed Systems, 36*(2), 69–79.

Hamed, A., & Khalek, A. A. (2019). Acoustic Attacks in the Era of IoT - A Survey. *2019 Amity International Conference on Artificial Intelligence (AICAI)*, 855-858. 10.1109/AICAI.2019.8701340

Haroon, A., Akram, S., Shah, M. A., & Wahid, A. (2017, September). E-Lithe: A lightweight secure DTLS for IoT. In *2017 IEEE 86th Vehicular Technology Conference (VTC-Fall)* (pp. 1-5). IEEE.

He, S., He, Y., & Li, M. (2019, March). Classification of illegal activities on the dark web. In *Proceedings of the 2019 2nd International Conference on Information Science and Systems* (pp. 73-78). 10.1145/3322645.3322691

He, S., He, Y., & Li, M. (2021). Classification of illegal activities on the dark web. In *Proceedings of the 2019 2nd International Conference on Information Science and Systems (ICISS 2019). Electronics.* Association for Computing Machinery.

Heistracher, C., Mignet, F., & Schlarb, S. (2020). Machine Learning Techniques for the Classification of Product Descriptions from Darknet Marketplaces. In *International Conference on Applied Informatics* (pp. 128-137). Academic Press.

Hendricks, C., Hendricks, J. E., & Kauffman, S. (2000). *Literacy, Criminal Activity, and Recidivism.* https://www.americanreadingforum.org/yearbook/yearbooks/01_yearbook/pdf/12_hendricks.pdf

Hinton, G. E., Srivastava, N., Krizhevsky, A., Sutskever, I., & Salakhutdinov, R. R. (2012). *Improving neural networks by preventing co-adaptation of feature detectors.* arXiv preprint arXiv:1207.0580.

Hofer-Schmitz, K., & Stojanović, B. (2019, November). Towards formal methods of IoT application layer protocols. In *2019 12th CMI conference on cybersecurity and privacy (CMI)* (pp. 1-6). IEEE.

Holt, T. J., & Lampke, E. (2010). Exploring stolen data markets online: Products and market forces. *Criminal Justice Studies, 23*(1), 33–50. doi:10.1080/14786011003634415

Holt, T. J., Strumsky, D., Smirnova, O., & Kilger, M. (2012). Examining the social networks of worm writers and hackers. *International Journal of Cyber Criminology, 6*(1), 891–903.

Honnibal, M., & Montani, I. (2017). spaCy 2: Natural language understanding with Bloom embeddings, convolutional neural networks and incremental parsing. *To Appear, 7*(1), 411–420.

Huang, C., Guo, Y., Guo, W., & Li, Y. (2021). HackerRank: Identifying key hackers in underground forums. *International Journal of Distributed Sensor Networks, 17*(5). doi:10.1177/15501477211015145

Huang, C., Zong, Y., Chen, J., Liu, W., Lloret, J., & Mukherjee, M. (2021). A deep segmentation network of stent structs based on IoT for interventional cardiovascular diagnosis. *IEEE Wireless Communications, 28*(3), 36–43.

Huang, G., Zhu, Q., & Siew, C. (2006). Extreme learning machine: Theory and applications. *Neurocomputing, 70*(1–3), 489–501. doi:10.1016/j.neucom.2005.12.126

Hu, C., Yin, M., Liu, B., Li, X., & Ye, Y. (2021). Identifying Illicit Drug Dealers on Instagram with Large-scale Multimodal Data Fusion. *ACM Transactions on Intelligent Systems and Technology, 12*(5), 1–23. doi:10.1145/3472713

Hussain, F., Abbas, S. G., Shah, G. A., Pires, I. M., Fayyaz, U. U., Shahzad, F., Garcia, N. M., & Zdravevski, E. (2021). A Framework for Malicious Traffic Detection in IoT Healthcare Environment. *Sensors (Basel)*, *21*, 3025. https://doi.org/10.3390/s21093025

Hutcheon, P. D., & Warren, R. (2021). *Under the Cover of Darkness: Insider Trading and the Dark Web*. https://www.natlawreview.com/article/under-cover-darkness-insider-trading-and-dark-web

Hu, W., Li, M., Yuan, C., Zhang, C., & Wang, J. (2020). Diversity in neural architecture search. n *Proceedings of the 2020 International Joint Conference on Neural Networks (IJCNN)*, 1–8.

Hyndman, R. J., & Athanasopoulos, G. (2018). *Forecasting: Principles and practice* (2nd ed.). OTexts.

IEC 61784-1:2014: Industrial communication networks – Profiles – Part 1: Fieldbus profiles. 2014https://webstore.iec.ch/publication/5878

Iliou, C., Kalpakis, G., Tsikrika, T., Vrochidis, S., & Kompatsiaris, I. (2017). Hybrid focused crawling on the Surface and the Dark Web. *EURASIP Journal on Information Security*, *2017*(1), 1–13.

innefuLabs. (n.d.). *How artificial intelligence in policing helps crime detection*. Innefu.Com.

Iqbal, N., Technology, C., & Lanka, S. (2020). *COVID-19 Outbreak Forecast Model using FbProphet*. Academic Press.

Irwin-Rogers, K. (2019). Illicit drug markets, consumer capitalism and the rise of social media: A toxic trap for young people. *Critical Criminology*, *27*(4), 591–610. doi:10.100710612-019-09476-2

ISA99. Developing the ISA/IEC 62443 Series of Standards on Industrial Automation and Control Systems (IACS). 2017http://isa99.isa.org/ISA9920Wiki/ Home.aspx/

ISA99. Developing the Vital ISA/IEC 62443 Series of Standards on Industrial Automation and Control Systems (IACS) Security. 2001http://isa99.isa.org/

ISO/IEC 27019 Information technology – security techniques – information security controls for the energy utility industry. 2017https://www.iso.org/standard/68091.html

ISO/IEC 27033-1:2015 Preview Information Technology-Security techniques –Network security – Part 1: Overview and concepts. 2015https://www.iso.org/standard/63461.html

ISO/IEC 29180: 2012 Information technology – Telecommunications and information exchange between systems – Security framework forubiquitous sensor networks. 2012https://www.iso.org/standard/45259.html

ISO/IEC TR 27019:2013: Information technology – security techniques – information security management guidelines based on ISO/IEC 27002 for process control systems specific to the energy utility industry. 2013https://www.iso.org/standard/43759.html

Jacobs, G., Lefever, E., & Hoste, V. (2018, July). Economic event detection in company-specific news text. In *Proceedings of the First Workshop on Economics and Natural Language Processing* (pp. 1-10). 10.18653/v1/W18-3101

Jagadeesan, S., & Amutha, B. (2021). An efficient botnet detection with the enhanced support vector neural network. *Measurement*, *176*, 109140–109151. doi:10.1016/j.measurement.2021.109140

Jain, A. K., Goel, D., Agarwal, S., Singh, Y., & Bajaj, G. (2020). Predicting Spam Messages Using Back Propagation Neural Network. *Wireless Personal Communications*, *110*(1), 403–422. doi:10.100711277-019-06734-y

Jamali, M. A. J., Bahrami, B., Heidari, A., Allahverdizadeh, P., & Norouzi, F. (2020). IoT security. In *Towards the Internet of Things* (pp. 33–83). Springer.

Jameel, F., Wyne, S., Kaddoum, G., & Duong, T. Q. (2019). A comprehensive survey on cooperative relaying and jamming strategies for physical layer security. *IEEE Communications Surveys and Tutorials*, *21*(3), 2734–2771.

James, J. Q. (2020). Sybil attack identification for crowdsourced navigation: A self-supervised deep learning approach. *IEEE Transactions on Intelligent Transportation Systems*.

Janze, C. (2017). Are cryptocurrencies criminals best friends? Examining the co-evolution of bitcoin and darknet markets. *Amer. Conf. Inf. Syst. (AMCIS)*. https://aisel.aisnet.org/amcis2017/InformationSystems/Presentations/2

Jawbone Announces New UP App for Smartphones, Smartwatches and Wearables. (2021). Retrieved 20 December 2021, from https://www.prnewswire.com/news-releases/jawbone-announces-new-up-app-for-smartphones-smartwatches-and-wearables-274541851.html

Ji, H., & Grishman, R. (2008). Refining event extraction through cross-document inference. *Proceedings of the 46th Annual Meeting of the Association for Computational Linguistics*, 254–262.

Jin, H., Song, Q., & Hu, X. (2019). *Auto-keras: An efficient neural architecture search system*. https://arxiv.org/abs/1806.10282

Jordan, T., & Taylor, P. (1998). A sociology of hackers. *The Sociological Review*, *46*(4), 757–780. doi:10.1111/1467-954X.00139

Joshi, A., Fidalgo, E., Alegre, E., & Al Nabki, M. W. (2018). Extractive text summarisation in dark web: A preliminary study. *International Conference of Applications of Intelligent Systems*.

Jump, M. (2019). Fighting Cyberthreats with Technology Solutions. *Biomedical Instrumentation & Technology*, *53*(1), 38–43. doi:10.2345/0899-8205-53.1.38 PMID:30702913

Kadar, C., Iria, J., & Pletikosa, I. (2016). KDD - Urban Computing WS '16. doi:10.1145/1235

Kamble, A., & Bhutad, S. (2018, January). Survey on Internet of Things (IoT) security issues & solutions. In *2018 2nd International Conference on Inventive Systems and Control (ICISC)* (pp. 307-312). IEEE.

Kamel, M., Keyvani, N., & Yazdi, H. S. (2018). Sentimental content analysis and knowledge extraction from news articles. arXiv preprint arXiv:1808.03027

Karie, N. M., Kebande, V. R., & Venter, H. (2019). Diverging deep learning cognitive computing techniques into cyber forensics. Academic Press.

Karmakar, K.K., Varadharajan, V., Nepal, S., & Tupakula, U. (2019). SDN enabled secure IoT architecture. In *2019 IFIP/IEEE symposium on integrated network and service management (IM)* (pp. 581-585). IEEE.

Kasim, M., Zhang, F., & Wang, Q. (2013). Estrada Index of Graphs. Academic Press.

Kasongo & Sun. (2019). *A Deep Long Short-Term Memory based classifier for Wireless Intrusion Detection System*. Academic Press.

Kawaguchi, Y., & Ozawa, S. (2019, December). Exploring and identifying malicious sites in dark web using machine learning. In *International Conference on Neural Information Processing* (pp. 319-327). Springer.

Kerschke, P., Hoos, H. H., Neumann, F., & Trautmann, H. (2019). Automated algorithm selection: Survey and perspectives. *Evolutionary Computation*, *27*(1), 3–45. doi:10.1162/evco_a_00242 PMID:30475672

Keshavarz, S., Saleemi, I., & Atia, G. (2017, September). Exploiting probabilistic relationships between action concepts for complex event classification. In *2017 IEEE International Conference on Image Processing (ICIP)* (pp. 1572-1576). IEEE. 10.1109/ICIP.2017.8296546

Kester, Q.-A., & Afoma, E. J. (2021). Crime Predictive Model in Cybercrime based on Social and Economic Factors Using the Bayesian and Markov Theories. *2021 International Conference on Computing, Computational Modelling and Applications (ICCMA)*, 165-170. 10.1109/ICCMA53594.2021.00034

Khan, A. F., & Anandharaj, G. (2020). A Multi-layer Security approach for DDoS detection in Internet of Things. *International Journal of Intelligent Unmanned Systems*.

Khandpur, R. P. (2017). Crowdsourcing cybersecurity: Cyber-attack detection using social media. In *Proceedings of the 2017 ACM on Conference on Information and Knowledge Management*. ACM.

Khandpur, R. P., Ji, T., Jan, S., Wang, G., Lu, C. T., & Ramakrishnan, N. (2017, November). Crowdsourcing cybersecurity: Cyber attack detection using social media. In *Proceedings of the 2017 ACM on Conference on Information and Knowledge Management* (pp. 1049-1057). 10.1145/3132847.3132866

Khare, A., Dalvi, A., & Kazi, F. (2020, July). Smart Crawler for Harvesting Deep web with multi-Classification. In *2020 11th International Conference on Computing, Communication and Networking Technologies (ICCCNT)* (pp. 1-5). IEEE. 10.1109/ICCCNT49239.2020.9225369

Khattak, H. A., Shah, M. A., Khan, S., Ali, I., & Imran, M. (2019). Perception layer security in internet of things. *Future Generation Computer Systems*, *100*, 144–164.

Khattak, H. A., Shah, M. A., Khan, S., Ali, I., & Imran, M. (2019). Perception layer security in Internet of Things. *Future Generation Computer Systems*, *100*, 144–164.

Kim, B.-H., & Pyun, J.-Y. (2020). ECG identification for personal authentication using LSTM-based deep recurrent neural networks. *Sensors (Basel)*, *20*(11), 3069. doi:10.339020113069 PMID:32485827

Kim, J. D., Ohta, T., Pyysalo, S., Kano, Y., & Tsujii, J. I. (2009, June). Overview of BioNLP'09 shared task on event extraction. In *Proceedings of the BioNLP 2009 workshop companion volume for shared task* (pp. 1-9). 10.3115/1572340.1572342

Kim, J., Sim, A., Kim, J., & Wu, K. (2020). Botnet Detection Using Recurrent VariationalAutoencoder. *GLOBECOM IEEE Global Communications Conference IEEE*, 1-6.

Koehler, E., & Van, P. (2021). *Shop Award-Winning Smart Thermometers | Kinsa Health*. Retrieved 27 November 2021, from https://kinsahealth.com/shop

Ko, I., Chambers, D., & Barrett, E. (2020). Adaptable feature-selecting and threshold-moving complete autoencoder for DDoS flood attack mitigation. *Journal of Information Security and Applications*, *55*, 102647–102657. doi:10.1016/j.jisa.2020.102647

Kolliakou, A., Ball, M., Derczynski, L., Chandran, D., & Stewart, R. (2015). *Mephedrone annotations for Twitter*. Figshare.

Koloveas, P., Chantzios, T., Alevizopoulou, S., Tryfonopoulos, S., & Tryfonopoulos, C. (2021). INTIME: A machine learning-based framework for gathering and leveraging web data to cyber-threat intelligence. *Electronics (Basel)*, *10*(7), 818.

Koloveas, P., Chantzios, T., Tryfonopoulos, C., & Skiadopoulos, S. (2019). A crawler architecture for harvesting the clear, social, and dark web for IoT-related cyber-threat intelligence. *Proceedings of the 2019 IEEE World Congress on Services*, 3–8.

Kozma, L. (2008). k Nearest Neighbors algorithm (kNN). Helsinki University of Technology.

Krishna, B. S., & Gnanasekaran, T. (2017, February). A systematic study of security issues in Internet-of-Things (IoT). In *2017 International Conference on I-SMAC (IoT in Social, Mobile, Analytics and Cloud)(I-SMAC)* (pp. 107-111). IEEE.

Krizhevsky, A., Sutskever, I., & Hinton, G. E. (2012). Imagenet classification with deep convolutional neural networks. *Advances in Neural Information Processing Systems, 25*, 1097–1105.

KumariS. (n.d.). https://timesofindia.indiatimes.com/readersblog/legal-writing/cyber-crimes-in-india-and-its-legal-remedies-35244/

Kunang, Y. N., Nurmaini, S., Stiawan, D., & Suprapto, B. Y. (2021). Attack classification of an intrusion detection system using deep learning and hyperparameter optimization. *Journal of Information Security and Applications, 58*, 102804–102814. doi:10.1016/j.jisa.2021.102804

Kwon, D., Kim, H., Kim, J., Suh, S. C., Kim, I., & Kim, K. J. (2019). A survey of deep learning-based network anomaly detection. *Cluster Computing, 22*(S1), 949–961. doi:10.100710586-017-1117-8

Lacey, D., & Salmon, P. M. (2015). It's dark in there: Using systems analysis to investigate trust and engagement in dark web forums. In D. Harris. In E. Psychology & C. Ergonomics (Eds.), *Lecture Notes in Computer Science* (Vol. 9174, pp. 117–128). Springer International Publishing.

Ladegaard, I. (2018). Instantly hooked? freebies and samples of opioids, cannabis, MDMA, and other drugs in an illicit E-commerce market. *Journal of Drug Issues, 48*(2), 226–245. doi:10.1177/0022042617746975

Lafferty, J., McCallum, A., Pereira, F., & Duh, K. (2002). Probabilistic models for segmenting and labeling sequence data. *International Conference on Machine Learning*.

Lashkari, A. H., Kaur, G., & Rahali, A. (2020). DIDarknet: A contemporary approach to detect and characterize the Darknet traffic using deep image learning. In *Proceedings of the 10th International Conference on Communication and Network Security (ICCNS 2020)* (pp. 1–13). Association for Computing Machinery.

Lawrence, H., Hughes, A., Tonic, R., & Zou, C. (2017). D-miner: A framework for mining, searching, visualizing, and alerting on darknet events. *2017 IEEE Conference on Communications and Network Security (CNS)*, 1–9. 10.1109/CNS.2017.8228628

Lee, S., Yoon, C., Kang, H., Kim, Y., Kim, Y., Han, D., . . . Shin, S. (2019, February). Cybercriminal minds: an investigative study of cryptocurrency abuses in the dark web. In *26th Annual Network and Distributed System Security Symposium (NDSS 2019)* (pp. 1-15). Internet Society. 10.14722/ndss.2019.23055

Lee, Bartlett, & Williamson. (1996). Efficient agnostic learning of neural networks with bounded fan-in. *IEEE Transactions on Information Theory, 42*(6), 2118–2132. doi:10.1109/18.556601

Lekamalage, C. K. L., Song, K., Huang, G., Cui, D., & Liang, K. (2017). Multi layer multi objective extreme learning machine. *Proceedings of the 2017 IEEE International Conference on Image Processing (ICIP)*, 1297–1301.

Leon, F. (2014). Optimizing neural network topology using Shapley value. *Proceedings of the 18th International Conference on System Theory, Control and Computing (ICSTCC)*, 862–867.

Le, Q., & Mikolov, T. (2014). Distributed representations of sentences and documents. *International Conference on Machine Learning*, 1188–1196.

Leukfeldt & Holt. (2020). Examining the social organization practices of cybercriminals in -e Netherlands online and offline. *International Journal of Offender 'erapy and Comparative Criminology, 64*(5), 522–538.

Leukfeldt, R., Kleemans, E. R., & Stol, W. P. (2017). Cybercriminal networks, social ties and online forums: Social ties versus digital ties within phishing and malware networks. *British Journal of Criminology, 57*(3), 704–722.

Leyden, J. (2021). *Tor Project unveils plans to route device traffic through Tor anonymity network with new VPN-like service* [Blog]. Retrieved 24 January 2022, from https://portswigger.net/daily-swig/tor-project-unveils-plans-to-route-device-traffic-through-tor-anonymity-network-with-new-vpn-like-service

Li, Chen, Jin, Shi, Goh, & Ng. (2019). Mad-gan: Multivariate anomaly detection for time series data with generative adversarial networks. In *International Conference on Artificial Neural Networks*. Springer. 10.1007/978-3-030-30490-4_56

Li, W., & Chen, H. (2014). *Identifying top sellers in underground economy using deep learning-based sentiment analysis*. Presented at the IEEE Joint Intell. Security Informatica Conference.

Liang, J., Ma, M., Sadiq, M., & Yeung, K.-H. J. K.-B. S. (2019). A filter model for intrusion detection system in Vehicle Ad Hoc Networks: A hidden Markov methodology (Vol. 163). Academic Press.

Liggett, Lee, Roddy, & Wallin. (2020). -e dark web as a platform for crime: an exploration of illicit drug, firearm, CSAM, and cybercrime markets. In *Palgrave Handbook of International Cybercrime and Cyberdeviance*. Palgrave Macmillan.

Lightfoot, S., & Pospisil, F. (2017). *Surveillance and privacy on the deepWeb*. ResearchGate.

Lim, Abdullah, Jhanjhi, & Khan. (2019). *Situation-Aware Deep Reinforcement Learning Link Prediction Model for Evolving Criminal Networks*. Academic Press.

Lim, M., Abdullah, A., Jhanjhi, N., Khan, M. K., & Supramaniam, M. (2019). *Link Prediction in Time-Evolving Criminal Network With Deep Reinforcement Learning Technique*. Academic Press.

Lin, Z., Feng, M., Santos, C. N. D., Yu, M., Xiang, B., Zhou, B., & Bengio, Y. (2017). *A structured self-attentive sentence embedding*. arXiv preprint arXiv:1703.03130.

Lindsey, N. (2019). Cyber criminals have turned social media cyber crime into a $3 billion business. *CPO Magazine*. https://www.cpomagazine.com/cyber-security/cyber-criminalshave-turned-social-media-cyber-crime-into-a-3-billion-business/

Lin, J., Yu, W., Zhang, N., Yang, X., Zhang, H., & Zhao, W. (2017). A survey on internet of things: Architecture, enabling technologies, security and privacy, and applications. *IEEE Internet Things J., 4*(5), 1125–1142.

Li, P., Su, J., & Wang, X. (2020). iTLS: Lightweight Transport-Layer Security Protocol for IoT With Minimal Latency and Perfect Forward Secrecy. *IEEE Internet of Things Journal, 7*(8), 6828–6841.

Lipoaie & Shortis. (n.d.). *From dealer to doorstep-How drugs are sold on the dark net*. GDPO Situation Anal. Swansea University, Global DrugsPolicy Observatory.

Liu, J., Hu, Q., Suny, R., Du, X., & Guizani, M. (2020, June). A physical layer security scheme with compressed sensing in OFDM-based IoT systems. In *ICC 2020-2020 IEEE International Conference on Communications (ICC)* (pp. 1-6). IEEE.

Liu, J., Chen, Y., Liu, K., & Zhao, J. (2018). Event detection via gated multilingual attention mechanism. *ThirtySecond AAAI Conference on Artificial Intelligence*.

Liu, S., Chen, Y., He, S., Liu, K., & Zhao, J. (2016). Leveraging Frame net to improve automatic event detection. In *Proceedings of the 54th Annual Meeting of the Association for Computational Linguistics (Volume 1: Long Papers)* (pp. 2134–2143). 10.18653/v1/P16-1201

Liu, S., Chen, Y., Liu, K., & Zhao, J. (2017, July). Exploiting argument information to improve event detection via supervised attention mechanisms. In *Proceedings of the 55th Annual Meeting of the Association for Computational Linguistics (Volume 1: Long Papers)* (pp. 1789-1798). 10.18653/v1/P17-1164

Li, Z., Zou, D., Xu, S., Jin, H., Qi, H., & Hu, J. (2016). VulPecker: an automated vulnerability detection system based on code similarity analysis. In *Proceedings of the 32nd Annual Conference on Computer Security Applications* (pp. 201–213). ACM.

Louis Columbus. (2016). *Roundup Of Internet Of Things Forecasts And Market Estimates*. https://www.forbes.com/sites /louiscolumbus/2016/11/27/roundup-ofinternet-of-things-forecasts-and-market-estimates-2016/

Lundberg, S., & Lee, S.-I. (2017). *A unified approach to interpreting model predictions*, arXiv:170507874, Ar.Xiv.

Maddox, M. J., Barratt, M. J., Allen, M., & Lenton, S. (2016). Constructive activism in the dark Web: Cryptomarkets and illicit drugs in the digital demimonde. *Information Communication and Society, 19*(1), 111–126. doi:10.1080/136 9118X.2015.1093531

Mahor, V., Rawat, R., Kumar, A., Chouhan, M., Shaw, R. N., & Ghosh, A. (2021). Cyber Warfare Threat Categorization on CPS by Dark Web Terrorist. *2021 IEEE 4th International Conference on Computing, Power and Communication Technologies (GUCON)*, 1–6.

Mahor, V., Rawat, R., Kumar, A., Chouhan, M., Shaw, R. N., & Ghosh, A. (2021, September). Cyber Warfare Threat Categorization on CPS by Dark Web Terrorist. In *2021 IEEE 4th International Conference on Computing, Power and Communication Technologies (GUCON)* (pp. 1-6). IEEE.

Mahor, V., Rawat, R., Kumar, A., Chouhan, M., Shaw, R. N., & Ghosh, A. (2021, September). Cyber Warfare Threat Categorization on CPS by Dark Web Terrorist. In *2021 IEEE 4th International Conference on Computing, Power and Communication Technologies (GUCON)* (pp. 1-6). IEEE. 10.1109/GUCON50781.2021.9573994

Mahor, V., Rawat, R., Kumar, A., Chouhan, M., Shaw, R. N., & Ghosh, A. (2021, September). Cyber Warfare Threat Categorization on CPS by Dark Web Terrorist. In *2021 IEEE 4th International Conference on Computing, Power and Communication Technologies (GUCON)* (pp. 1-6). IEEE. doi:10.1201/9781003140023-6

Mahor, V., Rawat, R., Telang, S., Garg, B., Mukhopadhyay, D., & Palimkar, P. (2021). Machine Learning based Detection of Cyber Crime Hub Analysis using Twitter Data. *2021 IEEE 4th International Conference on Computing, Power and Communication Technologies (GUCON)*, 1–5.

Mahor, V., Rawat, R., Telang, S., Garg, B., Mukhopadhyay, D., & Palimkar, P. (2021, September). Machine Learning based Detection of Cyber Crime Hub Analysis using Twitter Data. In *2021 IEEE 4th International Conference on Computing, Power and Communication Technologies (GUCON)* (pp. 1-5). 10.1109/GUCON50781.2021.9573736

Mahor, V., Rawat, R., Telang, S., Garg, B., Mukhopadhyay, D., & Palimkar, P. (2021, September). Machine Learning based Detection of Cyber Crime Hub Analysis using Twitter Data. In *2021 IEEE 4th International Conference on Computing, Power and Communication Technologies (GUCON)* (pp. 1-5). IEEE.

Makmal, A., Melnikov, A. A., Dunjko, V., & Briegel, H. J. (2016). Meta-learning within projective simulation. *IEEE Access: Practical Innovations, Open Solutions, 4*, 2110–2122. doi:10.1109/ACCESS.2016.2556579

Mamdouh, M., Awad, A. I., Khalaf, A. A. M., & Hamed, H. F. A. (2021). Authentication and Identity Management of IoHT Devices: Achievements, Challenges, and Future Directions. *Computers & Security, 111*. doi:10.1016/j.cose.2021.102491

Manjunath, G., & Jaeger, H. (2013). Echo state property linked to an input: Exploring a fundamental characteristic of recurrent neural networks. *Neural Computation, 25*(3), 671–696. doi:10.1162/NECO_a_00411 PMID:23272918

Manyumwa, T., Chapita, P. F., Wu, H., & Ji, S. (2020). Towards Fighting Cybercrime: Malicious URL Attack Type Detection using Multiclass Classification. *2020 IEEE International Conference on Big Data (Big Data)*, 1813-1822. 10.1109/BigData50022.2020.9378029

Marin, E., Diab, A., & Shakarian, P. (2016, September). Product offerings in malicious hacker markets. In *2016 IEEE conference on Intelligence and Security Informatics (ISI)* (pp. 187-189). IEEE.

Marin, E., Almukaynizi, M., Nunes, E., Shakarian, J., & Shakarian, P. (2018). Predicting hacker adoption on Darkweb forums using sequential rule mining. *Proceedings of the 2018 IEEE International Conference on Parallel and Distributed Processing with Applications, Ubiquitous Computing and Communications, Big Data and Cloud Computing, Social Computing and Networking, Sustainable Computing and Communications (ISPA/IUCC/BDCloud/SocialCom/SustainCom)*, 1183–1190.

Marin, E., Almukaynizi, M., Nunes, E., & Shakarian, P. (2018). Community finding of Malware and exploit vendors on Darkweb marketplaces. *Proceedings of the 2018 1st International Conference on Data Intelligence and Security (ICDIS)*, 81–84.

Marin, E., Almukaynizi, M., & Shakarian, P. (2019). Reasoning about future cyber-attacks through socio-technical hacking information. *Proceedings of the 2019 IEEE 31st International Conference on Tools with Artificial Intelligence (ICTAI)*, 157–164.

Mars, D., Gammar, S. M., Lahmadi, A., & Saidane, L. A. (2019). Using information centric networking in internet of things: A survey. *Wireless Personal Communications*, *105*(1), 87–103.

Masi, D., Fischer, M. J., Shortle, J. F., & Chen, C.-H. (2011). Simulating network cyber-attacks using splitting techniques. ACM. In *Proceedings of the Winter Simulation Conference* (pp. 3217–3228). Winter Simulation Conference.

Ma, W., Chen, X., & Shang, W. (2012, June). Advanced deep web crawler based on Dom. In *2012 Fifth International Joint Conference on Computational Sciences and Optimization* (pp. 605-609). IEEE.

McCallum, A. K. (2002). *Mallet: A machine learning for language toolkit.* http://mallet. cs. umass.edu

Medjek, F., Tandjaoui, D., Romdhani, I., & Djedjig, N. (2017, June). A trust-based intrusion detection system for mobile RPL based networks. In *2017 IEEE International Conference on Internet of Things (iThings) and IEEE Green Computing and Communications (GreenCom) and IEEE Cyber, Physical and Social Computing (CPSCom) and IEEE Smart Data (SmartData)* (pp. 735-742). IEEE.

Meidan, Y., Bohadana, M., Mathov, Y., Mirsky, Y., Breitenbacher, D., Shabtai, A., & Elovici, Y. (2018). N-BaIoT: Network-based Detection of IoT Botnet Attacks Using Deep Autoencoders. *IEEE Pervasive Computing*, *17*(3), 12–22. doi:10.1109/MPRV.2018.03367731

Meland, P. H., & Sindre, G. (2019, December). Cyber-attacks for sale. In *2019 International Conference on Computational Science and Computational Intelligence (CSCI)* (pp. 54-59). IEEE. 10.1109/CSCI49370.2019.00016

Meng. (2016). *Column store for gwac: a High-cadence, High-density, Large-scale astronomical light curve pipeline and distributed Shared-nothing database.* Astronomical Society of the Pacific.

Meng, W., Chao, W., & Zhang, Y. (2016). A Pre-research on GWAC Massive Catalog Data Storage and Processing System. *Tianwen Yanjiu Yu Jishu*, (3), 373–381.

Mercaldo & Santone. (2020). Deep learning for image-based mobile malware detection. *Journal of Computer Virology and Hacking Techniques*, 1-15.

Mercaldo, F., Martinelli, F., & Santone, A. (2019). Real-time SCADA attack detection by means of formal methods. *Proceedings of the 2019 IEEE 28th International Conference on Enabling Technologies: Infrastructure for Collaborative Enterprises (WETICE)*.

Messalas, A., Kanellopoulos, Y., & Makris, C. (2019). Model-agnostic interpretability with Shapley values. *Proceedings of the 2019 10th International Conference on Information, Intelligence, Systems and Applications (IISA)*, 1–7.

Michael, T., & Akbik, A. (2015, July). SCHNÄPPER: A Web Toolkit for Exploratory Relation Extraction. In *Proceedings of ACL-IJCNLP 2015 System Demonstrations* (pp. 67-72). 10.3115/v1/P15-4012

Middleton, P., Graham, C., Blackmore, D., Sharpington, K., Singh, H., Velosa, A., & Lheureux, B. (2021). *Forecast: IT Services for IoT, Worldwide, 2019-2025*. Retrieved 28 October 2021, from https://www.gartner.com/en/documents/4004741/forecast-it-services-for-iot-worldwide-2019-2025

Mikolov, T., Chen, K., Corrado, G., & Dean, J. (2013). *Efficient estimation of word representations in vector space*. arXiv preprint arXiv:1301.3781.

Millenson, M. (2021). *'The Matrix' Meets Medicine: Surveillance Swoops Into Health Care*. Retrieved 20 December 2021, from https://khn.org/news/matrix-meets-medicine/

Mirea, M., Wang, V., & Jung, J. (2019). The not so dark side of the darknet: A qualitative study. *Security Journal*, *32*(2), 102–118. doi:10.105741284-018-0150-5

Mitamura, T., Liu, Z., & Hovy, E. H. (2015). Overview of TAC KBP 2015 event nugget track. In *Text Analysis Conference*. National Institute of Standards and Technology.

Molnar, D., Piotrowski, M., Schultz, D., & Wagner, D. A. (2005). The program counter security model: Automatic detection and removal of control-flow side channel attacks. *Information Security and Cryptology - ICISC 2005 8th International Conference*, 156-168.

Molnar, C. (2020). *Interpretable machine learning*. Lulu Press.

Montieri, A., Ciuonzo, D., Bovenzi, G., Persico, V., & Pescapé, A. (2020). A dive into the DarkWeb: Hierarchical traffic classification of anonymity tools. *IEEE Transactions on Network Science and Engineering*, *7*(3), 1043–1054. doi:10.1109/TNSE.2019.2901994

Moodi, M., Ghazvini, M., & Moodi, H. (2021). A hybrid intelligent approach to detect Android Botnet using Smart Self-Adaptive Learning-based PSO-SVM. *Knowledge-Based Systems*, *222*, 106988–106996. doi:10.1016/j.knosys.2021.106988

Moore, D., & Rid, T. (2016). Cryptopolitik and the Darknet. *Survival*, *58*(1), 7–38.

Motoyama, M., McCoy, D., Levchenko, K., Savage, S., & Voelker, G. M. (2011). An analysis of underground forums. In *Proceedings of the 2011 ACM SIGCOMM conference on Internet measurement conference* (pp. 71–80). ACM.

Mrabet, H., Belguith, S., Alhomoud, A., & Jemai, A. (2020). A survey of IoT security based on a layered architecture of sensing and data analysis. *Sensors (Basel)*, *20*(13), 3625.

Müller, J.-W. (2014). On Conceptual History. In Rethinking Modern European Intellectual History. Oxford University Press. https://doi.org/10.1093/acprof:oso/9780199769230.003.0004.

Musavi, S. A., & Hashemi, M. R. (2019). HPCgnature: A hardware-based application-level intrusion detection system. *IET Information Security*, *13*(1), 19–26. doi:10.1049/iet-ifs.2017.0629

Nair, V., & Hinton, G. E. (2010, January). Rectified linear units improve restricted boltzmann machines. ICML.

Namazifar, M. (2017). *Named Entity Sequence Classification*. arXiv preprint arXiv:1712.02316.

NarnoliaN. (n.d.). https://www.legalserviceindia.com/legal/article-4998-cyber-crime-in-india-an-overview.html

Nastase, L. (2017). Security in the internet of things: a survey on application layer protocols. In *2017 21st International Conference on Control Systems and Computer Science (CSCS)* (pp. 659-666). IEEE.

Nastase, L. (2017, May). Security in the internet of things: A survey on application layer protocols. In *2017 21st international conference on control systems and computer science (CSCS)* (pp. 659-666). IEEE.

Natale, S., & Ballatore, A. (2014). The web will kill them all: New media, digital utopia, and political struggle in the Italian 5-Star Movement. *Media Culture & Society, 36*(1), 105–121. https://doi.org/10.1177/0163443713511902

Nazah, S., Huda, S., Abawajy, J., & Hassan, M. M. (2020). Evolution of Dark Web threat analysis and detection: A systematic approach. *IEEE Access: Practical Innovations, Open Solutions, 8*, 171796–171819. doi:10.1109/ACCESS.2020.3024198

Nebbione, G., & Calzarossa, M. C. (2020). Security of IoT application layer protocols: Challenges and findings. *Future Internet, 12*(3), 55.

Nguyen, Q. P., Lim, K. W., Divakaran, D. M., Low, K. H., & Chan, M. C. (2019). GEE: A Gradient-based Explainable VariationalAutoencoder for Network Anomaly Detection. *IEEE Conference on Communications and Network Security*, 91-99. 10.1109/CNS.2019.8802833

Nguyen, T. H., Fu, L., Cho, K., & Grishman, R. (2016, August).A two-stage approach for extending event detection to new types via neural networks. In *Proceedings of the 1st Workshop on Representation Learning for NLP* (pp. 158-165). 10.18653/v1/W16-1618

Nguyen, T. H., & Grishman, R. (2016). Modelling skip grams for event detection with convolutional neural networks. *Conference on Empirical Methods in Natural Language Processing*, 886–891.

Nicholls, J., Kuppa, A., & Le-Khac, N.-A. (2021). Financial Cybercrime: A Comprehensive Survey of Deep Learning Approaches to Tackle the Evolving Financial Crime Landscape. *IEEE Access: Practical Innovations, Open Solutions, 9*, 163965–163986. doi:10.1109/ACCESS.2021.3134076

NIST. (2015). *TAC KBP event track.* http://tac.nist.gov/- 2015/KBP/Event/

No Title. (n.d.). http://www.deeplearningbook.org

Norbutas, L. (2018). Offline constraints in online drug marketplaces: An exploratory analysis of a cryptomarket trade network. *The International Journal on Drug Policy, 56*, 92–100. doi:10.1016/j.drugpo.2018.03.016 PMID:29621742

Norbutas, L., Ruiter, S., & Corten, R. (2020). Reputation transferability across contexts: Maintaining cooperation among anonymous cryptomarket actors when moving between markets. *The International Journal on Drug Policy, 76*, 102635. doi:10.1016/j.drugpo.2019.102635 PMID:31972474

Nozomi Networks. (2020). *Webinar: OT/IoT Security Report 2020.* https://www.nozominetworks.com/past-events/webinar-ot-iot-security-report-2020/

NTT Com confirms possible information leak due to unauthorized access. (2021). Retrieved 19 October 2021, from https://www.ntt.com/en/about-us/press-releases/news/article/2020/0702.html

O'hare, J. (2020). *Machine learning and artificial intelligence for online investigations.* Read.Nxtbook.Com. https://read.nxtbook.com/wordsmith/evidence_technology/april_2020/machine_learning_and_artifici.html

O'Neill, M. (2016). Insecurity by design: Today's IoT device security problem. *Engineering, 2*(1), 48–49.

Okutan, A., Yang, S. J., & McConky, K. (2017). Predicting cyber-attacks with bayesian networks using unconventional signals. In *Proceedings of the 12th Annual Conference on Cyber and Information Security Research* (p. 13). ACM.

Om Kumar, C. U., & Ponsy, R. K. (2019). Detecting and confronting flash attacks from IoT botnets. *The Journal of Supercomputing*, *75*(12), 8312–8338. doi:10.100711227-019-03005-2

Owenson, G., Cortes, S., & Lewman, A. (2018). The darknet's smaller than we thought: The life cycle of Tor Hidden Services. *Digital Investigation*, *27*, 17–22. https://doi.org/10.1016/j.diin.2018.09.005

Oz, M., Zheng, P., & Chen, G. M. (2018). Twitter versus Facebook: Comparing incivility, impoliteness, and deliberative attributes. *New Media & Society*, *20*(9), 3400–3419. https://doi.org/10.1177/1461444817749516

Pacheco, F., Exposito, E., Gineste, M., Baudoin, C., & Aguilar, J. (2018). Towards the deployment of machine learning solutions in network traffic classification: A systematic survey. *IEEE Communications Surveys and Tutorials*, *21*(2), 1988–2014. doi:10.1109/COMST.2018.2883147

Padia, A., Roy, A., Satyapanich, T. W., Ferraro, F., Pan, S., Park, Y., & Finin, T. (2018). *UMBC at SemEval-2018 Task 8: Understanding text about malware*. UMBC Computer Science and Electrical Engineering Department.

Paffenroth, R. C., & Zhou, C. (2019). Modern Machine Learning for Cyber-Defense and Distributed Denial-of-Service Attacks. *IEEE Engineering Management Review*, *47*(4), 80–85. doi:10.1109/EMR.2019.2950183

Pandeeswari, N., & Kumar, G. (2016). Anomaly detection system in cloud environment using fuzzy clustering based ANN. *Mobile Networks and Applications*, *21*(3), 494–505. doi:10.100711036-015-0644-x

Pankaj, Lovekesh, & Gautam. (2015). Long Short Term Memory networks for anomaly detection in time series. *European Symposium on Artificial Neural Networks*, 89-94.

Pantelis, G., Petrou, P., Karagiorgou, S., & Alexandrou, D. (2021, August). On Strengthening SMEs and MEs Threat Intelligence and Awareness by Identifying Data Breaches, Stolen Credentials and Illegal Activities on the Dark Web. In *The 16th International Conference on Availability, Reliability and Security* (pp. 1-7). Academic Press.

Patel, N., Saridena, A. N., Choromanska, A., Krishnamurthy, P., & Khorrami, F. (2018). Adversarial learning-based online anomaly monitoring for assured autonomy. *IEEE/RSJ International Conference on Intelligent Robots and Systems (IROS)*, 6149–6154. 10.1109/IROS.2018.8593375

Patnaik, R., Padhy, N., & Raju, K. S. (2021). A systematic survey on IoT security issues, vulnerability and open challenges. In *Intelligent System Design* (pp. 723–730). Springer.

Pennington, J., Socher, R., & Manning, C. D. (2014). Glove: Global vectors for word representation. *Proceedings of the 2014 Conference on Empirical Methods in Natural Language Processing (EMNLP)*, 1532–1543. 10.3115/v1/D14-1162

Personal, M., & Archive, R. (2009). *Munich Personal RePEc Archive Determinants of crime rates : Crime Deterrence and Growth in*. Academic Press.

Phalaagae, P., Zungeru, A. M., Sigweni, B., Chuma, J. M., & Semong, T. (2020). Iot sensor networks security mechanisms/techniques. In *Green Internet of Things Sensor Networks* (pp. 97–117). Springer.

Phillips, M., & Marden, J. R. (2018). Design tradeoffs in concave cost-sharing games. *IEEE Transactions on Automatic Control*, *63*(7), 2242–2247.

Pustokhina, I. V., Pustokhin, D. A., Gupta, D., Khanna, A., Shankar, K., & Nguyen, G. N. (2020). An effective training scheme for deep neural network in edge computing enabled Internet of medical things (IoMT) systems. *IEEE Access: Practical Innovations, Open Solutions*, *8*, 107112–107123. doi:10.1109/ACCESS.2020.3000322

Puthal, D., Ranjan, R., Nepal, S., & Chen, J. (2017). IoT and big data: An architecture with data flow and security issues. In *Cloud infrastructures, services, and IoT systems for smart cities* (pp. 243–252). Springer.

Qian, Y., Jiang, Y., Chen, J., Zhang, Y., Song, J., Zhou, M., & Pustišek, M. (2018). Towards decentralized IoT security enhancement: A blockchain approach. *Computers & Electrical Engineering, 72*, 266–273.

Qiu, X., Lin, X., & Qiu, L. (2016, October). Feature representation models for cyber attack event extraction. In *2016 IEEE/WIC/ACM International Conference on Web Intelligence Workshops (WIW)* (pp. 29-32). IEEE. 10.1109/WIW.2016.020

Queiroz, A. L., Mckeever, S., & Keegan, B. (2019). Detecting hacker threats: performance of word and sentence embedding models in identifying hacker communications. *Proceedings of the 27th AIAI Irish Conference on Artificial Intelligence and Cognitive Science AICS 2019*, 116–127.

Quest, L., Charrie, A., & Roy, S. (n.d.). *The Risks And Benefits Of Using AI To Detect Crime.* Oliver Wyman. https://www.oliverwyman.com/our-expertise/insights/2018/dec/risk-journal-vol-8/rethinking-tactics/the-risks-and-benefits-of-using-ai-to-detect-crime.html

Raghuvanshi, A., & Singh, U. K. (2020). Internet of Things for smart cities-security issues and challenges. *Materials Today: Proceedings*.

Rahman, M. A., Asyhari, A. T., Wen, O. W., Ajra, H., Ahmed, Y., & Anwar, F. (2021). Effective combining of feature selection techniques for machine learning-enabled IoT intrusion detection. *Multimedia Tools and Applications, 2021*(20), 1–19. doi:10.100711042-021-10567-y

Rajaharia, R. (2022). Covid-19 Related Data Of 20,000 Indians Leaked Online. *Outlook India*. Retrieved 24 January 2022, from https://www.outlookindia.com/

Rajawat, A. S., Rawat, R., Barhanpurkar, K., Shaw, R. N., & Ghosh, A. (2021). Blockchain-Based Model for Expanding IoT Device Data Security. *Advances in Applications of Data-Driven Computing*, 61.

Rajawat, A. S., Rawat, R., Barhanpurkar, K., Shaw, R. N., & Ghosh, A. (2021). Vulnerability Analysis at Industrial Internet of Things Platform on Dark Web Network Using Computational Intelligence. *Computationally Intelligent Systems and their Applications*, 39-51.

Rajawat, A. S., Rawat, R., Barhanpurkar, K., Shaw, R. N., & Ghosh, A. (2021a). Blockchain-Based Model for Expanding IoT Device Data Security. *Advances in Applications of Data-Driven Computing*, 61.

Rajawat, A. S., Rawat, R., Barhanpurkar, K., Shaw, R. N., & Ghosh, A. (2021b). Vulnerability Analysis at Industrial Internet of Things Platform on Dark Web Network Using Computational Intelligence. *Computationally Intelligent Systems and Their Applications*, 39–51.

Rajawat, A.S., Rawat, R., Barhanpurkar, K., Shaw, R.N., & Ghosh, A.(2021). Vulnerability Analysis at Industrial Internet of Things Platform on Dark Web Network Using Computational Intelligence. *Computationally Intelligent Systems and their Applications*, 39-51.

Rajawat, A. S., Rawat, R., Mahor, V., Shaw, R. N., & Ghosh, A. (2021). Suspicious Big Text Data Analysis for Prediction—On Darkweb User Activity Using Computational Intelligence Model. In *Innovations in Electrical and Electronic Engineering* (pp. 735–751). Springer. doi:10.1007/978-981-16-0749-3_58

Rajawat, A. S., Rawat, R., Mahor, V., Shaw, R. N., & Ghosh, A. (2021). Suspicious Big Text Data Analysis for Prediction—On Darkweb User Activity Using Computational Intelligence Model. In *Innovations in Electrical and Electronic Engineering*. Springer.

Rajawat, A. S., Rawat, R., Shaw, R. N., & Ghosh, A. (2021). Cyber Physical System Fraud Analysis by Mobile Robot. In *Machine Learning for Robotics Applications* (pp. 47–61). Springer. doi:10.1007/978-981-16-0598-7_4

Rajawat, A. S., Rawat, R., Shaw, R. N., & Ghosh, A. (2021). Cyber Physical System Fraud Analysis by Mobile Robot. In *Machine Learning for Robotics Applications*. Springer.

Ramirez-alcocer, U. M., Tello-leal, E., & Mata-torres, J. A. (2019). *Predicting Incidents of Crime through LSTM Neural Networks in Smart City Domain*. Academic Press.

Ransomware Impacting Pipeline Operations | CISA. (2021). Retrieved 20 October 2021, from https://us-cert.cisa.gov/ncas/alerts/aa20-049a

Rantos, K., Drosatos, G., Demertzis, K., Ilioudis, C., & Papanikolaou, A. (2021). *Blockchain-based consents management for personal data processing in the IoT ecosystem*. https://www.scitepress.org/PublicationsDetail

Rantos, K., Drosatos, G., Demertzis, K., Ilioudis, C., Papanikolaou, A., & Kritsas, A. (2019). *ADvoCATE: A consent management platform for personal data processing in the IoT using Blockchain technology*. In Lecture Notes in Computer Science. Springer. doi:10.1007/978-3-030-12942-2_23

Rao, B. T., Patibandla, R. L., & Murty, M. R. (2020). A comparative study on effective approaches for unsupervised statistical machine translation. In *Embedded Systems and Artificial Intelligence* (pp. 895–905). Springer.

Rawat, Chouhan, Garg, Telang, Mahor, & Pachlasiya. (2021). *Malware Inputs Detection Approach (Tool) based on Machine Learning [MIDT-SVM]*. Available at SSRN: https://ssrn.com/abstract=3915404

Rawat, Kumar, Telang, Pachlasiya, Garg, Mahor, & Chouhan. (2021). Drug Trafficking crime analysis using Systematic literature Review (SLR) within Darkweb. *AIBM - 2nd International Conference on "Methods and Applications of Artificial Intelligence and Machine Learning In Heterogeneous Brains"*. Available at SSRN: https://ssrn.com/abstract=3903797

Rawat, Mahor, Pachlasiya, Garg, Telang, Chouhan, & Kumar. (2021). Twitter Crime analysis and categorization. *AIBM - 2nd International Conference on "Methods and Applications of Artificial Intelligence and Machine Learning In Heterogeneous Brains"*. Available at SSRN: https://ssrn.com/abstract=3896252

Rawat, R., Dangi, C. S., & Patil, J. (2011). Safe Guard Anomalies against SQL Injection Attacks. *International Journal of Computer Applications*, 22(2), 11-14.

Rawat, R., Garg, B., Mahor, V., Chouhan, M., Pachlasiya, K., & Telang, S. Cyber Threat Exploitation and Growth during COVID-19 Times. In Advanced Smart Computing Technologies in Cybersecurity and Forensics. CRC Press.

Rawat, R., Kumar, A., Chouhan, M., Telang, S., Pachlasiya, K., Garg, B., & Mahor, V. (2021). *Systematic literature Review (SLR) on social media and the Digital Transformation of Drug Trafficking on Darkweb*. Available at SSRN 3903797.

Rawat, R., Mahor, V., Chirgaiya, S., Shaw, R. N., & Ghosh, A. (2021). Sentiment Analysis at Online Social Network for Cyber-Malicious Post Reviews Using Machine Learning Techniques. *Computationally Intelligent Systems and their Applications*, 113-130.

Rawat, R., Mahor, V., Chirgaiya, S., Shaw, R. N., & Ghosh, A. (2021b). Sentiment Analysis at Online Social Network for Cyber-Malicious Post Reviews Using Machine Learning Techniques. *Computationally Intelligent Systems and Their Applications*, 113–130.

Rawat, R., Mahor, V., Garg, B., Telang, S., Pachlasiya, K., Kumar, A., Shukla, S. K., & Kuliha, M. (2021). Analyzing Newspaper Articles for Text-Related Data for Finding Vulnerable Posts Over the Internet That Are Linked to Terrorist Activities. International Journal of Information Security and Privacy, 16(1). Doi:10.4018/IJISP.285581

Rawat, R., Mahor, V., Rawat, A., Garg, B., & Telang, S. (2021). Digital Transformation of Cyber Crime for Chip-Enabled Hacking. In Handbook of Research on Advancing Cybersecurity for Digital Transformation (pp. 227-243). IGI Global.

Rawat, R., Dangi, C. S., & Patil, J. (2011). Safe Guard Anomalies against SQL Injection Attacks. *International Journal of Computers and Applications, 22*(2), 11–14. doi:10.5120/2558-3511

Rawat, R., Garg, B., Mahor, V., Chouhan, M., Pachlasiya, K., & Telang, S. Cyber Threat Exploitation and Growth during COVID-19 Times. In *Advanced Smart Computing Technologies in Cybersecurity and Forensics* (pp. 85–101). CRC Press.

Rawat, R., Mahor, V., Chirgaiya, S., & Garg, B. (2021). Artificial Cyber Espionage Based Protection of Technological Enabled Automated Cities Infrastructure by Dark Web Cyber Offender. In *Intelligence of Things: AI-IoT Based Critical-Applications and Innovations* (pp. 167–188). Springer. doi:10.1007/978-3-030-82800-4_7

Rawat, R., Mahor, V., Chirgaiya, S., & Rathore, A. S. (2021). Applications of Social Network Analysis to Managing the Investigation of Suspicious Activities in Social Media Platforms. In *Advances in Cybersecurity Management* (pp. 315–335). Springer. doi:10.1007/978-3-030-71381-2_15

Rawat, R., Mahor, V., Chirgaiya, S., Shaw, R. N., & Ghosh, A. (2021). Analysis of Darknet Traffic for Criminal Activities Detection Using TF-IDF and Light Gradient Boosted Machine Learning Algorithm. In *Innovations in Electrical and Electronic Engineering* (pp. 671–681). Springer. doi:10.1007/978-981-16-0749-3_53

Rawat, R., Mahor, V., Rawat, A., Garg, B., & Telang, S. (2021). Digital Transformation of Cyber Crime for Chip-Enabled Hacking. In *Handbook of Research on Advancing Cybersecurity for Digital Transformation* (pp. 227–243). IGI Global. doi:10.4018/978-1-7998-6975-7.ch012

Rawat, R., Rajawat, A. S., Mahor, V., Shaw, R. N., & Ghosh, A. (2021). Dark Web— Onion Hidden Service Discovery and Crawling for Profiling Morphing, Unstructured Crime and Vulnerabilities Prediction. In *Innovations in Electrical and Electronic Engineering* (pp. 717–734). Springer.

Rawat, R., Rajawat, A. S., Mahor, V., Shaw, R. N., & Ghosh, A. (2021). Dark Web—Onion Hidden Service Discovery and Crawling for Profiling Morphing, Unstructured Crime and Vulnerabilities Prediction. In *Innovations in Electrical and Electronic Engineering* (pp. 717–734). Springer. doi:10.1007/978-981-16-0749-3_57

Rawat, R., Rajawat, A. S., Mahor, V., Shaw, R. N., & Ghosh, A. (2021). Dark Web—Onion Hidden Service Discovery and Crawling for Profiling Morphing, Unstructured Crime and Vulnerabilities Prediction. In *Innovations in Electrical and Electronic Engineering.* Springer.

Rawat, R., Rajawat, A. S., Mahor, V., Shaw, R. N., & Ghosh, A. (2021). Surveillance Robot in Cyber Intelligence for Vulnerability Detection. In *Machine Learning for Robotics Applications* (pp. 107–123). Springer. doi:10.1007/978-981-16-0598-7_9

Rehurek, R., & Sojka, P. (2011). Gensim--python framework for vector space modelling. NLP Centre, Faculty of Informatics, Masaryk University.

Reksna, T. (2017). *Complex network analysis of Darknet black market forum structure.* Academic Press.

Reporting and Analysis Centre for Information Assurance MELANI. (2021). *Situation in Switzerland and internationally* . National Cybersecurity Centre NCSC & Federal Intelligence Service FIS. Retrieved from https://www.newsd.admin.ch/newsd/message/attachments/63536.pdf

Ribeiro, J., Saghezchi, F. B., Mantas, G., Rodriguez, J., & Abd-Alhameed, R. A. (2020). Hidroid: Prototyping a behavioral host-based intrusion detection and prevention system for android. *IEEE Access: Practical Innovations, Open Solutions, 8*, 23154–23168. doi:10.1109/ACCESS.2020.2969626

Ribeiro, J., Saghezchi, F. B., Mantas, G., Rodriguez, J., Shepherd, S. J., & Abd-Alhameed, R. A. (2020). An autonomous host-based intrusion detection system for android mobile devices. *Mobile Networks and Applications*, *25*(1), 164–172. doi:10.100711036-019-01220-y

Rizvi, S., Kurtz, A., Pfeffer, J., & Rizvi, M. (2018, August). Securing the internet of things (IoT): A security taxonomy for IoT. *2018 17th IEEE International Conference On Trust, Security And Privacy In Computing.*

Robertson, J., Paliath, V., Shakarian, J., Thart, A., & Shakarian, P. (2016). Data driven game theoretic cyber threat mitigation. IAAI.

Rodríguez-Ruiz, J., Mata-Sánchez, J. I., Monroy, R., Loyola-González, O., & López-Cuevas, A. (2020). A one-class classification approach for bot detection on Twitter. *Computers & Security*, *91*, 101715–101727. doi:10.1016/j.cose.2020.101715

Rosenberg, J. (2017). Embedded security. *Rugged Embedded Systems*, e1-e74. doi:10.1016/b978-0-12-802459-1.00011-7

Rousseau, F., Kiagias, E., & Vazirgiannis, M. (2015, July). Text categorisation as a graph classification problem. In *Proceedings of the 53rd Annual Meeting of the Association for Computational Linguistics and the 7th International Joint Conference on Natural Language Processing (Volume 1: Long Papers)* (pp. 1702-1712). Academic Press.

Rumi, S. K., Deng, K., & Salim, F. D. (2018). Crime event prediction with dynamic features. *EPJ Data Science*, *7*(1), 43. doi:10.1140/epjds13688-018-0171-7

Russell, S., & Norvig, P. (2002). *Artificial intelligence: A modern approach.* Academic Press.

S, D., & S, R. (2014). Performance Comparison for Intrusion Detection System using Neural Network with KDD dataset. ICTACT Journal on Soft Computing, 4(3), 743–752. doi:10.21917/ijsc.2014.0106

Sabbah, T., & Selamat, A. (2014, December). Modified frequency-based term weighting scheme for accurate dark web content classification. In *Asia Information Retrieval Symposium* (pp. 184-196). Springer. 10.1007/978-3-319-12844-3_16

Sadaf, K., & Sultana, J. (2020). Intrusion detection based on autoencoder and isolation Forest in fog computing. *IEEE Access: Practical Innovations, Open Solutions*, *8*, 167059–167068. doi:10.1109/ACCESS.2020.3022855

Sadek, I., Rehman, S. U., Codjo, J., & Abdulrazak, B. (2019). Privacy and Security of IoT Based Healthcare Systems: Concerns, Solutions, and Recommendations. In J. Pagán, M. Mokhtari, H. Aloulou, B. Abdulrazak, & M. Cabrera (Eds.), Lecture Notes in Computer Science: Vol. 11862. How AI Impacts Urban Living and Public Health. ICOST 2019. Springer. https://doi.org/10.1007/978-3-030-32785-9_1.

Saha, H. N., Roy, R., Chakraborty, M., & Sarkar, C. (2021). IoT-Enabled Agricultural System Application, Challenges and Security Issues. *Agricultural Informatics: Automation Using the IoT and Machine Learning*, 223-247.

Salmon, P. M., Lane, B. R., Desmond, D., Cherney, A., Kulatilleke, G., Matthews, A., Lacey, D., & Stanton, N. A. (2019). Breaking bad systems with Human Factors and Ergonomics: Using Work Domain Analysis to identify strategies to disrupt trading in dark net marketplaces. *Proceedings of the Human Factors and Ergonomics Society Annual Meeting*, *63*(1), 458–462. https://doi.org/10.1177/1071181319631315

Samrin, R., & Vasumathi, D. (2017). Review on anomaly based network intrusion detection system. *Proceedings of the 2017 International Conference on Electrical, Electronics, Communication, Computer, and Optimization Techniques (ICEECCOT).*

Samtani, S., Abate, M., Benjamin, V., & Li, W. (2020). Cybersecurity as an industry: a cyber threat intelligence perspective. In Palgrave Handbook of International Cybercrime and Cyberdeviance. Palgrave Macmillan.

Samtani, S., Chinn, R., & Chen, H. (2015). Exploring hacker assets in underground forums. In *Intelligence and Security Informatics (ISI), 2015 IEEE International Conference on* (pp. 31–36). IEEE.

Samtani, S., Li, W., Benjamin, V., & Chen, H. (2021). Informing Cyber Threat Intelligence through Dark Web Situational Awareness: The AZSecure Hacker Assets Portal. *Digital Threats: Research and Practice, 2*(4), 1–10. doi:10.1145/3450972

Samtani, S., Zhu, H., & Chen, H. (2020). Proactively identifying emerging hacker threats from the dark web: A diachronic graph embedding framework (d-gef). *ACM Transactions on Privacy and Security, 23*(4), 1–33.

Sandberg, H. (2021). *A Risk Management Approach to Cyber-Physical Security in Networked Control Systems.* Retrieved 19 October 2021, from https://cnls.lanl.gov/External/GSSlides2021/Sandberg.pdf

Sandeep, C. H., Naresh Kumar, S., & Pramod Kumar, P. (2020). Significant Role of Security in IOT Development and IOT Architecture. *Journal of Mechanics of Continua and Mathematical Sciences, 15*(6), 174–184.

Sangani, A., Sampat, C., & Pinjarkar, V. (2019). Crime Prediction and Analysis. SSRN *Electronic Journal*. doi:10.2139/ssrn.3367712

Sarker, I. H. (2021). Machine Learning: Algorithms, Real-World Applications and Research Directions. *SN Comput. Sci., 2*, 160. doi:10.1007/s42979-021-00592-x

Sarma, M. K., & Mahanta, A. K. (2019, April). Clustering of Web Documents with Structure of Webpages based on the HTML Document Object Model. In *2019 IEEE International Conference on Intelligent Techniques in Control, Optimization and Signal Processing (INCOS)* (pp. 1-6). IEEE.

Sarma, P. K., Liang, Y., & Sethares, W. A. (2018). Domain adapted word embeddings for improved sentiment classification. arXiv preprint arXiv:1805.04576. doi:10.18653/v1/P18-2007

Satyapanich, T., Finin, T., & Ferraro, F. (2019). Extracting rich semantic information about cybersecurity events. *Second Workshop on Big Data for CyberSecurity*. 10.1109/BigData47090.2019.9006444

Schäfer, M., Fuchs, M., Strohmeier, M., Engel, M., Liechti, M., & Lenders, V. (2019). BlackWidow: Monitoring the Dark Web for Cyber Security Information. *2019 11th International Conference on Cyber Conflict (CyCon),* 1-21. doi: 10.23919/CYCON.2019.8756845

Schäfer, M., Fuchs, M., Strohmeier, M., Engel, M., Liechti, M., & Lenders, V. (2019, May). BlackWidow: Monitoring the dark web for cyber security information. In *2019 11th International Conference on Cyber Conflict (CyCon)* (Vol. 900, pp. 1-21). IEEE.

Schmidt, H. C. (2015). Student Newspapers Show Opinion Article Political Bias. *Newspaper Research Journal, 36*(1), 6–23.

Schwartz, H. (2022). *Significant Cyber Incidents*. Center for Strategic and International Studies. Retrieved 24 January 2022, from https://www.csis.org/programs/strategic-technologies-program/significant-cyber-incidents

ScreenCloud – Digital Signage Software for Any Screen or TV. (2021). Retrieved 27 November 2021, from https://screencloud.com/

Searle, J. (2021). *Industrial Control Systems (ICS)*. SANS Institute. Retrieved 20 October 2021, from https://www.sans.org/industrial-control-systems-security/

Seenivasagam, V., & Chitra, R. (2016). Myocardial Infarction Detection Using Intelligent Algorithms. *Neural Network World, 26*(1), 91–110. doi:10.14311/NNW.2016.26.005

Sha, K., Errabelly, R., Wei, W., Yang, T. A., & Wang, Z. (2017, May). Edgesec: Design of an edge layer security service to enhance iot security. In *2017 IEEE 1st International Conference on Fog and Edge Computing (ICFEC)* (pp. 81-88). IEEE.

Shahid, M. R., Blanc, G., Zhang, Z., & Debar, H. (2019). Anomalous Communications Detection in IoT Networks Using Sparse Autoencoders. *International Symposium on Network Computing and Applications IEEE*, 1-5. 10.1109/NCA.2019.8935007

Shaikh, F., Bou-Harb, E., Crichigno, J., & Ghani, N. (2018). A machine learning model for classifying unsolicited IoT devices by observing network telescopes. *Proceedings of the 14th International Wireless Communications and Mobile Computing Conference (IWCMC)*, 938–943.

Sharma, P. K., Singh, S., Jeong, Y. S., & Park, J. H. (2017). Distblocknet: A distributed blockchains-based secure sdn architecture for IoT networks. *IEEE Communications Magazine*, *55*(9), 78–85.

Shaukat, K., Luo, S., Chen, S., & Liu, D. (2020). Cyber Threat Detection Using Machine Learning Techniques: A Performance Evaluation Perspective. *2020 International Conference on Cyber Warfare and Security (ICCWS)*, 1-6. 10.1109/ICCWS48432.2020.9292388

Shaukat, K., Rubab, A., Shehzadi, I., & Iqbal, R. (2017). A Socio-Technological analysis of Cyber Crime and Cyber Security in Pakistan. *Transylvanian Review*, *1*(3).

Shipping, F. W. (2017). The dark web: Breakthroughs in research and practice. *The Dark Web: Breakthroughs in Research and Practice*. doi:10.4018/978-1-5225-3163-0

Shone, N., Ngoc, T. N., Phai, V. D., & Shi, Q. (2018). A Deep Learning Approach to Network Intrusion Detection. *IEEE Transactions on Emerging Topics in Computational Intelligence*, *2*(1), 41–50. doi:10.1109/TETCI.2017.2772792

Simpson, S. S., Adams, N., Brugman, C. M., & Conners, T. J. (2018). Detecting novel and emerging drug terms using natural language processing: A social media corpus study. *JMIR Public Health and Surveillance*, *4*(1), e2. doi:10.2196/publichealth.7726 PMID:29311050

Sinaeepourfard, A., Sengupta, S., Krogstie, J., & Delgado, R. R. (2019). Cybersecurity in Large-Scale Smart Cities: Novel Proposals for Anomaly Detection from Edge to Cloud. *2019 International Conference on Internet of Things, Embedded Systems and Communications (IINTEC)*, 130-135. 10.1109/IINTEC48298.2019.9112114

Singh, S. (2018). *Natural language processing for information extraction.* arXiv preprint arXiv:1807.02383.

Singh, P., & Venkatesan, M. (2018). Hybrid approach for intrusion detection system. *Proceedings of the 2018 International Conference on Current Trends Towards Converging Technologies (ICCTCT)*, 1–5.

Siswanto, A., Syukur, A., Kadir, E. A., & Suratin, E. A. (2019). Network traffic monitoring and analysis using packet sniffer. *Proceedings of the 2019 International Conference on Advanced Communication Technologies and Networking (CommNet)*.

Sivakumar, P. (2021). Real Time Crime Detection Using Deep Learning Algorithm. *2021 International Conference on System, Computation, Automation and Networking (ICSCAN)*, 1-5. 10.1109/ICSCAN53069.2021.9526393

Smart Wearable, E. C. G. (2021). *EKG Monitor - QardioCore*. Retrieved 26 November 2021, from https://www.qardio.com/qardiocore-wearable-ecg-ekg-monitor-iphone/

Song, H., Jiang, Z., Men, A., & Yang, B. (2017, November 15). A hybrid semi-supervised anomaly detection model for high-dimensional data. *Computational Intelligence and Neuroscience*, *8501683*. Advance online publication. doi:10.1155/2017/8501683 PMID:29270197

Soni, A., Upadhyay, R., & Jain, A. (2017). Internet of Things and wireless physical layer security: A survey. In *Computer communication, networking and internet security* (pp. 115–123). Springer.

Soysal, M., & Schmidt, E. G. (2010). Machine learning algorithms for accurate flow-based network traffic classification: Evaluation and comparison. *Performance Evaluation, 67*(6), 451–467. doi:10.1016/j.peva.2010.01.001

Spitters, M., Verbruggen, S., & Van Staalduinen, M. (2014, September). Towards a comprehensive insight into the thematic organisation of the tor hidden services. In *2014 IEEE Joint Intelligence and Security Informatics Conference* (pp. 220-223). IEEE.

Stalidis, P., Semertzidis, T., & Daras, P. (2021). Examining Deep Learning Architectures for Crime Classification and Prediction. *Forecasting, 3*(4), 741–762. doi:10.3390/forecast3040046

Suchanek, F. (2007). a core of semantic knowledge. *Proceedings of the 16th international conference on World Wide Web ACM,* 697–706. 10.1145/1242572.1242667

Summerville, D. H., Nwanze, N., & Skormin, V. A. (2004). Anomalous packet identification for network intrusion detection. *Proceedings of the Fifth Annual IEEE SMC Information Assurance Workshop,* 60–67.

Sun, X., Gui, G., Li, Y., Liu, R. P., & An, Y. (2018). ResInNet: A novel deep neural network with feature Re-use for Internet of things. *IEEE Internet of Things Journal, 6*(1), 679–691. doi:10.1109/JIOT.2018.2853663

Swamy, S. N., Jadhav, D., & Kulkarni, N. (2017). Security threats in the application layer in IOT applications. In *2017 International Conference on ISMAC (IoT in Social, Mobile, Analytics and Cloud (I-SMAC)* (pp. 477-480). IEEE.

Swamy, S. N., Jadhav, D., & Kulkarni, N. (2017, February). Security threats in the application layer in IOT applications. In *2017 International conference on i-SMAC (iot in social, mobile, analytics and cloud)(i-SMAC)* (pp. 477-480). IEEE.

Symantec. (2018). *Internet Security Threat Report.* https://www.symantec.com /content/dam/symantec/docs/reports/istr23-2018-en.pdf

Szakonyi, A., Leonard, B., & Dawson, M. (2021). Dark Web: A Breeding Ground for ID Theft and Financial Crimes. In Handbook of Research on Theory and Practice of Financial Crimes (pp. 506-524). IGI Global. doi:10.4018/978-1-7998-5567-5.ch025

Takaaki, S., & Atsuo, I. (2019, March). Dark web content analysis and visualisation. In *Proceedings of the ACM International Workshop on Security and Privacy Analytics* (pp. 53-59). ACM.

Tariq, H., Hanif, M. K., Sarwar, M. U., Bari, S., Sarfraz, M. S., & Oskouei, R. J. (2021). Employing Deep Learning and Time Series Analysis to Tackle the Accuracy and Robustness of the Forecasting Problem. *Security and Communication Networks, 2021,* 1–10. doi:10.1155/2021/5587511

Tavabi, N., Goyal, P., Almukaynizi, M., Shakarian, P., & Lerman, K. (2018). *DarkEmbed: Exploit prediction with neural language models.* https://ojs.aaai.org/index.php/AAAI/article/view/11428

Tavallaee, M., Bagheri, E., Lu, W., & Ghorbani, A. A. (2009). A detailed analysis of the KDD CUP 99 data set. *Electronics, 10*(781), 1–6.

Taylor, M., & Bing, C. (2021). *Exclusive: China-backed hackers 'targeted COVID-19 vaccine firm Moderna'.* Retrieved 20 October 2021, from https://www.reuters.com/article/us-health-coronavirus-moderna-cyber-excl/exclusive-china-backed-hackers-targeted-covid-19-vaccine-firm-moderna-idUSKCN24V38M

Tewari, A., & Gupta, B. B. (2020). Security, privacy and trust of different layers in Internet-of-Things (IoTs) framework. *Future Generation Computer Systems, 108,* 909–920.

The Guardian. (2021). *How the Colonial Pipeline hack is part of a growing ransomware trend in the US.* Retrieved from https://www.theguardian.com/technology/2021/may/13/colonial-pipeline-ransomware-attack-cyber-crime

The Week in Dark Web. (2022). *Access Sales and Data Leaks.* SOCRadar® Cyber Intelligence Inc. Retrieved 24 January 2022, from https://socradar.io/the-week-in-dark-web-17-january-2022-access-sales-and-data-leaks/

Thiyagarajan, P. (2020). A Review on Cyber Security Mechanisms Using Machine and Deep Learning Algorithms. In *Handbook of Research on Machine and Deep Learning Applications for Cyber Security* (pp. 23–41). IGI Global. doi:10.4018/978-1-5225-9611-0.ch002

Thompson, M. (2013). Iranian Cyber Attack on New York Dam Shows Future of War. *TIME*, 1-2. Retrieved from https://time.com/4270728/iran-cyber-attack-dam-fbi/

Tijana, J., & Lars, N. (2011). On domain localization in ensemble-based Kalman filter algoithms. *Monthly Weather Review*, *139*(7), 2046–2060.

Todorof, M. (2019, July). FinTech on the dark web: The rise of cryptos. In *Era Forum* (Vol. 20, No. 1, pp. 1-20). Springer Berlin Heidelberg.

Tomić, I., & McCann, J. A. (2017). A survey of potential security issues in existing wireless sensor network protocols. *IEEE Internet of Things Journal*, *4*(6), 1910–1923.

ToppiReddy, H. K. R., Saini, B., & Mahajan, G. (2018). Crime Prediction & Monitoring Framework Based on Spatial Analysis. *Procedia Computer Science*, *132*, 696–705. doi:10.1016/j.procs.2018.05.075

Tounsi, W. (2019). *What is cyber threat intelligence and how is it evolving? In Cyber-Vigilance and Digital Trust: Cyber Security in the Era of Cloud Computing and IoT*. ISTE Ltd.

Tsogbaatar, E., Bhuyan, M. H., Taenaka, Y., Fall, D., Gonchigsumlaa, K., Elmroth, E., & Kadobayashi, Y. (2021). DeL-IoT: A deep ensemble learning approach to uncover anomalies in IoT. *Internet of Things*, *14*, 100391–100403. doi:10.1016/j.iot.2021.100391

Tudisco, F., & Higham, D. J. (2021). *Node and Edge Eigenvector Centrality for Hypergraphs.* arXiv preprint arXiv:2101.06215.

Tu, E., Zhang, G., Rachmawati, L., Rajabally, E., Mao, S., & Huang, G. (2017). A theoretical study of the relationship between an ELM network and its subnetworks. *Proceedings of the 2017 International Joint Conference on Neural Networks (IJCNN)*, 1794–1801.

Tyagi, N. (2016). A reference architecture for IoT. *Int J Comput Eng Appl., 10*(1).

Unwala, I., Taqvi, Z., & Lu, J. (2018, April). Thread: An iot protocol. In *2018 IEEE Green Technologies Conference (GreenTech)* (pp. 161-167). IEEE.

van der Sanden, R., Wilkins, C., Romeo, J. S., Rychert, M., & Barratt, M. J. (2021). Predictors of using social media to purchase drugs in New Zealand: Findings from a large-scale online survey. *The International Journal on Drug Policy*, *98*, 103430. doi:10.1016/j.drugpo.2021.103430 PMID:34487954

Vashi, S., Ram, J., Modi, J., Verma, S., & Prakash, C. (2017, February). Internet of Things (IoT): A vision, architectural elements, and security issues. In *2017 international conference on I-SMAC (IoT in Social, Mobile, Analytics and Cloud) (I-SMAC)* (pp. 492-496). IEEE.

Vaughan, S. (2020). Random time series in astronomy. Philosophical Transactions of the Royal Society of London, 371(1984).

Venger, O. (2019). The use of experts in journalistic accounts of media events: A comparative study of the 2005 London Bombings in British, American, and Russian newspapers. *Journalism*, *20*(10), 1343–1359.

Vyas, P., Liu, J., & El-Gayar, O. (2021). Fake News Detection on the Web: An LSTM-based Approach. *AMCIS 2021 Proceedings*, 5. https://aisel.aisnet.org/amcis2021/virtual_communities/virtual_communities/5

Vyas, P., Reisslein, M., Rimal, B. P., Vyas, G., Basyal, G. P., & Muzumdar, P. (2021). Automated Classification of Societal Sentiments on Twitter with Machine Learning. *IEEE Transactions on Technology and Society*, 1–1. doi:10.1109/TTS.2021.3108963

Walker Orr, J., Tadepalli, P., & Fern, X. (2018). *Event Detection with Neural Networks: A Rigorous Empirical Evaluation.* arXiv e-prints, arXiv-1808.

Walker, C., Strassel, S., Medero, J., & Maeda, K. (2006). *ACE 2005 multilingual training corpus.Technical report.* Linguistic Data Consortium.

Wang, R., Zhou, D., & He, Y. (2019). Open event extraction from online text using a generative adversarial network. arXiv preprint arXiv:1908.09246. doi:10.18653/v1/D19-1027

Wang, W. (2012, April). Chinese news event 5W1H semantic elements extraction for event ontology population. In *Proceedings of the 21st International Conference on World Wide Web* (pp. 197-202). 10.1145/2187980.2188008

Wang, W., Du, X., Shan, D., Qin, R., & Wang, N. (2020). *Cloud Intrusion Detection Method Based on Stacked Contractive Auto-Encoder and Support Vector Machine. IEEE Transactions on Cloud Computing.* doi:10.1109/TCC.2020.3001017

Wang, X., Peng, P., Wang, C., & Wang, G. (2018). You are your photographs: Detecting multiple identities of vendors in the darknet marketplaces. *Proceedings of the 2018 on Asia Conference on Computer and Communications Security*, 431–442. 10.1145/3196494.3196529

Werner, G., Yang, S., & McConky, K. (2017). Time series forecasting of cyber-attack intensity. In *Proceedings of the 12th Annual Conference on cyber and information security research* (p. 18). ACM.

Wetschoreck, F., Krabel, T., & Krishnamurthy, S. (2020). *Ppscore:* Zenodo *release* (1.1.2 version). *Zenodo.*

Wikipedia Average path length. (n.d.). https://bit.ly/3b8hwxn

William, P., & Badholia, A. (2021). Analysis of personality traits from text based answers using HEXACO model. In *International Conference on Innovative Computing, Intelligent Communication and Smart Electrical Systems (ICSES), 2021* (pp. 1–10). 10.1109/ICSES52305.2021.9633794

William, P., & Dr Badholia, A. (2021). A review on prediction of personality traits considering interview answers with personality models. *International Journal for Research in Applied Science and Engineering Technology, 9*(5), 1611–1616. doi:10.22214/ijraset.2021.34613

William, P., Kumar, P., Chhabra, G. S., & Vengatesan, K. (2021). Task allocation in distributed agile software development using machine learning approach. In *International Conference on Disruptive Technologies for Multi-Disciplinary Research and Applications (CENTCON), 2021* (pp. 168–172). 10.1109/CENTCON52345.2021.9688114

William, P., & Dr Badholia, A. (2020). Evaluating efficacy of classification algorithms on personality prediction dataset. *Elementary Education Online, 19*(4), 3400–3413. doi:10.17051/ilkonline.2020.04.764728

William, P., & Dr Badholia, A. (2021, July). Assessment of Personality from Interview Answers using Machine Learning Approach. *IJAST, 29*(08), 6301–6312.

William, P., & Patil, V. S. (2016). Architectural challenges of cloud computing and its security issues with solutions. *International Journal for Scientific Research and Development, 4*(8), 265–268.

Winder, D. (2022). Hack Attack Takes Down Dark Web Host: 7,595 Websites Confirmed Deleted. *Forbes*. Retrieved 24 January 2022, from https://www.forbes.com/sites/daveywinder/2020/03/30/hack-attack-takes-down-dark-web-7595-websites-confirmed-deleted/?sh=4b96a9241435

Wu, Y., Sun, H., & Yan, C. (2017, March). An event timeline extraction method based on news corpus. In *2017 IEEE 2nd International Conference on Big Data Analysis (ICBDA)* (pp. 697-702). IEEE. 10.1109/ICBDA.2017.8078725

Xiao, L., Wan, X., & Han, Z. (2018, March). PHY-Layer Authentication With Multiple Landmarks With Reduced Overhead. *IEEE Transactions on Wireless Communications*, 17(3), 1676–1687. doi:10.1109/TWC.2017.2784431

Xing, L., Demertzis, K., & Yang, J. (2020). Identifying data streams anomalies by evolving spiking restricted Boltzmann machines. *Neural Computing & Applications*, 32(11), 6699–6713. doi:10.100700521-019-04288-5

Xu, Z., Cao, L., & Chen, X. (2019). Learning to learn: Hierarchical meta-critic networks. *IEEE Access: Practical Innovations, Open Solutions*, 7, 57069–57077. doi:10.1109/ACCESS.2019.2914469

Yadav, R., & Kumari Sheoran, S. (2018). Crime Prediction Using Auto Regression Techniques for Time Series Data. *2018 3rd International Conference and Workshops on Recent Advances and Innovations in Engineering (ICRAIE)*, 1–5. 10.1109/ICRAIE.2018.8710407

Yang, L., Yang, Y., Yu, H., & Zhu, G. (2019, December). Anonymous market product classification based on deep learning. In *Proceedings of the International Conference on Artificial Intelligence, Information Processing and Cloud Computing* (pp. 1-5). 10.1145/3371425.3371467

Yang, L., Yang, Y., Yu, H., & Zhu, G. (2019, December). Edge-Based Detection and Classification of Malicious Contents in Tor Darknet Using Machine Learning. *Mobile Information Systems*.

Yang, Y., Yang, L., Yang, M., Yu, H., Zhu, G., Chen, Z., & Chen, L. (2019). Article. In *Proceedings of the 2019 IEEE 8th Joint International Information Technology and Artificial Intelligence Conference (ITAIC)* (pp. 1216–1220). IEEE.

Yang, Y., Yang, L., Yang, M., Yu, H., Zhu, G., Chen, Z., & Chen, L. (2019, May). Dark web forum correlation analysis research. In *2019 IEEE 8th Joint International Information Technology and Artificial Intelligence Conference (ITAIC)* (pp. 1216-1220). IEEE. 10.1109/ITAIC.2019.8785760

Yang, Y., Yu, H., Yang, L., Yang, M., Chen, L., Zhu, G., & Wen, L. (2019). Hadoop-based dark web threat intelligence analysis framework. *Proceedings of the IEEE Publications 3rd Advanced Information Management, Communicates, Electronic and Automation Control Conference (IMCEC)*.

Yang, B., & Liu, D. (2019). Research on Network Traffic Identification based on Machine Learning and Deep Packet Inspection. *Proceedings of the 2019 IEEE 3rd Information Technology, Networking, Electronic and Automation Control Conference (ITNEC)*, 1887–1891.

Yang, Q. (2018). *Open schema event profiling for massive news corpus. CIKM'18*.

Yang, S., Shu, K., Wang, S., Gu, R., Wu, F., & Liu, H. (2019, July). Unsupervised fake news detection on social media: A generative approach. *Proceedings of the AAAI Conference on Artificial Intelligence*, 33(01), 5644–5651. doi:10.1609/aaai.v33i01.33015644

Yang, Y., Wu, L., Yin, G., Li, L., & Zhao, H. (2017). A survey on security and privacy issues in Internet-of-Things. *IEEE Internet of Things Journal*, 4(5), 1250–1258.

Yang, Y., Zheng, K., Wu, B., Yang, Y., & Wang, X. (2020). Network intrusion detection based on supervised adversarial variational auto-encoder with regularization. *IEEE Access: Practical Innovations, Open Solutions*, 8, 42169–42184. doi:10.1109/ACCESS.2020.2977007

Yan, Y. (2019). *Side Channel Attacks on IoT Applications (Ph.D)*. The University of Bristol.

Yar, M., & Steinmetz, K. F. (2019). *Cybercrime and society*. SAGE Publications Limited.

Yarrabelly, N., & Karlapalem, K. (2018, June). Extracting predictive statements with their scope from news articles. *Twelfth International AAAI conference on web and social media.*

Yerima, S. Y., Sezer, S., & McWilliams, G. (2013). Analysis of Bayesian classification-based approaches for Android malware detection. *IET Information Security, 8*(1), 25–36. doi:10.1049/iet-ifs.2013.0095

Yerima, S. Y., Sezer, S., & Muttik, I. (2015). High accuracy android malware detection using ensemble learning. *IET Information Security, 9*(6), 313–320. doi:10.1049/iet-ifs.2014.0099

Yilmaz, Y., Gunn, S. R., & Halak, B. (2018, July). Lightweight PUF-based authentication protocol for IoT devices. In *2018 IEEE 3rd international verification and security workshop (IVSW)* (pp. 38-43). IEEE.

Yu, X., & Jin, Z. (2017, October). Web content information extraction based on DOM tree and statistical information. In *2017 IEEE 17th International Conference on Communication Technology (ICCT)* (pp. 1308-1311). IEEE.

Yuki, J. Q., Sakib, M. M. Q., Zamal, Z., Habibullah, K. M., & Das, A. K. (2019). Predicting Crime Using Time and Location Data. *Proceedings of the 2019 7th International Conference on Computer and Communications Management,* 124–128. 16/1210.1145/3348445.3348483

Yu, X. (2020). Design of Cross-border Network Crime Detection System Based on PSE and Big Data Analysis. *2020 IEEE International Conference on Power, Intelligent Computing and Systems (ICPICS),* 480-483. 10.1109/ICPICS50287.2020.9202004

Yu, X., & Guo, H. (2019). A survey on IIoT Security. *Proceedings of the 2019 IEEE VTS Asia Pacific Wireless Communications Symposium (APWCS),* 1–5.

Zanero, S. (2008). Ulisse, a network intrusion detection system. In *Proceedings of the 4th annual workshop on Cyber security and information intelligence research: developing strategies to meet the cyber security and information intelligence challenges ahead* (p. 20). ACM.

Zavrak, S., & İskefiyeli, M. (2020). Anomaly-Based Intrusion Detection From Network Flow Features Using Variational Autoencoder. *IEEE Access: Practical Innovations, Open Solutions, 8,* 108346–108358. doi:10.1109/ACCESS.2020.3001350

Zeadally, S., Adi, E., Baig, Z., & Khan, I. A. (2020). Harnessing artificial intelligence capabilities to improve cybersecurity. *IEEE Access: Practical Innovations, Open Solutions, 8,* 23817–23837.

Zenebe, A., Shumba, M., Carillo, A., & Cuenca, S. (2019). Cyber threat discovery from dark web. *Proceedings of the 28th International Conference on Software Engineering and Data Engineering.*

Zhang, L., & Gao, Z. (2011). The Shapley value of convex compound stochastic cooperative game. *Proceedings of the 2011 2nd International Conference on Artificial Intelligence, Management Science and Electronic Commerce (AIMSEC).*

Zhang, M., Cui, Z., Neumann, M., & Chen, Y. (2018, April). An end-to-end deep learning architecture for graph classification. *Thirty-Second AAAI Conference on Artificial Intelligence.*

Zhang, X., & Chow, K. P. (2020). A framework for dark Web threat intelligence analysis. In Cyber Warfare and Terrorism: Concepts, Methodologies, Tools, and Applications (pp. 266-276). IGI Global.

Zhang, J., Rajendran, S., Sun, Z., Woods, R., & Hanzo, L. (2019). Physical layer security for the internet of things: Authentication and key generation. *IEEE Wireless Communications, 26*(5), 92–98.

Zhang, J., & Zulkernine, M. (2006). Anomaly based network intrusion detection with unsupervised outlier detection. *Proceedings of the 2006 IEEE International Conference on Communications, 5*, 2388–2393.

Zhang, K., Wang, Q., Liu, X., & Giles, C. L. (2020). Shapley homology: Topological analysis of sample influence for neural networks. *Neural Computation, 32*(7), 1355–1378. doi:10.1162/neco_a_01289 PMID:32433903

Zhang, N., Chen, D., Ye, F., Zheng, T. X., & Wei, Z. (2019). Physical layer security for internet of things. *Wireless Communications and Mobile Computing, 2019*, 1–2.

Zhang, X. D. (2020). Machine learning. In *A Matrix Algebra Approach to Artificial Intelligence* (pp. 223–440). Springer. doi:10.1007/978-981-15-2770-8_6

Zhang, Y., Fan, Y., Song, W., Hou, S., Ye, Y., Li, X., Zhao, L., Shi, C., Wang, J., & Xiong, Q. (2019). Your style your identity: Leveraging writing and photography styles for drug trafficker identification in darknet markets over attributed heterogeneous information network. *The World Wide Web Conference*, 3448–3454. 10.1145/3308558.3313537

Zhang, Y., Qian, Y., Fan, Y., Ye, Y., Li, X., Xiong, Q., & Shao, F. (2020). dStyle-GAN: Generative Adversarial Network based on Writing and Photography Styles for Drug Identification in Darknet Markets. *Annual Computer Security Applications Conference*, 669–680. 10.1145/3427228.3427603

Zhao, F., Skums, P., Zelikovsky, A., Sevigny, E. L., Swahn, M. H., Strasser, S. M., Huang, Y., & Wu, Y. (2020). Computational approaches to detect illicit drug ads and find vendor communities within social media platforms. *IEEE/ACM Transactions on Computational Biology and Bioinformatics*. PMID:32149652

Zhong, S., Liu, D., Lin, L., Zhao, M., Fu, X., & Guo, F. (2020). A novel anomaly detection method for gas turbines using weight agnostic neural network search. *Proceedings of the 2020 Asia-Pacific International Symposium on Advanced Reliability and Maintenance Modeling (APARM)*, 1–6.

Zhou & Paffenroth. (2017). Anomaly detection with robust deep autoencoders. *Proceedings of the 23rd ACM SIGKDD International Conference on Knowledge Discovery and Data Mining*, 665–674.

About the Contributors

Romil Rawat is currently working as Assistant Professor in Shri Vaishnav Vidyapeeth Vishwavidyalaya, Indore, India. He attended several research programs and received research grants from USA, Germany, Italy and UK. The Author has research alignment towards Cyber Security, IoT, Dark Web Crime analysis and investigation techniques, and working towards tracing of illicit anonymous contents of cyber terrorism and criminal activities. He also chaired International Conferences and Hosted several research events including National and International Research Schools, PhD colloquium, Workshops, training programs. He also published several Research Patents.

Upinder Kaur is working as an Assistant Professor in the Department of Computer Science and Engineering, Akal University, Bathinda, Punjab, India. She received her Ph. D. Degree at Department of Computer Science and Applications, Kurukshetra University, Kurukshetra. She is in teaching since October 2006. She holds Master of Technology (M. Tech.) degree in Computer Science and Engineering from MMEC, Mullana, Ambala, India .Her main research interests are in the areas of Distributed Computing, Distributed Data Structures, Cloud Computing, Data Science and Analytics, ML/DL. Currently working on the research issues in applications of deep learning in agriculture and health care. She has attended many National and International Conferences/workshops and she has more than 25 research papers in national / international journals and conferences. She has also a member of IEEE, ACM and supervising three Ph.D. Scholars and several graduate and undergraduate students in multi-cloud domain and data science in agriculture and deep learning in bio-signals.

* * *

Anusha Bamini A. M. received her PhD in Computer science and Engineering in 2018 from Noorul Islam Centre for Higher Education, Tamilnadu, India. She received Master of Engineering (M.E) in Anna University Tirunelveli, India in 2010, with University First Rank. She received Bachelor of Engineering (B.E) with distinction in Anna University, Chennai, India in 2008. Now she is working as an Assistant Professor in Karunya Institute of Technology and Sciences. Her area of interest is Cloud Computing, Scheduling and Security in Cloud Computing, IoT, Image Processing, Deep Learning and Data Science. She has published more number of papers in Conference, SCIE, SCOPUS and Peer reviewed Journals.

Stuti Asthana is acting as Independent Researcher and Analyst in the domain of Artificial Intelligence . In 2019, she received doctoral degree, Doctor of Philosophy with specialization in Artificial Intelligence from Suresh Gyan Vihar University (NAAC "A" Grade), Jaipur, India. In 2012, she received

Master's degree, Master of Technology with specialization in Computer Science and Engineering from Rajiv Gandhi Prodhyogiki Vishwavidhyalaya, Bhopal, M.P., India. Within the period of her doctoral-level studies at the Doctor of Philosophy of Computer Engineering, she has demonstrated herself extraordinary as disciplined and dedicated research scholar. As an unwavering dedicated researcher, she has published 12 Research Papers in various reputed Web of Science, SCOPUS, DBLP indexed International Journals and flagship international Scopus Indexed Conferences. Her doctoral research investigates the design and development of Multiscript Handwriting Recognition Using Neural Network. She is an active Editorial Board member for various reputed international journals. She has also published National and International Patents in the areas of Data Mining, Machine Learning, IoT and Neural Network.

Sunil G. Bhirud is working as a Professor at Computer Engineering and Information Technology department, Veermata Jijabai Technological Institute (VJTI) Mumbai. He is having vast experience of 29 years in Academics, Research and Administration. His specialization is in mainly Digital signal processing & Artificial neural networks. He has authored more than 100 research articles, journals and guided more than 20 research scholars. He has also handled additional charge as a Registrar, Mumbai University. He has also worked as an advisor for All India Council for Technical Education (AICTE), Delhi.

Dashank Bhoir is a Management Trainee at ICICI Prudential. He holds a bachelor's degree in Computer Engineering from VJTI Mumbai. His research interests are Machine Learning and Data Science.

Rakesh Kumar Bhujade completed Ph.D. in Artificial Intelligence in 2016 and currently working as Head of the Information Technology Department in Government Polytechnic, Daman. He has published 01, Australian Government Patent, 05 Indian patents, 03 Books, 02 AWS Global Certifications, 01 Research Grant (TEQIP III) and more than 30 papers in Scopus Indexed International Journal/ Conferences. He also acted as Advisory Board member in many International Journals and conferences.

Rahul R. Bibave is currently an Assistant Professor in the department of Electrical Engineering at Sanjivani College of Engineering, Kopargaon. He received his M.E.(Electrical Machines and Drives) from Government College of Engineering, Aurangabad in October, 2018 and B.E.(Electrical Engineering) from Pune University in August 2016. He has teaching experience of more than 3 years in all areas of Electrical Engineering. His current research interests include Electrical Vehicles, MPPT in renewable energy.

Sadhna Bijrothiya is currently PhD Pursuing from MANIT Bhopal, MP, India, attend the workshop, seminars, national and international labeled.

Prathap Rudra Boppuru is an Assistant Professor in Computer Science and Engineering at CHRIST (Deemed to be University) India. He has completed his B.Tech In information technology, M.Tech in Software Engineering and PhD in Crime analysis using machine learning algorithms. He exhibits a solid commitment toward continued career development embracing every opportunity to achieve educational excellence. Prathap writes Research articles on crime analytics. He has published articles on Crime analysis in Indian context using social media data.

Deepika Chauhan received the Master's of Engineering from DAVV, Indore in 2017. She is a reviewer and member of the editorial board of several Journals. She has supervised 50 postgraduate students. She serves in the educational field for the last 10 years. Her main research interest includes machine learning, image processing, the Internet of Things, Cloud Computing, and Blockchain. She has published more than 10 books in various publications. She has published more than 20 research articles in various national and international conferences and journals.

Akhilesh Chauhan is a Ph.D. student of Information Systems at the College of Business and Information Systems, Dakota State University, USA. He received his master's degree in Analytics from the Dakota State University, USA. His current research interest includes Association Rule Mining, Machine Learning, Healthcare Informatics, Transfer Learning, Text Mining, and Data Mining.

Siddhartha Choubey, M.Tech., Ph.D. (Computer Science and Engineering), LMISTE, MCSI, is working as Professor in Computer Science and Engineering in Shri Shankaracharya Technical Campus Bhilai, India.. He has published more than 60 research papers in various international and national journals and conferences. His areas of interest includes Networking , Parallel Processing, image processing, biomedical imaging, nano-imaging, neural network, fuzzy logic, pattern recognition ,Bio informatics , AI , Machine Learning , Deep Learning and IOT.

Ashwini Dalvi is pursuing her Ph.D. Degree from VJTI, affiliated to Mumbai University. She joined the Department of Information Technology, K. J. Somaiya College of Engineering, Mumbai in 2006 as an Assistant Professor. She has published over 25 journal and conference papers in the areas of Security, Intelligent applications.

Jigyasu Dubey has more than 21 years of Academic, Research and Industry experience, and currently working as Professor & Head, Department of Information Technology of Shri Vaishnav Vidyapeeth Vishwavidyalaya, Indore. He is also serving as Faculty In-charge of Network Establishment & Internet Cell, Coordinator - SVVVERP System, Deputy Controller of Examinations, Coordinator – Learning Resource Centre, and Coordinator – Centre of Excellence in Simulation and Gaming at the University. He is Ph. D. in the Faculty of Computer Engineering in the field of Computer Networking and Peer-to-Peer Computing. He obtained M.E. in Computer Engineering with specialization in Software Engineering from Devi Ahilya Vishwavidyalaya (DAVV) Indore in year 2007. He also holds B.E. in Computer Science & Engineering from Vikram University, Ujjain in year 2000. His areas of research interest are Computer Networking, Cyber & Network Security, Peer-to-Peer Computing, Software Engineering, and Object Oriented Analysis and Design. He has more than forty publications in peer-reviewed International/National journals, and International /National Conferences. Dr. Dubey also coordinated 52nd annual conference of International Simulation and Gaming (ISAGA 2021). He worked as reviewer of IEEE Transaction on Network and Service Management and Journal of Experimental & Theoretical Artificial Intelligence published by Taylor and Francis. Mr. Jigyasu also worked as reviewer for various International and National journals and conferences. Currently 05 Research Scholars are registered for Ph. D. under him.

Madhu Gottumukkala is a technology professional with 21 years of domestic and international experience in Software Development, Software Quality Assurance, IT Service Management, Enterprise

Architecture, Information Security, Risk Management and Project/Program Management. He has a MBA in engineering and technology management and a masters in computer science engineering. He is currently pursuing his PhD is information systems with healthcare specialization. His domain expertise is in Healthcare, Telecom/Wireless, Mobile Applications, Infrastructure, Internet Technologies and Unified Communications. He has experience in establishing major technology initiatives, developing and managing multi-disciplined engineering organizations over the last two decades. Madhu Gottumukkala is PMI certified Project Management Professional, Agile Certified Practitioner and a Scrum Alliance Certified Scrum Professional with an agile mindset. He is also CISSP Certified Information Security Professional, ITIL4 Managing Professional, ITIL4 Strategic Leader & ITIL3 Expert, TOGAF 9.2 Certified, and ISTQB Certified Tester Advanced Level (CTAL-FULL). He has a patent as Inventor in Automation Test Systems (PatentNo:US7,519,864B2).

Yu-Chen Hu received his Ph.D. degree in computer science and information engineering from the Department of Computer Science and Information Engineering, National Chung Cheng University, Chiayi, Taiwan. Currently, Dr. Hu is a distinguished professor at Providence University, Taiwan. He is a senior member of IEEE. He is also a member of Computer Vision, Graphics, and Image Processing (CVGIP), Chinese Cryptology and Information Security Association (CCISA), Computer Science and Information Management (CSIM), and Phi Tau Phi Society of the Republic of China. He joints the editorial boards of several international journals. He publishes more than 120 journal papers and more than 100 conference papers. His research interests include digital forensics, information hiding, image and signal processing, data compression, information security, computer network, artificial intelligence, and Information management.

Uddhav Jambhalkar is an Assistant Software Engineer at Montran Corporation. His interests lie in Java Development, Blockchain and Machine Learning. He has completed a B.Tech in Computer Engineering from VJTI Mumbai.

M. A. Jawale received the degree in Ph.D. in Computer Science and Engineering, in 2015. She is currently working as Professor in Information Technology and Head of IT Dept. in Sanjivani College of Engineering, Kopargaon. She is a Best Teacher Award Recipient of SPPU, Pune. She is also a life member of ISTE and member of IE, India. She worked on various Committees, reviewer, and jury at national as well as international level. She is also worked and completed research projects in opinion mining, cyber security, data mining, Internet of Things (IoT) for which she has been received research grants from BCUD, SPPU Pune, AICTE. She has been published more than 30 + journal and conference research papers in well-reputed journal, including IEEE Explore, Springer. Her main research interest includes Opinion Mining, Cyber Security, Machine Learning, Internet of Things (IoT).

Nirmit Joshi is graduated from Veermata Jijabai Technological Institute (VJTI) in 2021. He obtained his Bachelor of Technology in Computer Engineering from VJTI.

Padmaveni K. completed her Ph.D in Cloud computing in 2018. She is working as Associate professor in the department of Computer Science and Engineering.

Dnyaneshwar Kudande had received his M.Tech from Pune University and having 10plus years of teaching experience in Engineering and Science. Area of Interest is Data Science. He published 10 papers in international journals and many books with various publication houses.

Vinod Mahor is currently working as Assistant Professor in IES College of Technology, Bhopal, Madhya Pradesh India. He attended several research programs from IIT, NIT, NITTTR and other organization. The Author has research alignment towards Cyber-security, IoT, Dark Web Crime research and investigative tactics, as well as efforts to trace unlawful anonymous materials of cybercrime and criminal operations He also presided over national international conferences.

Harshita Mandloi completed her ME from Information Technology Department of Institute of Engineering &Technology (IET), a UTD of Devi Ahilya University, Indore, Madhya Pradesh, India. She has more than 13 year of teaching experience at UG and PG level presently working as Assistant professor in in CSE Department of ShriVaishnav Vidyapeeth Vishwavidyalaya Indore. She has published 2 international and one national paper in the reputed journal of CSE & IT.

Jasvant Mandloi is research scholar at Information Technology Department of Institute of Engineering & Technology (IET), a UTD of Devi Ahilya University, Indore, Madhya Pradesh, India and the author of 6 refereed publications. He was Head of the department at one of the prestigious Engineering college of Central India. He was secretory of CSI Indore chapter for year 2016-17. He served as National Co-Coordinator for Vidyarthi Vigyan Mantahn (A Project for School Level Students by Vigyan Bharati, an NGO working for National Science Movement). He has done his graduation in Information Technology from JIT Borawan Madhya Pradesh in year 2006. He has received Master's degree MTech IT from UTD RGPV Bhopal in year 2008.He has membership oftechnical association ISTE and CSE and received awards at National level from IBM and NEN India. He has recently cleared the UPSC interview and get selected as T&P officer in the Daman Technical Department. His areas of research interest are Blockchain, Smart Contract, Cloud computing, Cybersecurity and Machine learning.

Priyanka Narode received the degree in MCA in Computer Application and Engineering, in 2015. She worked as an assistant teacher in SSGM, Senior College Kopargaon. She is currently working as a lecturer for Information Technology at Sanjivani Junior College, Kopargaon. She has been published more than 10+ journal and conference research papers in well-reputed journal. Her main research interest includes Information Technology, Machine Learning

A. B. Pawar received the degree in Ph.D. in Computer Science and Engineering, in 2015. He is currently working as Professor in Computer Engineering and Dean Academics in Sanjivani College of Engineering, Kopargaon. He is a Best Teacher Award Recipient of ISTE, New Delhi in year 2016. He is a recognized research guide at SPPU, Pune India. He is also a life member of ISTE and member of IE, India. He worked on various IEEE Technical Advisory Committees, reviewer, and jury at national as well as international level. He is also worked and completed research projects in cyber security, data mining, Internet of Things (IoT) for which he has been received research grants from BCUD, SPPU Pune, AICTE. He has been published more than 35+ journal and conference research papers in well-reputed journal, including IEEE Explore, Springer. His main research interest includes Artificial Intelligence, Cyber Security, Machine Learning, Internet of Things (IoT), IOT Security, malware analysis and detection.

Varun Pawar is a Senior Developer at ICICI Lombard. He is interested in Software Development and Machine Learning. He has completed a bachelor's degree in Computer Engineering from Veermata Jijabai Technological Institute, Mumbai.

Chitra R. is currently working as Associate Professor of Computer Science and Engineering at Noorul Islam Centre for Higher Education and has 18 years of experience in the field of Computer Science and Engineering. She received B.E degree in Electrical and Electronics Engineering and M.E degree in Computer Science and Engineering, PhD degree in Computer Science and Engineering from Manonmaniam Sundaranar University. She has published 14 papers in the field of Data mining, Artificial Intelligence and Soft Computing. Her research area of include data mining, intelligent technique, and bioinformatics.

Saurabh Raut is a graduate student at University of Pennsylvania majoring in Computer and Information Science. He is passionate about machine learning and applying it to real world problems.

Kunjal Shah is an Associate Developer at SAP Labs India Pvt Ltd. He has completed a B.Tech in Computer Engineering from Veermata Jijabai Technological Institute, Mumbai. His interests are Deep Learning, Machine Learning, and Computer Vision. With an excellent academic record, he has authored multiple publications in reputed journals and conferences.

Chaitanya Singh completed his Ph.D. degree from Bhagwant University Ajmer in 2017. M.Tech. in Computer Science and Engineering from Rajiv Gandhi Proudyogiki Vishwavidyalaya (RGPV), Bhopal, India in 2017 and B.E. Degree in Computer Science and Engineering from Rajiv Gandhi Proudyogiki Vishwavidyalaya (RGPV), Bhopal India in 2005. He started his academic career from Shree Institute of college in 2005 and served various reputed colleges and universities in India. Currently, he holds the position of Associate Professor at the department of Computer Science and Engineering in Swarrnim Startup and Innovation University, Gandhinagar Gujarat, India. He worked at various positions in academic institutions and serving in educational field from last 15 years. He has authored or co-authored over more than 50+ technical papers published in national and international journals and conferences and also published 3 patents in India and abroad. His research interests include applications of Blockchain, Artificial Intelligence, Machine Learning, Deep Learning and IOT in Smart cities, automobile, healthcare, etc.

Shrikant Telang is currently working as Assistant Professor in Shri Vaishnav Vidyapeeth Vishwavidyalaya, Indore, India. He attended several research programs. The Author has research alignment towards Cyber Security, IoT, Dark Web Crime analysis and investigation techniques, and working towards tracing illicit anonymous contents of cyber terrorism and criminal activities. He also joins International Conferences and several research events including National and International Research Schools, Workshops, training programs. He also published several Research Patents.

Arun Kumar Tripathi completed Ph. D. in Computer Applications with specialization in Mobile IPv6 from NIT Kurukshetra in 2018, M. Tech. in Computer Science & Engineering from Dr. A.P.J. Abdul Kalam Technical University, Lucknow (Formerly known as Gautam Buddha Technical University, Lucknow) in 2010, MCA from LNCT Bhopal affiliated to Rajiv Gandhi Proudyogiki Vishwavidyalaya, Bhopal in 2002 and B.Sc. Electronics from Dr. Hari Singh Gour Central University (Formerly known as

Sagar University). At present he is appointed as Professor and Head Cyber Security and Forensic Science Division. His research interests include Computer Network, Network Security, IoT, machine Learning, Blockchain etc. He has more than fifty research publications in reputed Journals and Conferences. He reviewed more than 12 SCI-Indexed journal papers. He is a life member of various professional societies like ACEEE, IACSIT, IAENG, CSTA etc. He guided 02 M. Tech. thesis in Computer Science and Engineering and at present 01 Ph.D. thesis is on-going. He is a CISCO certified academy instructor.

Chandrika V. S. is a B.E. in EEE from Madras University in 2001, M.E. in PED from Anna University, Chennai in 2005 and Ph.D in Electrical Engineering from Anna University, Chennai in May 2015. Started career as lecturer in EEE in 2001 and currently working as Associate Professor in EEE at KPR Institute of Engineering and Technology, Coimbatore. Published 15 papers in national and international journals, 24 papers in national and international conferences and own a patent in solar powered wireless robotic vehicle. Currently working in the area of intelligent drives for electric vehicles, Machine learning and Image Processing.

Apurv Verma was born in Raipur, Chhattisgarh on July 14, 1990. He has received his B.E. in Computer Science and Engineering from CSVTU, Bhilai in 2012 and M. Tech. in Computer Science and Engineering from MATS University, Raipur in 2016. He is currently working as an Assistant Professor in the department of Computer Science and Engineering, School of Engineering and I.T., MATS University, Raipur.

Gitika Vyas is a self-employed researcher and has received her Master's in renewable energy from Rajasthan Technical University (RTU) India. She received her Bachelor's degree in Electronic Instrumentation and Control from RTU, India. She has published research papers in various premium conferences such as IEEE, MWAIS, and Journals like IIS. Her research areas include data analysis in social networking, renewable energy, and solar energy.

Piyush Vyas is a Ph.D. candidate in Information Systems at the College of Business and Information Systems, Dakota State University, USA. He received his master's degree in Information Systems from the Dakota State University, USA. He has a master's and bachelor's degree in Information Technology from State Technical University-Bhopal, India. His current research interest includes Association Rule Mining, Machine Learning, Healthcare Informatics, Transfer Learning, Text Mining, and Data Mining. He has received best paper awards for premier conferences- AMCIS and has published papers in journals from IEEE, AIS, and IJCA research societies. He has more than eight years of teaching, research, and academic service experience.

P. William is working as an Assistant Professor, Department of Information Technology, Sanjivani College of Engineering, SPPU Pune. He received his Bachelor of Engineering in Computer Science and Engineering from CSVTU, Bhilai in 2013 and Master of Technology in Computer Science and Engineering from CSVTU, Bhilai in 2017. He is currently pursuing his Ph. D. in the Department of Computer Science and Engineering from School of Engineering & Information Technology, MATS University, Raipur. He has published many papers in Scopus indexed journals and IEEE Conferences. His field of research include Natural Language Processing, Machine learning, Soft Computing, Cyber Security and Cloud Computing. He has been associated with numerous Multi-National Companies including IBM,

TCS etc. and Educational Groups. A focused and hardworking professional with experience in taking Corporate Trainings. He is a Life Member of Quality Circle Forum of India (QCFI) and member of various other professional bodies.

Index

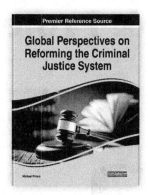

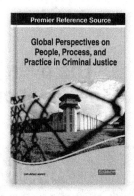

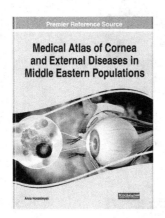

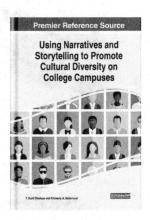

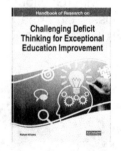

Printed in the United States
by Baker & Taylor Publisher Services